This book provides an understanding of memory development through an examination of the scientific contributions of eminent developmental scientist Peter A. Ornstein. His fifty-year career not only coincided with but also contributed to a period of extraordinary progress in the understanding of children's memory. The volume describes this historical context, constructs a theoretical structure for understanding memory development, and emphasizes research applications for educational and forensic practice. Organized around Ornstein's four influential research programs in children's memory strategies, children's event memory, family socialization of memory, and classroom socialization of memory, the chapters examine contemporary directions in each area, with commentaries addressing each program provided by internationally renowned developmental psychologists. The book presents a comprehensive overview of memory development for psychologists and educators at all levels of training and practice, and also provides a model of a generative life in science.

LYNNE E. BAKER-WARD is Professor of Psychology at North Carolina State University, USA, where she teaches courses in developmental psychology and ethics. Her research examines how children interpret, remember, and share their experiences.

DAVID F. BJORKLUND is Professor of Psychology at Florida Atlantic University, USA, where he teaches courses in developmental and evolutionary psychology. His research interests include children's cognitive development and evolutionary developmental psychology.

JENNIFER L. COFFMAN is Associate Professor of Human Development and Family Studies at the University of North Carolina at Greensboro, USA, where she teaches developmental science and studies the socialization of cognition.

T0384710

# THE DEVELOPMENT OF CHILDREN'S MEMORY

## The Scientific Contributions of Peter A. Ornstein

EDITED BY

**LYNNE E. BAKER-WARD**

*North Carolina State University*

**DAVID F. BJORKLUND**

*Florida Atlantic University*

**JENNIFER L. COFFMAN**

*University of North Carolina at Greensboro*

CAMBRIDGE
UNIVERSITY PRESS

Shaftesbury Road, Cambridge CB2 8EA, United Kingdom

One Liberty Plaza, 20th Floor, New York, NY 10006, USA

477 Williamstown Road, Port Melbourne, VIC 3207, Australia

314–321, 3rd Floor, Plot 3, Splendor Forum, Jasola District Centre, New Delhi – 110025, India

103 Penang Road, #05–06/07, Visioncrest Commercial, Singapore 238467

Cambridge University Press is part of Cambridge University Press & Assessment, a department of the University of Cambridge.

We share the University's mission to contribute to society through the pursuit of education, learning and research at the highest international levels of excellence.

www.cambridge.org
Information on this title: www.cambridge.org/9781108819046

DOI: 10.1017/9781108871105

First published 2021
First paperback edition 2023

*A catalogue record for this publication is available from the British Library*

*Library of Congress Cataloging-in-Publication data*
NAMES: Baker-Ward, Lynne E., editor. | Bjorklund, David F., 1949 – editor. | Coffman, Jennifer L., editor.
TITLE: The development of children's memory : the scientific contributions of Peter A. Ornstein / edited by Lynne E. Baker–Ward, North Carolina State University, David F. Bjorklund, Florida Atlantic University, Jennifer L. Coffman, University of North Carolina at Greensboro.
DESCRIPTION: New York : Cambridge University Press, 2021. | Includes bibliographical references and index.
IDENTIFIERS: LCCN 2021012011 (print) | LCCN 2021012012 (ebook) | ISBN 9781108836456 (hardback) | ISBN 9781108819046 (paperback) | ISBN 9781108871105 (epub)
SUBJECTS: LCSH: Memory in children. | Ornstein, Peter A. | BISAC: PSYCHOLOGY / Developmental / General | PSYCHOLOGY / Developmental / General
CLASSIFICATION: LCC BF723.M4 D478 2021 (print) | LCC BF723.M4 (ebook) | DDC 155.4/1312–dc23
LC record available at https://lccn.loc.gov/2021012011
LC ebook record available at https://lccn.loc.gov/2021012012

ISBN    978-1-108-83645-6    Hardback
ISBN    978-1-108-81904-6    Paperback

To Peter A. Ornstein – developmental scientist, scholar, mentor, friend, and true mensch.

# Contents

vii

*Contents*

# Figures

# *Tables*

# Contributors

DIANA I. ACOSTA is a psychology doctoral student at Loyola University Chicago. Her adviser is Catherine A. Haden, making her an Ornstein "grand-student."

LYNNE E. BAKER-WARD is an Alumni Distinguished Undergraduate Professor of Psychology at North Carolina State University. She completed her PhD under the direction of Peter A. Ornstein.

PATRICIA J. BAUER is Asa Griggs Chandler Professor of Psychology at Emory University.

DEBORAH L. BEST is William L. Poteat Professor of Psychology at Wake Forest University. She completed her PhD under the direction of Peter A. Ornstein.

DAVID F. BJORKLUND is a professor of psychology at Florida Atlantic University. He completed his PhD under the direction of Peter A. Ornstein.

MAGGIE BRUCK is a professor of child and adolescent psychiatry at the Johns Hopkins School of Medicine.

JENNIFER L. COFFMAN is an associate professor in human development and family studies at the University of North Carolina at Greensboro. Her dissertation adviser was Peter A. Ornstein.

DEBORAH A. CONNOLLY is a professor of psychology at Simon Fraser University.

OLIVIA K. COOK is completing her PhD in human development and family studies at the University of North Carolina at Greensboro. Her adviser is Jennifer L. Coffman, making her an Ornstein "grand-student."

BRIAN D. COX is professor of psychology at Hofstra University. His dissertation was supervised by Peter A. Ornstein.

ALENA G. ESPOSITO is an assistant professor of psychology at Clark University. She completed her dissertation under the direction of Lynne E. Baker-Ward at North Carolina State University, making her an Ornstein "grand-student."

ROBYN FIVUSH is Samuel Candler Dobbs Professor of Psychology and Director of the Institute for the Liberal Arts, Emory University.

TRISHA H. FOLDS-BENNETT is currently Provost, The University of Virginia's College at Wise. She was previously Dean of the Honors College at the College of Charleston. She received her PhD under the supervision of Peter A. Ornstein.

JENNIE K. GRAMMER is an assistant professor in the School of Education and Information Studies, University of California, Los Angeles. She completed her doctorate under the direction of Peter A. Ornstein.

CATHERINE A. HADEN is a professor of psychology at Loyola University Chicago. She completed a postdoctoral fellowship at the Center for Developmental Science under the supervision of Peter A. Ornstein.

AMY M. HEDRICK is an associate professor of psychology at Lenoir-Rhyne University. She completed a postdoctoral fellowship at the Center for Developmental Science under the supervision of Peter A. Ornstein.

KESHA N. HUDSON is a postdoctoral fellow at RTI International. Peter A. Ornstein was her doctoral adviser.

ANDREA M. HUSSONG is a professor of psychology and neuroscience at the University of North Carolina at Chapel Hill and former Director of the Center for Developmental Science.

HILLARY A. LANGLEY is an assistant professor of psychology at Sam Houston State University. Her doctoral studies were directed by Peter A. Ornstein.

FREDERICK J. MORRISON is a professor emeritus of psychology at the University of Michigan.

LAUREN C. PAGANO is a psychology doctoral student at Loyola University Chicago. Her adviser is Catherine Haden, making her an Ornstein "grand-student."

HEATHER L. PRICE is Canada Research Chair in Culture and Communities: Children and the Law and Professor of Psychology at Thompson Rivers University. She was a postdoctoral fellow in the Ornstein Laboratory.

GABRIELLE F. PRINCIPE is professor of psychology at the College of Charleston. Her dissertation was directed by Peter A. Ornstein.

WOLFGANG SCHNEIDER is a professor emeritus of psychology at the Department of Psychology, University of Würzburg.

TAYLOR E. THOMAS recently completed her PhD under the direction of Peter A. Ornstein.

REMI TORRES is a graduate student in the School of Education and Information Studies, University of California, Los Angeles. Her mentor is Jennie K. Grammer, making her an Ornstein "grand-student."

KEADIJA C. WILEY is completing her PhD in human development and family studies at the University of North Carolina at Greensboro. Another Ornstein student, Jennifer L. Coffman, is co-directing her dissertation, making her an Ornstein "grand-student."

# PART I

## *Backdrop*

# CHAPTER I

# The Emergence of the Developmental Science of Memory
## A Festschrift for Peter A. Ornstein

*Lynne E. Baker-Ward, David F. Bjorklund, and Jennifer L. Coffman*

This volume had its origins in a celebration. In May 2019, dozens of Peter Ornstein's former and current students, colleagues, and friends gathered to commemorate a significant milestone. After 45 years on the faculty of the University of North Carolina at Chapel Hill and a total of 100 semesters in academia, Professor Ornstein had accepted emeritus status as the F. Stuart Chapin Distinguished Professor of Psychology and Neuroscience. In addition to social activities, including a lively roast and the announcement of a distinguished professorship named in Ornstein's honor, the festivities involved a series of scientific talks by alumni of his laboratory. Ornstein's four distinct programs of research formed the organizational structure for these presentations, with each topic represented by an overview of his work and a description of on-going research that continued and extended the original contributions. It was immediately apparent that Ornstein's 50-year research career not only reflected advancements in the understanding of memory development but also constituted a driving and enduring force in the field. This edited volume, structured around Ornstein's separate but interrelated programs of research, provides a perspective on the emergence and growth of the developmental science of memory as well as a Festschrift for a widely revered academician.

## The Developmental Context

There is continuity as well as change in Peter Ornstein's scientific development. He was trained as an experimental psychologist, earning his PhD under the direction of David A. Grant at the University of Wisconsin–Madison in 1968. As discussed by Brian Cox (Chapter 2), Ornstein's initial research exemplified the on-going transition in psychology from verbal learning to information processing. Whereas work in the Ornstein Laboratory moved over the decades from the application of a mechanistic model emphasizing control processes to a more sociocultural approach addressing interactions with others as a source of change in memory development, his rigorous training as an experimental psychologist has been consistently apparent in his research. With his students, he devoted attention to the conduct of investigations that incorporated appropriate control conditions and careful procedures, built in replications of previous findings, and provided systematic extensions of prior studies, as exemplified throughout this volume.

Pronounced change is notable alongside this continuity. Ornstein's scientific identity formally shifted from experimental psychology to developmental psychology when he moved from Princeton University to the University of North Carolina at Chapel Hill (UNC-CH) in 1973. However, corresponding to changes within the field, Ornstein's approach to developmental psychology changed dramatically over time. He made a transition from a more experimental-child approach, with an emphasis on identifying age differences in a particular independent variable, to an increasingly well-articulated focus on understanding the process of development and the factors that drive it. As described in an influential article (Ornstein & Haden, 2001a), this approach addressed the *development* of memory in comparison to *memory* development. In Chapter 3, Catherine A. Haden provides an update of this report, with an emphasis on longitudinal research and the role of parent–child interactions in the development of skilled remembering over time. Her discussion documents the central contributions of work conducted by researchers trained in the Ornstein Laboratory in advancing the understanding of the development of memory.

The colleagues whom Ornstein came to know in Chapel Hill were instrumental in his continuing growth as a developmental psychologist. Harriet L. Rheingold, who served as a research professor at UNC-CH from 1964 to 1978, was an internationally recognized scientist whose work emphasized bidirectionality in the interactions between mothers and infants (see Lipsitt & Ornstein, 2002). This focus on young organisms as competent and active, rather than the passive recipients of stimulation, represented a profound change in the field (see Sameroff, 2009). Robert B. Cairns, with whom Ornstein worked closely from the time he arrived at UNC-CH until Cairns's death in 1999, was instrumental in establishing developmental science. This perspective emphasized the importance of multidisciplinary approaches to the study of development over time, the incorporation of multiple levels of analysis in understanding stability and change, and the vital importance of applied contributions (see Cairns, Elder & Costello, 1996). Cairns's roles as a cofounder of the Carolina

Consortium on Human Development in 1989 and subsequently as the founding director of the Center for Developmental Science in 1994 provided Ornstein with a stimulating community for the exploration of development. The Center tangibly contributed to Ornstein's work through the support of postdoctoral fellows, including Catherine A. Haden (Chapters 3 and 12), Amy M. Hedrick (Chapter 11), and Heather L. Price (Chapter 8), as well as a number of predoctoral students. Representing the latter group in this volume are Jennifer L. Coffman (this chapter, Chapters 13, 15, and 16), Jennie K. Grammer (Chapter 17) Kesha N. Hudson (Chapter 16), and Taylor E. Thomas (Chapter 7).

In addition to his important relationships with local colleagues and students, Ornstein has long enjoyed a rich network of national and international colleagues. Four of these distinguished researchers – Wolfgang Schneider, Maggie Bruck, Robyn Fivush, and Fredrick J. Morrison – have each provided a valuable commentary on the research program most closely aligned with their work. We are grateful to them for sharing their expertise. A final chapter, authored by David F. Bjorklund, whose dissertation was directed by Ornstein, discusses advances in the conceptualization and application of memory development over the past 50 years and examines the impact of this work on the understanding of cognitive development broadly defined.

The great importance of his professional colleagues notwithstanding, Ornstein's understanding of development has also certainly been inspired and informed at home. Marilyn Reichwald Ornstein, his spouse of 55 years, is a highly regarded early childhood educator whose contributions have extended well beyond her own classrooms. The Ornsteins have reared two exceptional daughters who share their parents' commitment to careers involving children. Miriam Ornstein has followed in her mother's footsteps in early education, and Naomi Ornstein Davis is a clinical psychologist. The Ornsteins are active participants in the lives of their five grandchildren.

## The Research Programs

Ornstein's body of work falls easily into four extensive programs of research, each addressing age-related changes in skilled remembering and reflecting increasing attention over time to the *development* of memory (see Haden, Chapter 3). These endeavors both addressed highly salient contemporary questions, reflecting the field at the time, and contributed to the understanding of the issues under examination, furthering the study of memory development. The quality of each program is indicated by the continuing extramural funding that supported the work, and the impact of the research is reflected in part by the large number of publications – over 150 – listed on Ornstein's CV.

These four programs are discussed in turn in Parts II through V of this book. Each part begins with an overview of Professor Ornstein's research provided by former PhD or postdoctoral students who contributed to the body of work. Additional chapters in each part, also authored by a former Ornstein student or a researcher trained by a former trainee (i.e., an Ornstein "grand-student"), provide contemporary perspectives on the issues under examination. Some of these chapters include work that directly builds on the research discussed in the overview, whereas others discuss applications of the accumulated knowledge to novel research problems or to practice. Each part concludes with a commentary by a distinguished scholar in the field. These commentaries elucidate the con-tributions of the research to the emerging understanding of the develop-ment of memory over the past half-century.

### Children's Memory Strategies

Ornstein's initial research as a developmentalist addressed age-related changes in children's deliberate remembering. This work conveyed an understanding of children as active thinkers, developing techniques such as rehearsal and organization for remembering items, as well as the role that children's world knowledge has upon their memory. An overview of this research is presented by two Ornstein PhDs, Deborah L. Best and Trisha H. Folds-Bennett. Alena G. Esposito, who is an Ornstein "grand-student," and Patricia J. Bauer continue the investigation of prior knowl-edge, emphasizing the way that knowledge representations are built, remodeled, and updated as a function of additive learning. Wolfgang Schneider, an internationally recognized expert in memory development, provides the commentary on the chapters included in this part.

### Children's Event Memory

A subsequent focus of Ornstein's research was on children's abilities to report personally experienced events involving some degree of stress or discomfort. A particular goal of this research, motivated by societal issues, was understanding the implications of developmental changes in memory capabilities on young children's involvement as witnesses in legal proceedings. The work of Ornstein and his students and collaborators contributed substantially to a better understanding of the development of autobiographical memory and contributed to changes in how children are interviewed in legal contexts (see Cox, Chapter 2; Bruck, Chapter 10). Lynne E. Baker-Ward, an Ornstein PhD, and Taylor E. Thomas, a recent doctoral graduate who is Ornstein's last formal advisee, provide an overview of this research. In the second chapter in this part, Heather L. Price, a former Ornstein postdoctoral fellow, and Deborah L. Connolly explore continuing basic research on children's memory for instances of repeated events and the legal context to which such knowledge is applied. In the third chapter of this part, Gabrielle F. Principe, who earned her doctorate under Ornstein's supervision, summarizes a programmatic series of studies that examines how conversations with peers and adults can shape children's recollections. This work complements Ornstein's primary focus on children's provision of accurate information under specific conditions. Maggie Bruck, an expert in children's eyewitness memory and suggestibility, shares her perspective on this research in the commentary, emphasizing the forsenic relevance of the research.

## *Family Socialization of Memory*

Reflecting his increasing commitment to developmental science, Professor Ornstein next initiated longitudinal research programs elucidating the socialization of memory. One area of inquiry examined the contributions of language-based interactions within the family on the origins and development of children's skills in independent remembering. Professor Ornstein with his students and colleagues identified important linkages between "joint talk" in parent–child conversations about previous and ongoing events and preschoolers' developing skills in reporting their experiences. His former postdoctoral fellow, Amy M. Hedrick, summarizes research on young children's emerging language and memory skills and their socialization through conversations with adults. Another former postdoc, Catherine A. Haden, and her doctoral students, Diana L. Acosta and Lauren C. Pagano, examine an extension of the original research – an exploration of how parent–child conversations about experiences in museums can advance children's learning and retention of STEM knowledge. In the third chapter of this part, Hillary A. Langley and Jennifer L. Coffman, two Ornstein PhDs, and Andrea M. Hussong examine parent–child conversations within the context of the development of gratitude. This work emphasizes the significance of components of autobiographical memory, as established through such conversations, for interpreting the past and forming expectations for the future. Robyn Fivush, whose own extensive research was foundational in the study of the family socialization of memory, discusses the implications of this research.

## Classroom Socialization of Memory

In his most recent work, Professor Ornstein began a second longitudinal investigation, addressing the influence of teacher–child interactions within the elementary school classroom on children's subsequent capabilities in deliberate memory. His former doctoral student and continuing collaborator in this endeavor, Jennifer L. Coffman, and her graduate student Olivia K. Cook, contribute the overview of this research program, charting the evolution of this work across longitudinal and experimental designs and toward the possibility of creating interventions that could influence classroom teaching as well as children's learning. Another Ornstein advisee, Kesha N. Hudson, along with Keadija C. Wiley and Jennifer L. Coffman, present research that extends the original findings to mathematics by demonstrating that the types of language parents and teachers use during the course of instruction and conversation affect children's academic performance in this domain. In the third chapter in this part, Jennie K. Grammer, who earned her doctorate under Ornstein's direction, and her student (and Ornstein "grand-sudent") Remi Torres discuss research that establishes links between memory skills and self-regulated learning as assessed through both behavioral and neuropsychological measures and examine the relation between aspects of teacher language and children's self-regulated learning skills. Fredrick Morrison, a highly influential researcher in developmental psychology and education, shares his expertise in providing a perspective on these chapters and Ornstein's career.

Although these programs of research clearly mark transitions in Ornstein's career-long development as a scholar and constitute distinct epochs in his work, their interconnectedness is notable. The early research on memory strategies, as summarized by Best and Folds-Bennett (Chapter 4), not only informs contemporary investigations of learning and knowledge and the applications of these findings as discussed in Part II but is also integral to on-going research on the classroom socialization of memory, as reviewed in Part V. Similarly, research on the socialization of memory within the context of the family, as presented in Part IV, informs a lively, on-going program of research on children's suggestibility, as reviewed by Principe (Chapter 9), as well as the work on the ways in which teacher talk influences children's memory performance, as examined in Part V. This integration of knowledge across research programs motivated by different questions reflects Ornstein's scholarly commitment to understanding the development of memory throughout his career (see also Haden, Chapter 3).

## Generativity across Contexts

A review of his work readily establishes that Peter Ornstein has been a meticulous and creative researcher who has modeled intellectual generativity in all his scientific endeavors. In even briefly examining the full extent of his accomplishments, it is clear that his contributions to the profession and to broader society have extended well beyond the laboratory. Ornstein has been a dedicated citizen of his institution and his discipline throughout his long career. Notably, at UNC-CH, Ornstein completed several terms as coordinator of the developmental area, served as department chair, and fulfilled multiple leadership roles within the Center for Developmental Science from its very beginning. His professional service, along with other activities, included his dedicated work as an associate editor for the journal *Developmental Psychology*, his active membership on the American Psychological Association's (APA) Publications Committee (which included his advocacy for the Oxford comma), and his involvement with APA's Division 7.

Ornstein's commitment to "giving psychology away" was particularly apparent with regard to his research on children's event memory, which he undertook in response to the urgent needs of legal and clinical professionals to better understand children's testimony in legal proceedings (see Chapters 2 and 7). His scientific expertise and personal integrity enabled him to fulfill the demanding role of co-chair of the American Psychological Association's Working Group on the Investigation of Memories of Childhood Abuse and to play a key role in the dissemination of its findings to the profession (see APA Working Group on Investigation of Memories of Childhood Abuse, 1998). Given his expertise and professional accomplishments, he was soon in demand as an expert witness, and as discussed by Bruck (Chapter 10), reluctantly took on this role because he believed it was his responsibility to do so.

The importance of these components of his legacy notwithstanding, Ornstein's generativity is particularly apparent in his work with students across settings and time. Ornstein has been a dedicated and successful classroom teacher, but it seems fair to say that his most important teaching has occurred within the context of his on-going investigations. His teaching and research have been beautifully integrated. Each of Ornstein's research programs has involved students who were the fortunate recipients of not only his extraordinary skill and insights but his dedicated guidance and multidimensional support. With the research training he provided and his model of a fully engaged career, Ornstein's students have gone on to make their own significant contributions to the field of cognitive development. Evidence that their experiences in the Ornstein laboratory were formative is apparent in his former students' continuing contributions to issues they first addressed under his direction, as represented in this book. The authors and coauthors of the chapters in this volume include ten researchers who earned their doctorates under Ornstein's direction between 1976 and 2020, and three former postdoctoral trainees. In several cases, pre- and postdoctoral students' involvement in these research endeavors evolved into sustained collaborative endeavors, with former students emerging as full partners who served as principal or co-principal investigators. As these contributors will attest, Ornstein valued his students' ideas even when they were in the early phases of their training, and the further articulations of his research questions reflect his students' and postdoctoral fellows' contributions to on-going research. Ornstein has often quoted Rabbi Hanina, who said, "I have learned much from my teachers and more from my friends, but the most from my students" (Talmud Bavil Ta'anit 7a).

As Ornstein's former students, we hope the readers of this volume – including Peter himself! – find new information and insights that enrich their understanding of the development of memory.

# CHAPTER 2

# Mechanism or Meaning?
## The Ornstein Lab and Memory in Historical Context

### Brian D. Cox

Over a century of memory research has swung between the two poles of the mechanistic model of Ebbinghaus (1885/1913) and the adaptive, sociocultural, and organismic view of Bartlett (1932), neither of which were developmental. The Ornstein Lab has, over the last half century, with experimental rigor, explored how growing children use memory adaptively in meaningful contexts. To begin this book commemorating and analyzing the 50 years of contributions of Peter Ornstein and his collaborators to the study of memory development, it is important to take a long view. As it is the job of later contributors to go through his oeuvre in detail, this chapter will focus on the *really* long view of historical changes in conceptualizations in memory that preceded his work, provided conceptual underpinnings during it, and continue to this day.

Peter Ornstein began his career in the Hullian behaviorist paradigm and published some work on verbal classical conditioning of differential eye-blink response (Perry et al., 1971). This work was completed in the waning days of the hegemony of conditioning and learning just as that paradigm was shifting.[1] From the transitional era of "verbal learning" in the 1950s to the cognitive revolution of the information-processing period in the 1980s, models of memory focused on the deployment and control of strategic processes of remembering that operate to store and retrieve memory content, models that, despite their modern sophistication, owe something to Ebbinghaus. But children grow up ecologically embedded in cultural structures of meanings, ranging from the doctor's office to the courtroom, aided or hindered by the people in them, intent on helping developing children to use memory adaptively within those cultural narratives. The purpose of this chapter is not to review all of the specific research of the

---

[1] Indeed, Peter told me that the fall from grace of Hullian theory was so complete that in the late 1970s, he found one of Hull's major works on a bookstore remainder table for 9 cents!

Ornstein Lab but instead to describe the historical shifts that carried it along and to which it significantly contributed.

## "Memory Proper" Separated from "Reminiscence": Ebbinghaus and the Pure Mechanisms of Memory

> The nonsense material, just described, offers many advantages, in part because of this very lack of meaning. First of all, it is relatively simple and relatively homogeneous. In the case of the material nearest at hand, namely poetry or prose, the content is now narrative in style, now descriptive, or now reflective; it contains now a phrase that is pathetic, now one that is humorous; its metaphors are sometimes beautiful, sometimes harsh; its rhythm is sometimes smooth and sometimes rough. There is thus brought into play a multiplicity of influences which change without regularity and are therefore disturbing. Such are associations which dart here and there, different degrees of interest, lines of verse recalled because of their striking quality or their beauty, and the like. All this is avoided with our syllables. Among many thousand combinations there occur scarcely a few dozen that have a meaning, and among these there are again only a few whose meaning was realized while they were being memorized
>
> (Ebbinghaus, 1885/1913, p. 23).

The experimental study of memory has undergone several paradigm shifts since it began 135 years ago in the work of Hermann Ebbinghaus (1885/1913), whose habilitationsschrift *Über das Gedächtnis* (*On Memory*) bears the literal signature of Hermann Helmholtz (Cahan, 2019) and deliberately follows in the footsteps of Gustav Fechner. Ebbinghaus's methods, which separated the mechanisms of memory from meaning, provided the metatheory not only for the memory-drum period of verbal learning but also for the information-processing period that succeeded it.

According to Danziger's masterful history of memory, *Marking the Mind* (2008), Ebbinghaus was well aware that the memory processes for which he justly became famous were not all of memory. In fact, he made a distinction between *Erinnerung* (reminiscence, self-conscious recollection) and *das blosse Behalten, das eigenliche Gedächtnis* (mere retention, pure retention, memory proper; Danziger, 2008, p. 128; his translations). Ebbinghaus's forgetting curves refer only to the second kind of remembering, and it is this kind of meaningless "memory proper" that has come down to us in memory experiments, as a mechanism that is underneath meaning or a carrier of it. As is well known, he painstakingly created 2,300 pronounceable "nonsense" trigram syllables grouped into lists that he used in experiments on himself as subject, following Fechner's individual method, and consistent with Wundt's focus on individual highly controlled experimental self-observation. Ebbinghaus was skeptical of artificial forms of memorization (*mnemotechnik*) and believed his methods allowed the study of natural memory.

For the purposes of our discussion, two of Ebbinghaus's innovations have made it into the current conceptions of memory. First, his method involved matching a well-defined item list with the criterion of performance. This conversion of subjective memory experiences into measurable bits ("items") of experience (trigrams, words, pictures, etc.) is such an obvious move today that we forget that someone had to invent it. Second, each repetition represented an amount of mental work (*Arbeit*) that was necessary to reach a criterion. Danziger points out that in earlier drafts of *Gedächtnis* and later publications, Ebbinghaus conceived this as something like potential energy saved up when something is memorized. Something must therefore be *applied to* the items to cement them at least temporarily into memory. If that something is a set of procedures, operations, or programs, we have the dichotomy between items and processes that underlies the verbal-learning period and the information-processing work that followed it.

Appreciation for Ebbinghaus's achievement thereafter continued, with crucial modifications. Ebbinghaus, like Fechner, did his experiments on himself; in 1894, the experimenter became separated from the subject in the lab of G. E. Müller at Göttingen. It was here that the presentation of stimuli was standardized by the invention of the *memory drum*. In her article on association in 1896, Mary Whiton Calkins cited primacy, recency, and frequency of presentation as factors in memory for paired associates. In education, E. L. Thorndike cited Ebbinghaus's masterwork in detail in volume 2 of *Educational Psychology: The Psychology of Learning* (1913). He cited the work of Ernst Meumann from Hamburg on the use of Ebbinghaus's methods for children's memorization (Ebert & Meumann, 1905); this work included use of similar methods on syllables, but also words, poetry, and sentences.

Thorndike's broader educational philosophy, while based on experimental procedures, was actually against rote learning and in favor of meaningfully contextualized knowledge transfer. At the beginning of the twentieth century, the "formal discipline" approach to education had suggested that the mind was like a muscle; therefore, their reasoning went, memorizing Latin declensions by rote allowed children to deal with other difficult subjects. To Thorndike and Woodworth (Thorndike & Woodworth, 1901;

Woodworth & Thorndike, 1900), this was nonsense; instead, they believed transfer occurred because of the commonality of the identical elements of thought required to transfer content from situation A to situation B. The teaching of any adaptive skill, including memory, therefore, involved developing connections to the place where that skill should be used. Math problems, for example, should include units of measurement and should never be the kind of abstract problem that a child would never encounter (see Cox, 1997).

So it would seem that the study of memory and learning broadly construed was heading toward a more meaningful future from Ebbinghaus to a functional description of memory in context. But not yet. First, we must discuss the verbal-learning period of memory research, followed by the developmental information-processing period – a school that shares many metatheoretical commitments with verbal learning.

### The Verbal Discrimination–Verbal Learning Interlude

When an episode in the history of science or psychology has been retrospectively classified as a wrong turn or dead end in the progress of the field – or on the wrong end of a paradigm shift – at least one of the following is probably true: First, we had to go through it to find out that it was wrongheaded. Second, even wrongheaded activities leave behind data or methods that, reinterpreted under a newer paradigm, turn out to be useful. Such it was for the verbal-learning paradigm.

Verbal learning typically involved the conversion of memory processes to classically conditioned stimulus associations among items or words. Often, this meant that the term "memory" disappeared entirely. For example, Eleanor J. Gibson's (1940) published doctoral dissertation supervised by Clark L. Hull at Yale framed her discussion of transfer, interference, intra-list effects, and retroactive interference as a process of establishing discrimination among items to be learned by generalization and differentiation, specifically differential inhibition as reinforced by practice. However, there was no reference to the meaning of items in this or other verbal-learning work, with associative connections only being attributed to mechanical presentation conditions such as pairing or chaining, which is essentially sequential pairing. Yet, verbal-learning research uncovered many well-known memory phenomena well before the advent of information processing, including, for example, the serial-position effect (e.g., Deese & Kaufman, 1957; Robinson & Brown, 1926) and, of course, Weston Bousfield's (1953) work on clustering in recall, including at least one rudimentary developmental study (Bousfield, Esterson, & Whitmarsh, 1958).

Once verbal-learning research got going, it was prolific. The *Journal of Verbal Learning and Verbal Behavior*, founded and edited by Benton J. Underwood in 1962, was a veritable factory of such work in adults, and it published work in short, largely theory-free bites, for the only theory underlying verbal learning was association. If it looked like a Kuhnian paradigm producing normal science, it was a paradigm that was about to be overthrown. Tulving and Madigan (1970) examined 540 studies on verbal learning and memory, roughly half of the total of such studies between 1940 and 1970, and were brutal in their evaluation of them. They evaluated each study in terms of what they called its "contributions to knowledge" and judged two-thirds of them as "utterly inconsequential." Future research and understanding of verbal learning and memory would not be affected at all if none of the papers in this category had seen the light of day"(Tulving & Madigan, 1970, p. 441). A quarter of the total was technically competent "run-of-the-mill" studies; only 10 percent were considered "worthwhile." And most of the worthwhile studies were in the camp of cognitive rather than behavioral associative memory.

Looking back from the present, several of Tulving and Madigan's suggestions were prescient indeed for the Ornstein Lab. First, Tulving and Madigan identified the notion of *elaboration coding*: When subjects remember the serial position of an item in the free-recall task, when they use initial letters of words to retrieve those words, when their behavior at the time of recall suggests that implicit associative responses were elicited by input items at the time of presentation, "to give but a few examples of an infinitely large number of possibilities, we have evidence of elaboration coding" (p. 462). And there is this: "What is the solution to the problem of lack of genuine progress in understanding memory? . . . [O]ne possibility does suggest itself: why not start looking for ways of experimentally studying, and incorporating into theories and models of memory, one of the truly unique characteristics of human memory: its knowledge of its own knowledge" (Tulving & Madigan, 1970, p. 477). That's metamemory, of course.

What was the status of knowledge of children's memory processes at the end of the verbal-learning period? Scattershot at best. Keppel's (1964) review of the subject found only a smattering of studies, rather unsystematically constructed with no real developmental aim in mind: "To know that the memory span increases with chronological age is certainly of interest to the educational and developmental psychologist, but unless this relationship can be translated into extant theories and produce predictions that will provide reasonable tests of these theories, the finding is of no immediate use to the verbal learning theorist" (Keppel, 1964, p. 77). But no such predictions could have been made from verbal learning, for the simple reason that associationism has no developmental theory to speak of; no developing structures had yet been postulated that could influence or impede the gradual build-up of associative strength.

Thus, at the end of the verbal-learning heyday there were experimental paradigms for learning lists of items, some associationist attempts at dealing with meaning, and findings concerning memory interference and serial-position curves, but few useful explanations for the findings. But, to use a grandiose historical comparison, in the same sense that the theory of natural selection could not have been confirmed without masses of data having been collected under the umbrella of natural theology, the methods and findings of verbal learning provided a framework for the cognitive information-processing period to come.

### The Era of Developmental Studies of Strategic Memorization

The most likely candidate for a paradigm-shifting publication from the verbal-learning to an information-processing approach to cognition is Atkinson and Shiffrin (1968), in which the multistore model of memory was first comprehensively reviewed. This chapter is so well-known to readers of this volume that it hardly needs to be reviewed here. Atkinson and Shiffrin integrated information from the classic verbal-learning tradition on adults, such as interference, serial-position curves, and paired-associate learning, with the cognitive work on the sensory store and short-term memory. Crucially, this research was sorted into structural registers, or stores, and control processes to operate on items (coding procedures, rehearsal operations, and search strategies). But the words "meaning" and "semantic" were nowhere to be found in this article, and "meaningfulness" was used as a vague placeholder. Although the computer metaphor was explicitly mentioned, much of the metatheory behind the multistore model – the operation of work or processes on "items" – still owes something to Ebbinghaus. Peterson and Peterson's (1959) seminal explication of the serial-position curve as dependent on the separate structures of the short-term versus the long-term store, after all, used meaningless pronounceable trigrams, just as Ebbinghaus did. And of course, there were no studies concerned with the growth and development of memory stores or processes.

Thus, around 1970, as Peter Ornstein was beginning his career, it appears in retrospect that everything was in place for a boom in research on developmental information processes in memory. The experimental methodology for list learning experiments of "items" was well established. Furthermore, the creation of the dichotomy of memory structures from memory processes made a partial developmental explanation possible in ways that a straight associationist explanation did not; indeed, the theories seemed to positively exclude developmental accounts because they provided nothing to grow.

The first step toward a developmental information-processing account of memory did rise from the verbal-learning literature. In the article that introduced the famous *mediation deficiency* in young children, Reese (1962) cited Kendler and Kendler (1959) but also Kuenne's (1946) work, which suggested that children can immediately reverse a discrimination rule if they have verbal labels to help them remember it. Vygotsky and Luria's notion that language acts as a mediator – a tool for thought – was also cited (Luria, 1961).

The classic connections between memory and strategy use were cemented in three articles around 1970 by Flavell and his colleagues. In addition to citing Luria and Vygotsky, Flavell, Beach, and Chinsky (1966) alluded to Eleanor Maccoby's (1964) suggestion that the inability to produce mediators that may be useful is different than the inability to use mediators to improve memory, which Flavell et al. (1966) coined as a *production deficiency*. Flavell et al.'s article documented that the incidence of rehearsal was nearly absent in five-year-olds but increased with age and in picture-naming conditions. Keeny, Cannizzo, and Flavell (1967) crisply proved the distinction between production and mediation deficiency: First graders who verbalized spontaneously remembered more than those who did not; those who were trained to use the strategy could do so, and when they did it worked, but the majority of children declined to use the rehearsal strategy on later trials. In his review of these studies and others, Flavell (1970), after examining and confirming the existence of production deficiencies for several strategies and modalities, expanded the concept of mediation beyond its verbal-learning roots: "Present evidence suggests … 'mnemonic mediation' may encompass an unexpectedly large and varied assortment of different cognitive activities, an assortment for which the classical schematization *r-s* (e.g., Kendler & Kendler, 1962) somehow seems an inadequate rubric" (p. 194). And, "In our view, a memory task can profitably be regarded as a type of problem-solving situation in which efforts at mnemonic mediation constitute the means or problem-solving strategy, and recall the goal or problem-solving solution . . . Should 'mediation' ever be dropped from the psychological lexicon, 'thinking' or one of its numerous synonyms might well replace it" (p. 195). In the same year, Flavell, Friedrichs, and Hoyt (1970) tested first-graders' predictions of their own memory spans, in what must be the first study of metamemory, without the name, citing Tulving and Madigan (1970). Finally, on April 1, 1971, Flavell served as a discussant at a Society for Research in Child Development (SRCD) symposium entitled "What Is Memory Development the Development of?," a presentation that Baker-Ward and Ornstein (2014) justly interpret as seminal.

The reason for declaring Flavell's presentation as being seminal, however, was not because it applied information-processing ideas to developmental processes but rather because it broadened memory development to the development of functional, adaptive problem solving. First, Flavell leveraged his knowledge of Piaget to argue that memory and intelligence, broadly conceived, cannot be separated; then he noted that memory development is simply another adaptive task of the mind, that it does its job with the general equipment with which the mind does other things. A general research strategy was suggested: Take interesting adult processes of memory as the end point and see how various components of this process are built through development. "To a cognitive developmental type, deliberate memorizing looks like a clear instance of planful, intentional, goal-directed, future-oriented behavior, and such behavior is hardly the stock in trade of the average 4-year old" (Flavell, 1971, p. 276). This implies that the study of the growth of strategy use and metamemory (a term coined in this article) is essential, and even gives a plan of action; but it also implies that memory may not be a separate faculty at all. "Memory development is largely the development of the mind itself, but the mind as viewed from a certain angle, or with respect to one of its numerous adaptational acts" (Flavell, 1970, p. 275).

Thus, in the same year that Tulving and Madigan drove a nail into the coffin of pure behaviorist verbal learning, developmental cognitive memory study was born and a research strategy laid down, but again, all the way back to Reese (1962), the route of this history went through Vygotsky, Luria, and Piaget, problem solving, and adaptation. Fortunately, the results could still often be interpreted in terms of multistore models – e.g., that children's serial-position recency effect disappears with distraction, just like adults', suggesting the existence of a short-term store.

What followed this breakthrough was a series of systematic explorations into the development of list-learning deliberate memory processes, or strategies, such as categorization (e.g., Bjorklund, Ornstein, & Haig, 1977; Corsale & Ornstein, 1980; Liberty & Ornstein, 1973) and elaborative rehearsal (e.g., Ornstein, Naus, & Liberty, 1975; Ornstein, Naus, & Stone, 1977). There were studies of what children knew about memory and metamemory (Kreutzer, Leonard, & Flavell, 1975), and studies that attempted to provide information about strategy use, feedback, and self-testing (e.g., Pressley, Levin, & Ghatala, 1984). Concomitant to this development was an examination of the effect of knowledge about the to-be-remembered domains on the use of strategies or metamemory knowledge. Domain knowledge (or "knowledge base") did not just make items from that domain easier to remember; it also facilitated the elicitation of the use of strategies themselves, even without direct instruction (e.g., Bjorklund, 1987; Corsale & Ornstein, 1980; Cox et al., 1989; see Best & Folds-Bennett, Chapter 4).

If this is the case, then it represents a breakdown of the dichotomy between processes and meaning that goes back to Ebbinghaus's *eigenlichte Gedächtnis* (memory proper). There was considerable bleed-over of the effect of meaningful items on the use of strategies. More seriously, as Flavell (1970) had hinted, transfer even of obviously effective strategy use was difficult to maintain; even elaborate methods to inculcate strategy transfer (such as those of Pressley and his colleagues) did not seem to work long term, or at least worked only in a subset of learners (e.g., Cox, 1989; Cox, Ornstein, & Valsiner, 1991). Or, when they were used, they were used inefficiently (e.g., Bjorklund et al., 1997). Another way of putting this would be to say that attempts to overcome production deficiencies themselves have production deficiencies.

By the early 1990s, the research on memory as a set of procedures underneath and separate from meaning was waning, in part because of the failure of transfer to meaningful contexts. In addition, there was little evidence that metamnemonic information was being taught in schools (e.g., Moely et al. 1992). More recently, work associated with the Ornstein Lab has found that most memory language in elementary school classes involves deliberate requests for facts in structured ways that require use of memory, and reflection on it, rather than instruction in strategies themselves. Strategic suggestions still make up a small part of instruction, but teachers vary considerably in their use (Coffman et al., 2008). When teachers use, or are taught to use, such suggestions (Grammer, Coffman, & Ornstein, 2013), they are associated with children's better use of the strategies, although not necessarily better recall than direct requests for meaningful information would allow. This work moved away from the time-honored list memorization studies to embedded meaningful activity. In other words, when metacognitive instruction is given to organize young children's knowledge of subjects such as engineering and math, that metacognition is evident in later sessions with that material, but not necessarily with abstract materials (e.g., Grammer et al., 2016). Indeed in this most recent work, there is a recognition that effective memory use may arise out of classroom experience with Cognitive Processing Language (CPL) that includes more than metamemory and may be closer to thinking itself, as Flavell (1970) predicted (Coffman et al., 2019; Hudson, Coffman, & Ornstein, 2018; see Coffman & Cook, Chapter 15) .

In the remainder of this chapter, I argue that meaning makes the difference, and by that I do not mean the memorization of meaningful materials alone, but also memory in the service of culturally valued and understood goals that serve to structure learning.

## The Development of the Adaptive Use of Memory in Meaningful Contexts

> [T]he experimental psychologist has only to consider that he is professing to deal with biological responses, and he will at once realise that so-called 'literal', or accurate, recall is an artificial con-struction of the armchair, or of the laboratory. Even if it could be secured, in the enormous majority of instances it would be biologi-cally detrimental. Life is a continuous play of adaptation between changing response and varying environment.... Remembering is a function of daily life, and must have developed so as to meet the demands of daily life. So our memories are constantly mingled with our constructions, are perhaps themselves to be treated as construc-tive in character (Bartlett, 1932, pp. 15–16).

At the beginning of his classic work *Remembering* (1932), Frederic Bartlett took Ebbinghaus's methods to task for dangerously oversimplifying mem-ory. Bartlett did not believe that meaning could be stripped from any stimulus, even nonsense words. To the extent that one seemingly succeeds in stripping meaning from a stimulus, an experimenter would then neces-sarily call forth from the subject artificial responses suitable only for that experimental situation. Moreover, just because a stimulus seems simplified does not mean that the stimulus necessarily calls forth a simple response free of subjectivity. Indeed, since people rarely encounter meaningless stimuli – which are useless by definition – they are forced to laboriously create new behaviors to deal with them (see Bartlett, 1932, pp. 3–7).

Bartlett's approach was a combination of perspectives almost diametrically opposite to the psychophysical methods that had inspired Ebbinghaus. First was the importance of culture. In Bartlett's first book, *Psychology and Primitive Culture* (1923), he had already moved beyond memory as contents in one person's head. In the chapter "Psychology and the Folk Story," Bartlett argued that stories are a social product, often without a known beginning, created in social fashion for a social purpose. Second, Bartlett was strongly influenced by functionalism, a school that, incorporating evolutionary insights with the ongoing electrical nature of nervous impulses, focused on the adaptive, fluid, and recurrent nature of thought (James, 1890; see also Cox, 2019, chapter 7). With this in mind, it is not hard to understand Bartlett's famous functional notion of *schema*, which, he apologized, is a term "at once too definite and too sketchy," and which he defined as an "active organization of past reactions or of past experiences which must always be supposed to be operating in any well-adapted organic response" (Bartlett, 1932, p. 201).

How then should we use Bartlett's insights in developmental memory studies? How and why do we convert the laboratory experiment into a field or ecologically valid study? Bartlett's point, I think, was that the meaning and goal structure of an experiment must connect in some way with the stories of the culture in which it is conducted. Elegant experimental and control conditions speak to the culture of science, but to a child, a control condition in which the child is not offered help to perform a memory task may be quite unusual (see Cox et al., 1991). Bartlett's preference to sacrifice rigid uniformity in stimuli for functional similarity in response – a "well-adapted organic response" – has puzzled many researchers, who find his experiments to be unforgivably sloppy (like a similar group of methodologists who were exasperated by Piaget), but developmentalists are usually taught that all subjects must understand the tasks in a similar way, and experimenters will bend instructions as written (slightly) to achieve that goal; it's just not often written up that way in our scientific narratives.

By cultural story, I do not mean a folktale or "The War of the Ghosts." I mean to ask instead, is the task a game or a school assignment, like a lesson or a test? Is it a task where the child is an expert or the adult? Is the recall required in a special cultural setting, such as a courtroom? Culture need not be exotic; it is simply what we do where we live. Culture provides the goal structure of virtually all of our actions, in a way that much of the information-processing research was ill-equipped to handle because of its reliance on computer metaphors. In contrast to the verbal-learning paradigm, which attempted to reinterpret memory as conditioned responses, the information-processing approach often put everything – storage and strategies – in the head. Culture is not confined to either place; we could therefore say that a child's use of memory depends on, or is elicited by, the context, relieving him or her from the burden of carrying everything in the head. If we know the purpose, we know the cultural context. It seems clear that for Bartlett, memory was not a faculty but an adaptive function; adaptation requires goals, and the goals of memory – and the definition of memory itself – is culturally bound.

In the remainder of this chapter, I argue that the considerable successes in developmental memory research in recent years are largely based on tasks that at micro and macro levels are bound by cultural expectations and meanings, albeit expectations such as what it means for boys and girls to tell stories about past events in exotic locations such as Disneyland, doctors' offices, and courtrooms. Then, and only then, if we want the results to replicate, the armamentarium of experimental structure and methodology dictated by the culture of scientific rigor can be brought to bear.

### Event Memory and Meaning: The Foundations

The place to start any contemporary functionalist, meaning-making account of memory-making is with the work of Katherine Nelson. Two delightful, classic studies of children's linguistic productions, "At Morning It's Lunchtime: A Scriptal View of Children's Dialogue" (Nelson & Gruendel, 1976) and *Narratives from the Crib* (Nelson, 1989), highlight the centrality of narratives for a functionalist account of the development of memory. Nelson and Gruendel make the point that scripts are constructed in dialogic social interactions with caregivers and friends, within a culture.

*Narratives* (Nelson, 1989) used a corpus of recordings of a 2-year-old named Emily as she talked to herself before bedtime every night, apparently going over the events of the day and preparing for future events. These monologues show that although a child might need an elementary sense of self to begin the project of constructing linguistic scripts of what to expect in specific situations, she does not always need an interlocutor, only a recursive feedback loop to refine and expand her knowledge. The urge to construct story frames appears natural and necessary, but a young child's script knowledge must be built from experience and negotiated through dialogue. If the scripts of say, two 4-year-olds do not match (such as a script about lunchtime), Nelson and Gruendel (1976) point out, their discourse will look more like two egocentric monologues than one conversation.

As Reese and Fivush and Haden discovered, children can form scripts by extracting material from what is common and what is less so in an event in repeated experiences and placing this in sentence frames to talk about those experiences; they determine the difference between what happens in a situation and what happened in a situation early, and with few experiences (Fivush, 1984). Talking about past events itself is constructed in dialogue with parents, and the style of discussing present events matters for how well children recall them later; parents who link a current event to a past event – linking memory experiences to autobiography – are likely to have children who remember new experiences later (e.g., Reese & Fivush, 1993; Reese, Haden, & Fivush, 1993; Fivush, Haden, & Reese, 2006). Such interactions can also be gendered, leading to a difference between boys and girls in, for example, recall of emotional material (e.g. Fivush, 1993; Fivush et al., 2000).

In a longitudinal study, researchers associated with the Ornstein Lab extended the linkages between the kinds of talk between parent and child and later memory development by establishing not only that parents with high elaboration and engagement had children who respond more correctly consistently to *wh*-questions between 36 and 42 months but also that that parental style led to an increase in correct responses with time (Hedrick, San Souci et al., 2009). Then, in a randomized training study, children who interacted with researchers who used a high-elaboration strategy during and after an event provided more features and elaborations on a 3-week posttest than those who had been given a low-interactive interlocutor (Hedrick, Haden, & Ornstein, 2009; see Hedrick, Chapter 11).

### *"Tell me What Happened": Event Memory in Natural Cultural Contexts*

By the 1990s, it was time for the researchers associated with the Ornstein Lab to craft a major study of children's memory of life events, and it was decided to study children's memory for doctors' office visits (Baker-Ward, Gordon et al., 1993). A doctors' office visit is a rich, slightly stressful real-life routine that most children repeatedly experience every few months that therefore has an expected script-like structure, with subtle differences in multiple small actions and people for each visit and child. Memory for this meaningful event was then subjected to rigorous experimental control: 3-, 5-, and 7-year-olds were randomly assigned to conditions with one versus two interviews, immediately in the waiting room, and at 1-, 3-, or 6-week delays, probed at recall by open-ended and yes–no questions. Standardized vocabulary, the child's stress, and any confounding intervening events were measured. This study was preceded by methodological studies on a sensitive, open-ended interview protocol followed by careful probing (Ornstein, Gordon, & Larus, 1992), and with studies of children's underlying knowledge structure of such visits (Clubb et al., 1993), and a later examination of the implications of systems for coding open-ended recall (Baker-Ward et al., 1995). Unlike many other studies that examined children's recall under conditions of repetitive attempts to mislead them (see below), this study showed that when sensitive interviewing is used, even 3-year-old children can recall accurately over 80 percent of such events, and will only give a small fraction of that in response to general prompts. Judicious probing is necessary to get a full account, and, of course, such probing can introduce errors. Also, at long delays, young children can insert script-consistent events that they did not experience (Ornstein et al., 1998). A more elaborate study using the same methodology (Ornstein, Baker-Ward et al., 2006) replicated these results. Interestingly, this latter study included a check of office-visit script knowledge for half of the children; it also noted that between the ages of 4 and 7 years, memory decay in recall did occur, but it was similar in rate and amount for children of all ages, and children were able to correctly deny yes–no prompts about events that might occur in that setting about 85 percent of the time even after a 6-month delay. Prior knowledge of the doctors' office script varied greatly at the youngest age and contributed to recall over and above expected increases due to age (see Baker-Ward & Thomas, Chapter 7).

This set of studies was near the beginning of a surge of research surrounding children's recall of medical visits – in the dental office (e.g., Baker-Ward et al., 2015); in the emergency room (e.g., Peterson & Bell, 1996); after traumatic injury (e.g., Burgwyn-Bailes et al., 2001); and in unusual, stressful, and embarrassing medical procedures, such as a voiding cystourethragram (VCUG; e.g., Brown et al., 1999). Rather than calling this work merely a step in the right direction for increasing ecological validity, which it was, I would rather call it bringing the lab to the field, because many such studies were conducted with at least some random assignment, use of nontrivial control groups, validity and manipulation checks, signal detection methodology, and so on. These methods allow the culture of science to address questions such as "Are repeated interviews harmful?" (No, if information has been elicited by open-ended questions: Baker-Ward, Gordon et al., 1993; Poole & White 1991, 1993; see Price &

Connolly, Chapter 8), or "Do children remember more or less about stressful medical procedures than about a typical office visit?". (Compared to a full well-visit control, a VCUG procedure elicited both more accurate *and* more inaccurate details, e.g., Brown, et al., 1999.)

Although children in these studies were presumably using whatever basic memory processes they had, these are not studies of "memory proper"; they are studies in the context of culturally valuable events, with the child adapting to whatever social expectations, pressures, and goal structures are operating in those events. Separating "memory" from "context" seems beside the point. It is about using memory adaptively in response to the meaningful goals of the situation, and the result is a more articulated knowledge of what happens in medical settings, of scripts, and their exceptions. Memory for the child's central experience of these events is surprisingly good, unless the child is distraught; and stress can be surprisingly low, probably because the script is preceded by preparatory explanations from parents and medical personnel, professional calm and empathy, and the promise of a lollipop or ice cream afterward. As any parent knows, stressful events may then be talked about frequently thereafter in dialogues or monologues as a kind of rudimentary self-regulation. In this way, the event is integrated into the child's autobiographical narrative, to be relatively remembered, folded into script knowledge, or forgotten as the story's usefulness dictates.

### Children in Court: Caught in a Web of Suggestion

There was another reason for this set of studies of memory in real, albeit stressful contexts: The medical setting is virtually the only one that children are permitted and expected to take their clothes off in front of a relative stranger and that meets the ethical requirements for research. In the late 1980s through the mid-1990s, a rash of legal cases alleging sexual abuse of children in daycare settings broke out. These cases were extensively discussed in Ceci and Bruck's (1995) now-classic *Jeopardy in the Courtroom*. The Little Rascals case began in North Carolina as the finishing touches were put on the research grant for what became Baker-Ward, Gordon et al. (1993). Each of these cases, and many more, showed officers of the court, parents, and other family members using egregiously leading and coercive questioning tactics on children about alleged abuse having possibly happened to children as young as three. Confirmatory bias, numerous repeated questions within and across sessions, overuse of directed yes–no questions, and even the use of tag-questions (e.g., "He did this, didn't he?") were seen. Stereotype induction, implied bribing and threatening of children, and drilling on inconsistencies within children's reports were rife in interviews. As it had been estimated that children caught up in our adversarial justice system are interviewed an average of 11 times over the course of up to two years before trial (Ceci & Bruck, 1995), this was an urgent problem that, at the time, psychologists were ill-equipped to ameliorate. Clinicians often made the problem worse by using play therapy, guided imagery, or anatomically correct dolls. Adaptive memory use, in a world of anxious adults, is memory under pressure (see, e.g., Poole & Bruck, 2012).

The studies on memory for medical contexts, discussed thus far, including most of those from Ornstein and his colleagues, were intent on maximizing accurate reports from children. The Ornstein Lab only ever misled children in the gentlest of ways. In keeping with the urgency of the times, Ceci, Bruck, and their colleagues were more interested in how to use the paradigm and other designs to sound the alarm of how inaccurate children's reports can be under pressure. For example, Bruck, Ceci, Francoeur, and Barr (1995) tried to influence 5-year-old children's reports of pain they had experienced during an inoculation with pain-affirming or pain-denying feedback compared to no feedback; the children's reports were all accurate one week later. They were then invited back nearly a year later and given three sessions of misleading information about the events they experienced as well as their reactions to the shot itself. Under misleading conditions, this design boosted errors to 50%; in the condition with no misleading information, however, errors were around 10%. This finding, that children can be relatively easily misled by administering biased information before or after an event – especially if the recall is of an innocuous event that happened long ago – is common. But it is also common for errors in control conditions to be quite low (e.g., Leichtman & Ceci, 1995; Lepore & Sesco, 1994).

Early on, the tendency was to label young children, especially those under the age of about 7, as *suggestible*. But in actuality, it was the often well-meaning adults conducting the interviews who were *suggestive*. Children can be accurate under the right conditions, but they are *vulnerable to suggestion*, as are people of any age, when enough pressure is applied. In fact, we should remember that the cultural expectations of any modern legal system are not based on accurate psychology; the system sets an unrealistically high bar for memory accuracy for anyone caught in it, and children are at a disadvantage.

The literature on interviewing children for court built up over the last 25 years is vast and beyond the scope of this chapter. But there is a happy ending. Over the past 20 years, methodical, empirically based procedures done in the spirit of bringing control conditions and rigorous methodology to the field have coalesced around the U S National Institute for Child Health and Development (NICHD) interview protocols (see Lamb et al., 2018 for these protocols and a research-rich description of their development).

The interview procedure used to promote an accurate account of the alleged incident of interest is, perhaps surprisingly, almost the same gentle questioning methodology found in Ornstein, Gordon, and Larus (1992) and Baker-Ward, Gordon et al. (1993), and carried forward by Poole and Lamb (1998); that is, begin with open invitations, then move to narrower open-ended prompts, followed by careful probes for specific information. Only if essential information has not yet been given would yes–no or option-posing questions be used. Try to avoid repeated questions about what has already been mentioned, and speak only about what is in the child's own open-ended answers until a full account of each event has been given.

## Bringing a Lab to the World

In the areas of memory strategies, script development, and use of memory in real-world cultural settings, Ornstein and his colleagues asked these questions: First you see if you can elicit something from children. Then you see whether it works when they use a cognitive strategy (e.g., Ornstein, Naus, & Stone, 1977, with rehearsal). If it works, you see if it can be taught (e.g., memory-relevant instructional techniques: Grammer, Coffman, & Ornstein, 2013). Then you see how it is taught in the world and by whom. Finally, you examine the longitudinal developmental consequences over time of its being taught (e.g., mother–child talk: Hedrick, San Souci, et al. 2009). As I see it in retrospect, the course of the study of the development of memory diverged from studies of memory on adults – research conducted without the assumption of development – around 1971, the year of Flavell's famous SRCD symposium discussed earlier; this is a divergence that Ornstein has noted in a number of publications. Flavell's comments on what develops in children's memory placed memory squarely in the center of thinking itself, and others took it further. The behavioral, verbal-learning, and information-processing approaches each provided new and rigorous methods to apply to memory development, and providing rigor and clarity of design for studying children's memory are some of Ornstein's significant contributions to the field; he always knows what method to apply to the problem, and what are the theoretical consequences of doing so. But Peter Ornstein did not stop there; he and the many students influenced by him (and who, in turn, influenced him) took that rigor and applied it to the study of the development of memory as an adaptive skill in the world. As the other chapters in this volume will confirm, it is an impressive contribution indeed.

# CHAPTER 3

# Memory *Development or the* Development *of Memory?*
## An Update

### Catherine A. Haden

In 2001, Peter Ornstein and I published a paper in *Current Directions in Psychological Science,* entitled "*Memory* Development or the *Development* of Memory?" In it, we acknowledged the considerable progress of research on memory development in advancing understanding of the mnemonic skills of children of different ages. Nevertheless, we argued what was missing was a focus on the *development* of memory, that is, studies that shed light on the processes that drive the development of skilled remembering (Ornstein & Haden, 2001a). In this chapter, I begin by recapping the position we took in our 2001 paper. Then I turn to offer an update on movements in the field that reflect our vision of expanding research paradigms to track developmental changes within individual children over time using different tasks and designs (i.e., multi-task assessments), and attending to the social context in which children's memory skills are developing.

## What Is Memory Development the Development of?

The first studies of children's memory were published more than 125 years ago (e.g., Binet & Henri, 1884b; Jacobs, 1887). Nonetheless, programmatic work on memory development did not begin in earnest until the middle 1960s, with John Flavell's pivotal explorations of children's use of naming and rehearsal *strategies* in the service of remembering (e.g., Flavell, Beach, & Chinsky, 1966; see Cox, Chapter 2). A few years later, the title of Flavell's now-celebrated symposium at the 1971 meeting of the Society for Research in Child Development posed a question that defined research on children's memory for several decades to come: "What Is Memory Development the Development Of?"

By the late 1970s, research on age-related changes in children's mnemonic skills was increasing in a dramatic fashion. This growth was reflected in the publication of several volumes (e.g., Kail & Hagen, 1977), including Ornstein's (1978/2014) *Memory Development in*

*Children*, and by the rise in the number of peer-reviewed journal articles on children's memory (see Baker-Ward & Ornstein, 2014). Information-processing approaches that had gained acceptance in the 1960s provided the theoretical underpinnings for this research that offered a detailed picture of age-related differences in children's memory skills (Schneider & Ornstein, 2015). Studies focused on the deployment and effectiveness of children's use of strategies such as rehearsal and organization in tasks that required children to engage in deliberate remembering. The research participants were primarily school-aged children. The design of the studies was almost all cross-sectional, involving comparisons of groups of children of different ages, who were asked to remember sets of words, pictures, or objects. When older children engaged in more strategy use and remembered more relative to younger children, the findings were attributed to developmental differences between the groups.

To be sure, the answers to Flavell's "what develops" question have changed over time, as have the conceptual frameworks characterizing the nature of remembering, the methods for studying memory development, and the ages of the children involved in memory research. Nevertheless, we maintained in our 2001 piece that the major thrust of research on children's memory remained largely aimed at characterizing that *something* (e.g., mnemonic strategies, underlying knowledge, basic memory capacity) was thought to be changing with age. Indeed, a voluminous research literature documents the contrasting memory skills of children of different ages. However, we asserted that there had been too little attention paid to addressing questions about the process of development. For example, how do early manifestations of a skill (e.g., a naming strategy) give way to later and more sophisticated examples of that skill (e.g., a more complex rehearsal strategy), and what can be said about the rate of change that is observed? Most importantly, what factors are responsible for bringing about this developmental change? This state of the field at the time led us to make the following statement: "it is as if researchers have focused on *memory* development and have not been concerned with the *development* of memory" (Ornstein & Haden, 2001a, p. 202).

## Toward the Study of the Development of Memory

The main objective of our 2001 paper was to offer a vision for the type of research we thought was necessary to advance understanding of the *development* of memory (Ornstein & Haden, 2001a). I briefly summarize our vision here.

From our perspective, a developmental analysis of memory (or any other set of skills, for that matter) requires researchers to (1) make a cognitive diagnosis, (2) describe developmental changes within individuals, and (3) identify mediators of developmental change. Cognitive diagnosis involves description of memory abilities of children of different ages. This is not necessarily easy, because children's performance may vary from setting to setting as a function of the information-processing requirements and level of support or scaffolding that is available. The paradigm-driven nature of work on children's memory limits understanding of linkages across tasks that vary in their demands. There were, however, some notable exceptions. For example, Bauer (e.g., Bauer et al., 2000) compared infants' abilities to imitate modeled sequences of actions that were arbitrary (i.e., no inherent constraints on the temporal position of the actions) versus enabling (i.e., actions performed in a temporally invariant pattern to reach an end state). Guttentag, Ornstein, and Siemens (1987) compared children's use of a rehearsal strategy to remember sets of items under conditions that were typical (i.e., each item removed from view after being presented) versus scaffolded (i.e., each item remained visible after being presented). In both of these studies, the within-subjects, across-task contrasts provided important diagnostic information about the nature of memory and its development.

Further limiting understanding of developmental change was the fact that the bulk of the memory development literature remained based on cross-sectional experiments. Cross-sectional studies present useful accounts of average-level competence on specified tasks at particular ages. However, there is nothing in a cross-sectional study design that enables inferences about the course of development for an individual child, or the contrasting patterns of change for different groups of children. Therefore, the cross-sectional literature can say nothing about how early skill in, for example, elicited imitation of previously modeled action sequences relates to later abilities recalling past events, and still later competency in tasks that require deliberate memorization.

Charting developmental change within individuals over time requires longitudinal research methods. Longitudinal studies are essential for describing the ways in which early demonstrations of skills relate to later articulations of cognitive competence. However, we argued that insights into development will still be limited unless longitudinal studies are expanded to include appropriate across-task comparisons and designed to consider potential mediators of developmental change. Within-individual descriptions of change across tasks and over time, as difficult as they may be to obtain, may not provide sufficient insights into the factors that drive development. Indeed, paradoxically, not all longitudinal studies are developmental in the sense of addressing the difficult question of "What are the forces that propel development and served to mediate developmental change?"

Therefore, the challenge is for a commitment to longitudinal research designs that can truly increase understanding of the development of memory. Such a commitment requires a willingness to move across conceptual boundaries, such as those of the information-processing and social-constructivist traditions. It is useful to think about the encoding, storage, and retrieval of information in information-processing terms. Nonetheless, the social-constructivist perspective – emphasizing as it does social and communicative interactions between children and adults – seems ideal for facilitating the discovery of mediators of developmental change. By bridging across these approaches, it should be possible to obtain precise cognitive diagnosis of changing skills of individual children over time, as well as some insights into the social forces that drive development (Ornstein & Haden, 2001a).

## Longitudinal Research on the Development of Memory

Until the mid-1980s, there were few longitudinal studies of children's memory. This is perhaps not surprising when one considers the myriad challenges of conducting longitudinal research (see Reese, 2014 and Schneider, 2014, for discussion). Longitudinal investigations are laborious. Research teams need to not only conduct the research activities but also engage in (often Herculean) efforts to retain the sample across the multiple assessment points. There is also the challenge of identifying assessments that can provide valid measures across multiple ages. Further, as Bauer (2014) put it, "Longitudinal studies are the Lamborghinis of developmental science" (p. 944). They are expensive. But unlike Lamborghinis, longitudinal studies are not fast. One must wait for children to age in order to observe and explain developmental change. It can take considerable time to get to the point of publishing findings across multiple age points in a longitudinal study. These pragmatic issues notwithstanding, we argued that longitudinal studies are crucial for a developmental analysis of memory in which the progression of skills are traced within individual children and factors that may drive developmental change are explored (Ornstein & Haden, 2001a).

In the following three sections, I illustrate the vision we offered in Ornstein and Haden (2001a) with some of the very exciting ways recent longitudinal research contributes to understanding both children's memory skills at specific points in development and the development of memory over time. It is important to note that Peter Ornstein and his former students have contributed a great deal to this body of work. There are recent comprehensive reviews of research in each of these areas that provide detailed testament to the ways the field has advanced (see Bauer & Fivush, 2014). My purpose here, therefore, is to highlight in a very brief and selective fashion, some significant ways longitudinal work is contributing to understanding the development of memory and shedding light on social mediators of developmental change.

### Longitudinal Research on Strategy Development

Until the 1980s, there was a real absence of longitudinal research on strategy development (see Schneider, 2014). Guttentag et al. (1987) conducted one of the first longitudinal studies of children's memory strategies – a short-term investigation of changes in children's use of deliberate rehearsal techniques from third to fourth grade. Interestingly, Guttentag et al. showed that fourth graders' use of an active rehearsal strategy under typical item-by-item presentation conditions was better predicted by what they could do a year earlier in a scaffolded task compared with their performance in third grade on the typical version of the task. Although limited in scope, this study is an important illustration of research tracing changes in individual children's performance over time, as well as the diagnostic utility of a multi-task assessment strategy.

Two other longitudinal studies, one launched in 1984 (the Munich Longitudinal Study on the Genesis of Individual Competencies [LOGIC]) and another beginning in 2001 (the Würzburg-Göttingen longitudinal memory study [WGLS]; see Schneider, 2014, for review), offer major insights into developmental changes in children's strategic competence. The LOGIC study tracked children over annual waves of data collection between 4 and 13 years of age. (Two additional assessments occurred when participants were 18 and 23 years old.) In the WGLS study, children were presented with several memory tasks every six months, for nine waves of data collection between 6 and 9 years of age. Although these two longitudinal studies were different in several respects, both revealed that at the level of individual children, strategy development is not as linear as would be expected based on group-level, cross-sectional results. In particular, in both investigations, the improvements in children's strategy use offered a picture of dramatic leaps in performance, not gradual increases in sophistication with age. Moreover, in both the LOGIC and WGLS studies, acquiring new strategies was not simply a matter of "out with the old and in with the new." Simple and less-effective strategies resided alongside more sophisticated and efficient ones, and individual children discovered, then lost, then rediscovered the same strategy at different points in time.

LOGIC and other longitudinal studies also contributed to understanding factors that may account for the variability observed in strategy acquisition (Grammer et al., 2011; Schneider, 2014). For example, paralleling age-related developments in children's strategy use are changes in their metamemory functioning, that is, their understanding of the demands of various memory tasks and the operation of the memory system (Flavell & Wellman, 1977). By tracking strategy use and metamemory across tasks in the same children over time, it is possible to address developmental links between metamemory and strategy use. The results point to earlier metamemory being associated with later use of strategies. Metamemory connects more strongly to strategy use than to recall performance. Furthermore, the links among metamemory, strategy use, and recall grow stronger with age (Schneider, 2014).

Longitudinal research now also provides insights into social contexts that support the emergence and refinement of children's strategy development. Given evidence of the importance of schooling for the development of deliberate skills for remembering (e.g., Morrison, Smith, & Dow-Ehrensberger, 1995), Ornstein, Coffman, and colleagues have carried out extensive observations in elementary school classrooms (e.g., Coffman et al., 2019; Coffman et al., 2008; Ornstein, Grammer, & Coffman, 2010). Their aim is to understand what about the early school context is important. The work demonstrates that teachers differ in the extent to which they use memory-relevant talk – what they called *cognitive processing language* (CPL) – during the course of instruction (see Coffman & Cook, Chapter 15 for details). By spring of the first-grade year, children with teachers using high levels of CPL in their classroom instruction evidenced better skills in the use of deliberate strategies than first graders taught by teachers using low levels of CPL. Moreover, there were long-lasting associations between first-grade teachers' use of CPL and children's strategy skills in second and fourth grade (when different teachers taught the children). To a considerable extent, this longitudinal work suggests that memory-relevant teacher language is one potential mechanism for the development of children's strategy discovery and utilization that has implications for children's deliberate skills for remembering years later.

*Longitudinal Research on Event Memory Development*

Although longitudinal work on children's deliberate remembering has increased over the years, research on children's autobiographical and event memory offers many more examples of the application of longitudinal methods (Baker-Ward & Ornstein, 2014; Reese, 2014). Several longitudinal case studies of individual children's early verbal memories describe how almost as soon as children start talking, they begin referencing past events (e.g., Nelson, 1989; Reese, 1999). Studies in which the same children were interviewed by researchers about a range of novel past events at several ages during early childhood document the tremendous progress young children make in providing well-organized and detailed verbal accounts of past experiences (e.g., Fivush, Haden, & Adam, 1995). From around the age of three, children begin to go beyond reporting what happened, as in simple script reports of routine and familiar events, to providing increasingly coherent accounts that place novel past experiences in context and evaluate their personal meaning. By following the same children over time, these studies also provide important information about stability and change in the level of detail and coherence of children's autobiographical memory narratives.

Longitudinal designs are also essential in research focused on the fate of early individual memories over time. These investigations involve the same children reporting about the same events at multiple age points. Some of these studies address whether and under what conditions individual children are able to verbally recall specific events they experienced prior to the onset of language (e.g., Bauer, Wenner, & Kroupina, 2002; Cheatham & Bauer, 2005; Jack, Simcock, & Hayne, 2012; Morris & Baker-Ward, 2007; Peterson & Rideout, 1998; Simcock & Hayne, 2002). Other work considers children's long-term retention of salient and emotional events, including stressful medical procedures (e.g., Brown et al., 1999; Merritt, Ornstein, & Spicker, 1994), injuries requiring an emergency room visit and/or surgery (Burgwyn-Bailes et al., 2001; Peterson, 2002), and destructive hurricanes (e.g., Fivush et al., 2004; Sales et al., 2005). The longitudinal nature of these studies enables the identification of important factors – such as children's ages at the time of events, their language and narrative skills, and the emotional valence and stress associated with the experiences – that are potent predictors of how detailed and accurate children's reports of early memories are across many years. Longitudinal research has also revealed how the child's age, the nature of the event, and repeated interviewing and event reinstatement at different points over the retention interval can extend individual event memories across long delays (e.g., Bauer et al., 2000; Hudson & Grysman, 2014).

Increasingly, longitudinal research also provides insights into the mediating role that social-communicative interactions between parents and children can play in bringing about developmental changes in children's autobiographical and event memory. In one of the first of these studies, Robyn Fivush, Elaine Reese, and I observed children talking about the past with their mothers and fathers, as well as researchers, at multiple age points between 40 and 70 months of age (Reese, Haden, & Fivush, 1993). We found that in contrast to mothers demonstrating a low-elaborative reminiscing style, mothers with a high-elaborative reminiscing style elicited long, embellished discussions of past events with their children. Maternal elaborativeness during early conversations about the past when the children were 40 months old was positively associated with children's recall of past experiences in later conversations at 58 and 70 months of age (Reese et al., 1993). The children of more elaborative mothers also expressed more detailed and coherent memory reports as much as a year-and-a-half later during unscaffolded interviews conducted by a researcher (e.g., Haden, Haine, & Fivush, 1997). Thus, early maternal reminiscing style is associated with children's subsequent, across-task memory for personally experienced events.

A substantial body of longitudinal work has replicated and extended these findings (see Fivush, 2014; Fivush et al., 2006, for reviews). Some have started with the very earliest conversations between mothers and children about events they experienced together (e.g., Farrant & Reese, 2000; Harley & Reese, 1999). For example, we (Haden et al., 2009) observed mother–child reminiscing over three age points beginning when children were 18 months old. Our work featured detailed analyses of mothers' use of open-ended question elaborations (e.g., "What did we do?", "Where were we when we heard that noise?") and statement elaborations ("We saw lots of dinosaurs at the museum."), as well as children's provision of memory information over time. Whereas statement elaborations were in fact negatively associated with children's memory reports over time, mothers' early use of open-ended elaborative questions to elicit children's participation was uniquely predictive of children's later reporting skills. This work is important in speaking to what specific conversational techniques are potential mechanisms by which maternal reminiscing style affects children's developing memory skills.

Cross-cultural longitudinal studies also find positive associations between maternal elaborative reminiscing and preschool children's autobiographical memory skills, although parent–child reminiscing seems to be most frequent in Western cultures (Fivush & Haden, 2003; Wang, 2013). Moreover, in two different New Zealand samples, Reese traced linkages between mothers' natural use of elaborative reminiscing style and children's developing autobiographical memory skills from early childhood through adolescence (Jack et al., 2009; Reese, Jack, & White, 2010; Reese & Roberston, 2019). A remarkable aspect of this work that is not possible in cross-sectional studies is the effort to test how multiple different factors – including children's self-awareness, and social-cognitive and socioemotional development – may be important at different points in development and contribute to individual differences in autobiographical memory over time. The main findings from this work are that a host of early childhood factors are associated with autobiographical memory development. Nevertheless, maternal reminiscing style is a strong and unique predictor of adolescents' earlier memories of their childhoods, as well as their longer, more insightful, and emotionally expressive autobiographical memory narratives from adolescence. Longitudinal work over the very long term such as this provides tremendous insights into the ways that early social interactions between parents and children may serve to mediate the development of children's autobiographical memory.

### Developmental Linkages among Autobiographical and Deliberate Memory Skills

Because of the largely paradigm-driven nature of research on children's memory, only recently has longitudinal research considered the ways in which the development of skills for reporting past events may set the stage for the emergence and refinement of deliberate memory strategies. Despite the largely separate treatment in the literature, Ornstein, Haden, and Elischbeger (2006; see also Ornstein & Haden, 2001a) proposed that we should expect to see developmental linkages because event memory and strategic memory share the same underlying processes of encoding, storage, retrieval, and reporting of information. Moreover, we speculated that autobiographical and deliberate memory might also share similar underlying mechanisms that drive development in adult–child conversational interactions. To test these claims, it is necessary to conduct longitudinal research that characterizes the social-communicative milieu of the home and school contexts in which these two forms of memory develop.

A few studies have made steps in this direction by linking mother–child conversational interactions and children's autobiographical and deliberate memory skills. Consider, for example, a longitudinal study in which we (Haden et al., 2001) observed children engage in activities we staged in their living rooms at each of three age points, when the children were 2.5, 3, and 3.5 years old. We found strong associations between the ways mothers and children talked about the events as they were unfolding and children's subsequent memory for these experiences. This study was unique, on the one hand, for considering how mother–child conversations *during* events might affect children's event memory at different ages. On the other hand, we included an assessment of the children's deliberate memory at the final age point to explore potential linkages between early forms of event and deliberate remembering. We found that the children's recall of objects in the deliberate memory task at 3.5 years of age was associated with their recall of the events they had jointly experienced with their mothers as much as one year earlier. Moreover, in separate analyses, we found that mothers who were more elaborative (Ornstein, Haden, & Coffman, 2011) and who talked more about the process of remembering (Rudek & Haden, 2005) when reminiscing with their children had children who engaged in more strategic behaviors in a deliberate memory task a year later.

Importantly, the strongest evidence to date of shared social-conversational mechanisms in the development of autobiographical and deliberate memory comes from a large-scale longitudinal study reported by Langley, Coffman, and Ornstein (2017). In this project, when the children were 3, 5, and 6 years old, they were observed both reminiscing with their mothers and engaging in a deliberate memory task. In addition to the associations between maternal elaborative reminiscing and children's autobiographical memory performance, there were also strong associations between maternal reminiscing style and children's deliberate memory recall. It may be that engaging with a mother with a highly elaborative reminiscing style provides children with practice in searching their memories to retrieve information to report about events. This practice may not only advance children's event memory performance but also be key to developing skills required for recalling and reporting information in a deliberate memory task as well (Haden et al., 2001; Langley et al., 2017).

## A Marriage of Methods

It is important to point out that longitudinal research is inherently correlational in nature, and as such, it precludes statements of causation. From our perspective (Ornstein, Haden, & Hedrick, 2004), it is essential, therefore, to supplement these within-subjects approaches with experimental interventions in which variables of theoretical importance – such as the nature of the conversations to which children are exposed – are brought under experimental control. There are a few examples of such a "marriage" of methodological approaches, whereby factors that emerge in longitudinal work as potential mediators of developmental change are paired with training studies in which these mediators are explored experimentally (e.g., Hedrick, Haden, & Ornstein, 2009; McGuigan & Salmon, 2004; see Reese, 2018, for review). As we see it (e.g., Ornstein, Haden, & San Souci, 2008), such efforts present another important way by which to meet the challenge of studying both memory development and the development of memory.

Consider, for example, an experimental project carried out by Grammer, Coffman, and Ornstein (2013) to follow up the findings of Coffman et al. (2008) regarding the linkages between teachers' use of CPL and children's memory skills. Interestingly, whereas all children in this study learned new factual information from lessons delivered with high or low levels of CPL, children exposed to high CPL instruction exhibited greater strategic knowledge and engaged in more sophisticated strategy use to remember lesson content than children exposed to low CPL instruction. Likewise, in Boland, Ornstein, and Haden (2003), following a baseline assessment of children's language skills, children were randomly assigned to either a maternal-style training or no-training condition. Trained mothers were instructed to use four conversational techniques associated with an elaborative style as they were experiencing an event with their children. Even though this study was short term, we found substantial effects of both maternal training and children's language skill on remembering the event at two delay intervals.

Other work involving training mothers in elaborative reminiscing indicates that the impact of reminiscing may not be apparent at short delays (Peterson, Jesso, & McCabe, 1999; Van Bergen et al., 2009). Rather, long-term follow-ups may be necessary to observe effects of reminiscing training that may be evident only once children have had the time to internalize the skills that elaborative reminiscing promotes (Reese, 2018). Therefore, to evaluate fully the role of maternal reminiscing with young children experimentally, it seems important to undertake longitudinal training studies that can examine long-term benefits. A conspicuous example of this approach is Reese and colleagues' (Reese & Newcombe, 2007; Reese et al., 2020) *Growing Memories* intervention that involved training mothers in elaborative reminiscing across multiple age points in early childhood and identified effects of training even as the children reached early adolescence.

## Looking Ahead

This update to our 2001 paper, albeit selective in scope, elucidates the unmistakable contributions of longitudinal work to our understanding of the development of memory, characterizing both the nature of what is changing with age and the factors that bring about such change. Recent longitudinal work features attention to social contexts, in some cases, integrating across social-constructivist and information-processing approaches, and providing precise cognitive diagnoses of children's changing skills, along with some insights into what propels development. Indeed, movements in the field over the past two decades have led to a substantially more developmental account of children's memory than was available in 2001. I have focused on longitudinal studies that – consistent with the social-constructivist perspective – emphasize children's conversational interactions with their parents and teachers as sources of key mediators of developmental change. In the next 20 years, it will be critically important for researchers to cast a wider net, as work from the cognitive developmental neuroscience of memory (Ghetti & Bauer, 2012; Riggins et al., 2016), for example, encourages consideration of how biological, cognitive, and social factors may co-act at different ages to advance developmental changes in memory skills.

Although much of the focus in longitudinal research has been on the ways parent–child reminiscing supports memory, parents engage with their children in memory-relevant talk in other conversational contexts as well – such as when playing board games or grocery shopping (e.g., Bjorklund, Hubertz, & Reubens, 2004). Güler et al. (2010) found differences in mothers' talk with their children during a collaborative (i.e., mothers and children worked together) deliberate memory task that were associated with children's performance on an independent (i.e., child worked alone) deliberate memory task over time. More specifically, mothers who emphasized categorization in their talk with their children in the collaborative task had children who engaged in more sorting in the independent task a year later. Future work should take a broader look at the ways that parents are encouraging memory skills in different everyday conversational contexts. Doing so will expand understanding of the sorts of parent–child conversational interactions that can mediate the development of event memory and deliberate skills for remembering over time.

There is also convincing need for longitudinal research that bridges the social-communicative milieu of home and school contexts. With rich characterizations of the home and classroom environments for the same children over time, it will be possible to address the interplay between child, family, and classroom factors that enable children to take advantage of the richness of the linguistic environment provided by their teachers. For example, we could learn if children with high-elaborative mothers come to school especially ready to take advantage of cognitively rich teacher talk. Moreover, we could determine whether having a first-grade teacher who is high in the use of cognitively rich language has special bearing on children of low-elaborative mothers, who may have further to grow in their metamemory and deliberate memory skills at school entry (Langley et al., 2017; see also Hudson, Coffman, & Ornstein, 2018). This work will also likely yield important information we should be "giving away" to teachers and parents, to support their engagement in practices that can foster the development of skilled remembering.

Finally, whereas correlational findings from longitudinal research are of considerable significance, they nonetheless represent a starting point in a systematic developmental analysis (Ornstein et al., 2011). As admittedly challenging as it is to do, it is necessary to combine longitudinal and experimental methodologies so we can make causal connections between, for example, parent and teacher "talk" and the development of children's memory skills. We should continue efforts to look across event and deliberate memory tasks to determine if training parents in elaborative talk may have effects beyond event memory to influence deliberate memory-skill development as well. In this regard, longitudinal training studies that trace the impacts of interventions across tasks at different points in development would seem to offer an especially fruitful approach. By further bridging across methods and paradigms, it should be possible to make significant new advances in understanding both *memory* development and the *development* of memory.

.

PART II

*Children's Memory Strategies*

# CHAPTER 4

# Overview
## Deliberate Remembering in Children
### Deborah L. Best and Trisha H. Folds-Bennett

## The Development of Deliberate Remembering: Fundamental Questions

Using the career of Peter Ornstein as the framework for understanding the evolution of research on memory strategies from the 1970s to the present, one is immediately struck by both the creativity and the tedium of the research. Whether the focus of discovery has been on the information-processing demands or the nature of the memory task, individual and age-related differences in the approach to remembering, or the intentional strategic processes necessary for successful remembering, a community of researchers has contributed to a much more complex and nuanced understanding of the development of memory than we once had. These collaborative efforts have enhanced our understanding of what children are able to remember, the factors that affect their ability to remember, and how intentional memory abilities change over time.

Studies of children's memory have a long history in psychology (e.g., Binet & Henri, 1884a, b; Jacobs, 1887; Kirkpatrick, 1894), but the focus of that research has evolved over the years (for a recent overview of memory development research, see Bauer & Fivush, 2014; Schneider, 2015). During the 1960s, when cognition became of interest in experimental psychology (e.g., Atkinson & Shiffrin, 1968; Broadbent, 1958), researchers began to examine memory processes in free recall. In fact, Bousfield, Esterson, and Whitmarsh (1958) found both perceptual (object color) and conceptual (object category) clustering in third and fourth graders' free recall of stimulus pictures, a finding that echoes into the 1970s and 1980s when researchers focused systematically on the study of organizational strategies in recall.

In 1993, Flavell and colleagues (Flavell, Miller, & Miller, 1993) described memory as the most researched aspect of children's cognition and pondered a range of questions that researchers had asked for decades prior. With the assumption that some sort of processing happens between the point when children encounter information and when they recall it, researchers examined questions such as the following: Does successful remembering have to do with the child's attentional capacity? Their knowledge base? The intentionality of their memory? The sophistication and effectiveness of the strategies they use? One area of focus was the distinction between storage and retrieval: What happens as words are encoded? What type of information is being stored? Do the task instructions impact retrieval? Do memory cues enhance recall? Other researchers focused explicitly on the space between storage and retrieval: What do children "do" with the information that is to be recalled? These are but some of the fundamental questions that researchers have asked in the study of memory, whether focused on adults or children. Incorporating the developmental questions about whether and how memory success changes with age creates a complex set of issues that can only be addressed through many different studies over years of research.

Early research in the 1970s tended to take a mechanistic approach, focusing on the basic information-processing aspects of memory (e.g., memory capacity) and individual differences in memory performance (for a review, see Schneider & Ornstein, 2019). These studies highlighted age-related differences in children's recall, but the factors responsible for them were not fully identified. The information-processing approach investigated what children do when dealing with certain types of information and how their systems allocate attention to the most critical aspects of the task at hand. Flavell (1970) influenced this information-processing, neo-behaviorist approach with his work on the emerging intentionality of children's memory and the strategies they use to aid memory. Emphasizing the distinction between implicit (nonconscious processes) versus explicit (conscious recollection) memory, he suggested there might be a *mediation deficiency* defined by young children's attempts to use strategies, but ineffectively and inefficiently, such that strategies do not serve as adequate mediators between the encoding of information and its subsequent recall. This limitation contrasted with a *production deficiency* characterized by young children's failures to produce strategies in situations where they would likely facilitate recall. At the Society for Research in Child Development conference in 1971, Flavell organized a symposium entitled "What Is Memory Development the Development of?," a session that inspired many researchers who had started to think about age-related changes in deliberate memory. By Schneider and Ornstein's (2019) account, the symposium opened a new vein of research focused on an analysis of the role of cognitive resources relative to the functions of memory, particularly strategy use.

The orientation toward research on strategy use casts the spotlight on a deeper understanding of the intentionality of memory and the range of factors that influence how much effort an individual devotes to remembering certain information (e.g., Folds et al., 1990). Siegler (1991), for example, argued that age-related differences in the quality of children's thinking depend on the types of information they encounter, how much of the information they are able to hold in memory, and the tools they have to work on the information to achieve a particular goal. Siegler concluded that the age-related increase in memory capacity is not the most critical factor; however, age-related changes in the speed of processing do seem to be a contributing factor. More recently, Vergauwe and colleagues (2015) argued that biological maturation factors (e.g., development of the inferior frontal junction involved in working memory functioning) limit how quickly children can process and retain information in short-term memory. Interestingly, Rabinowitz and colleagues (1994) explored the capacity issue in an experiment where they de-confounded age and experience by presenting items in a lexical-decision task in the participants' native language (German) and in a second language (English). Participants were German youth, some of whom (ninth graders) had experienced five years of instruction in English, some three years (seventh graders), and some only one year (ninth graders). Results showed that experience, not age, had the most important effect on the participants' speed of processing, revealing the influence of experiential knowledge and motivational factors.

Findings such as these demonstrate the dynamic interaction between biology and experience, but they also beg the question, "If capacity and speed are not the primary factors underlying age-related differences in recall performance, what are the most important influencers?" Siegler (1991) suggested that deliberate actions – memory strategies and knowledge about memory strategies and how to use them (metamemory) – are the most critical factors in predicting developmental changes in memory performance.

## Children's Deliberate Remembering: The Acquisition of Mnemonic Strategies

For the first 15 years of work on deliberate memory, researchers examined age-related differences in specific strategies (e.g., rehearsal, organization, elaboration). With the exception of elaboration, the primary research findings revealed increased complexity in use of strategies and their effectiveness across the elementary and middle school years (e.g., Flavell, 1970; Naus & Ornstein, 1983; Pressley & Levin, 1977). Harkening back to the 1800s, most of this research was done in a laboratory setting where memory tasks were systematically stripped of various features so that researchers could begin to isolate the factors that most influence memory success (Schneider, 2015; see Cox, Chapter 2). Even then, researchers recognized that contextual factors – such as task demands and situational conditions – as well as individual factors – such as motivation, prior knowledge, and metamemory – likely contribute to the effectiveness of children's strategy use (e.g., Bjorklund, 1990; Schneider & Ornstein, 2015). These early studies ignited interest in examining the differential sophistication of the strategies older children deploy relative to younger children. Research focused on how children use various patterns of rehearsal to hold information in memory, the relation between the existing semantic structure of to-be-remembered information and subsequent recall, the types of strategies children use in situations with high versus low structure, and what internal and external factors (e.g., knowledge, metamemory) affect strategies and their impact on recall (e.g., Bjorklund, 1985; Folds et al., 1990).

In an overview of research on children's strategy use, Ornstein and his colleagues (Folds et al., 1990) outlined three dimensions of strategic behavior that are critical to understanding children's deliberate attempts to remember: the extent to which a strategy is intentionally directed toward a goal, the consistency of strategy use across settings, and the effectiveness of the strategies that are deployed. They argued that a careful diagnosis of strategic competence that recognizes the full range of usage – from automatic to intentional, context-specific to general, ineffective to effective – is essential. In fact, they suggested that a taxonomy of memory tasks and the ways that various conditions facilitate or interfere with children's memory success should be developed to advance understanding of children's deliberate memory. Based on their assessment of current research at the time, they argued that memory is maximized if 1) the goal of remembering is explicit; 2) the semantic structure of the materials to be remembered encourages strategy use; 3) the instructions and other task procedures guide the child to use strategies; 4) the information-processing demands of the task are low; and 5) the child has considerable knowledge about the materials to be remembered. Likewise, Flavell and his colleagues (1993) described a similar progression of strategy development with age.

They claimed that children move from having a poor grasp on strategy execution to being very good at it, from no strategy use to spontaneous strategy use, and from not responding well to training instructions to easily transferring new strategies across various tasks. As a result, over time, the child's retrieval improves linearly as strategy use improves.

Although researchers have examined several types of strategies in an attempt to understand developmental patterns in their usage, the two strategies that have received the most attention and have yielded the most insight into the development of intentional memory are rehearsal and organization. Thus, in the next sections we dive into the research in these areas, highlighting work that examines age-related changes in the deliberate and effective use of the strategy, the role of contextual variables in inducing strategy use, and the effects of training on use of the strategy across various conditions. We also introduce several methodological innovations that have been critical to a more refined analysis of children's emerging memory ability.

## The Legacy of Two Strategies: The Influence of Research on Rehearsal and Organization

### *Rehearsal*

Early research on memory strategies was focused on the use of rehearsal to facilitate the recall of information. As early as the 1960s, studies demonstrated that the use of spontaneous rehearsal emerges at around 6 years old and increases with age (e.g., Flavell, Beach, & Chinsky, 1966). Flavell and his colleagues created a game situation to examine children's spontaneous rehearsal, having them wear a brightly colored toy space helmet with a visor that had tape across it to minimize looking, but that exposed their mouths. Experimenter Beach, seated directly across from the child, listened and "lip read" children's rehearsal activities before they were asked to recall the pictures they had seen. The researchers found that rehearsal increased with age, such that few 5-year-olds rehearsed, almost all 10-years-olds did so, and about half of the 7-year-olds rehearsed. Ten-year-olds showed the highest levels of recall. More importantly, 7-year-olds who rehearsed recalled more pictures than the 7-year-olds who did not rehearse, suggesting that rehearsal strategy use influences memory performance.

Using the Atkinson and Shiffrin (1968) information-processing model of memory, rehearsal studies throughout the 1970s examined such phenomena as the influence of rehearsal on the shape of the serial position curve in various recall situations (e.g., Palmer & Ornstein, 1971). A primary finding was that the passive style of rehearsal (e.g., repeating words one at a time or in minimal combination with other words) used by young children yields a clear recency effect in recall, but almost no primacy effect, such that words at the end of a to-be-remembered list are more frequently recalled than words at the beginning. Arguments were made about how more active styles of rehearsal, such as rehearsing words cumulatively by combining each new word with previous ones, might spur the transfer of information from short-term to long-term storage, keeping information in memory long enough to be integrated with existing knowledge (Miller, 2014). Indeed, further research found that cumulative rehearsal strengthens inter-item associations based on the temporal order of words in the to-be-remembered list, and this contiguity effect develops with age (Lehmann & Hasselhorn, 2012).

Methodologically, refining the Flavell and colleagues (1966) "space helmet game," researchers focused on the externalization of rehearsal strategies by asking children to rehearse aloud so that differences in the quality of the strategy might be observed directly. Generally, findings showed that children progress from more passive types of rehearsal strategies to more active, cumulative types, and that as the quality of the rehearsal strategy improves, recall is enhanced. In a study by Ornstein, Naus, and Liberty (1975), third graders who were asked to rehearse aloud items from a list of to-be-remembered words used a passive style, repeating each word in isolation from other words. Sixth graders, on the other hand, used an active style, rehearsing strings of words, adding new words as they were presented, and mixing the order to keep as many words alive in memory as possible. The older children remembered more words on average than the younger children and had a more pronounced primacy effect, suggesting that the quality of the rehearsal strategy at storage had a positive effect on retrieval. Interestingly though, third graders who were given lists of words that were blocked according to taxonomic associations during presentation showed improved recall, even though their rehearsal style was still passive. Such findings suggested that the quality of rehearsal was not the only factor affecting the child's memory success. The salience of the associations among items may have tapped into the child's knowledge base in some automatic fashion, perhaps serving as cues during retrieval (Ornstein & Naus, 1978).

Naus, Ornstein, and Kreshtool (1977) explored this idea by comparing rehearsal patterns on recall and recognition tests. They questioned whether rehearsal activity influences the transfer of information from short- to long-term memory or whether it is mostly relevant in the retrieval of information from long-term storage. On a recognition task that occurred 24 hours later, results showed no difference in performance for third graders versus sixth graders. However, performance on the recall test revealed age-related differences, suggesting that rehearsal activity has its effect on the retrieval of information from long-term storage rather than on the transfer of information from short- to long-term storage. Naus and colleagues argued that passive and active rehearsal may have similar effects on the transfer of information, but active rehearsal leads to different, stronger representations of the information in long-term storage, thus facilitating recall.

Follow-up studies examined the quality of children's rehearsal and its impact on memory performance. Some studies used training paradigms instructing children who do not spontaneously use strategies how to rehearse in a more active style. Naus, Ornstein, and Aivano (1977) instructed third and sixth graders to rehearse items in sets of three and gave them either 5 or 10 seconds to rehearse each item. Their results showed that younger participants' recall was improved with increased study time, and that they benefited from the rehearsal instructions. However, the rehearsal quality of the younger children showed subtle differences in their rehearsal style. Whereas older children were more varied in their rehearsal patterns, younger children were more constrained in their rehearsal. Ornstein and his colleagues concluded that with more contextual support (e.g., more time, more obvious taxonomic structure), younger children show memory improvement, suggesting that young children suffer from a production deficiency. They can use strategies, but they do not use a mature version of the strategy that creates strong representation of items in memory. They adapt their rehearsal style nominally when given basic instructions on how to rehearse more actively. However, the quality of their rehearsal does not match that of older children, and seemingly as a result, they do not have equivalent retrieval success.

In the Ornstein Lab, this revelation led to a series of studies that explored the impact of simply rehearsing items to keep them alive in memory relative to the emerging ability to use categorical information to improve the quality of rehearsal. These training studies systematically manipulated the task conditions within which children were encouraged to use a rehearsal strategy (e.g., Ornstein et al., 1985). In an early study, Belmont and Butterfield (1971) had let children control the amount of time they spent looking at serially presented letters to be recalled.

Thirteen-year-olds took more time per item than 9-year-olds, which Belmont and Butterfield assumed was an indication they were using more active and deliberate rehearsal. Some years later, Ornstein et al. (1985) built on Belmont and Butterfield's finding by instructing second graders with visual access to the to-be-remembered items to rehearse aloud cumulatively. The children who rehearsed in a cumulative fashion had better recall. In a subsequent study, Guttentag, Ornstein, and Siemens (1987) gave visual access to items and found that some younger children (third graders) were more likely to use a cumulative rehearsal strategy spontaneously, even without instructions to do so. They labeled these children "transitional" and found that when they were tested a year later (in grade 4), they were more likely than their peers, who had persisted in single-word rehearsal despite visual access, to use cumulative rehearsal spontaneously even when not given visual access. These researchers stressed the importance of examining children's strategy use in conditions with low and high support, as well as using both within-subjects and longitudinal research designs to determine individual patterns in the developmental progression toward more effective strategy use.

This early focus on rehearsal strategies revealed a number of important characteristics and trends in children's memory development. Although the methodology was mechanistic and reductionist, isolating memory performance from its everyday context, critical factors that influence age differences in recall were identified. Most importantly, researchers discovered that with low support for the use of a rehearsal strategy (e.g., random list items, no instructions or cues to rehearse, quick presentation of materials), children in early elementary school are not likely to use rehearsal, or if they use it, they rehearse passively. With more semantic structure among list items, instructions on how to engage in more active rehearsal, and more time to rehearse, younger children are able to use the strategy and to improve their recall, although not always at the same level as older children. Overall, findings led to the conclusion that young children have both capacity limitations (Guttentag, 1984) and production deficiencies (Naus et al., 1977), consistent with Atkinson and Shiffrin's model and Flavell's work. However, the fundamental question that Flavell had asked – "If children can use strategies, why don't they?" – was not answered completely by the research on rehearsal strategies. Clearly, a full understanding of memory development and the role of strategies would require a more contextualized approach. On the path toward that goal, researchers turned to analysis of the role of organizational strategies in memory – an attempt to explore connections between children's existing knowledge base and their efforts to remember.

## Organization

Ornstein's original foray into examining the role of organization in memory occurred during his dissertation work where, with adult participants, he investigated Tulving's explanation for the lack of positive transfer in part-whole free-recall learning (Ornstein, 1970). Consistent with Tulving's organizational hypothesis, Ornstein found that recall was a function of how participants organized to-be-remembered lists. At the time, Ornstein was not looking at memory explicitly but was focused on how semantic associations influenced information processing. Years later, Ornstein and his lab (e.g., Best & Ornstein, 1986; Bjorklund, Ornstein, & Haig, 1977; Corsale & Ornstein, 1980) focused on organization to understand how children use existing knowledge to facilitate memory. They were spurred by studies focused on rehearsal strategies and intrigued by the classic study by Bousfield, Esterson, and Whitmarsh (1958) that found clustering in children's free recall of stimulus pictures. Ornstein and his colleagues investigated whether clustering in recall was the operation of deliberate organizational strategies at storage or retrieval or was simply a result of strong inter-item relations between category items represented in the child's knowledge base – a rather automatic process.

The early studies focused on organization at recall and recall performance, assuming how items were clustered in recall reflected the way "things go together" in one's knowledge base. Consistent with the organizational theories of Tulving (1962, 1968) and Mandler (1967), using one's knowledge structure to organize memory was expected to improve recall performance. A necessary methodological contribution to this work involved the development of clustering measures; quantitative measures – such as category clustering, the ratio of repetition (Bousfield & Bousfield, 1966), and the adjusted ratio of clustering (Roenker, Thompson, & Brown, 1971) – and qualitative measures, such as proximity analyses (Friendly, 1977) and multidimensional scaling analyses (Caramazza, Hersh, & Torgerson, 1976). These measures aimed to quantify the extent to which category items are recalled adjacent to each other (Lange, 1978). According to Lange, these clustering measures were superior to early work that used paired-associates because these new measures allowed for a more sensitive assessment of the age at which children actually begin to search for category structure among a group of stimuli and then use that structure to enhance recall.

Generally, developmental studies of clustering at recall after the study of taxonomically related items showed age-related improvement in the use of the semantic associations among items (e.g., Moely et al., 1969; Ornstein, Hale, & Morgan, 1977). Flavell and colleagues argued that this was evidence of a production deficiency, in that young children (early elementary school) do not spontaneously use semantic structure to guide their recall, and thus their memory performance is poor compared with older children. However, in these clustering studies, without knowing what the child was "doing" with the information at input, the source of the memory deficit was hard to pinpoint. Therefore, researchers developed a sorting methodology at input so as to externalize the ways participants were creating an organizational plan to enhance recall (Naus & Ornstein, 1978). By using this sort–recall methodology, researchers gained considerable insight into how participants perceived and used the categorical structure of to-be-remembered items (e.g., Best & Ornstein, 1986; Liberty & Ornstein, 1973; Ornstein & Corsale, 1979).

With the sort–recall methodology firmly established, factors such as type of materials and instructions to use an organizational strategy were examined. In an early study, Liberty and Ornstein (1973) compared the memory performance of adults and fourth graders after a free-sorting task. Along with the expected age-related differences in recall and category clustering, they found that fourth graders' sorting patterns were idiosyncratic (e.g., some semantically associated items were sorted together, but not all), whereas adult patterns demonstrated predictable use of categorical structure and little variability. Interestingly, when fourth graders were constrained to adult sorting patterns, their clustering in recall and the items recalled increased. Similarly, recall was impaired for adults when they were constrained to fourth graders' sorting patterns. These findings revealed that more meaning-based organization during encoding is related to improved recall performance and contributed to evidence that young children's memory performance is hampered by a production deficiency.

As researchers explored various manipulations of the stimulus materials and other contextual factors, a clearer understanding of the deliberate nature of children's memory was exposed. Indeed, studies demonstrated the effectiveness of direct instruction and organizational training for improving children's strategy use and recall performance (Bjorklund et al. 1977; Corsale & Ornstein, 1980; Schneider & Pressley, 1989). Research established that as children grow older, their sorting patterns become more similar to adults when given lists of words to remember that have obvious semantic or taxonomic relations between items (e.g., Best & Ornstein, 1986; Corsale & Ornstein, 1980). Not surprisingly, with weaker inter-item semantic relations, children have a more difficult time creating a subjective organizational structure that would facilitate remembering the words (Ornstein & Corsale, 1979). In one study, using relatively unrelated stimulus items in a sort–recall task, Corsale and Ornstein (1980) found that the seventh graders, regardless of instructions, sorted items into meaning-based groupings and had higher recall than the third graders. Third graders instructed to sort items to facilitate recall formed random groupings and had lower recall than third graders who were instructed to sort items into meaning-based groups and were unaware of a subsequent recall trial. In fact, the meaning-based third graders recalled as many items as did the seventh graders. Although the younger children were aware of the relations between the unrelated items and thought a related-item list would be easier to remember, they did not use this semantic knowledge spontaneously, consistent with a production deficiency.

Looking more closely at the types of materials that may induce children to use organizational strategies during study and during recall, Best and Ornstein (Best, 1993; Best & Ornstein, 1986) investigated a more indirect form of strategy support by using an induction manipulation. They gave children a series of sort–recall tasks with different sets of to-be-remembered items. Without explicit instruction, third graders developed meaning-based sorting patterns using taxonomically related materials and even transferred that organizational orientation to a later list of unrelated items. In fact, they showed greater organization in sorting and recalling the low-associated lists than did third graders who had previous experience with functionally related or other unrelated lists. Regardless of the materials they were given, sixth graders sorted more meaningfully, recalled more, and showed greater use of sorting organization in their recall than did third graders. In contrast to the third graders, previous experience with functionally related materials facilitated sixth graders' sorting and recall. These older children may have been sensitive to the subtle differences in the types of organization linking related items. Best and Ornstein argued that exposure to functionally related items may have induced them to search for functional or thematic relations that may be found more readily with low-associated materials.

Clearly, the contrast between younger children's sorting patterns with relatively unrelated and categorical materials demonstrates the importance of context in children's memory performance, a point supported by Ornstein and his colleagues (Ornstein, Baker-Ward, & Naus, 1988). Explicitly instructing children to group items by meaning (e.g., Bjorklund & Buchanan, 1989) or constraining younger children to the sorting patterns of older subjects (e.g., Liberty & Ornstein, 1973) are examples of supportive task contexts that lead to enhanced strategy use and recall performance. Indeed, children may be instructed to use an organizational strategy but fail to do so (i.e., mediation deficiency), and if they do use it, they may or may not benefit from it (i.e., production deficiency, Flavell, 1970). Memory strategies are demanding and often require a great deal of a child's cognitive resources, sometimes to the extent that they do not have sufficient resources for recall (Bjorklund & Coyle, 1995). However, as children become more efficient with strategy use, they may choose to combine multiple strategies from their repertoire, similar to Siegler's (1996) overlapping wave model of memory strategy choice. With age and experience, children begin to understand how particular strategies work and how they may be used together in service of improved memory.

## Universal or Individual Trajectories in the Development of Deliberate Memory?

Although early studies of children's strategy development tended to focus on age comparisons of strategy use and the task conditions that increased or decreased differences among age groups, some studies examined factors related to individual differences in strategy use and recall performance (Bjorklund, 1988; Corsale & Ornstein, 1980). Two factors, in particular, have received attention: the knowledge base and metamemory.

### *Knowledge Base*

In research focused on the role of knowledge in memory performance, the prevailing assumption is that a rich system of knowledge related to the to-be-remembered items facilitates integration of those items into long-term storage (Miller, 2014). The importance of drawing on existing knowledge to enhance strategy effectiveness is illustrated in studies where lists of taxonomically related items have been presented (Best & Ornstein, 1986; Ornstein et al., 1975). Ornstein and colleagues found that younger children will use a more active rehearsal style spontaneously if presented items are blocked according to taxonomic relations. Best and Ornstein found that taxonomically related lists facilitate the use of organizational strategies in younger children, which is correlated with higher levels of recall. The role of the knowledge base is even clearer if comparisons are made between category typical (for clothing: shirts and pants) and atypical lists (for clothing: socks and ties; Bjorklund, 1988).

In her classic study on the role of domain-specific knowledge in memory performance, Chi (1978) found that typical age trends in memory success were reversed when memory for chessboard arrangements in elementary school–aged children with advanced knowledge of chess was compared with that of adults who were chess novices. The children had superior recall, although in a task focused on digit memory, adults had more recall success. Other studies have demonstrated similar facilitating effects of domain-specific knowledge, such as dinosaurs, music, and sports, on memory performance (e.g., Chi & Koeske, 1983; Oura & Hatano, 1988; Schneider, Korkel, & Weinert, 1989).

In 1987, Bjorklund suggested that knowledge can affect memory in three ways: 1) by making specific items more accessible so less attentional focus is necessary to remember them; 2) by activating relations among items, as with categorically related items, in an automatic manner that frees up capacity to process less-familiar items; and 3) by facilitating the use of deliberate strategies and metacognitive processes. As these processes mature, Bjorklund suggested, more functional capacity is available for children to hold and manipulate information in active memory so that memory traces and cues can be strengthened. Similarly, Ornstein and Naus (1985) contended that age-related changes in children's knowledge base and in the accessibility of that knowledge likely contribute to a more efficient use of memory strategies. Theoretically and methodologically, researchers acknowledged that knowledge acquisition and age are usually confounded, exposing the possibility that age-related differences in memory performance could be as much about individually specific experiences, such as with expert domain knowledge, as about universal developmental trajectories defined by chronological age.

## Metamemory

In the research on metamemory – knowledge about how to approach a memory task and which strategies are better tools for remembering certain types of information – the original assumption was that children need to have some knowledge of strategies and what makes them effective before they can use them deliberately in the service of memory (Schneider, 1985; Wellman, 1983). In a classic study, Kreutzer, Leonard, and Flavell (1975) created the first comprehensive questionnaire to assess children's metamemory, and a clear age trend was found in children's responses. Older children (fifth graders) displayed a more sophisticated understanding of the situations and actions that would predict successful memory than did third graders and kindergartners. More importantly, other researchers showed that young children who do not spontaneously use mnemonic strategies to improve their recall respond to metamemory questions in a way that suggests they are able to recognize when to-be-remembered materials may be harder or easier to remember (Corsale & Ornstein, 1980; Roebers, 2014).

Suspecting that children may have more implicit metacognitive knowledge than they express explicitly in response to metamemory questions, Best and Ornstein (1986) created a memory task "teaching" procedure to evaluate children's metamemory. When asked to instruct a younger child how to "play" a sort–recall game, children stressed the importance of organization in both sorting and recall in the directions that they gave to the younger child. In contrast with their performance in the teaching task, these same children displayed lower levels of metamemory in questions similar to the ones that Flavell had used, suggesting that the peer-tutoring task was a more sensitive index of children's metamemory knowledge than the standard interview questions.

Other researchers have focused on situations that facilitate memory success in preschoolers – an age group that traditional memory-strategy studies would categorize as "nonstrategic." Given the right context, even young children can display some understanding of what they need to do to remember. Baker-Ward, Ornstein, and Holden (1984) contrasted children's use of strategies when they were asked to remember versus play with a set of items. They found that the 3- and 4-year-olds acted as if they were deliberately exerting effort to recall the items they were asked to remember by repeatedly looking at the items. This repeated looking was not evident when the children were asked to play with the items. Even with this seemingly intentional behavior, however, the children's recall was not enhanced. These findings suggest that children develop intuitions about what they should do to remember before they are able to put those actions to effective use.

Research looking at general knowledge about the world and specific knowledge about how the memory system works leads to the conclusion that memory development is not simply about strategy usage. Memory development is the product of not only universal maturational processes but also individual experiences that build knowledge and awareness. Decades of research suggest that performance on memory tasks reveals a developmental progression that has both practical and theoretical implications as the foundation for a more complex model of memory development (Schneider & Pressley, 1989).

## Conclusions: Methodological Lessons

Over the course of the elementary school years, research demonstrates that children become facile users of an impressive array of techniques for remembering information (Folds et al., 1990). Clearly, there are age-related differences in mnemonic strategy use and its effectiveness. Equally clear is the fact that various task conditions have differential effects on memory performance, even to the extent that typical developmental patterns can be disrupted in highly supportive situations that map onto the individual's knowledge base. Although it is tempting to focus on arguments about when strategic activities are truly intentional, Folds, Ornstein, and colleagues (1990) argue that the relevant question concerns strategic competence and its relation to increased memory success. In other words, what does it mean to "have" a cognitive ability (Miller, 2014)?

From the outset, researchers have tried to determine whether young children have comprehensively immature memory systems and change in memory competence occurs along a universal and linear trajectory, or whether various aspects of the memory system develop at different times and in ways that are unique to the individual. The cross-sectional studies that typified research on the development of children's memory strategies in the 1960s and 1970s led to the conclusion that children gradually develop strategic competence as they develop more control over their behavior (Bjorklund, Dukes, & Brown, 2009). However, the "snapshot in time" approach of these cross-sectional studies did not fully reflect the complex nature of memory development, nor did it allow for a deeper understanding of the underlying mechanisms of change (Schneider, 2014). Schneider argues that the computer metaphor borrowed from the information-processing theorists and focused on the hardware of the system (e.g., capacity) and the software (e.g., strategies) provided insight into the workings of the memory system, but it ultimately limited what researchers could understand about the multiplicity and interaction of factors that underlie change in memory ability across time.

Understanding the complexity of memory and all the factors that influence recall success led to longitudinal research as a means to a more comprehensive understanding of memory and its development. Findings from the Munich Longitudinal Study on the Genesis of Individual Competencies (LOGIC, Sodian & Schneider, 1999) and the Würzburg–Göttingen longitudinal memory studies (Kron-Sperl, Schneider, &

Hasselhorn, 2008) showed that the overall arc of memory development is gradual. However, a microgenetic approach measuring different facets of memory over short segments of time revealed that for most children, nonstrategic to strategic use of mnemonic strategies occurs rather quickly over early elementary school years, and that individual differences do exist (Bjorklund et al., 2009; Schneider & Ornstein, 2019). Furthermore, the components of memory – different types of strategies, metamemory, knowledge – do not develop at the same pace. Kron-Sperl, Schneider, and Hasselhorn (2008) found a great deal of variability in the development of organizational and rehearsal strategies, suggesting that memory development does not simply involve moving from noneffective to effective strategy use. Children can display considerable sophistication in one strategy but not in another. Also, children can use strategies quite proficiently early in development, but display no improvement in recall, a phenomenon that Miller (1990) called a *utilization deficiency*.

These longitudinal studies have provided more insight regarding the linkages or interaction among factors, such as knowledge base, metamemory, and strategy use. Whereas cross-sectional studies only allow documentation of correlations (or lack thereof) among these factors, longitudinal studies facilitate the study of their co-emergence in development. In fact, Schlagmüller and Schneider (2002), in a microgenetic longitudinal study tracking change across shorter intervals of time, verified that individuals who show early metamemory are the first individuals to display effective strategy use. Longitudinal studies have also shown that the linkages among knowledge, metamemory, strategy use, and recall grow stronger with age (Schneider & Ornstein, 2019).

The bottom line is that research focused on understanding the developmental progression in the intentionality of memory laid a strong foundation for current research that is more relevant to children's everyday need to remember information. The mechanistic approach that isolated factors that influence memory performance has contributed to a more refined analysis of when children become deliberate in their attempts to remember. These previous studies underscore the importance of understanding the interplay among neurological capacities, strategic learning, knowledge base, and motivation in determining memory performance and development (Pressley, Borkowski, & Schneider, 1989). Understanding such basic mechanisms of memory opened the doors for a new sort of research, extending from infancy into adulthood and focusing on memory in everyday, ecologically valid contexts. These critical applications of memory development research are explored throughout chapters in this volume and verify that the detailed attention over more than five decades to the factors that underlie memory performance continues to have relevance today.

# CHAPTER 5

# Strategies and Self-Derivation
## Means of Maintaining and Extending Knowledge

### Alena G. Esposito and Patricia J. Bauer

Learning is a lifelong and consistent part of human existence. In the immortal words of Theodor "Dr. Seuss" Geisel, "The more that you read, the more things you will know. The more that you learn, the more places you'll go" (Geisel, 1990). Indeed, knowledge is fundamental to success. Children, especially, have much to learn about the world to build the knowledge base needed for later occupations and participation in society. This task is so great that children spend the majority of their waking hours in pursuit of knowledge – both in formal educational settings as well as in their extracurricular activities.

Much effort and research has been devoted to understanding how children learn and the strategies they use to acquire knowledge. The work of Dr. Peter Ornstein and colleagues over the past 50 years has illuminated the developmental progression of emerging memory strategy use and effectiveness in children. Through this extensive body of research, Ornstein and colleagues laid out the course of developmental change in how children employ strategies when presented with an expectation to remember, such as through classroom lessons, books, or in experimental conditions. In this chapter, we review Ornstein's contributions to the study of strategy use to maintain new information that is explicitly provided. We then use our own research to build on the discussion of how children accumulate a knowledge base. In our research, we examine how children use productive processes to extend beyond what was explicitly provided and self-derive new knowledge through integration of separate learning episodes.

This work has been funded by grants from the Spencer Foundation (201500118, PI: Lynne Baker-Ward), National Science Foundation (BCS 1528091, PI: Patricia J. Bauer), and Institute of Education Sciences (R305A 160240; PI: Patricia J Bauer).

## Strategy Use to Maintain Information

*Memory Strategies*

Memory strategies are behaviors intended to increase the quantity and quality of retention of target information (Roebers, 2014). Although strategies can be employed without conscious effort, they are, in theory, under the control of the individual. Thus, the individual can choose to maintain, cease, or change tactics (for reviews, see Ornstein, Haden, & Elischberger, 2006; Best & Folds-Bennett, Chapter 4). Adults employ memory strategies with apparent ease. For example, we use rehearsal to remember items on our grocery list. We may even organize the items into categories to help us remember. The work of Ornstein and colleagues has aided our understanding of how we use strategies to maintain explicitly provided material, how strategy use develops over childhood, and what factors influence the successful use of strategies. In this section, we briefly review key findings from Ornstein and colleagues as well as those inspired by his work.

Three common strategies that are well researched are rehearsal, elaboration, and organization. *Rehearsal* refers to repeating items in memory, such as grocery items. When children use rehearsal, especially active rehearsal of multiple items intermixed, they show superior recall (e.g., Naus, Ornstein, & Aivano, 1977; Ornstein et al., 1985; Ornstein, Naus, & Stone, 1977). Children as young as four have been observed repeating items as though attempting rehearsal. However, effective use of the strategy emerges later in childhood (e.g., Baker-Ward, Ornstein, & Holden, 1984). *Elaboration* involves creating an episode in memory that forms a connection between two or more items (see Pressley, 1982, for a review). For example, to remember that you need milk and paper towels, you may form an image of spilling milk and cleaning it up with the paper towels to help you remember the two items. Elaboration may be in the form of an image or verbalization and can increase recall for the target items. Elaboration, especially use of imagery, comes into use in early adolescence (Willoughby et al., 1999).

Both rehearsal and elaboration are encoding strategies; they are observed during learning of new information. In contrast, *organization* is observed at retrieval. Organization involves arranging or categorizing to-be-remembered information into groups. For example, in trying to retrieve animal names, one might group them taxonomically into mammals, birds, and reptiles. Organizational strategies are more typically employed by older children, but younger children can benefit from them when they are trained or prompted to do so (e.g., Bjorklund, Ornstein, & Haig, 1977; Bjorklund et al., 1994).

Children learn early on that maintaining information in memory requires active effort. For example, even children as young as four behave differently when told to try to remember (Baker-Ward et al., 1984). In this study, an experimenter told children either to "play with" or to "remember" target items. Children in the "remember" condition spent less time playing and more time naming and looking at the target objects. However, knowing that memory takes effort does not necessarily lead to benefits in performance. Knowing what strategy to employ as well as when and how to employ it effectively takes time to develop. For example, children initially attempt a rehearsal strategy with single-item rehearsal (cat-cat-cat) before moving to a cumulative rehearsal strategy (cat-rug-dog-hat-chair) and eventually, in adolescence, to a semantically organized rehearsal (cat-dog-rug-chair-hat), showing more advanced use of the strategy over time (e.g., Naus et al. 1977; Ornstein, Naus, & Liberty, 1975; Ornstein, Naus, & Miller, 1977).

### Barriers and Supports to Memory Strategy Use

Failures in strategy use can be grouped into at least two categories. First, the initial use of strategies does not benefit memory performance, referred to as a *utilization deficiency* (Miller, 1990). In the Baker-Ward et al. (1984) study described earlier, for example, although the 4-year-olds in the remember and play conditions behaved differently, their memory performance did not differ. It was not until 6 years of age that the behaviors yielded higher memory performance. Thus, early attempts at strategy use often fail.

Second, even when children have the skill set to effectively use a strategy, they often fail to do so. Evidence for these *production deficiencies* comes from studies in which a prompt or reminder to use the strategy improves performance (see Schneider & Pressley, 1997, for a review). For example, Naus et al. (1977) found that 8-year-old children could effectively use a rehearsal strategy when instructed to do so, but they did not spontaneously employ the strategy; they were dependent on a prompt. Over development, deployment becomes more robust and, with practice, the strategies begin to support memory performance.

Whether strategy use is effective is also influenced by factors such as task demands, prior knowledge, and metacognitive awareness. (For reviews, see

Ornstein, Haden, & Elischberger, 2006; Best & Folds-Bennett, Chapter 4.) Strategies are more likely to be implemented and implemented effectively when task demands are low, freeing up more mental space to implement the strategy. Examples include the previously discussed studies that found higher performance when support was offered such as in the form of availability of target items during study (Guttentag, Ornstein, & Siemens, 1987) or categorically related target items (Best & Ornstein, 1986).

Prior knowledge supports effective memory strategy use because it provides a foundation for organization and easier access to stored information due to greater interconnections between and within concepts (see Bjorklund, 1987; Ornstein, Haden, & San Souci, 2008; Ornstein & Naus, 1985, for reviews). Knowledge of categories and concepts provides a structure for effective organization of information to be retrieved from memory. Children with greater knowledge in a subject area are better able to employ strategies that result in benefits to remembering. For example, when baseball experts were compared to novices on lists of either baseball terms or non-baseball terms, experts utilized more sophisticated sorting strategies and recalled more of the baseball terms (Gaultney, Bjorklund, & Schneider, 1992). There were no differences in performance on the non-baseball terms, indicating that it was the domain-specific knowledge that drove the advanced strategy use. Prior knowledge also automatizes the organization process such that older children with both more knowledge and more experience do not have to be explicitly told to use the strategy. This also frees cognitive resources that do not have to be devoted to deliberate strategy use (e.g., Roebers, 2014).

Metacognition development is another factor that improves strategy performance. Metacognition refers to understanding the demands of cognition and typically includes both monitoring and control factors (Flavell, 1979; Nelson & Narens, 1990). Metamemory is metacognition specific to understanding memory. Children with greater metamemory are better able to assess the need for a strategy and to choose appropriately (see Schneider, 1999, for review). For example, Schneider, Schlagmüller, and Visé (1998) examined the unique effects of both domain knowledge and metamemory on strategy use in third- and fourth-grade children. They found that both domain knowledge and metamemory predicted unique variance in successful use of an organizational strategy for recall of pictures, although this effect was limited to experts in their area of expertise, indicating the formation of a knowledge base is a prerequisite for metamemory to be able to direct the use of said knowledge.

*Application*

The fact that metamemory can be trained is especially interesting for educational purposes. This aspect of metamemory led to investigations of children's strategy use in classrooms (see Coffman et al., 2019, for a discussion). In studies conducted with first-grade teachers and students, Coffman and colleagues found that teachers' use of Cognitive Processing Language and direct references to metacognition predicted students' gains over the school year in effective memory strategy use (e.g., Coffman et al., 2008; Grammer, Coffman, & Ornstein, 2013). Thus, the relation between strategy use and metamemory was observed not only in the laboratory but also in the classroom. (See Coffman & Cook, Chapter 15, for discussion of this line of research.)

In summary, use of strategies to maintain explicitly provided information improves over childhood in terms of recognition that a strategy can be used, selection of the appropriate strategy, and effective deployment of the strategy. As knowledge and experience increase, strategy use becomes more spontaneous and less effortful. In this way, children become more efficient in maintaining explicitly taught information in memory.

## Building Knowledge through (Productive) Extension

A notable feature of the work of Ornstein and colleagues is that the strategies are applied to explicitly taught information, or information that is presented with the expectation of remembering. Children acquire knowledge through many means of explicit instruction, including teaching, books, television, museum exhibits, and experimenter-directed sources. Yet for knowledge to build quickly and efficiently, we must go beyond what is explicitly given. If every piece of knowledge had to be directly and explicitly taught, learning would be a slow and tedious process indeed. Even the use of memory strategies, which clearly aids learning, cannot eliminate the burden of laboriously learning each needed fact through explicit instruction. Instead, we employ complementary processes that also support the construction of knowledge by going beyond what was explicitly provided. For example, children identify language patterns rather than learning each and every possible word combination in their language (Studdert-Kennedy, 1998). This capacity allows for the infinite generativity of human language and is far more efficient than acquiring specific combinations. This example can be extended to mathematical formulas that can then be applied to infinite number combinations and to the extension of taxonomic categories based on salient features. Indeed, productive processes permeate learning across content areas and are assumed to be a major mechanism of cognitive development (e.g., Bauer, 2012; Brown et al., 1983; Siegler, 1989; Sloutsky, 2010). Research on the productive processes of deductive reasoning, analogy, and transitive inference has contributed to our general understanding of factors supporting learning. Similar to the factors contributing to strategy use in maintaining explicitly taught material, productive processes show a developmental progression such that older children and adults are better able to use these processes successfully (see Goswami, 2002, for a review). The context of learning, such as the child's prior knowledge, affects performance as does the development of metacognition.

One productive process especially relevant to the study of knowledge accumulation is that of self-derivation of new factual knowledge through the integration of separate episodes of learning, or *self-derivation through integration* (e.g., Bauer & San Souci, 2010). Self-derivation through integration occurs when information acquired in one learning episode (e.g., dolphins live in groups called *pods*) is integrated with information presented in a separate episode (e.g., dolphins talk by clicking and squeaking). Integrating the two separate learning episodes can then result in the productive extension of new knowledge (e.g., pods talk by clicking and squeaking) – information that was not directly or explicitly taught.

Self-derivation through integration has particular relevance to how children build knowledge over time and media for at least three reasons. First, self-derivation through integration is an ecologically relevant process. Children and adults engage in this process across multiple test paradigms, contexts, and subject areas (e.g., Esposito & Bauer, 2019a; Varga, Esposito, & Bauer, 2019). Self-derivation is a process through which real-world content, such as that included in school curricula, is extended. Second, the real-world nature of the stimuli also enables tests of retention of the newly derived information. New knowledge gained through self-derivation through integration is retained over time. In both the laboratory and the classroom, children show evidence for retention over at least one week (Bauer, Esposito, & Daly, 2020; Varga & Bauer, 2013). In fact, there is little forgetting. In a laboratory study, 6-year-old children correctly answered 63% self-derivation questions in Week 1 and 60% a week later (Varga & Bauer, 2013). Third, individual variability in self-derivation through integration predicts academic performance in elementary school children and college students (Esposito & Bauer, 2017; Varga et al., 2019).

This relation holds in elementary school children even when differences in parent education level are controlled (Esposito & Bauer, 2017).

There is substantial evidence supporting self-derivation through integration as a reliable process for accumulating knowledge. Indeed, we have observed successful self-derivation through integration across different environmental settings such as the laboratory and the classroom (e.g., Bauer & Larkina, 2017; Esposito & Bauer, 2019a, respectively), in different content areas such as science and history (Bauer et al., 2020; Varga et al., 2019, respectively), and with different measurement paradigms including verbal and nonverbal media (e.g., Bauer & San Souci, 2010; Bauer et al., 2016; Esposito & Bauer, 2017, 2019a; Esposito, Lee, Dugan, et al., under review). Evidence for success has been observed in children as young as four, with performance improving across the school years (e.g., Bauer & Larkina, 2017; Esposito & Bauer, 2017) and considerable individual variability remaining even in adult college student performance (3%–93% correct; Varga & Bauer, 2017). Self-derivation through integration has emerged as a robust process that adds to the accumulation of knowledge.

## Parallels in Maintaining and Extending Knowledge

Maintaining explicitly provided information through memory strategies and knowledge extension through self-derivation are complementary processes for knowledge accumulation. Children acquire information through explicit instruction (from a multitude of sources) and maintain it in memory through the implementation of strategies. They also productively extend information in memory thereby building knowledge beyond what was directly provided. These two processes have several underlying similarities. In this section, we highlight one similarity that promotes learning, namely, that both processes benefit from prior knowledge in the domain of instruction. We also discuss similarities in production deficiencies that limit successful learning. Our review illustrates the spiral of knowledge accumulation in that knowledge begets additional knowledge.

### Prior Knowledge

Prior knowledge in a subject area supports effective strategy use, as reviewed above. According to Bjorklund (1987), prior knowledge supports memory performance because it provides easier access, activates information effortlessly, and frees cognitive resources for deliberate use of memory strategies. Regarding access, information related to the memory target will be more easily recalled due to more fully developed interconnections and a greater number of potential cues (Baker-Ward, Ornstein, & Principe, 1997). These same interconnections facilitate activation of related content without the need for extensive effort. Based on an information-processing framework, the combination of easy access and effortless activation that comes with prior knowledge also reduces the cognitive load of a task because the interconnections between concepts have already been forged, freeing more of the cognitive resources for other mental processes (Bjorklund, 1987).

Self-derivation through integration also is supported by prior knowledge as evidenced by relations with measures of verbal comprehension (e.g., Bauer et al., 2016; Esposito & Bauer, 2019b; Varga & Bauer, 2014). Verbal comprehension is an index of existing semantic knowledge and how well an individual uses that knowledge base for reasoning. Across several studies with different measurement paradigms and age groups, verbal comprehension has emerged as a unique predictor of self-derivation through integration. For example, Esposito and Bauer (2018) found that across two laboratory-based studies of children aged 6–10 years including measures of working memory, executive functions, verbal and nonverbal intelligence, the only unique predictor of self-derivation performance was verbal comprehension (as measured by the Woodcock–Johnson Test of verbal comprehension; Schrank, 2011). The consistency was observed despite different self-derivation test paradigms for the 6–8- and 8–10-year-olds (story and single sentence, respectively). A follow-up study with 8-year-olds in a classroom setting yielded the same results across two samples and with two different study paradigms (again, story and single sentence; Varga et al., 2019). Importantly, the content on which children were tested also varied across these four studies. A laboratory-based study with college students using a different test paradigm and different content also found verbal comprehension to be a unique predictor of self-derivation through integration performance, further supporting the robust relation with prior knowledge (Varga et al., 2019). Thus, prior knowledge supports the maintenance of explicitly taught information as well as the process of self-derivation through integration.

One way in which prior knowledge supports memory strategy use is that it provides a structure for organizing information. For learning new explicitly taught information, organizing items into groups that are semantically related aids recall. Evidence in support of the relation between prior knowledge and organization comes from studies of expertise (for example, see above discussion regarding baseball experts compared to novices, Gaultney et al., 1992).

In self-derivation through integration, the relation with organization strategies is in the very name of the process. Integration refers to recognizing that one or more concepts overlap and putting them together, or linking them, in memory. This organizational strategy creates an interconnected network of semantic knowledge. In studies of self-derivation, we have found that integration is supported by contextual cues that concepts are related and can be organized together. If stories conveying related semantic content share surface similarities in addition to the deeper-level conceptual content, children are more likely to integrate and subsequently self-derive new knowledge. For example, Bauer et al. (2012) tested 6-year-old children's self-derivation through integration in a story paradigm when the main character in paired stories was the same (high surface similarity) or different (low surface similarity). Children had higher performance when the characters in paired stories were the same compared to when they differed (63% vs. 37%, respectively), presumably because there was an additional and salient cue to integrate the material. Thus, prior knowledge supports self-derivation through memory integration just as it supports memory strategy use. We hypothesize that it does so through similar mechanisms, namely, by freeing cognitive resources that otherwise would be spent accessing and organizing information.

*Production Deficiencies*

As discussed earlier, prior to the deployment of memory strategies, children may be capable of using a strategy effectively but they fail to recognize the opportunity to do so. Similar to these so-called production deficiencies in memory strategy use (e.g., Naus et al., 1977), early in development, self-derivation through integration may be dependent on prompts. Consider that in most tests of self-derivation through integration, production deficiencies are not apparent because the key measure for assessing successful performance typically is prompted. Recall the earlier example in which to test whether children have successfully self-derived the new knowledge that pods talk by clicking and squeaking, a direct question is posed, "How does a pod talk?" This question provides the prompt to engage in memory integration. Nevertheless, there is indirect evidence that for children, self-derivation of new knowledge is prompt-dependent, whereas for adults it is not.

Here we describe two sources of indirect evidence that children require a prompt to engage in self-derivation through integration. First, Varga and

Bauer (2013) found that if 6-year-old children were presented with the to-be-integrated facts, but then not tested for self-derivation through integration until after a week-long delay (i.e., they were not prompted), performance suffered compared to children who were prompted immediately and then retested a week later (21% vs. 63%, respectively). Thus, the issue was not retention of the self-derived information, but instead a production deficiency in doing the cognitive work without an immediate prompt to do so. The second source of indirect evidence of production deficiencies in self-derivation through integration comes from a study we conducted in classrooms with second graders (approximately 8-years-old; Bauer et al., 2020). Children were presented with to-be-integrated information through a story. Children were prompted to integrate the semantic target information contained within the stories through questions for self-derivation through integration. A week later, children were asked to judge whether episodic information was in the stories they heard the week before. Information presented was 1) true and derived directly from the story (old); 2) plausible, but not included in the story (new); or 3) a blend of content from the paired stories such that details of one story were blended inaccurately into the other story (hybrid). The children were not prompted to integrate the episodic content of the stories. We reasoned that if they did so unprompted, they would be more likely to endorse the hybrid statements as true. Children correctly endorsed the old information and correctly rejected the new information, indicating good memory for the episodic content after one week. They also rejected the hybrid statements, indicating that the unprompted episodic information had not been integrated.

In contrast to the status of the process of integration in children, adults seemingly spontaneously engage in self-derivation through integration. In Varga and Bauer (2017), for example, scalp-recorded electrical oscillations in the brain that are time-locked to the processing of a stimulus (Event Related Potentials, i.e., ERP) revealed different patterns at the time of encoding of related facts based on whether the adult subsequently correctly self-derived the new fact through integration or not. Specifically, on trials on which they successfully integrated, as evidenced by self-derivation, adults showed a different ERP pattern when they were exposed to the second fact in a related pair, indicating that they were engaging in the process unprompted at the time of fact exposure.

In summary, maintenance of explicitly taught material through the use of memory strategies and knowledge extension through self-derivation through integration are learning processes supported by prior knowledge and organization. In addition, both show evidence for production deficiencies in childhood that are overcome by adulthood. Although the timeline for this process of "automatization" is well studied in memory strategy use, it remains an area for future research for self-derivation through integration. Overall, the data indicate that there are parallel supports for these learning processes. Next, we explore the lessons learned from the work of Dr. Peter Ornstein and how these lessons can be applied to our work on knowledge extension.

## Lessons Learned

There are three broad approaches for future research that are inspired by lessons learned from Ornstein and colleagues' work in the development of memory strategy use: (1) move the research into ecologically relevant and even "high-stakes" contexts, (2) conduct longitudinal work, and (3) investigate the role of metacognition. In this section, we elaborate on how these lessons can and do apply to our work with self-derivation through memory integration. We focus primarily on the first lesson, where we have made the most progress in application to our own work, and discuss lessons 2 and 3 as interesting future directions.

### *Lesson 1: Get into Ecologically Relevant Contexts*

The first lesson we take from Ornstein and colleagues is to move the research out of the laboratory. In addition to Ornstein's contributions to our understanding of children's strategy use in memory, he and his colleagues have made substantial contributions to research paths that blend laboratory and field work to better understand the applications of the work (see Baker-Ward & Ornstein, 2014). This balance of field and laboratory work can be seen in Ornstein and colleagues' work in memory reports for interactions with healthcare providers (e.g., Baker-Ward, Gordon, Ornstein, Larus, & Clubb, 1993; Baker-Ward, Ornstein, & Starnes, 2009; Baker-Ward & Thomas, Chapter 7) and in teachers' use of Cognitive Processing Language (CPL) in the classroom (e.g., Coffman et al., 2008; Grammer, Coffman, & Ornstein, 2013; see Coffman & Cook, Chapter 15).

After years of research on memory strategies conducted in the laboratory, Ornstein and colleagues began research on medical procedures as a way to understand children's eyewitness testimony in cases of abuse (see Baker-Ward & Thomas, Chapter 7). Forensic contexts clearly are exceptionally "high stakes," such that the report of information (accurate or not) could lead to adult prosecution. The examination of medical procedures can be considered an ethical analogue to abusive situations in that medical procedures involve an adult touching a child's body and are sometimes stressful situations, such as in the case of an emergency room visit or dental procedure (e.g., Baker-Ward et al., 2015; Burgwyn-Bailes et al., 2001). From these field-contexts, Ornstein and colleagues were able to provide guidance for interviewing procedures to use with children who may have suffered abuse. For example, in an experimental study of 3–5-year-old children's recall of a physical exam (Principe et al., 2000), children were interviewed immediately after the exam and again at 12 weeks post exam. At the six-week mark, children participated in one of four conditions: additional interview, view a video of a child receiving a physical exam, visit to the pediatrician's office, or the no-manipulation control. The results showed that the events that intervened between an initial and later interview impacted recall. Specifically, the children in the additional interview condition recalled more accurate information compared to children in the control condition without additional inaccuracies. Those who viewed the video recalled more accurate information, but also more inaccuracies, and those who returned to the pediatrician's office had poorer recall compared to the control. Thus, by extending research to ecologically relevant, and even high-stakes, contexts, we can better understand the processes involved and the application for policy and practice.

The educational contexts can also be considered high stakes. In educational contexts, children are tested on the knowledge they have gained, such as in annual tests that determine grade promotion and class placement, among other outcomes. Ornstein and colleagues have examined the maintenance of explicitly taught memory strategies for the purpose of informing educational applications and implications. (See Coffman et al., 2019, for review and discussion.) From this field work, they have learned that there is natural variability in teachers' use of CPL that impacts children's strategy deployment in first grade and continues to predict their strategy use and study strategies when they are in fourth grade. These findings provide important insights into sources of variability in children's performance in the classroom.

We also have taken our work on self-derivation through memory integration into the field – the classroom. With the cooperation of participating schools, we visit classrooms and teach guest lessons. In these lessons, we teach children fact pairs that could be integrated to support self-derivation of new knowledge. There is a delay between related facts and between fact presentation and test. In our first foray into the class-room, we tested children in grades K-3 with a story paradigm (Esposito & Bauer, 2017). We saw evidence for self-derivation through integration in Grades 1–3, with third graders significantly outperforming both first- and second-grade students. Importantly, and as noted earlier, children's performance on the self-derivation questions predicted their academic achievement as measured by school-based assessments. This relation remained when we accounted for parents' level of education.

Anything in the classroom is "high stakes," but some classrooms have higher stakes than others. One such context is when children are required to navigate academic content that is presented in more than one language. This may happen because children's home language and language of instruction differ, or because they are enrolled in a dual-language educational model. Children in a dual-language educational program are required to learn through two languages, one of which they are not likely yet proficient in. If they are not successful in learning and integrating across the languages, they will fall behind academically. Given the importance of success and the expansion of dual-language programs in the United States (http://webapp .cal.org/duallanguage/), we have been testing self-derivation through mem-ory integration across languages in dual-language programs. We originally hypothesized that learning through two different languages would present a significant challenge because different languages have different surface fea-tures, thus making it more challenging to recognize overlap in content. As described previously, Bauer et al. (2012) found that 6-year-olds performed better on a self-derivation-through-integration task when characters between paired stories were the same (high surface similarity) compared to when they differed (67% accuracy vs. 37%, respectively). We reasoned that a change in language between related facts would be similarly challenging.

The potential consequences of this high-stakes environment were evident in a field study (Esposito & Bauer, 2019b). We tested children enrolled in third grade (9-year-olds) with a paradigm in which facts were presented as blocks of single sentences. Half of the students were enrolled in a dual-language program in which instruction was provided through both Spanish and English (50% of the time for each) and the other half of the students were enrolled in an English monolingual program. Within the dual-language program, children received half of the fact pairs in English only and the other half included a language manipulation that required integration not only across facts but across languages. We expected the low surface similarity of the language manipulation would be a challenge to students. As hypoth-esized, children performed significantly better in the English-only condition compared to the language manipulation. Indeed, performance in the cross-language condition did not exceed chance in a forced-choice test.

In contrast to third graders, fourth graders (10-year-olds) in the same study performed similarly in the English-only and cross-language conditions. Although we might assume that the differences in grades represent differences in language proficiency such that gains in language proficiency supported self-derivation through integration performance across language contexts, the data do not support this possibility. The third-grade children actually had nominally higher language proficiency scores in Spanish and English compared to fourth graders. Instead, we interpreted the difference in performance to reflect the added experience of integrating across languages for an additional year in their educational setting.

The challenge of integrating across low surface similarity conditions is not absolute; it can be overcome with contextual support. Similar to support provided by teachers high in the use of CPL as studied by Ornstein and colleagues, stories and illustrations provide support to integrate in self-derivation. In the same series of studies, we examined second graders' (approximately 9 years of age) self-derivation-through-integration performance in a paired story paradigm. Again, half of the students were enrolled in a dual-language (Spanish/English) program; and children in this program received half of the story pairs through English only and the other half included the language manipulation. The story paradigm provided contextual support in the form of a familiar structure as well as illustrations to aid comprehension. With the added contextual supports, there were no differences in performance between the English-only and cross-language conditions. This indicates that the contextual supports mitigated the challenges of integrating and subsequently self-deriving new knowledge across language contexts. Thus, just as high-CPL teachers facilitate their children's performance, our "high-context" story paradigm facilitates self-derivation through memory integration. At this point, the research conducted in classrooms indicates the importance of contextual support, but more work is needed to clarify and refine guidelines for educational practice.

### *Lesson 2: The Need for Longitudinal Work*

Ornstein and colleagues have underscored the importance of longitudinal studies (see Haden, Chapter 3). Longitudinal work on strategy use has largely confirmed the developmental transitions and trajectories found in cross-sectional studies. (See Schneider & Sodian, 1999, for review.) However, longitudinal work indicates that the utilization deficiencies are not nearly as common as previously thought from cross-sectional work (e.g., Schneider et al., 2004; see also Schneider & Sodian, 1999, for review). Rather than utilization deficiencies, memory strategy use is predicted by memory capacity and the ability to use multiple strategies effectively, which takes time and experience to emerge (e.g., Kron-Sperl, Schneider, & Hasselhorn, 2008). Indeed, many studies have confirmed that the use of multiple strategies improves performance but is more likely to be effectively employed by older children. In a cross-sectional study, Schwenck, Bjorklund, and Schneider (2009) found that even some 4-year-olds employed multiple strategies, but it was 8-year-olds who were more likely to use and benefit from the use of multiple strategies. Thus, there are areas where we see agreement between longitudinal and cross-sectional work and other areas that show the necessity of longitudinal work to elucidate developmental trajectories.

Longitudinal work also is needed to further elucidate individual differences in performance. The longitudinal studies on memory strategy use indicate substantial individual differences in performance (e.g., Schneider et al., 2004; see also Schneider & Sodian, 1999, for review). Understanding these differences and what can be done to support low-performers is a continued area of investigation (e.g., Schwenck et al., 2009).

The lesson we take from this is that longitudinal work is an important next step for understanding self-derivation through integration. Longitudinal work will help to elucidate when in development self-derivation through integration becomes less dependent on a prompt as well as what supports are most appropriate for different developmental periods. Longitudinal work will also help to identify the concurrent and lagged predictors of individual differences in self-derivation performance. Of particular interest are the malleable factors that predict performance and those that predict less dependency on a prompt. These factors will clarify the role of self-derivation through integration on education and academic outcomes. We have just completed data collection for a five-year longitudinal study of self-derivation through integration in classrooms with children across Kindergarten–Grade 5 (ages 5–11). We are excited to examine how this process develops over time and the concurrent and lagged contributing cognitive factors.

### Lesson 3: Explore the Role of Metacognition

The third direction we take from Ornstein's work is to understand the role of metacognition. The development of metacognition, and specifically metamemory, supports effective strategy use, as previously discussed (see Schneider, 1999, for review). In addition, high-CPL teachers foster development of metacognition in their students by reflecting on memory use and encouraging students to do the same (Coffman et al., 2019). This could also be the case for self-derivation through integration.

To date, the self-derivation-through-integration literature has not elucidated to what extent individuals are aware that they are engaging a productive process when they successfully self-derive new knowledge through integration. We have some evidence that adults who are aware of the process have higher performance compared to those who are not. Varga and Bauer (2017) presented young adults with a single-sentence testing paradigm in which they were not told that some facts were related and could be used to self-derive new information. After presentation of facts and the test for self-derivation, the participants were asked if they noticed anything about the facts. Over half (62%) reported being aware that some of the facts were related and this awareness was correlated to task performance. Interestingly, explicit awareness also was correlated to response time on unsuccessful self-derivation trials, indicating those with awareness that the facts were related spent longer searching for an answer.

In another laboratory-based study, college students were provided with single-sentence paired facts in four blocks with testing taking place after each block (Dugan et al., 2017). The facts were original in each block, but performance significantly improved after the first block. This suggests that whatever information participants derived about the structure of the first block of trials – whether in the form of explicit awareness or something more implicit – aided their performance in the subsequent three blocks. A future direction is to examine to what extent metacognition generally and awareness of the relation between facts specifically impacts self-derivation-through-integration performance. We are poised to address this question. Across three years of longitudinal data collection, we included measures of metacognition in the form of both feeling of knowing and judgments of learning. We anticipate the longitudinal analyses of these data will elucidate the relation between the development of metacognition and self-derivation through integration.

## Conclusions

The work of Dr. Peter Ornstein and colleagues over the past 50 years has laid out the developmental progression of children's use of memory strategies for maintaining information presented with an expectation to remember. This extensive body of work has revealed the developmental timeline and the challenges and supports for efficient deployment of strategies, as well as the educational implications of Cognitive Processing Language in classrooms. The implications of Ornstein's work extend beyond the study of memory strategies and their development. His career has taught us the importance of moving our research out of the laboratory and into ecologically relevant and even "high-stakes" contexts, of conducting longitudinal work, and of investigating the role of metacognition.

The work we have been conducting on self-derivation through memory integration is complementary to that of Ornstein. Rather than focusing on maintenance of information explicitly provided, we have focused on how children and adults integrate information gained from separate learning episodes and use it as a basis to derive new knowledge. In this work we have found pronounced age-related differences and individual variability. The variability relates to academic achievement. Like use of memory strategies, self-derivation through integration is influenced by prior knowledge. There also are what we might gloss as "productive deficiencies" in self-derivation through integration. Just as in the memory strategy literature, children are dependent on prompts to engage the cognitive processes that eventually result in self-derivation of new knowledge, whereas adults employ strategies seemingly spontaneously. We hope that similar to Ornstein and colleagues, our research on the process of knowledge extension through self-derivation based on memory integration will inspire inquiry and follow a trajectory that leads to translation into educational policy and practice.

CHAPTER 6

# Commentary
## Children's Memory Strategies
### Wolfgang Schneider

The two chapters on memory strategy development included in Part II of this volume provide a rather comprehensive account of initial research trends and subsequent developments in this field. Overall, the views presented in these chapters square well with my own perception of major outcomes. In the following, I focus on several core findings outlined in these chapters, trying to elaborate on basic assumptions and implications of major research outcomes. One important aspect of my comments concerns the contribution of Peter Ornstein and his colleagues to the progress we have observed in this research area over the past 50 years.

## Early Research on Memory Strategy Development

As noted by Best and Folds-Bennett in their overview of memory strategy development in children (Chapter 4), research on children's memory has a long history. The vast majority of studies since the mid-1960s have been carried out with schoolchildren, mainly dealing with declarative (explicit) memory, that is, conscious remembering of facts and events. It was repeatedly found that particularly clear improvements in declarative memory can be observed for the age range between 6 and 12 years, which roughly corresponds to the elementary school period in most countries. In order to explain these rapid increases in memory performance over time, different sources or determinants of memory development have been identified. According to most contemporary memory researchers, changes in *basic capacities, memory strategies, metacognitive knowledge,* and *domain knowledge* all contribute to developmental changes in memory performance. There is also broad agreement that some of these sources of development contribute more than others, and that some play an important role in certain periods of childhood but not in others (Schneider, 2015).

## Development of Rehearsal Strategies

The pioneering work carried out by John Flavell and coworkers from the mid-1960s on demonstrated the important role of strategies for children's memory development. In particular, rehearsal and organization were established as major memory strategies that develop between 5 and 10 years of age (e.g., Flavell, 1971). Memory strategies were broadly defined as mental or behavioral activities that achieve cognitive purposes and are effort-consuming, potentially conscious, and controllable (Roebers, 2014). Whereas rehearsal is an encoding strategy, organization can be observed both at encoding and retrieval.

The classic study on the development of rehearsal by Flavell, Beach, and Chinsky (1966; described in more detail by Best and Folds-Bennett, Chapter 4) permitted the experimenter to determine if 5- to 10-year-olds were verbally rehearsing the materials when preparing for serial recall of picture lists. As a main result, Flavell and colleagues demonstrated that production of the rehearsal strategy increased with age (as indicated by primacy effects) and was positively correlated with recall. They concluded from their findings that frequency of rehearsal determines level of memory performance.

Similar research subsequently carried out by Peter Ornstein and his coworkers (Ornstein, Naus, & Liberty, 1975) used an overt rehearsal procedure that required children to repeat the items of a word list aloud. This permitted the experimenter to determine exactly what the children were doing. Ornstein et al. (1975) found that younger elementary school children tended to rehearse each item singularly as it was presented (passive rehearsal style), whereas older children rehearsed each item with several previously presented ones (active, or cumulative rehearsal style). Ornstein and colleagues thus questioned Flavell's frequency interpretation, asserting that the important developmental changes are in terms of *style* rather than *frequency* of rehearsal. This position has been validated in a number of studies carried out by Ornstein and colleagues as well as in other labs (for details, see Chapters 4 and 5).

Another important finding (also described in these two chapters) was first demonstrated in studies by Flavell and colleagues and later on by Ornstein and coworkers, indicating that there are barriers to children's strategy use. That is, deliberate strategies were not observed in children younger than 5 or 6 years of age. The lack of strategic behaviors in very young children was labeled *mediation deficiency*, indicating that children of a particular (preschool) age do not benefit from memory strategies, even after having been instructed how to use them. Although slightly older children such as kindergarteners and young schoolchildren also did not use strategies spontaneously, their problem was different. These children were shown to suffer from a *production deficiency*. That is, they failed to use (or to produce) strategies when given "neutral" instructions but could be easily trained to do so, usually with corresponding improvements in memory performance. For instance, Naus, Ornstein, and Aivano (1977) provided evidence that the differences in rehearsal between younger and older elementary school children reflected a production deficiency by the younger children. (See also Guttentag, Ornstein, & Siemens, 1987; Ornstein & Naus, 1985.) This training study as well as others (e.g., Cox et al., 1989) demonstrated the strong relationship between rehearsal style and memory performance, noting improvements in young children's recall following cumulative rehearsal training. Yet, rehearsal training for young children rarely eliminated developmental differences, and generalization of the trained strategy was typically weak. These findings led to the conclusion that a critical developmental difference concerns children's inclination to implement a particular strategy rather than their ability to use it, which indicates that young schoolchildren are typically production-deficient (Bjorklund, Dukes, & Brown, 2009).

## The Development of Organizational Strategies

As noted in Chapters 4 and 5, the developmental story for organizational strategies is much the same as for rehearsal. That is, older schoolchildren are more likely to employ organizational strategies spontaneously than younger children, whereas performance of younger children varies considerably as a function of type of materials, prior knowledge, and instruction. In most cases, preschoolers and young elementary children show a production deficiency when given "neutral" instructions to remember. However, several studies demonstrated the effectiveness of direct prompts and organizational training for improving young children's strategy use and recall (e.g., Corsale & Ornstein, 1980; Lange & Pierce, 1992).

## Locus of Effect: Encoding or Retrieval?

One interesting aspect of research carried out by Ornstein and colleagues (e.g., Bjorklund, Ornstein, & Haig, 1977; Corsale & Ornstein, 1980) concerned the question of whether memory for randomly presented but semantically clusterable lists of items substantially benefit from deliberate categorization strategies or is simply a result of strong semantic inter-item associations (and thus the result of rather automatic processes). Ornstein and his colleagues developed a sort–recall methodology that involved organizing pictures or words into semantic categories. Children were given randomly ordered lists of categorizable items (e.g., animals, furniture, and the like). They were then told that their task was to remember the items later on, and that they were free to do anything with the materials that might help their recall. Following a short study period, children were asked to recall as many items as they could. Children's organization of items during study (sorting) and recall (clustering) was then measured using various clustering indices.

Overall, findings indicated that sorting strategies are more important for memory performance than clustering during recall (Liberty & Ornstein, 1973; Kee, Bell, & Davies, 1981). For instance, Kee and colleagues (1981) assessed sorting during studying and clustering during recall in second and sixth graders as well as in university students. Whereas the university students' clustering scores for both encoding and recall were similarly high, the sorting scores of the children were lower than their clustering scores at output. When children were instructed to use sorting strategies during encoding, positive effects on sorting scores and recall were found. In contrast, instructions to use categories at the time of retrieval had only small effects on clustering and recall. Kee and colleagues (1981) concluded from their findings that effects of organization at input and not during testing produced differences in memory performance.

There are now many demonstrations that the degree of output organization systematically covaries with association and typicality of the list items (e.g., Bjorklund, 1985; Hasselhorn, 1992). These researchers argue that young children's clustering during free recall may be automatically determined by the structure of the task materials and is less an indicator of conscious strategic operations. Typically, correlations between sorting during study and recall turned out to be higher than correlations between clustering during recall and memory performance.

## Can Very Young Children Benefit from Strategy Use?

There is evidence that young children have already developed a rough understanding of the importance of strategies in list-learning tasks. As shown by Baker-Ward, Ornstein, and Holden (1984), even preschoolers can develop some understanding of what they need to remember. When asked to remember a set of items, children repeatedly looked at the items, a behavior not shown when asked to play with items. However, as emphasized by Bjorklund et al. (2009), the organizational abilities of preschoolers, kindergartners, and young schoolchildren resemble their rehearsal abilities in that they are capable of organizing information for recall, but they rarely do so spontaneously. As with rehearsal, training children to use an organizational strategy can be effective but rarely eliminates age differences. Moreover, young children also typically fail to generalize the strategy to new situations or new sets of materials (Cox & Waters, 1986). Thus, a salient feature of young children's deliberate use of memory strategies is the context specificity that characterizes many aspects of their performance.

Does this imply that young children benefit from the use of memory strategies whenever the context is favorable? The evidence is mixed. On the one hand, several memory researchers have observed that higher levels of organization spontaneously demonstrated by young children are not always accompanied by higher levels of recall. Such *utilization deficiencies* (UD) have been shown in several studies with both preschoolers and young elementary schoolchildren (for reviews, see Bjorklund & Coyle, 1995; Miller & Seier, 1994). It appears from this research that using a strategy such as organization is only a first step. Once the mechanics of the strategy are learned, children need more time before they can execute it proficiently. Although there is plenty of evidence supporting the utilization-deficiency paradigm, it seems important to note that findings are not always consistent, depending on the particular definition and on certain characteristics of the task (Schneider & Sodian, 1997). Research findings concerning utilization deficiencies with regard to organizational strategies are particularly difficult to reconcile, given that the UD phenomenon was found for some children but not for others (e.g., Kron-Sperl, Schneider, & Hasselhorn, 2008; Schwenck, Bjorklund, & Schneider, 2009). There seems reason to conclude from recent research that utilization deficiencies are context-dependent and only one of several patterns of strategy use/recall relations (Bjorklund et al., 2009).

On the other hand, several training studies carried out with young children indicate that even preschoolers and kindergarten children are able to use intentional strategies, both in ecologically valid settings such as hide-and-seek tasks and in the context of a laboratory task (Schneider, 2015). Thus, memory strategies can be effectively taught to young children. For example, young children trained to use an active (cumulative) rehearsal strategy increased levels of recall substantially (Cox et al., 1989), and even preschool children used organizational strategies and demonstrated enhanced levels of recall when instructions emphasized the importance of grouping (Carr & Schneider, 1991; Lange & Pierce, 1992).

Taken together, the empirical evidence on the development of rehearsal and organizational strategies summarized by Best and Folds-Bennett as well as by Esposito and Bauer in Chapters 4 and 5, respectively, indicates that memory strategies are rarely found in preschool children but develop rapidly over the elementary school years. Older children are more likely to actively rehearse items and to group items on the basis of meaning and to study same-category items together, with higher levels of sorting and clustering yielding higher levels of recall. However, the ages of strategy acquisition are relative and variable within and between strategies. As noted by Folds and colleagues (1990), memory performance is maximized if the semantic structure of task materials to be remembered and the instructions encourage strategy use, and if children possess considerable knowledge about task materials and requirements. In particular, age-related changes in children's domain knowledge and their task-specific strategy knowledge should contribute to more efficient strategy use (Ornstein & Naus, 1985). This insight stimulated a second wave of studies on memory strategy development (starting in the late 1980s) that focused on interrelationships between knowledge and strategy use.

## Effects of Metacognitive Knowledge and Domain Knowledge on Strategy Use

Chapters 4 and 5 both emphasize the importance of metacognitive knowledge (metamemory) and domain knowledge for the development of memory strategies, In the following paragraphs, I briefly comment and elaborate on this issue.

### Metamemory and Strategy Development

Flavell and Wellman (1977) introduced the term *metamemory* for knowledge about memory processes. From a developmental perspective, this concept seemed well suited to explain young children's production deficiencies on a broad variety of memory tasks. Whereas young children usually do not learn much about the advantages of memory strategies, schoolchildren are regularly confronted with various memory tasks that should eventually help them to discover the advantages of strategies and improve their strategy knowledge. In turn, this should positively affect memory behavior (i.e., strategy use) and performance on future memory tasks. Thus, the expectation was that clear developmental trends in the relationship between metamemory and memory should be found across childhood and adolescence.

Two broad categories of metacognitive knowledge have been distinguished in the literature (Flavell & Wellman, 1977; Schneider & Pressley, 1997). *Declarative metacognitive knowledge* refers to what children factually know about their memory. This type of knowledge is explicit and verbalizable and includes knowledge about the importance of person variables (e.g., age or IQ), task characteristics such as task difficulty, and strategy knowledge. In comparison, *procedural metacognitive knowledge* is mostly implicit (subconscious) and refers to children's self-monitoring and their control strategies (e.g., self-testing after a study period).

There are a variety of measures that have been used to capture what children know about memory. Most measures of declarative, factual knowledge have used interviews or questionnaires that focus on knowledge about person variables, task demands, and strategies. Whereas earlier instruments predominantly used in the memory domain suffered from methodological problems, more recent interviews and questionnaires showed better psychometric properties such as sufficient reliability and validity (Schneider, 2015). Moreover, nonverbal techniques helped in assessing young children's declarative knowledge. For instance, Best and Ornstein (1986) developed a useful procedure (peer-tutoring task) in which older children were asked to tutor younger children about how to do a certain memory task in order to maximize learning. Peer tutoring is likely more motivating to young children than interviews, and children tend to be more explicit when answering a question of an older child as compared with that of an adult (who already seems to know everything).

There is much evidence for the position expressed in Chapters 4 and 5 that metamemory development is a factor that facilitates strategy use and improves memory performance. Empirical research exploring the development of declarative metamemory revealed that children's knowledge of facts about memory increases considerably over the primary-grade years. Numerous studies showed that increases in knowledge about strategies are paralleled by the acquisition of strategies, and that metamemory–memory behavior relationships tend to be moderately strong. In a statistical meta-analysis of empirical studies addressing this issue (based on 60 studies and more than 7,000 participants), an overall correlation of .41 between metamemory and memory was found. Correlations between metamemory and strategy use were about the same size from Grade 3 on but considerably lower for younger elementary school children (Schneider & Pressley,

1997). Obviously, what older schoolchildren and adolescents know about their memory frequently influences how they try to remember.

There is evidence that task-specific metamemory can be trained effectively in younger schoolchildren. One procedure that was used in several studies (e.g., Pressley et al., 1984) involved the comparison of effective versus ineffective strategies and their effects on memory performance. For instance, in studies designed to train organizational strategies, young schoolchildren were first asked to memorize a set of picture cards without any prompts to use a strategy. Next, children's recall was assessed, and they were informed about the outcome. In a second trial using a parallel list of items, children were instructed to first sort the items into semantic categories and then study them by category. Subsequently, children were asked to compare their memory performance on the two trials. According to my experiences with this paradigm, children were always impressed by the recall difference. This approach can be conceived of as a *metacognitive acquisition procedure* (Pressley, Borkowski, & Schneider, 1989), leading to the insight that the organizational strategy is more powerful than the children's original approach. In most cases, children used this information to guide future strategy use. Given this positive evidence, it seems unfortunate that systematic strategy training programs are rarely included in elementary school instruction, both in Europe and the United States (see Coffman & Cook, Chapter 15).

## The Importance of Domain Knowledge

As noted above, Ornstein and Naus (1985) were among the first to point out that age-related changes in children's knowledge base contribute to a more efficient use of memory strategies. Children with a rich knowledge base can access items of a given memory task more easily, will be able to quickly activate inter-item relationships, and thus are more likely to use memory strategies because less attentional focus and memory capacity are required (Bjorklund, 1987). Increasing domain knowledge improves efficiency of basic processes, acquisition and execution of strategies, and metacognitive knowledge. Thus, prior knowledge of related content not only influences how much and what children recall but also affects their execution of basic processes and strategies, their metacognitive knowledge, and their acquisition of new strategies. Rich domain knowledge can also have nonstrategic effects, that is, diminish the need for strategy activation.

Since the late 1970s, a large number of developmental studies have confirmed this assumption, demonstrating that the amount of knowledge in a particular domain such as chess, physics, or sports determines how much new information from the same domain can be stored and retrieved. (See the reviews by Bjorklund, 1987; Schneider & Bjorklund, 1998.) Evidence for the powerful effects of domain knowledge on memory performance comes from studies using the *expert–novice paradigm*. These studies compared experts and novices in a given domain (e.g., baseball, chess, or soccer) on memory tasks related to that domain. From a developmental perspective, the major advantage of the expert–novice paradigm is that knowledge and chronological age are not necessarily confounded, a problem inherent in most studies addressing knowledge-base effects. Several studies demonstrated that rich domain knowledge enabled a child expert to perform much like an adult expert and better than an adult novice – thus showing a disappearance and sometimes reversal of usual developmental trends (see review by Schneider, 2015).

Domain knowledge and metamemory may interact in facilitating strategy use. The study by Schneider, Schlagmüller, and Visé (1998), already described in Chapter 5, illustrated effects of both knowledge components on strategy use in third- and fourth-grade children. As noted by Esposito and Bauer, findings indicated that both domain knowledge and metamemory explained unique variance in the use of organizational strategies. Moreover, causal modeling procedures revealed that although there was only a modest direct contribution of metamemory to the prediction of recall, the indirect link via strategic behavior was much stronger. When the sort–recall task required the organization of soccer-related items and the sample was subdivided into soccer experts and novices, individual differences in domain knowledge explained most variance in recall. Interestingly, however, individual differences in strategy use were also significantly related to children's recall, accounting for a small portion of the variance in memory performance. These findings suggest that metamemory and domain knowledge facilitate the use of memory strategies, which substantially enhances memory performance.

## Recent Research Trends: Focus on Longitudinal Studies and Educational Contexts

Both Best and Folds-Bennett and Esposito and Bauer emphasize the need for longitudinal studies in order to understand the complexity of memory and all those factors that influence memory performance (see also Schneider & Ornstein, 2019). Although several longitudinal studies confirmed major outcomes of cross-sectional work, as far as general developmental trends were concerned, they also indicated a high degree of interindividual variability (e.g., Kron-Sperl et al., 2008; Lehmann & Hasselhorn, 2012). These longitudinal studies showed that memory strategies do not develop as straightforward as suggested by cross-sectional work, demonstrating considerable variability in the development of organizational and rehearsal strategies (Roebers, 2014; Schneider, 2014). Moreover, longitudinal research has shown that the process of strategy acquisition is not one of simply replacing an ineffective technique with a more effective procedure, and that early metacognitive knowledge indeed precedes effective strategy use.

Several studies on the development of memory strategies and metamemory have emphasized the *importance of educational contexts* for developmental changes (Coffman & Cook, Chapter 15; Hudson, Wiley, & Coffman, Chapter 16; Grammer & Torres, Chapter 17). Obviously, most of memory development is not so much a product of age but of education. One way in which parents and teachers facilitate cognitive development is by nurturing the development of children's metacognition. For instance, Kron-Sperl et al. (2008) repeatedly presented the children of their sample with a sort–recall memory task without giving any specific strategy cues. When performance of these children was compared with that of random samples of schoolchildren who received this task for the first time, substantial practice effects were found. Children of the longitudinal sample not only outperformed the control children regarding strategy use and memory performance but also showed better task-specific memory. Obviously, it does not require much effort to improve children's strategy knowledge.

However, research carried out in the classroom revealed that teachers do not always foster children's metacognitive knowledge and strategy use. For instance, Moely and colleagues observed in classrooms to find out how elementary teachers instructed strategy use and memory knowledge as they presented lessons to children in Grades K to 6 (see the overview by Moely, Santulli, & Obach, 1995). Teachers varied widely in the extent to which they focused on how children might adjust or regulate their cognitive activities in order to master a task. Efforts also varied widely depending on the subject matter under consideration. When Moely and colleagues first looked at a broad range of instructional effort, they found low levels of strategy instruction.

More recent longitudinal research on the impact of schooling on strategy development (e.g., Ornstein et al., 2010, Coffman et al., 2019; see Coffman & Cook, Chapter 15) confirmed the earlier finding that teachers rarely provide direct strategy instruction but nonetheless offer memory-relevant "talk." Interestingly, individual differences in the use of Cognitive Processing Language (high vs. low "CPL" teachers) were important for students' subsequent strategy development, with children instructed by high-CPL teachers demonstrating more sophisticated strategies. Ornstein and colleagues also showed that teachers can be easily instructed to use this memory-related (CPL) language.

Esposito and Bauer describe an interesting research program that goes beyond explicit strategy instruction. They labeled their approach *self-derivation through integration,* a phenomenon that occurs when information acquired in one learning episode is integrated with information presented in a separate episode. They illustrate parallels between the memory-strategy approach, where the major goal is to maintain information, and their new research program that focuses on knowledge extension. I fully agree with their conclusion that the self-derivation-through-integration approach could benefit from the inclusion of core issues of the memory-strategy approach, such as the analysis of production deficiencies, the assessment of metacognitive knowledge and its effect, and the consideration of ecologically relevant contexts.

Taken together, the various research programs described by Best and Folds-Bennett and by Esposito and Bauer in Chapters 4 and 5, respectively, have added considerably to our knowledge about memory development. The numerous studies carried out by Peter Ornstein and his research teams during a long academic career of about 50 years have significantly contributed to our knowledge about this issue and also ensured that it remained a very active/interesting component of research on cognitive development.

# PART III

# Children's Event Memory

# CHAPTER 7

# Children's Reports of Personal Experiences
## From the Laboratory to the Doctor's Office to the Courtroom

*Lynne E. Baker-Ward and Taylor E. Thomas*

In 1985, Peter Ornstein was thriving as a professor of psychology at the University of North Carolina at Chapel Hill, fully engaged in each of the tripartite realms of academic responsibility. His transition from experimental to developmental psychologist long complete, he served as the director of the Developmental Graduate Program and enjoyed the collegial exchanges that would soon become the Carolina Consortium of Human Development (see Baker-Ward, Bjorklund, & Coffman, Chapter 1). His research on children's use of strategies for deliberate memory (see Best & Folds-Bennett, Chapter 4) was supported by federal funding and published in prestigious journals (e.g., Ornstein et al., 1985; Best & Ornstein, 1986). He had also succeeded in integrating his research and teaching. A dedicated mentor, he actively involved his graduate students in his research programs, and often continued to collaborate with alumni of his laboratory. It clearly seemed reasonable to assume that this generative academician was not seeking new directions when a telephone call he received led to a new stage in his career.

The caller was Virginia Weisz, the director of the Guardian ad Litem program in North Carolina. This program provides alleged victims of child abuse and neglect with a trained community volunteer who, paired with an attorney, advocates for the best interest of the child. Weisz wanted to provide judges with information that would help them understand the statements that children made in legal proceedings regarding their reports of the alleged actions (P. Ornstein, personal communication, June 12, 2020). Her action was prompted in part by a judge's decision regarding a 3-year-old child's competence to testify. The child was found wandering outside alone, had obviously been assaulted, and spontaneously named the individual who she said was responsible for her injuries. Because of her age

The research described in this chapter was supported by grants MH 49304 and HD 33214 from the US Public Health Service to Peter A. Ornstein.

and the nature of the allegations, however, the judge did not allow her to take the stand. Ornstein quickly realized that, despite his stature as an internationally recognized expert on children's memory, the empirical support needed to inform legal practice was not available at the time in his own research or even in the collective knowledge base of the field.

## The Context

Ornstein was not alone in receiving requests to address children's testimony. Changes had recently taken place in state and federal policy that led to dramatic increases in reports of child abuse (see Poole & Lamb, 1998). Notably, in the 1970s most states had designated physicians as mandated reporters of child abuse. Congress would soon pass the Abuse and Prevention Act (Public Law 93–247, 1988), which extended the parameters of child abuse to include child sexual and emotional abuse in addition to physical abuse. Because of these changes, the prosecutions of child sexual abuse nearly doubled by the early 1990s (Brainerd & Reyna, 2012), increasing the admissibility of expert psychological testimony (see Ceci & Bruck, 1993).

### Societal Controversy

The prosecution of cases involving child sexual abuse extended beyond the courtroom to the public sphere. For example, the media closely documented a series of daycare abuse cases in which young children made allegations of sexual abuse against school teachers and staff (e.g., the McMartin Preschool trial, the Little Rascals trial; Bikel, 1993). In these cases, children's allegations were often bizarre (e.g., reports of being made to ingest feces), obtained through suggestive modes of questioning, and unaccompanied by physical evidence. The potential for memory distortion led to heated disagreements about the reliability of children's reports, with some individuals believing that children's accounts reflected their untainted, veridical experience and others concluding that social pressures led children to produce unreliable information. This debate grew increasingly heated in the absence of empirical results to inform practice. When should a child's testimony be admissible? Could a jury, as a bumper sticker advised, "Believe the Children"?

### Conceptual Underpinnings of a Research Program

Ornstein found himself increasingly intrigued by the issue of young children's abilities to report their significant personal experiences and embarked on a program of research that would continue for three decades (e.g., Ornstein, Gordon, & Larus, 1992; Ornstein, Baker-Ward et al., 2006; Baker-Ward, Ornstein, & Thomas, in press) and, in many regards, constitute a new stage in his career. But as every developmentalist knows, continuity as well as discontinuity characterizes stage transitions. Ornstein's interest in children's testimony was premised on the assumption that, although multiple factors affect children's accounts of their experiences, at a fundamental level, *children cannot report what they cannot remember* (Ornstein, Larus, & Clubb, 1991). Hence, research on children's memory for personal experiences would build on his laboratory's established skill in investigating memory within the context of strategic recall (see Best & Folds-Bennett, Chapter 4). Like memory for events, strategic memory represents a type of episodic recall (see Gordon, Baker-Ward, & Ornstein, 2001), i.e., memory for experiences that are located in time and space. Whereas episodic recall includes ordinary, prosaic experiences including the presentation of to-be-remembered words, children's memory for personal experiences represents autobiographical memory, which involves memory for events that involve the self and have personal significance (see Fivush, 2011).

Ornstein also brought his well-articulated conceptualization of memory and its development to this new endeavor. The perspective from which he pursued the understanding of children's memory for real-world events, such as their memory for experimenter-provided, to-be-remembered stimuli, was an information-processing framework (e.g., see Ornstein, Baker-Ward et al., 1997). This model directed researchers' attention toward the operation of the memory system at each of several stages in the flow of information from the initial encoding of components of an event to the reporting of information in memory. Further, the model encompassed the possibility of distortions in memory over time, hence facilitating efforts to address a central concern in evaluations of children's capacity to provide testimony in legal proceedings. The general themes that constitute the framework, as most typically applied by Ornstein and his colleagues were as follows: (1) Not everything gets into memory; (2) What gets into memory may vary in strength; (3) The status of information in memory changes over time; (4) Retrieval is not perfect; and (5) Not everything that can be retrieved is reported.

The emergence of developmental science, and the central role that Ornstein's home institution played in its emergence and establishment, further influenced the approach embodied in the developing research program (see Baker-Ward et al., Chapter 1). The investigation of children's event memory inherently involved the examination of multiple domains of performance and the exploration of individual differences. Further, Ornstein's research on children's event memory as informed by this perspective examined memory for events in children's everyday environments that held personal significance for children and their families.

### *"Bringing a Lab to the World"*

At the time, groundbreaking research conducted by Katherine Nelson, Robyn Fivush, Judith Hudson, and others was powerfully illustrating the contrast between preschoolers' memory as assessed in laboratory contexts and as demonstrated in their natural settings (Nelson, 1986; Fivush & Hudson, 1990). This research emphasized children's understanding and representation of their experiences. Consequently, the reliability of children's reports and the degree of correspondence between the accounts of children and adults were not central issues, which of course, are of paramount importance in assessing children's capacity to provide testimony in legal settings. Ornstein and his colleagues faced the challenge of examining children's accounts of meaningful personal experiences while assessing the extent and accuracy of the information they provided.

Examining children's memory for their experiences in medical settings provided the opportunity to overcome both of these challenges. Ornstein and his colleagues developed a basic research paradigm that they implemented in investigations of children's memory for a range of medical events ranging from routine physical examinations (e.g., Ornstein, Gordon, & Larus, 1992) to an invasive diagnostic procedure (Merritt, Ornstein, & Spicker, 1994). These naturally occurring events were salient components of children's lives. They involved appropriate, necessary contact with a child's body by an adult; were characterized by varying degrees of the child's understanding across event components; and, to differing degrees, evoked stress and discomfort. Hence, medical experiences constituted an analogue for child sexual abuse that, with parental consent and child assent, the researchers could ethically investigate. This analogue, of course, was not perfect; for example, parents and other adults sanctioned these experiences, and medical checkups, in contrast to episodes of abuse, are freely discussed within the family. Further, the work was conducted with children who had not been the subject of allegations of abuse or neglect. Thus, the generalizability of the findings to memory among children with these histories was unclear. Nonetheless, reporting medical experiences was, indeed, a long way from recalling word lists.

The involvement of collaborators representing different areas of expertise contributed to the success of the research program. Betty N. Gordon, a clinical psychologist, was a co-investigator from the planning of the initial investigation until her death in 2004. Kathy A. Merritt, a pediatrician, provided expertise in the use of biological measures and insights regarding children's and providers' experiences in medical settings. An additional developmental psychologist, Lynne Baker-Ward, also contributed to the research program from its inception. In consultation with medical professionals, Ornstein and his team defined standard components or *features* of the event, documented the actions included in individual exams and procedures at the time of their occurrence, and charted the child's retention of these features over a range of delay intervals. They could manipulate some aspects of the experience, including the nature of the memory assessment and the length of time between the event and the child's report of the experience, providing some degree of experimental control. In addition, the approach was programmatic, with replications of some conditions incorporated into the design of later investigations. In these regards, the methodology involved "bringing a lab to the world" (as described by Cox, Chapter 2).

### From Description to Optimization

Baltes and colleagues (e.g., Baltes, Reese, & Lipsitt, 1980) provide a model for the study of lifespan development that we have adopted in a simplified form to guide our overview of Ornstein's research on children's memory for personally experienced events. Baltes and his collaborators proposed that life-span developmental psychology involves three major functions in studying human development. The first is *description*, which consists of the systematic report of change as it occurs during development. The second, *explanation*, encompasses the explication or clarification of identified changes in behaviors in order to show their relationships to concurrent situations or components of the individual's history. The third function, *optimization,* involves the generation of a knowledge base that allows for the enhancement of development through the prevention or alleviation of developmental differences.

We see this model as applicable to Ornstein's research program, and apply it in structuring this overview of his work. We begin the next section with a description of children's reports of medical experiences across age, delay intervals, and event types. Next, we focus on a potential explanation of changes in the observed levels of memory performance across different ages, delays, and event types: prior knowledge. Finally, we explore the work of Ornstein and his colleagues with particular relevance to the optimization of children's testimony, focusing on attempts to enhance children's memory reports through the provision of interview procedures with enhanced supports for retrieval.

## Describing Children's Event Memory

In responding to the need to understand better the capacity of young children to report naturally occurring events that they had experienced, the first task for the Ornstein Lab was to define some basic parameters of memory performance within the context of the research paradigm that they had developed.

### Age Differences

The most pressing questions involved age differences in performance. Could even younger preschoolers provide information that could contribute to an understanding of what happened within the context of legal proceedings? How did memory performance differ across the preschool and early elementary school years? Would young children's accounts include significant distortions of events or products of imagination or fantasy? Given the extensive literature addressing these questions that has been amassed over the past three decades, it may be difficult to appreciate how little information was available at the time. To provide answers to these questions, Ornstein and his colleagues worked with community pediatric practices in two initial investigations. We summarize the second of these investigations from the Ornstein Laboratory, Baker-Ward, Gordon et al. (1993), in this section. This investigation replicated and extended the results of the first study, Ornstein, Gordon, and Larus (1992).

Consistent with the general research approach described above, Baker-Ward, Gordon et al. (1993) worked with the participating practices to define standard features of a pediatric examination. For example, the features comprising the visit with the nurse included testing the child's hearing; the interaction with the physician included listening to the heart. Parents and healthcare providers completed checklists to document variations in an individual child's examination. On average, each child experienced about 19 standard features of the examination. A researcher who provided increasingly specific prompts assessed the child's retention of these features in an individual interview. The interview began with open-ended requests for information ("Tell me what happened during your checkup") followed by increasingly delineated requests if information regarding a particular feature was not forthcoming ("Did the doctor check any parts of your face? What parts?"), and ended with a yes/no question if necessary ("Did the doctor shine a light in your eyes?").

Children ($N$ = 187) at three age levels – 3, 5, and 7 years – were interviewed immediately after their checkups and again after either 1, 3, or 6 weeks; an additional group that provided a control for any effects of the initial interview was interviewed only at 3 weeks. Figure 7.1 presents the percent of features correctly reported in response to open-ended and specific probes by test condition at ages 3 (panel A), 5 (panel B), and 7 (panel C) years. As indicated in this figure, even the 3-year-old children provided a great deal of information regarding the event, reporting on average about three-quarters of the features they experienced, and performance increased significantly with age. An age-related increase was also observed in the percent of features reported in response to general, open-ended prompts rather than yes/no questions. The 3-year-olds reported only about one-third of the features they recalled in response to general probes, whereas the 7-year-olds provided about two-thirds of the information in open-ended recall.

The ability to serve as a competent witness requires not only the provision of accurate information but also the capacity to avoid providing or endorsing inaccurate statements. At all ages, the children in Baker-Ward, Gordon et al. (1993) provided virtually no spontaneous reports of actions that they did not experience (i.e., intrusions). Rates of correct rejections of questions that referenced actions that did not occur (e.g., "Did the doctor cut your hair?") were about 90% among both the 5- and 7-year-olds, but significantly lower among the 3-year-old children, who succeeded in rejecting only about three-quarters of these questions in some conditions.

In an additional investigation in the Ornstein Laboratory, Gordon and Follmer (1994) conducted a reanalysis of the data from Baker-Ward, Gordon et al. (1993) to explore the implications for understanding children's testimony in legal proceedings. They concluded that 3-year-olds, in comparison to older children, were less likely to be seen as credible with reference to three widely applied criteria: the spontaneity with which information was reported, the extent to which the reported information included elaboration, and the consistency of the report across time. However, they established that although the youngest children reported

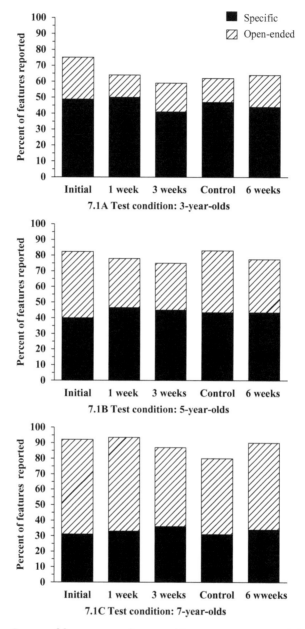

Figure 7.1    Percent of features correctly reported in response to open-ended and specific probes by test condition at ages 3 (panel A), 5 (panel B), and 7 (panel C) years. Note that the data presented for the initial test are averaged across the three delay groups.

From Baker-Ward, Gordon et al. (1993).

Used by permission of John Wiley & Sons.

less information in response to open-ended questions than the older children did, the accuracy of this information did not differ across age. Similarly, the elaborative detail the youngest children included in their reports was relatively limited but comparably accurate. However, Gordon and Follmer (1994) also found that younger children were not only more reliant on the interviewer's provision of specific (yes/no) questions, but also their answers to these questions were less likely to be correct than the yes/no responses produced by the older children. The findings indicate that the examiner's skill is particularly important in interviewing younger preschoolers. The successful interviewer must support open-ended recall to increase accuracy and avoid the risk of increased susceptibility to suggestion associated with specific questions.

## *Effects of Extended Delay Intervals*

The early work of Ornstein and his collaborators on the accuracy and completeness of children's event memory over delays of weeks extended the understanding of children's abilities to report personal experiences over time. However, children's testimony in legal proceedings involves much longer retention intervals. For example, in the Little Rascals case, the trial began two-and-a-half years after the first allegations of abuse (Ceci & Bruck, 1995). Hence, to inform the understanding of children's testimony, researchers had to explore long-term retention.

Ornstein, Baker-Ward, and colleagues (1997) examined retention in a large sample of children over delays of up to three months. They applied hierarchical linear modeling to calculate retention functions across several investigations, each of which involved children's reports of predefined features of pediatric checkups reported in response to hierarchically structured questioning (i.e., from very general to quite specific). This analysis included data from 232 children at three age levels – 3, 4–5, and 6–7 years – and included delays of 1, 3, 6, and 12 weeks. As expected, recall increased with age. Although total recall (open-ended recall + yes/no) decreased among the two younger groups over the delays, the 6- to 7-year-olds demonstrated generally consistent total recall over the 12-week interval. However, open-ended recall, while characterized as extensive at all time points, declined over time at each age level.

The Ornstein Lab extended the delay interval to 6 months in a subsequent investigation. Ornstein, Baker-Ward et al. (2006) examined 4- to 7-year-old children's memory ($N = 83$) for a well-child examination and reported findings that were generally consistent with Ornstein,

Baker-Ward et al. (1997). Whereas the expected age differences were observed, the effects of the delay interval did not differ by age. The children provided an extensive amount of information overall. After the 6-month delay, total recall ranged from 65% of the features at age 4 to 82% at age 7. Although total recall declined over the first 3 months of the delay interval, it remained constant from 3 to 6 months. Further, at the 6-month interview, the children had lost 18% of the features they initially reported in response to open-ended questions. In their discussion of the findings, Ornstein, Baker-Ward et al. (2006) suggested that forgetting appears most likely to occur for events involving relatively low levels of arousal, whereas memory for more salient experiences is likely to persist.

The results of a small investigation of children's memory for a highly salient event support this interpretation. Burgwyn-Bailes et al. (2001) examined 3- to 7-year-old children's memory for receiving treatment by a plastic surgeon for a facial laceration resulting from an injury. The procedure was an instantiation of the approach used in other investigations conducted in the Ornstein Lab, with the recall of features of the experience assessed in a hierarchically structured interview. Burgwyn-Bailes et al. (2001) interviewed the children a few days after the emergency treatment and again after 6 weeks and 1 year.

As expected, age accounted for variance in total recall at the 6-week and 1-year interviews, and to the variance in open-ended recall on all three occasions. Surprisingly, however, the length of the delay interval did not affect either total recall or open-ended recall. The children reported 78%, 73%, and 72% of the features in total recall across the initial, 6-week, and 1-year delays, respectively. The corresponding figures for open-ended recall were 40%, 41%, and 35%. Rates of false alarms to questions about features that did not occur increased significantly from the initial to the 6-week interview, but not from the 6-week to the 1-year interview. Other, larger-scale investigations of children's memory for injuries and resulting emergency room treatment have similarly reported that, at least under some conditions, young children can provide extensive information about salient experiences after lengthy delays. Notably, Peterson (1999, p. 1503) summarized her own results as indicating that "overall, the children seemed to recall as many accurate details of their experiences two years later as they had initially."

Although it is clear that even preschoolers can provide extensive amounts of information about events they have experienced after even lengthy delays, it is important to keep in mind that what happens during the delay interval affects the extent and the reliability of the child's subsequent report. In the investigations of children's long-term retention of medical experiences discussed above, children had unrestrained opportunities to discuss their experiences with others and were likely to have encountered some reminders (e.g., follow-up examinations, scars) in many cases. These naturally occurring experiences may have been important in maintaining event memory over time. In other instances, the child may be exposed to interactions with others that can distort their memory for a previous experience (see Principe, Chapter 9). It may also be the case that children's knowledge and expectations regarding an experience may alter aspects of their report of a particular instantiation of the event, as discussed later in this chapter (see also Price & Connolly, Chapter 8).

An investigation from the Ornstein Lab illustrates the influence of different types of experiences during the delay interval on children's subsequent reports of an event. Principe et al. (2000) examined 3- and 5-year-old children's memory for the details of a physical examination immediately after it occurred and again after a 12-week delay. Participants were assigned to one of four conditions that differed only with regard to their experiences 6 weeks after the checkup. Children in one condition were again interviewed about their checkups, whereas those in the other conditions either viewed a video of another child's checkup, returned to the pediatrician's office to complete some unrelated memory assessments, or acted as control groups. At the 12-week interview, children who had received an additional interview midway through the retention interval or who had seen the video (which included some features that were inconsistent with the child's own experience) provided higher levels of open-ended recall in comparison to children in the control condition. However, viewing the video or returning to the doctor's office resulted in a marked decrease among the 5-year-old children in their rates of correct rejections of questions addressing actions that were not included in the original examination.

Research by Ornstein and his colleagues has provided compelling descriptions of children's capacity to retain information over extended delays. However, this research also illustrates that the delay interval provides the opportunity for memory distortions. These findings, in conjunction with research from other investigators, indicate the importance of careful analyses of factors and experiences that may support children's reliable remembering or provide sources of memory distortion.

### Generalizability across Different Events

Although it is clear that children can provide extensive information about their experiences with a routine medical checkup even after extended delays (e.g., Ornstein, Baker-Ward et al., 2006), the generalizability of these findings to the types of events about which children testify in legal proceedings must be questioned. Most children are relaxed during pediatric examinations, as confirmed by ratings made by parents and medical personnel (e.g., Ornstein, Gordon, & Larus, 1992), with only brief moments of distress (e.g., when receiving an inoculation), whereas experiencing abuse or witnessing violence evokes high levels of fear and anxiety. Further, children develop extensive knowledge regarding routine medical care (e.g., through discussion with parents, exposure to media) but are likely to poorly understand at least some aspects of forensically relevant experiences. To examine the applicability of their findings to events that differed from the pediatric examination in important regards, the Ornstein Lab expanded their research to the investigation of memory for less-routine medical experiences.

In collaboration with pediatrician Kathy Merritt, Ornstein and his student Brenda Spicker examined 3- to 7-year-old children's memory for a voiding cystourethrogram (VCUG), an invasive and painful diagnostic procedure that may evoke some degree of shame in children (Merritt et al., 1994). The features of the VCUG include inserting a catheter into the bladder, filling the catheter with contrast fluid, conducting fluoroscopic filming, and instructing the child to expel the catheter through urination on the examination table. Hence, this procedure provides a much closer analogue to sexual abuse in comparison to the pediatric checkup. As anticipated, the VCUG event involved high levels of stress, as indicated by ratings, structured observations, and salivary cortisol assays. Nonetheless, the children demonstrated high levels of recall for features of the procedures in hierarchically structured interviews, reporting 88% and 83% of the features in their immediate and 6-week interviews, respectively. In addition to showing little forgetting over time, children required minimal prompting by interviewers; 65% and 60% of features were recalled in response to open-ended questions in children's immediate and delayed interviews, respectively. In contrast to children's reports of routine physical examinations (Baker-Ward, Gordon et al., 1993), age was only marginally correlated with children's reports of their procedures, and even the youngest of children were able to recall the majority of the features (Merritt et al., 1994). The results of this investigation are consistent with Burgwyn-Bailes et al.'s (2001) demonstration of extensive and enduring recall for the components of minor emergency medical treatment.

Having provided detailed descriptions of the basic parameters of children's memory and established the applicability of the findings from studies of children's memory for routine checkups to more intense medical experiences, Ornstein turned to the analysis of influences on differences in children's memory performance within age groups. Much of this research examined a predictor of memory performance he had investigated extensively in his research on the development of memory strategies (see Best & Folds-Bennett, Chapter 4). Specifically, how does the child's knowledge regarding an event affect the retention of the experience?

## Analyzing Influences on Event Memory Performance

Theoretical perspectives on the development of episodic memory emphasize the significance of the individual's knowledge regarding the to-be-remembered information on strategy use and recall performance (see Ornstein & Naus, 1985). With regard to memory for events, children's knowledge regarding what usually happens during routine events, i.e., their scripts, enhances their memory for repeated experiences but may also increase their errors in reporting variable components of a particular episode of a repeated event, especially over time (Price & Connolly, Chapter 8). Ornstein and his colleagues extended the understanding of domain-specific knowledge on children's event reports by addressing the role of continuous variation in prior knowledge on memory performance across delays (see Ornstein, Baker-Ward et al., 2006). Applying their information-processing framework, the Ornstein Laboratory was particularly interested in understanding the points in the flow of information through the memory system at which domain-specific knowledge affected children's accounts of what happened to them. Further, the extent to which constructive errors characterized children's event reports was of particular interest, in part because not even optimal interviewing can eliminate misrepresentations resulting from changes in memory representations over time.

### *Knowledge Predicts Memory Performance*

As an initial step, Ornstein and colleagues established the expected relation between children's knowledge of components of the event and their subsequent recall of the experience. Clubb et al. (1993) recruited a sample of 5-year-old children who received regular medical care but who had not been recently examined by their pediatricians, and assessed their knowledge of the features of pediatric examinations through their responses to open-ended questions (e.g., "What does the nurse do to check you?"). Knowledge scores were based on the proportion of children who reported the individual features in this interview. The researchers then examined the relation between knowledge scores for particular features of the examination and the proportion of 5-year-olds in a previous investigation (Baker-Ward, Gordon et al., 1993) who reported the features in response to open-ended questions for a specific visit to the doctor. The correlations between the knowledge and recall scores at each of the delay intervals included in the original investigation ranged from .63 to .74. Additional analyses of the language the children used in the two interviews indicated that the participants had not simply reverted to scripted representations of the doctor visit over time.

## Knowledge Influences Encoding

Ornstein, Baker-Ward et al. (2006) examined the understanding of the linkage between knowledge and open-ended recall performance in an investigation conducted with 4- to 7-year-old participants. Half of the children received a knowledge interview prior to their scheduled pediatric examination using the procedure developed by Clubb et al. (1993). Each child participated in a memory interview shortly after the examination and again after a delay of 6 months, with half of the sample also completing the interview three months after the examination. This design provided a more precise examination of the relation between knowledge and recall than the previous investigation did, and enabled the researchers to explore the contributions of knowledge scores in accounting for variance in open-ended recall, above and beyond the effects of age.

As expected, knowledge scores and open-ended recall were positively correlated with age. Regarding the knowledge–recall linkage, a strong association was observed at the initial interview ($r = .53$), but the correlation did not reach significance at either the 3- or 6-month interview. The knowledge scores continued to predict open-ended recall at the initial assessment even after age was accounted for in the model, indicating that knowledge is not simply a proxy for age. Moreover, the knowledge scores were unrelated to the amount of forgetting observed over the retention interval. Ornstein, Baker-Ward et al. (2006) suggested that knowledge influences recall at the level of the encoding of information. However, as discussed below, they pointed out that in other research, knowledge can contribute to errors in recall over time as memory fades.

## Knowledge Both Supports and Impairs Event Memory

Although prior knowledge clearly facilitates remembering (Clubb et al., 1993; Ornstein, Baker-Ward et al., 2006), it can also lead to errors in children's memory reports when components of the to-be-remembered experience conflict with their preexisting knowledge and expectations. That is, children can confuse what usually occurs within the context of similar experiences for what transpired in the to-be-remembered experience. Errors of this nature can become more likely over time as details stored in children's memory fade and constructive processes operate to fill in the gaps (Ornstein et al., 1998).

Consider research by Ornstein and colleagues (1998) that used a unique methodology to explore the magnitude of the potentially negative effects of prior knowledge on the accuracy of children's memory reports. In this experiment, 4- and 6-year-old children took part in a specially designed, simulated physical examination that included some typical features (Typical Present Features; e.g., listening to the lungs) while omitting other typical features of an examination (Typical Absent Features; e.g., looking in ears, listening to the heart). Further, the examination incorporated Atypical Present Features (e.g., measuring head circumference, wrapping bandage on leg, asking child to touch nose) that were unlikely to occur in a pediatric checkup (Atypical Present Features). Other atypical features (Atypical Absent Features) were not administered in the exam but were addressed in the interview. Both immediately after the event and after a delay of 12 weeks, the researchers used a hierarchically structured interview protocol to interview the children about the Typical and Atypical Features that had been either included or omitted from their mock physical examinations (Ornstein et al., 1998).

The results provided evidence that prior expectations serve to both enhance and depress memory performance. With regard to the open-ended recall of Present Features, Typical Features in comparison to Atypical Features were more likely to be recalled and maintained over the 12-week interval at both ages. However, knowledge derived from expectations was a source of spontaneous errors in memory performance. With regard to Absent Features, intrusions of Typical Features increased over the 12-week interview, especially among the 6-year-olds in comparison to the 4-year-olds, with 74% in comparison to 42% spontaneously reporting at least one Typical Absent Feature. Similarly, correct denials of Typical Absent Features in comparison to Atypical Absent Features were markedly lower, especially over time. This effect was again more pronounced among the older children, who presumably had a richer knowledge structure than the younger participants.

Ornstein's group conducted a follow-up study (Baker-Ward et al., 2020) in which 6-year-old children again experienced a mock physical examination with some typical features omitted and other atypical features included. A particular focus of the investigation was the extent to which errors in episodic memory represent children's limitations in differentiating episodic and generic representations. Hence, the researchers explored linkages between source-monitoring skill and memory errors. Children were again interviewed in a hierarchical manner immediately and 12 weeks after the event. Each of these interviews included questions about the features of the mock examinations (e.g., "Did the doctor check your eyes?"), their confidence in their reports of these features, and their understanding of what usually happens when visiting the doctor (e.g., "Does the doctor usually check your eyes?). One week after the delayed interview, the children completed a source-monitoring task, which measured their skill in identifying stimuli as old or new, and if judged as old, whether the initial presentation had been in the form of a picture or a word.

Consistent with previous research, generic knowledge had both positive and negative effects on memory performance. Children reported more Typical than Atypical Present Features in open-ended recall at both the immediate- and delayed-memory interviews. There were very few intrusions or false alarms in response to questions regarding Typical Absent Features at the immediate interview. However, at the delayed interview, children on average intruded about one-third of the Typical Absent Features in open-ended recall, whereas there were essentially no intrusions of Atypical Absent Features. Thus, even in the absence of external pressure, generic knowledge supported the report of plausible false memories over time. A similar pattern characterized the children's responses to yes/no questions across the delay. The results also provided some evidence that the ability to differentiate sources of information and levels of trace strength may be valuable in separating generic from episodic memories. Clearly, understanding children's testimony necessitates understanding development.

*Information in Memory Changes Over Time*

Given the considerable amount of evidence that shows the dramatic impact of knowledge and expectations on children's remembering, Ornstein's research group also has considered the consequences of changes in children's understanding over time. Specifically, in dissertation research conducted under Ornstein's direction, Greenhoot (2000) examined 5- and

6-year-old children's memory for a series of stories. Prior to hearing the stories, children's knowledge of the protagonist was manipulated, such that some children were led to believe that the protagonist was either antisocial and disliked or prosocial and liked. When children were questioned about the ambiguous actions of the protagonist, their answers largely aligned with the information that was provided to them.

Approximately one week later, Greenhoot (2000) established a second manipulation designed to again convince children that the protagonist was either antisocial or prosocial, which was consistent with some children's initial impressions but inconsistent with those of other children. Following the manipulation, children's memory for the original stories was again assessed. Regardless of the information provided at the beginning of the study, children's reports most often aligned with the information presented in the second manipulation. That is, children led to believe that the protagonist was antisocial at the end of the study reported negative information, whereas those convinced that the protagonist was prosocial reported positive information (Greenhoot, 2000).

These findings are consistent with research by Ross (1989) and suggest that changes in knowledge can prompt a reworking of earlier memories to be compatible with one's current understanding. Ornstein and his collaborators (Baker-Ward, Ornstein, & Starnes, 2009) have described changes in the representation of an event after it is entered into memory as *extended encoding*. Given subsequent information, for example, some aspects of a memory may be disregarded whereas others may be linked together in a coherent manner that increases the likelihood of subsequent retrieval. Such constructivist processes can represent the spontaneous and autonomous operation of cognitive processes internal to the child and may be important influences on children's reports of forensically relevant experiences.

## Optimizing Children's Testimony

Ornstein's research on children's memory for medical experiences was motivated in large part by the need for evidence-based information that would inform clinical and legal practice involving child witnesses. In this section, we first examine the contributions of experiments designed to address specifically an issue in interviewing young children. Then, we briefly explore the implications of the basic understanding of event memory in children resulting from the efforts of Ornstein and his colleagues on the involvement of children in the legal system.

*Enhanced Retrieval Support*

As discussed earlier, 3-year-old children in comparison to even slightly older interviewees have difficulty recounting their experiences in a credible manner. In particular, young preschoolers produce relatively little information in response to general, open-ended probes. The resulting reliance on specific probes can increase suggestibility and result in the provision of incorrect information (Gordon & Follmer, 1994). In many situations, however, the reports of young children are central to the case. Consequently, many examiners were interested in the development of interview techniques that could support preschoolers' performance. Because most interviews depend on verbal responding, it seemed possible that protocols that alleviate the impact of developmental limitations in receptive and expressive language could increase the amount of information that preschoolers could spontaneously report and accompany with elaboration. Ornstein and his colleagues provided experimental evidence regarding the effects of two alternative protocols: one providing dolls as a means of reporting bodily contact, and the other including props to enable children to reenact their experiences.

When the Ornstein Lab (Gordon et al., 1993) began their investigation, examiners used dolls extensively in investigations of allegations of child sexual abuse. Although 5- and 7-year-old children benefited from the practice, the effects of the use of dolls in interviews with younger children were not established. Reducing verbal demands by allowing children to demonstrate their experiences would appear to provide extensive support for younger children's reports, increasing retrieval support.

Adapting the method used in previous research in the Ornstein Laboratory, Gordon et al. (1993) examined 3- to 5-year-old children's reports of their checkups after a 3-week delay. However, children in only one condition were interviewed with the verbal protocol used in previous studies. Two additional conditions incorporated a doll as an interview aid. The children in the Representational group could use the doll as a model for the self, and the children in the Role Play condition were asked to pretend the doll was another child who was going to get a checkup and to demonstrate what would happen to the child. Children in the Verbal condition reported features of the examination in response to the interviewer's open-ended questions, followed by increasingly specific probes as needed, with requests for elaboration for each feature reported. In the doll conditions, participants were also presented with open-ended questions, but if they did not respond verbally, they were asked to "show me [or show the doll] what happened during your checkup." Similarly, if requests for elaboration were not provided in response to a question, children in these conditions were asked to "show me [the doll] how the doctor checked your heart." Questions about features that were not administered in the examination were also presented.

The presence of the doll did not reduce age effects in total memory. In fact, the use of the doll in the Role Play condition interfered with the recall of the 3-year-olds, in contrast to expectations, and increased memory performance of the 5-year-olds in the Representational condition. In addition, the effects of the interview condition on the proportions of features recalled in response to open-ended probes did not differ by age. It was also the case that the addition of the doll did not increase elaboration at either age. These results are consistent with DeLoache's (1990) research on developmental limitations in symbolic representation, which could make it difficult for younger children to view the doll as a toy and, at the same time, as a representation of the self. There was some evidence, however, that dolls may have facilitated the 3-year-olds' correct rejections of questions about features that were not included in the checkup.

Following up on Gordon et al.'s (1993) results, the Ornstein Lab (Greenhoot et al., 1999) examined the effects of extensive retrieval support enabling children to act out the details of a physical examination on age differences in recall. Sixty-two 3- and 5-year-old participants who received regular physical examinations were interviewed about this event after a few days and again after 6 weeks. Half of the children responded verbally to interview questions, whereas the others could act out the details of their examinations. The children in this Enactment condition were interviewed in a room that was outfitted as a pediatric examining room and contained a doll and 15 objects included in the child's own examination (e.g., a blood pressure cuff) along with 15 other objects never used during checkups (e.g., an eye dropper). Consistent with other studies of children's memories for doctor's visits, the interview protocol used hierarchically structured prompts to probe for the retention of features of the examination. Children in the Verbal condition were asked to tell the interviewer what happened, whereas children in the Enactment condition were asked to demonstrate the procedures involved in their examinations. Participants in both conditions also responded to yes/no questions about procedures the child did not experience (Non-administered Features), including typical features omitted from the individual's checkup, and a standard set of eight items addressing features unlikely to occur as part of pediatric checkups (e.g., "Did the nurse wrap a bandage around your leg?").

The Enactment manipulation enhanced the open-ended recall of present features, especially for the 3-year-olds. Further, children at both age levels provided more elaboration in the Enactment condition. However, the 3-year-olds in the Enactment condition in comparison to the Verbal condition reported a higher proportion of intrusions of Non-administered Features at the initial interview, and both age groups intruded more features in the Enactment condition at the 6-week interview. The 3-year-olds in the Enactment condition were much more likely to provide incorrect information in response to general probes. This provision of incorrect information in the Enactment condition is particularly noteworthy as it contrasts with the usual accuracy of spontaneously provided information in verbal interviews. For example, at the delayed interview, the younger children in the Enactment condition reported on average 4.31 actions that did not occur compared with a mean of 0.25 intrusions among the participants in the Verbal condition. This pattern of results raises concerns regarding the consequences of the use of props in interviews with young children in legal settings.

The judicious use of dolls and props in some assessment contexts may have merit. For example, children may point to a private body part that they hesitate to name (e.g., Saywitz et al., 1991). However, the evidence contributed by the Ornstein Laboratory supports the conclusion that the use of dolls and props with 3-year-old children does not eliminate age differences in recall and entails the risk of intrusions of inaccurate information. The results of research on the use of dolls and props as aids in forensic interviews is consistent with results reported by other researchers (see Poole, Bruck, & Pipe, 2011). The provision of empirical evidence regarding the risks associated with some techniques contributes to the avoidance of false accusations in interviews with younger preschoolers.

## Basic Understanding of Memory Development

The importance of empirical assessments of the risks and benefits involved in the use of controversial interview techniques notwithstanding, Ornstein and colleagues' most significant contribution for optimizing children's testimony may well be the enhanced understanding of children's event memory. As a notable example, Lamb and colleagues (2007) cited Ornstein's research on the effects of open-ended versus closed-ended prompts in their description of the development of the NICHD

Investigative Interview Protocol – an extensively researched and validated, internationally applied interview procedure. As Cox points out in Chapter 2, this protocol applies the same hierarchical structure used in programmatic research by Ornstein and colleagues.

The information-processing framework that has guided Ornstein's research program in children's event memory (e.g., Ornstein, Gordon, & Baker-Ward, 1992; Baker-Ward et al., in press) represents another significant contribution in service of understanding children's testimony. This framework not only provides an important scaffold for research but also helps structure forensic examiners' evaluation of the sequence of experiences that may have maintained or, alternatively, may have modified children's memory for a particular experience (e.g., Principe et al., 2000; Baker-Ward et al., 2020). Sharing this information with the clinicians who are working directly with child witnesses has always been an important activity of the Ornstein Lab (e.g., Gordon et al., 2001).

Important work with relevance to the informational needs of clinical and legal professionals remains to be accomplished (see Baker-Ward et al., in press). The complicated relation between children's stress at the time of an event and their subsequent memory for the experience remains incompletely understood, despite the attention devoted to this important topic. Further, despite intriguing suggestions of relations among individual-difference variables and memory outcomes, the understanding of variations in temperament, coping, and other factors deserves more attention. The findings accumulated by Ornstein and his colleagues have not definitively answered important questions regarding these critical influences on children's event memory but provide relevant contributions to future investigations.

## In Conclusion

A major contribution of the research program of Peter Ornstein and his colleagues is the documentation of just how good children's memory can be under some conditions. In general, the investigations conducted in the Ornstein Lab have involved supportive interviewers, carefully structured questions, and the absence of coercion or deception. In this regard, the work complements research including misinformation or suggestion (e.g., see Bruck & Ceci, 1999; Principe, Chapter 9). But while the work of Ornstein and his colleagues provides evidence of the capacity of young children to report accurately their experiences, it also identifies important questions to be asked regarding the conditions under which the child conveyed what happened. We should always listen to the children. We should also keep in mind the constraints and qualifications on the circumstances under which we should unquestioningly "Believe the Children."

This chapter began with the description of a telephone call Professor Ornstein received with an attorney's questions regarding a 3-year-old child's ability to provide a reliable account of an alleged assault. At the time, answers to the attorney's questions did not exist. Dozens of investigations and decades later, Ornstein would be able to respond immediately and authoritatively. Given the child's spontaneous disclosure, a short delay interval, and the absence of exposure to misleading information, it is likely that the child's report is reliable. Although a judge must determine the admissibility of testimony and a jury must evaluate the reliability of its content, a strong knowledge base would now support the inclusion of that child in the legal proceedings.

# CHAPTER 8

# Children's Memory for Instances of Repeated Events
## Applications to the Experience of Child Victims and Witnesses

*Heather L. Price and Deborah A. Connolly*

## Background

Imagine you are describing a typical restaurant experience to a community newcomer who has only ever prepared meals from his own vegetable garden. If you are like many busy parents, you might have a couple of different restaurant scripts you could rely on. You might be able to differentiate the peaceful, relaxed evenings out with only your significant other from the chaotic chain-restaurant disasters crammed between children's extracurricular activities. A description of either type of meal is probably rather easy to produce and would give your newcomer a sense of the range of experiences that restaurant dining provides. However, if you were instead asked to recall the details of the fourth most recent family dinner out, and distinguish that experience from the seventh most recent family dinner out, the task is likely to be considerably more challenging.

Children, like adults, tend to have a good memory for what usually happens during a routine event (Brubacher, Powell, & Roberts, 2014), but often struggle to identify which particular event details took place during one instance of a repeated event (Woiwod et al., 2019). The development of a script of usual happenings assists our comprehension of, and memory for, repeatedly occurring events, but can also lead to predictable memory errors (e.g., Erskine, Markham, & Howie, 2001). We use scripts to reconstruct what likely happened in the past (e.g., Myles-Worley, Cromer, & Dodd, 1986; Ornstein et al., 1998); understand what is happening during a routine instance of a repeated event (Farrar & Goodman, 1990, 1992); as well as to make predictions about how such events are likely to unfold in the future (Hudson, Fivush, & Kuebli, 1992). These processes can lead us to make educated guesses about a particular instance that occurred as part of a script, rather than rely directly on a specific memory trace for each instance. These guesses will often be correct because they are derived from the script that itself was created from extracting commonalities among experiences. However, there are also many ways in which they may be wrong. In this chapter, we review the state of our current understanding about children's memory for instances of repeated events.

## Application to the Legal System

Many children who interact with the legal system are victims of repeated abuse (Connolly et al., 2015; Trocmé et al., 2010). However, much of the research conducted on children's recall abilities in a forensic context has focused on children's ability to recall a single salient experience. Like many areas of basic developmental psychology, the disconnect between the empirical literature and the context to which the research was applied limited the applicability of the findings (e.g., Ornstein, Larus, & Clubb, 1991). Reaching outside the forensic context, the study of children's memory for repeated autobiographical experiences began in earnest in the 1980s with the important work on memory for routine events and scripts conducted by Katherine Nelson, Judith Hudson, Robyn Fivush, and colleagues (e.g., Fivush, 1984; Fivush & Hudson, 1990; Nelson, 1986). This work on understanding how memory for repeated similar experiences operated considerably advanced our understanding of children's memory, and was a catalyst for continued research on how such events are represented in memory.

Importantly, even when a routine of abuse is established, in many legal jurisdictions, children may be required to report not only the routine but also details of particular instances of abuse that took place within the routine (Woiwod & Connolly, 2017). In the United States, for example, the Supreme Court held, "it is not sufficient that the indictment shall charge the offense in the same generic terms as in the definition; but it must state the species, – it must descend to particulars" (*United States v. Cruikshank*, 1875, p. 558). Similarly, in Canada a complainant must describe each instance of abuse with sufficient detail to "lift it from the general to the specific" (*R. v. B. [G.]*, 1990). Such details might include specifics about time and place, as well as other contextual information such as clothing and weather that isolate particular instances of abuse (Guadagno, Powell, & Wright, 2006). This particularization is said to provide the defendant with enough detail to raise a defense against the allegations.

This important legal issue was identified in the late 1990s by researchers who embarked on a quest of understanding children's ability to pull an instance from a series for recall (Connolly & Lindsay, 2001; Powell et al., 1999). Now, more than 20 years into this exploration, we can confidently draw some conclusions from the work. Recent summaries of the relevant literature (e.g., Woiwod et al., 2019) allow us to answer questions about how memory for instances of repeated events is organized, which factors influence the ability to recall details from particular instances, and the general reasonableness of requests for children to recall details from a particular instance of a repeated event. We begin the chapter, however, with an overview of memory theories relevant to recall of instances of repeated events, followed by a discussion of the standard research paradigm upon which the field has typically relied.

## Theory

There are several theories that can be used to predict how children's memory for repeated events will differ from the better understood memory for single, or unique, events. Here we focus on script theory, instance-based theories, and fuzzy-trace theory.

According to script theory, after an event is experienced, a script, or overarching representation of the common elements of the event, is established (Fivush, 1984; Hudson & Mayhew, 2009 for a review). With repeated experience, the script becomes stronger. Although script theory allows for memory for the instance (Slackman & Nelson, 1984), it does not clearly articulate the fate of such memories; the theory focuses on memory for the script. This script typically quite accurately represents the central elements of the event and the elements of the event that do not change from instance to instance. Repeated experiences with similar events will strengthen the general event representation but lead to confusion about which details occurred during which instance.

According to instance-based theories (e.g., Alba & Hasher, 1983; Hintzman, 1986), each instance of a repeated event generates a distinct memory trace. Confusion across instances occurs because a retrieval cue that is meant to activate one instance actually activates all relevant instance traces. With multiple instances activated, distinguishing between them is difficult.

Fuzzy-trace theory implicates both schema- and instance-based theories. An experience generates two independent but parallel memory traces, one for the instance (verbatim) and one for the meaning of the experience (gist) (Brainerd & Reyna, 2012). When an event is experienced repeatedly, separate verbatim traces are formed but the same gist trace is strengthened.

Although either can be retrieved shortly after the experience, verbatim traces fade more quickly than gist traces. Accordingly, after a delay, only the gist trace is available. When a gist trace is relied upon for recall of an instance, an increase in suggestibility and the risk of confusion between experienced instances is likely.

Script theory and fuzzy-trace theory differ in the content of the general event representation (i.e., script memory or gist memory). According to script theory, some experienced details may reside in script memory, whereas, according to fuzzy-trace theory, experienced details reside in verbatim memory only, not in gist memory. All theories predict that under most circumstances, there will be an improvement in memory performance with age. In certain circumstances, described below as developmental reversal, both script theory and fuzzy-trace theory predict that memory performance will decline with age. Despite these differences and similarities, clear evidence has not supported the efficacy of one theory over the others. Researchers who are very active in this field are working on compiling large amounts of data to specifically test these theories – and potentially develop a distinct theory – but this work is ongoing and has not yet produced a clear theoretical path forward.

In addition to the above theories that are applied to recall of instances of repeated events, there is also a large complementary literature in which it has been demonstrated that prior knowledge about a single experience serves a similar, structural purpose to event repetition. This work, led by Peter Ornstein and his many collaborators (Baker-Ward, Gordon et al., 1993; Clubb, Nida, Merritt, & Ornstein, 1993; Ornstein, et al., 1998; Ornstein, Shapiro et al., 1997), has found compelling evidence that prior knowledge of an event influences children's ability to encode details of the experience. Much of this work has focused on children's recall of medical experiences, including routine pediatric checkups, and observed benefits to event encoding with higher levels of prior knowledge about checkups. There is also some evidence of the benefits of prior knowledge on retrieval (Bender, Wallsten, & Ornstein, 1996; Ornstein et al., 1998; but see Ornstein, Baker-Ward et al., 2006). Thus, both direct event repetition as well as event exposure through knowledge exert influences on children's recall of a single experience.

## Typical Paradigm

Early work on the study of event repetition in memory, like many areas of memory research, relied on word list paradigms to control and observe the phenomena. However, Nelson, Fivush, Hudson, and their colleagues (e.g., Fivush, 1984; Fivush & Hudson, 1990; Nelson, 1986) brought this laboratory-based work to naturally occurring events that children encountered in their everyday lives (e.g., attending school). This foundational work led to the current approach to studying memory for complex repeated events in controlled experimental settings.

Contemporary researchers studying children's memory for repeated events have primarily used a play activity paradigm in which children experience a series of play activity instances (most often four) that include a common structure, and then some (or all) of the target details experienced within that structure vary across instances. For example, children may begin with a warm-up exercise that is different for each instance (e.g., jumping jacks, stretching), followed by completing a puzzle of a different animal for each instance (e.g., lion, dog). These individual play activities, or instances, each follow a common general script and the instances take place minutes to days apart.

Within the general structure of the repeated event activities, the particular target details experienced by children may be fixed across instances (i.e., occur in exactly the same way each instance) or they may vary predictably across instances. When details vary predictably, all experienced details may belong to the same taxonomic category (e.g., a puzzle of a dog, cat, lion), or they may belong to different taxonomic categories (e.g., puzzle of a dog, umbrella, car). Some instances may also contain unpredictable variation (i.e., a deviation), as when something happens that could not be predicted from past experience (e.g., an interruption). Much of the extant literature has focused on memory for details that vary predictably. After some delay (from minutes to years), researchers question children about the overall event and/or details that occurred during a particular target instance (most often the final instance). This questioning typically begins with an open-ended free-recall prompt, followed by specific questions about particular activities. In some experiments, children are asked to recall everything that happened in each instance (e.g., Connolly et al., 2016), again with free-recall prompts and specific questions, or children are asked to nominate a particular instance for recall (e.g., Brubacher, Roberts, & Powell, 2012; Danby et al., 2017).

In a typical example of the paradigm, Connolly and Price (2006) compared the memory reports of 4- to 5-year-olds and 6- to 7-year-olds who had experienced either a single play session or who had experienced four similar play sessions, each of which included 16 critical to-be-remembered details.

Table 8.1. *Sample of details used in Connolly and Price (2006)*

| Activities | Session 1 | Session 2 | Session 3 | Session 4 | Suggestion |
|---|---|---|---|---|---|
| **Puzzle** | *Cow* | *Tiger* | *Pig* | *Mouse* | *Cat* |
| Shape of mat | *Blue* | *Waterfall* | *Fire* | *Big Bird* | |
| **Draw a picture** | *House* | *Mansion* | *Hut* | *Trailer* | |
| Think about | *Lemonade* | *Sunny* | *Don/Dawn* | *9* | *Tree* |
| **Build with clay** | *Pot* | *Can opener* | *Bowl* | *Knife* | *Fork* |
| Hold a lucky | *Jo* | *8* | *7:00* | *Hot chocolate* | |
| **Hide under cup** | *$10* | *$10,000* | *$1* | *$100* | |
| Find in treasure chest | *4* | *8:00* | *Ginger ale* | *Hot* | *Cotton balls* |

In addition, half of the critical details shared category membership (e.g., dog, cow, cat, pony) and half of the details were low in association (e.g., dog, tree, bicycle, violin). Sample details are provided in Table 8.1 (high-association categories are in bold, and were counterbalanced).

Two weeks later, children participated in a biasing interview in which they were misinformed about half of the critical details from the final (or only) play session, also known as the target event. The following day children participated in a memory interview that included free- and cued-recall questions about the target event. Older children and children who experienced a single event recalled more details about the target event than younger children and children who had experienced a repeated event, respectively. However, an additional interesting pattern emerged in relation to children's suggestibility: As can be seen in Figure 8.1, older children were more suggestible than younger children. Though typically younger children are more suggestible than older children (Brainerd, Reyna, & Ceci, 2008), the ability of the older children to make the connection between items that were associated categorically enhanced their acceptance of suggestions that were also category-consistent. In contrast, younger children were not as able to make such connections and thus were less suggestible. This study provided further evidence for the importance of children's existing knowledge and cognitive structures in their remembrances (Baker-Ward et al., 2020; Ornstein, Baker-Ward et al., 2006; Ornstein et al., 1998).

The repeated-event-activity paradigm provides researchers with knowledge of ground truth and allows for identification of both accurate

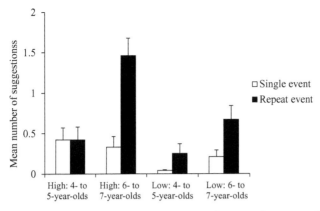

Figure 8.1    Mean numbers of suggested responses as a function of age, event frequency, and association of details
From Connally and Price (2006)
Used by permission of Elsevier Publishing Company

responses and the nature of the errors children report. Researchers most often code experienced details recalled from the target instance (correct details), experienced details recalled from nontarget instances (internal intrusion errors), details that were inaccurately suggested to children in post-event misinformation paradigms (suggested details), or details that were not suggested and never experienced (external intrusion errors).

## Recalling Instances of Repeated Events

One of the critical ways in which this area has advanced is via understanding how repeated events are organized in memory. In a recent meta-analysis of 31 experiments including more than 3,000 child participants, Woiwod et al. (2019) identified several key conclusions that can be drawn from the extant literature, as well as key variables that moderate some important relationships.

### *Response Profile of Repeated-Event Children*

Most of the research exploring children's memory for instances of repeated events has included a comparison group of children who experience only the target instance. Thus, researchers are able to compare recall for a single instance with recall of that same instance when it is surrounded by several other similar instances (i.e., repeated events). Relative to children who have experienced a single event, when children who have experienced a repeated event are asked to recount a single target instance from the series, they provide

- fewer correct details about the target instance;
- more internal intrusion errors (i.e., confusion across instances);
- fewer external intrusion errors (i.e., reports of details never experienced); and
- a similar number of "don't know" responses.

This pattern suggests that repeated-event children have difficulty distinguishing between the various experienced instances (i.e., increased internal intrusion errors), but that they are not more likely to confuse what did happen (correct details and internal intrusion errors) with what did not happen (external intrusion errors).

### Narrow versus Broad Definitions of Accuracy

As a result of the above-described pattern, we have recommended that researchers differentiate between narrow and broad definitions of accuracy (Connolly et al., 2008; Price, Connolly, & Gordon, 2016; Woiwod et al., 2019). Considered narrowly, evaluation of children's recall accuracy is based exclusively on their ability to recall details from the target instance. Thus, if a child reports a detail that was experienced in one of the instances but not in the target instance, this reported detail was considered incorrect (i.e., an internal intrusion error). In contrast, a broad definition of accuracy includes children's reports of details that were experienced but did not take place in the target instance (i.e., experienced in nontarget instances). When conceptualized broadly, the recall of children who experienced repeated events is as accurate as the recall of children exposed to a single event.

The distinction between narrow and broad definitions of accuracy becomes particularly important when children are repeatedly interviewed about their experiences. We explored children's consistency across multiple interviews when reporting a single event or an instance of a repeated event (Price et al., 2016). Most of the children reported at least one response pair that included apparently contradictory details, but both were actually experienced. For example, when asked to describe the final instance, in the first interview a child described completing a puzzle of a lion, whereas in the second interview a child described a puzzle of a dog. Both details were actually experienced (one detail was in the second play session, the other was in the final play session) but appear to contradict one another. When accuracy was defined narrowly, repeated-event children were less consistently correct and more consistently incorrect than single-event children. However, when accuracy was defined broadly, repeated-event children were as consistently correct across repeated interviews as single-event children. Thus, repeated interviews may exacerbate challenges faced by repeated-event children.

This important pattern suggests that repeated-event children may be equally accurate but also inconsistent in their reports, which creates a challenge for those seeking to evaluate the credibility of children's reports. It is critical that the reason for report inconsistencies is considered when evaluating repeated-event children's testimony. In an investigative context, this perspective will make particularization challenging, but if the aim is to determine what did and what did not happen to a particular child, conceptualizing accuracy as details that did and did not take place is a more just approach.

## Delay

Consistent with the notion that memory decays over time, the meta-analysis by Woiwod and colleagues (2019) revealed that more correct details were reported after shorter (less than 1 week) delays, relative to longer (more than 1 week) delays. Similarly, more internal intrusion errors were reported at a long delay, which is consistent with the expected decay of access to particular instance details.

Within the paradigm currently used to study instances of repeated events, there have been relatively few explorations of recall after more than a month (but see, for example, Powell & Thomson, 1996; Price et al., 2016; Price & Connolly, 2013). The few that have explored long-term memory indicate that recall of instances is even more challenging after a delay, a finding that is supported by predictions made by fuzzy-trace theory. Specifically, children who have experienced a repeated event were more likely to accept suggestions of details that never happened after a long delay than after a short delay (in response to yes/no recognition questions; Price & Connolly, 2013). We speculate that this increased susceptibility to suggestion may have been a result of the relatively degraded access to particular instance memory in repeated-event, relative to single-event children.

## Age Differences

Not unexpectedly, the Woiwod et al. meta-analysis revealed that older children recalled more correct details and responded with "I don't know" less often than did younger children. According to script theory, older children require fewer experiences to develop a script than younger children (Farrar & Boyer-Pennington, 1999; Farrar & Goodman, 1992). For instance, Farrar and Goodman (1990, 1992) found that 7-year-olds evidenced script memory after three experiences with the same event, whereas 4-year-olds did not. Importantly, when the event was simplified, both groups of children evidenced script memory for the event with the same amount of experience (Farrar & Boyer-Pennington, 1999). With the aid of script memory, attention is efficiently targeted to details that vary from the script, leading to better memory for variable details among older than younger children.

Adams and Worden (1986) concluded that younger children have "fuzzier" script boundaries than older children. In recall of stories about grocery shopping, getting up in the morning, and going to a restaurant (events for which young children have relevant scripts), younger children had more trouble than older children identifying details that were atypical of the script. That is, younger children tend to admit new details into an established script more readily than older children.

Scripts become more elaborate and complex with age and experience (Fivush, 1984, 1997; Price & Goodman, 1990). That is, with increases in age and experience, the script contains more details, more superordinate categories (you order food), more conditionals (if it is Wednesday, then we eat at McDonald's), more optionals (you might go to the playroom), and more variable details (you could order a hamburger, fish, chicken nuggets, etc).

## Separation of Instances

There are at least two ways in which instances can become more or less distinct in memory: temporal spacing and distinctiveness of instances. There is a large literature suggesting that learning is enhanced when repeatedly presented material is presented temporally distributed, rather than massed (i.e., presented in the same session; Braun & Rubin, 1998; Greene, 1989). The distributed presentation allows for greater processing of learned material. Applied to the memory for instances of repeated-events context, one would expect that increased temporal distribution of instances would increase the perception of instance distinctiveness, which may then enhance children's ability to accurately report details from an instance. Consistent with this notion, Price, Connolly, and Gordon (2006) found that when repeated events were experienced very closely together (e.g., four instances in one day), compared to more distant in time (e.g., four instances spread across two weeks), individuation of individual instances was easier after a short delay to recall (1 day; Price, Connolly, & Gordon, 2006). However, there was also evidence that the benefits of temporal spacing of repeated events diminished after 1 week (Price, Connolly, & Gordon, 2006).

Individual instances may also be differentiated from one another through manipulations of item or instance similarity (e.g., Connolly & Price, 2006; Danby et al., 2018). For instance, if a child completes a puzzle each day, the puzzle may be of four different animals (e.g., dog, cat, lion, tiger) or of four distinct items (e.g., tree, van, fence, ladybug). Highly similar events lead to increased confusion between instances, which results in a higher rate of internal intrusion errors, as well as reports of fewer correct details, narrowly defined. However, highly similar events also result in more overall correct details reported about the series of instances as well as more script deviations (Danby et al., 2018). As described earlier, item similarity can lead to a reverse developmental trend such that older children are more suggestible than younger children when items belong to the same taxonomic category (Connolly & Price, 2006).

## Deviations from the Script

There have also been a few studies that have explored the important question of the influence of an unpredictable variation – and the nature of that unpredictable variation – on children's recall of elements of a repeated event. This type of script interruption has been referred to as event deviations (see Brubacher, Glisic et al., 2011; Connolly et al., 2016). In Connolly et al. (2016, Experiment 3), children experienced four magic shows. During the fourth magic show, a deviation occurred (an interruption by a new magician) for some children but not for others. One or two days later, all children were asked questions about each magic show. Eight-year old children (but not 9- to 11-year-olds) who experienced a deviation during the fourth show recalled more about each magic show than 8-year-olds who did not experience a deviation. That is, the advantage was to memory for all instances; it was not targeted to the instance that contained the deviation. Connolly and colleagues also reported that children were more complete and more accurate in their description of the deviation itself than of the routine details that occurred in the instance that contained the deviation. In fact, children in the repeated- and single-event conditions recalled the deviation similarly.

*Emotionality of the Event*

In general, research within the repeated-events paradigm has focused on neutral to positive events. However, there are some exceptions (e.g., Price & Connolly, 2007) in which the focus has been on emotionally negative or stressful events, as well as complementary research that has observed the effects of repeated stressful medical experiences on children's recall (Goodman & Quas, 1997; Goodman et al., 1994; Ornstein, Baker-Ward et al., 1997). Using a variation of the established paradigm, Price and Connolly (2007) arranged swimming lessons for novice swimmers who were, or were not, afraid of the water. Some of the children received a single private lesson, whereas others received four private lessons. Price and Connolly observed that anxious and non-anxious children were equally likely to confuse details across multiple instances. However, anxious children were less likely to be suggestible than non-anxious children. In a call for more research, Price and Connolly (2008) reviewed the literature related to children's memory for repeated stressful experiences and noted there may be important theoretical reasons to predict differences in recalling repeated neutral or positive versus repeated stressful events. However, the methodological challenges associated with controlling such an event has made this work difficult to do and the question largely remains unanswered.

## What Does This Mean for Child Witnesses?

Like much of the work on children's memory that is applied to their experiences in the justice system, children's experiences will not change unless legal practices change. This may require an increase in expert testimony to inform triers of fact about what can reasonably be expected from children. More critically, however, is the understanding that what children are asked to do may not match their capabilities. Some jurisdictions have dealt with this challenge by instituting continuous abuse statutes that allow for a reduced level of particularity of each instance of alleged abuse and an increased focus on the continuous nature of the offense (see Woiwod & Connolly, 2017 for discussion). Such statutes typically require a minimum number (often three) of abuse acts to have occurred over a defined period of time. There is considerable debate about balancing the rights of a defendant to defend themselves with the (in) ability of children to provide specific details about individual instances of repeated abuse (Woiwod & Connolly, 2017).

A further challenge children who have experienced repeated abuse face is that, independent of accuracy, they are perceived as less credible than children reporting a unique event (Connolly et al., 2008; see Weinsheimer et al., 2017 for a similar result in adults). Researchers have speculated that this reduced credibility may be a result, at least in part, of differences in the confidence and consistency with which repeated-event children recall their experiences (Connolly et al., 2008; Roberts & Powell, 2005). Other research has indicated that children who have experienced a repeated event speak with less-specific language, describing how abuse usually occurs (e.g., "he does" rather than "he did"; Schneider, Price, Roberts, & Hedrick, 2011), which has itself been linked to reduced perceptions of credibility. The precise mechanisms underlying this important finding have not been identified yet, but it could be a combination of any one of the above possibilities, and/or many others. Identifying the mechanisms and working toward methods for mitigating the impact is a critical next step. Of course, the perception of a report as inconsistently or consistently reported will also depend on an understanding of which details are being confused. If there is understanding that confusing details across instances can lead to the appearance of inconsistency, without actually making errors in reporting things that never happened, children's reports will be much better understood. Given the importance of confidence and consistency in evaluations of credibility (Myers et al., 1999), this must be investigated further.

## Moving Forward

To date, the work on children's memory for instances of repeated events has allowed us to understand better (but not fully) the underlying structure of repeated-event memory. This is a critical first step and has allowed the field to establish some parameters around how memory is represented. Despite the important gains in knowledge, there are still many critical areas in which a substantial amount of work is required. We discuss three of the most urgent areas for exploration next.

### *How to Interview Children about Instances of Repeated Events*

Many of the studies in the area have introduced manipulations of prompt type within designs, including comparisons of prompts such as general and cued invitations (e.g., Danby et al., 2017). Much of this work has also focused on the type of memory that can be retrieved with a particular prompt type, such as generic or episodic (e.g., Schneider et al., 2011).

Brubacher et al. (2014) published a review that focused squarely on the implications of the repeated-event literature for investigative interviewing of children who have experienced repeated abuse. In the article, Brubacher et al. suggested several practical strategies that could be used to elicit recall of instances from a series. In addition to adhering to the widely recommended interviewing strategies, such as those provided by the National Institute of Child Health and Human Development Protocol (Lamb et al., 2011), Brubacher and colleagues offered several recommendations, including the following:

- Engage in a practice narrative prior to introducing the substantive phase of the interview (see Roberts et al., 2011). A practice phase builds rapport and allows children to acclimate to the request to provide narrative descriptions of their experiences. Brubacher et al. (2014) suggest that recalling at least one instance, but preferably two instances, of a past repeated (nontarget) event allows children to engage in providing episodic details of particular instances and to apply this strategy when recalling instances of repeated abuse.
- Allow an initial generic account of "what usually happens," if the child wishes to recall the script before individual instances. Several laboratory studies (e.g., Brubacher et al., 2012; Connolly & Gordon, 2014) have demonstrated that activation of the event script by recalling how an event typically unfolds can enhance recall of variable options within the script.
- Use language that matches the type of memory you would like to retrieve. When an interviewer seeks instance-specific details, use episodic language (e.g., "what happened") rather than generic language (e.g., "what happens"). There is clear evidence for the match between the retrieval cue and the nature of the child's response (e.g., Brubacher et al., 2011; Schneider et al., 2011).
- Use children's language to label individual instances within the script (e.g., "the time that the water spilled"). Children can help to determine if the label is appropriate and unique to the instance (e.g., Brubacher et al., 2018).

Despite this important piece of work by Brubacher and colleagues, the application of the repeated-event literature to the development of concrete strategies that match investigator needs with children's abilities still requires considerable work. As we move toward the development of clearer theoretical descriptions and predictions of memory for instances of repeated events, developing specific strategies for recommendations should become an increasing focus. To change inaccurate perceptions of the reliability of repeated-event children in the legal system, researchers can focus on eliciting narratives in ways that better reflect the strength of the underlying memory.

## Methodological Variability

Though there have been variations, most of the studies discussed in this chapter have used a very similar paradigm. Most methods include four positive play activities, target either the first or last event for recall (with some researchers allowing for self-nomination of instance; e.g., Brubacher et al., 2012; Danby et al., 2017), and have delays to a single recall of no more than a month. Obviously, extending this paradigm to a larger number of instances (see Powell & Thomson, 1997) experienced across months to years (see Price & Connolly, 2013; Price, Connolly, & Gordon, 2016), further exploring recall of all instances (see Brubacher et al., 2012; Danby et al., 2017), conducting multiple interviews spaced across time (see Price et al., 2016), and strategically increasing the delays both between instances and to recall (see Price et al., 2006) would enhance our understanding of the boundaries of the current conclusions on memory for instances of repeated events. Further, the degree to which a child is able to comprehend the entirety of the event, including their prior knowledge of the event, has not been considered. As Peter Ornstein's work reviewed earlier clearly demonstrates, there is considerable evidence that children's prior knowledge about an event can provide needed structure that enhances future remembering (Ornstein, Baker-Ward et al., 2006; Ornstein et al., 1998). However, the contribution of prior knowledge to script development, and the subsequent influence on memory for an instance within a script, has not been examined. Prior knowledge of a repeated event may make the script more flexible as knowledge about possible instantiations within the structured event already exists. A script that is based both on prior knowledge and on direct experience may form more quickly (e.g., Fivush, 1984 reported evidence of a school script in children after the first week of kindergarten) and may allow for increased acceptance of false, but plausible, details.

## Increasing the Ecological Validity of the Paradigm

As with many areas that study basic cognitive processes, the paradigms used in the repeated-event literature focus on neutral to pleasant experiences that, although distinct, fit well within the expected daily experience of most children. The experimental experiences are rich auto-biographical events that contain emotion, active engagement, and complex interpersonal interactions. However, they are typically not stressful (but see Price & Connolly, 2007), and do not involve other elements common to abuse, such as well-known adults in trusted roles, that may be commonly experienced in the "real world." This limitation, of course, is a direct result of the important ethical limitations on research. The extant research can clearly inform us about the structure of memory, and such structure should remain consistent across a wide variety of experiences. Children's willingness to report details of events, however, might differ depending on the nature of the experienced event. This variable has currently unknown impacts on the details children will report in response to interviewer prompts. Though incredibly challenging to do experimentally, consideration of factors such as the violation of trust between an adult and a child, escalation of the nature of abuse over repeated abuses, and offender grooming behavior are all important considerations when applying this basic memory paradigm to children's experiences with events that might bring them into contact with the justice system.

## Conclusion

Research on the application of children's basic memory processes to the legal system has grown in several substantive directions since the early work on eyewitness memory of the late 1970s. In all of this work, the aim has been to identify challenges that legal professionals encounter in interpreting and facilitating children's evidence provision in the justice system and to conduct research that helps to inform both a basic understanding of children's cognitive processes as well as the way in which such understanding can enhance the treatment of children who provide evidence as victims and witnesses in legal proceedings.

The early work on how children remember and report stressful experiences and on children's suggestibility to misleading questions formed the basis for much for the current adaptation of legal processes to children's needs. As this field has grown exponentially, the questions about children's capabilities have become more refined and researchers have been able to address challenges posed by the application of a legal system designed for adults to children's needs.

Over 20 years into the study of children's memory for instances of repeated events, it is clear that though substantive gains have been made, there is still much to learn. We are now able to articulate children's likely strengths in recall as well as their predictable errors. There are also developing recommendations on how best to conduct an investigative interview with a child who has experienced repeated abuse. The legacy of Peter Ornstein's early foray into applying memory theory to children's experience in the justice system continues to highlight both our growing areas of knowledge as well as the many fruitful areas of future inquiry.

# CHAPTER 9

# Everyday Conversations as a Source of False Memories in Children
## Implications for the Testimony of Young Witnesses

### Gabrielle F. Principe

A volume in honor of Peter Ornstein's scholarly contributions would be incomplete without highlighting the conceptual framework (see e.g., Gordon, Baker-Ward, & Ornstein, 2001; Ornstein, Larus, & Clubb, 1991) he developed to guide the application of findings from his research program on children's memory for medical experiences to discussions of the testimonial capabilities of young witnesses. At the center of this framework are five themes that characterize the flow of information in the memory system: 1) not everything gets into memory; 2) what gets into memory may vary in strength; 3) the status of information in memory changes over time; 4) retrieval is not perfect; and 5) not everything that can be retrieved is reported. Professor Ornstein and his colleagues have used this information-processing model to advance our understanding of the range of variables that can influence individual differences and developmental changes in children's abilities to attend to, encode, retrieve, and report experienced events over extended delays (e.g., Ornstein, 1995; Ornstein & Greenhoot, 2000; Ornstein, Baker-Ward et al. 1997). For instance, this conceptualization has afforded a useful means for framing discussions of how factors such as attention and knowledge can affect the initial encoding of information, how experiences encountered after an event can alter what is stored in memory, and how certain features of interviews such as the type of questions asked and the sorts of ancillary aids used can affect what is retrieved and reported (see Baker-Ward & Taylor, Chapter 7).

The utility of Professor Ornstein's model for conceptualizing how experienced events are represented and transformed in memory notwithstanding, my colleagues and I (Crossman et al., 2002) expanded his framework to include a sixth theme: Not everything that is reported was experienced. We added this theme to punctuate the legal significance of findings in the forensic developmental literature that demonstrate that a range of factors can lead children to provide accounts of things that never happened. Given that children's testimony is elicited during interviews, much of this research has centered on the mnemonic effects of suggestive techniques during formal interviews. This body of work has revealed that various forms of suggestion – such as repeated misleading questions, stereotype induction, guided imagery, and selective praise – can seriously derail children's accuracy and even lead to entirely fictitious accounts that are relayed with such believability that professionals wrongly judge them as true (see Bruck, Ceci, & Hembrooke, 2002; Bruck, Ceci, & Principe, 2006, for reviews). Indeed, this sixth theme is seen in some of Ornstein's own work. For example, when he and colleagues (Baker-Ward et al., 2020; Ornstein et al., 1998) modified children's routine medical checkups so that they excluded some typical procedures, such as listening to the heart with a stethoscope, most children offered subsequent accounts of expected-but-non-occurring procedures, demonstrating the potency of scripted knowledge to prompt false recollections of nonevents. This chapter provides a selective overview of a program of research inspired by this sixth theme and focused on a common experience that has much potential to induce reports of nonevents in children's recall, namely natural conversations with peers and parents.

Examination of factors that can engender accounts of non-experienced events is significant to discussions about young witnesses because memories of experience often play a central role in situations that bring children into the forensic arena. For instance, in civil and family court cases, children's reports of parental transgressions such as domestic violence and substance abuse, as well as their descriptions of everyday events such as daily home routines and interactions with family members, can impact decisions involving custody, visitation, and support (Crossman et al., 2002). Further, many of the criminal offenses that bring children to court, such as sexual abuse and other forms of molestation, often lack other witnesses or corroborating evidence. Consequently, children's testimony frequently serves as the sole piece of evidence against defendants in such cases (London et al., 2008). Clearly, in any of these contexts, reports of nonevents can have dire legal consequences ranging from fit parents losing custody of their children to innocent defendants spending their lives in prison to guilty perpetrators remaining free to abuse other children.

As noted above, the bulk of research on factors that can produce reports of nonevents has centered on suggestive interviewing practices. Despite the significance of this work for understanding children's testimonial capabilities, investigators have become increasingly interested in examining sources of suggestion outside of the formal interview environment that can bring about false accounts. The shift has been prompted by studies demonstrating that even when questioned in an optimally non-suggestive manner, children at times will report nonevents (Poole & Lindsay, 2001; Principe et al., 2000).

One potential source of extra-interview suggestion is informal conversations with others about events. Talking with others about experience is a typical and frequent part of children's everyday lives. During the course of such dialogues, however, children are constantly encountering others' versions of experience. When these versions differ from their own – either because conversational partners have unwittingly misremembered the past or deliberately invented new details – children may become prone to confuse those aspects of an event that are remembered as experienced and those that have been reconstructed or transformed in light of others' construals. Similarly, conversations before events transpire can create expectations about subsequent events. When accepted, such expectations can influence how children interpret and encode their experiences.

This conceptualization of memory as shaped by the contributions of others is consistent with the constructivist view of memory originally articulated by Bartlett (1932) (see Cox, Chapter 2). In this framework, memory is seen as a dynamic process where internal factors, such as beliefs, feelings, and goals, and external factors, such as the contributions of others, mix with perception to generate a representation of experience. Thus, event representations necessarily are imperfect reproductions of experience made up of more and different information than that available during the original event. This perspective is also in line with Professor Ornstein's concept of *extended encoding* that characterizes encoding processes as extending beyond the generation of the initial representation (see Baker-Ward, Ornstein, & Starnes, 2009; Ornstein, Haden, & Elischberger, 2006). When individuals are exposed to new information or novel motivations that prompt them to reconceptualize the past, they update extant memories to match their current understanding and needs. To illustrate, Greenhoot (2000) found that novel details encountered after an event about an individual's personality can lead to corresponding reconstructive changes of information already in memory.

The majority of research on the mnemonic influence of others has focused on the facilitative effects of conversations. For instance, work in the Ornstein Lab has shown that event-relevant information supplied by more-knowledgeable others can help children formulate better organized and more elaborated representations of novel experiences. To illustrate, when medical technologists helped children make sense of an unfamiliar radiological procedure by telling them what to expect, children were better able than others who received less preparation to later remember the details of their experience (Principe et al., 1996). This improvement in memory presumably occurred because the adult explanation promoted children's ability to understand and represent this novel event. Other research in the Ornstein Lab has shown that dialogues that take place after events also can aid memory. For example, children who talked with an interviewer about a recent routine check-up evidenced higher levels of spontaneous recall during a subsequent opportunity to discuss the examination (Principe et al., 2000).

The beneficial effects of conversations on memory notwithstanding, information gained from others also can lead to errors in remembering, especially when false information is shared. Several lines of research in our lab demonstrate that children's memories are surprisingly prone to misleading information gathered from others. In the remainder of this chapter, I discuss three strands of work focused on how everyday conversations with others can shape children's accounts of experience and at times lead to false recollections. The first line examines how details shared among co-witness peers can engender accounts of non-experienced events. The second centers on how input from mothers to their children can lead to reports of nonevents when mothers are exposed to false information about their children's experiences. The third explores how conversations that endorse fantasy can distort children's memory for certain types of events.

The forensic relevance of these studies comes from real-world examples demonstrating that young witnesses caught up in the legal system often discuss forensically relevant information with others before providing official reports (Bruck et al., 2006; London et al., 2005). For instance, witnesses to crimes or other violent acts commonly talk about the event to other witnesses before being questioned by legal professionals (Paterson & Kemp, 2006a). Further, in most reported maltreatment cases, children initially disclose to someone in their everyday lives, such as a non-offending parent (London et al., 2005). In addition, in some cases of alleged abuse, parents are instructed by law enforcement to talk with their children about allegations made by others (e.g., the case of *Lillie and Reed* v. *Newcastle City Council & Ors*, see Bruck et al., 2006; the McMartin Preschool case in Manhattan Beach, California, see Ceci & Bruck, 1995). Thus, considering that children often talk with others such as co-witnesses and parents prior to undergoing forensic interviews, how such exchanges can affect the accuracy of children's subsequent event reports is a critical question for child-witness research.

## Conversations with Co-witnesses

Consider the following exchange from a study where we asked 5-year-old Abby to recount an event that occurred in her preschool:

INTERVIEWER:   What else happened when Dr. Diggs visited?
CHILD:         He spilled it, his coffee, on the map and him. He made a big mess.
INTERVIEWER:   Then what happened?
CHILD:         He took off his pants.
INTERVIEWER:   He took off his pants?
CHILD:         Yeah and he put on new pants.
INTERVIEWER:   Why did he do that?
CHILD:         Cause the coffee it burned the hole.
INTERVIEWER:   The coffee burned a hole?
CHILD:         Yeah and he got a big boo-boo.
INTERVIEWER:   How do you know this happened?
CHILD:         Sophie told me.

There are several noteworthy aspects of this conversation. First, other children in Abby's classroom corroborated her story. So, other children told us that Dr. Diggs spilled coffee on himself, put on clean pants, and sustained a minor injury. Second, and more significant to our research, none of the things that Abby reports really happened during her visit with Dr. Diggs; her entire report is a fabrication. Third, we learn that the source of Abby's knowledge about Dr. Diggs' accident was Sophie rather than her own observation. Sophie, who is Abby's classmate, did witness Dr. Diggs spill a cup of coffee on a map, so it is possible that Sophie shared this information with Abby. But there is more to the story; during his visit to the school, Dr. Diggs never spilled his drink on himself, he never changed his pants, and he never sustained an injury. So how did these fictitious details become part of the story of Dr. Diggs' visit?

In this investigation (Principe & Ceci, 2002), 4- and 5-year-olds participated in a staged archeology dig with an archeologist named Dr. Diggs. Diggs instructed the children to use tools to dig pretend artifacts, such as dinosaur bones and gold coins, out of specially constructed blocks of sand. Each dig included two "target" artifacts: a bottle with a map to a buried treasure and a rock with a message written in a secret language. Some children, those in the Witness condition, saw Diggs ruin these artifacts. He "accidentally" spilled coffee on the map, rendered it unreadable, and said in an upset tone, "I messed up the map! Now I'll never find the buried treasure!" These children also saw Diggs shatter the rock and say, "I've broken the rock! Now I'll never know what the secret message says!" Other children, those in the Classmate condition, did not witness these accidents but were the classmates of those who did. Immediately after the dig, the Witness and Classmate children interacted naturally.

When later interviewed, most of the Witness children correctly reported seeing the two accidents. However, many of the Classmates also reported seeing these activities take place. In contrast, those in a Control condition, who participated in the dig but had no exposure to the accidents or witnesses, failed to report that the map or rock had been damaged. Further, the Witnesses generated relatively detailed narratives describing these experienced events. But many of the Classmate children also relayed elaborate reports of these occurrences that only the Witness children saw, with many, like Abby in the example above, embellishing with details that went beyond the Witnesses' experiences but nonetheless were consistent with them. In fact, the false accounts of those who heard about the accidents secondhand from peers were more voluminous than the true accounts of those children who actually saw the accidents. These findings demonstrate not only that natural contact with peer witnesses can induce reports of nonevents but also that false accounts engendered by peer interaction can be more elaborate than true recollections based on experience.

## Rumors as a Source of Suggestion

Considering these findings of peer-induced error, we (Principe et al., 2006) sought to determine whether peer interactions can shape children's reports even when *none* of them actually witnessed the occurrence in question. To do so, we planted a false rumor about an experienced event among some children in classrooms and examined the degree to which the rumored information leaked into children's subsequent recollections.

We turned to rumor transmission because the social literature demonstrates that rumors tend to emerge about events that are troubling and meaningful when the truth is uncertain (see Rosnow, 1991). These conditions resemble those created by the sorts of offenses that often bring children to court, such as sexual abuse and other forms of maltreatment, because such allegations are disconcerting and commonly lack corroborating evidence. In these cases, rumors may emerge to fill in gaps of missing details. Given that people readily accept information gained during everyday interactions as true (Gilbert & Malone, 1995), rumors have much potential to trigger revisions in memory in the direction of what is overheard.

In this investigation, 3- to 5-year-olds saw a scripted magic show in their preschools. During the show, a magician named Magic Mumfry attempted to pull a live rabbit out of his hat. After several unsuccessful tries, he apologized and left the building. Children were situated into three experimental groups that differed in their exposure to a false rumor spread immediately after the show about why Mumfry's trick failed. Children in the Overheard group overheard an adult tell another that the trick failed because Mumfry's rabbit had gotten loose in the school rather than residing in his hat. Children in the Classmate group did not overhear the adult rumor but were the classmates of those who did. These two groups of children interacted naturally after those in the first condition overheard the rumor. Children in the Control group had no exposure to the rumor or children who did.

When later questioned about the show, nearly all of the Overheard and Classmate children reported that the rumored event actually occurred, and most reported this nonevent in response to open-ended questions, showing not only that information overheard from adults can lead to high levels of spontaneous false reports but that rumors transmitted by peers can be as detrimental as those spread by adults. Importantly, the Control group made no false claims of a loose rabbit.

This study also included a fourth group who, rather than hearing the loose rabbit rumor following the failed rabbit trick, actually saw a live rabbit loose in their school. As expected, all these children recalled seeing the rabbit and generated quite elaborate narratives about this experience. However, children in both the Overheard and Classmate groups provided much more elaborate accounts describing their experiences with a loose rabbit than those who actually experienced a loose rabbit, documenting that rumors planted by adults can induce false accounts that are more detailed than reports of experience.

### Conflicting Rumors

These findings of the potency of rumor prompted us to consider whether rumor might be less damaging when it conflicts with the past than when it explains an ambiguous event. This is because when rumor simply fills a gap, overheard information can be imported into memory without displacing any experienced details. But when rumor conflicts with the past, children must resolve the contradiction between what was experienced and what was heard. Furthermore, older children may be more resistant to conflicting rumors given their more sophisticated ability to reason about conflicting mental representations. This prediction comes from studies in the theory-of-mind tradition that demonstrate a transition in representational understanding between ages 3 and 6 (Perner, 1991). This work shows that younger children presume that the mind directly records experience and that everyone therefore has the same accurate beliefs about it. By contrast, older children recognize the subjective nature of representation and consequently that different people can have conflicting representations of the same experience.

To examine this possibility, 3- to 6-year-olds experienced our usual magic show but half of the Overheard and Classmate children saw a plausible explanation for the failed "rabbit-out-of-the-hat" trick during the show that later would conflict with the loose rabbit rumor (Principe, Tinguely, & Dobkowski, 2007). Specifically, when Mumfry failed at the hat trick he uncovered a cage to find his rabbit still in it. He explained to the children that his rabbit must be too sick to come out to do the trick. To encourage belief in this explanation, he checked the rabbit with medical instruments and gave it "medicine." Next, all the Overhead children heard our original rumor that Mumfry's trick failed because the rabbit had gotten loose.

Replicating our earlier findings, nearly all Overheard and Classmate children reported that Mumfry's rabbit had gotten loose when they merely heard the rumor and did not experience a conflicting explanation for the failed trick. However, the 5- and 6-year-olds, but not the 3- and 4-year-olds, were better able to resist the rumor when it conflicted with their experiences (i.e., when they saw the sick rabbit) than when it merely filled a gap. Supporting the idea that an understanding of representational processes boosts resistance, stronger performance on a set of conflicting representation tasks was associated with reduced reports of the rumored event and lower levels of descriptive detail in line with the rumor.

### Child-Generated Rumor

Our findings demonstrating the mnemonic damage of rumors planted by adults prompted us to consider the effects of rumors generated by children themselves. Given children's tendencies to make causal inferences under certain conditions (Schmidt & Paris, 1978), we wondered whether children might propagate causal inferences made about their experiences in a manner that could affect their own and their peers' reports. To examine this question, 3- to 6-year-olds saw Mumfry fail at two tricks: pulling a rabbit out of his hat and producing a birthday cake from a baking pan

(Principe, Guiliano, & Root, 2008). Next, some children saw two sets of clues: carrot ends with "teeth marks" scatted throughout the school and a plate with cake crumbs and a dirty fork. We expected that these clues would induce two inferences about the causes of the failed tricks, namely that the rabbit had gotten loose in the school and that someone had eaten the cake.

When later interviewed, nearly 80 percent of the children who saw the clues reported that Mumfry's rabbit had gotten loose or that someone had eaten the cake, indicating that the clue manipulations prompted the generation of inferences about the failed tricks that some children later misattributed as events experienced on the day of the show. Further, nearly 40 percent of the children who were the classmates of those exposed to the clues reported that the rabbit had gotten loose or that someone had eaten the cake, showing not only that children propagated their inferences but also that their transmissions readily leaked into their peers' reports. Furthermore, the classmates produced more elaborate false reports describing the nonevents than those who saw the clues firsthand, suggesting that children may be more likely to embellish information picked up from others than that derived from their own reasoning.

We also found a reverse developmental effect among those who saw the clues. Specifically, 5- and 6-year-olds were more likely than 3- and 4-year-olds to mistakenly report experiencing what could have only been inferences, and their accounts of non-experienced-but-inferred occurrences were embellished with double the amount of detail compared to those of the younger children. This age trend makes empirical sense given that causal inferencing ability develops rapidly during the preschool years (Sophian & Huber, 1984). To the extent that the older children generated more relevant inferences from the clues, they likely had created for themselves more opportunities than the younger children did to mistake their inferences for actually witnessed events.

## Social Factors

In our rumor studies, levels of false reports and fictitious elaboration are greater than in most suggestibility investigations where children undergo coercive interviews (see Bruck et al., 2002). Demonstrations in the social influence literature that the very same misinformation produces more interference if picked up during social interactions than learned through nonsocial means (Paterson & Kemp, 2006b) suggest that the social experience of interacting with others after overhearing our rumor, rather than the rumor itself, may drive our exceptionally high error rates.

To test this possibility experimentally, we (Principe, Daley, & Kauth, 2010) permitted only half of the children in the Overheard condition to interact with peers following their exposure to the false rumor. When later questioned, the 3- to 5-year-olds who heard the rumor and then interacted with peers made substantially more false claims of the rumored occurrence, were more likely to report actually seeing this nonevent, and described this non-occurrence in more detail than those who did not have the opportunity to talk with their peers after overhearing the rumor, confirming that the opportunity for peer conversation following rumor amplifies its interfering effects. Furthermore, more than one-third of the false details reported by children who interacted overlapped with something at least one other class-mate claimed, whereas those who were denied an opportunity to interact evidenced negligible overlap in their reports, indicating that social interaction following exposure to a misinformation source such as rumor can lead to high levels of corroboration even when no members of the group are accurate. We also found that the rumor induced greater memory contamination and higher levels of corroboration if it was planted and shared among familiar peers than if encountered among strangers, demonstrating that a group's social history can augment the degree to which false narrative details invented during natural interactions leak into children's later individual reports.

## Representational Changes

The interfering effects of rumor notwithstanding, to what extent are false accounts following rumor driven by a genuine belief that the rumored information was actually experienced or merely the result of social demands to relay information children know has not been experienced but only overheard? This distinction is forensically important because if rumor can bring about errant beliefs about experiencing events that only were heard about, there may be little that interviewers can do to mitigate rumors' effects. But if reports of rumored occurrences are driven by compliance to social pressures, such errors may be reduced by protocols that increase the retrieval and reporting of experienced information, such as the National Institute of Child Health and Human Development (NICHD) Investigative Interview (see Lamb et al., 2007).

To determine if false reports following rumors can result from repre-sentational changes, we (Principe, Haines et al., 2010) replicated our original Overheard and Classmate groups with 3- to 6-year-olds. When interviewed, half of the children received a series of emphatic warnings that any information overheard after the show was wrong and therefore should not be reported. Thus, if children could determine the correct source of the loose rabbit (i.e., that they heard about it from someone), there were no social pressures to relay it. We found that the warning reduced false reports when the rumor was planted by an adult. However, when the rumor was picked up from peers, the warning decreased false reports among 5- and 6-year-olds, but not 3- and 4-year-olds. Interestingly, the warning had no effect on children's claims of seeing a loose rabbit.

This pattern suggests that social demands produced some false reports but that demand characteristics had little or nothing to do with children's claims of seeing the rumored occurrence. In fact, analyses of children's narratives suggest that representational changes underlaid children's reports of seeing. Specifically, children who recalled seeing the rumored event generated different narrative profiles than those who reported a loose rabbit but did not recall seeing it. Those who reported seeing the loose rabbit described this rumored event with more perceptual (e.g., color and sound) and contextual (e.g., spatial location and temporal order) detail than those who were unable to say how they knew about the rabbit or who reported another source. Because perceptual and contextual details in memory typically serve as cues that a representation is based on a real experience rather than a suggested or otherwise non-experienced source (Johnson, Hashtroudi, & Lindsay, 1993), the generation of these qualities in children's representation of the rumored event may have interfered with source-judgment processes and consequently led some children to misattribute it as a witnessed event. Importantly, these findings suggest that rumored events can come to be represented similarly to experienced events and that such representational changes put children at risk for developing false beliefs of seeing occurrences that were merely rumored.

Replicating Principe and colleagues (2006), we found that the Classmate children made more frequent reports of seeing and gave more lengthy descriptions of the rumored occurrence relative to the Overheard children. Examination of children's narratives indicated that the Classmates reported proportionately more perceptual and contextual detail than the Overheards, suggesting that what makes rumors picked up from peers particularly potent is that this mode of transmission can lead to an abundance of perceptual and contextual detail in memory that children are prone to judge as indicative of an authentic witnessed experience.

### Post-rumor Conversations

We (Principe et al., 2012) also sought to investigate directly the content of children's post-rumor conversations to better understand which qualities of these discussions are linked to later errors in memory. To do so, we followed our initial study by establishing three experimental groups: Overheard, Classmate, and Control. For 20 minutes following the Overheards' exposure to the rumor, all children wore a small digital recorder that captured their conversations. Children were interviewed at delays of 1 and 4 weeks.

Consistent with prior work, when questioned 1 week after the show, nearly all Overheard and Classmate children but none of the Control children reported that Mumfry's rabbit was loose. Likewise, many Overheard and Classmate children recalled seeing an escaped rabbit and many provided high levels of constructive embellishments in line with the rumor. Reports of the loose rabbit and recollections of seeing it remained high across the 4-week delay. These patterns indicate that the memory alterations engendered by false rumor do not dissipate rapidly but rather reflect more lasting changes in remembering. They also are in line with predictions made by fuzzy-trace theory that false memories of gist-consistent events are particularly resistant to forgetting (Brainerd & Reyna, 2019).

Examination of children's natural exchanges with peers in their class-rooms following the magic show revealed a remarkable amount of dialogue going on among those who heard the rumor directly from an adult as well as those who had picked it up secondhand from their peers. In fact, every child in both groups uttered at least one statement about the alleged loose rabbit, indicating that every Overheard and Classmate child encoded the rumor and was actively engaged, albeit in varying degrees, in circulating the rumored information. Indeed, children's unanimous participation in the propagation of stories about a loose rabbit provides some insight into the basis of the near-ceiling levels of reports of the rumored event in our work. Further, there was much overlap between the content of children's classroom dialogues and their interview reports at both delays, indicating that the very details invented and shared on the day of the show intruded into their own and their peers' later individual accounts.

Consistent with our earlier findings (Principe et al. 2006; Principe, Haines et al., 2010), the rumor was more damaging to memory when it was gleaned from agemates than when it was overheard from an adult. Specifically, at both interviews, the Classmate children made more frequent reports of seeing the rumored occurrence and offered lengthier false narratives than the Overheards. Examination of the classroom dialogues suggests that group differences in natural talk following the show may underlie this heighted peer suggestibility. Both groups improvised abundantly; overall 58 percent of children's transmissions in the classroom were new (i.e., no other child in the classroom had yet mentioned). However, the Classmate children relayed more than twice as many original details as the Overheard children, indicating that they invented and shared more novel embellishments than their peers. Further, the Classmate children were more affected than the Overheards by what went on in the classrooms on the day the rumor was planted. At both the 1- and 4-week delays, Classmates evidenced greater overlap between things they themselves said as well as things their classmates uttered and their subsequent interview reports. By contrast, at both interviews, the Overheard children relayed higher levels of nonoverlapping information, suggesting that they were more likely than the Classmate children to fabricate their interview reports on the fly. Taken together, these patterns suggest that rumors gleaned from peers may be particularly potent because they lead to deeper and more inventive rumor-mongering than rumors picked up from adults. But what happens if the source of misinformation is the most important adult in the child's life, namely a parent?

## Conversations with Parents

The developmental literature documents the importance of parent–child memory-sharing conversations in fostering children's autobiographical remembering skills (see e.g., Hedrick, Chapter 11; Ornstein, Haden, & Hedrick, 2004). Little attention, however, has been directed toward exploring what happens when parents share false information during such exchanges. To explore this issue, we (Principe, DiPuppo, & Gammel, 2013) interviewed 3- to 5-year-olds about our usual magic show with the failed rabbit trick. On the morning of the interview, mothers were asked to talk naturally with their children about the show. Some mothers were given a false suggestion that the magician's rabbit may have gotten loose during his visit to the school and were asked to query their children about this possibility. When interviewed, more than half of the children whose mothers were misinformed reported a loose rabbit, and many of these children described this nonevent with abundant detail, indicating that natural conversations with mothers can be a source of children's memory error.

Interestingly, not all misinformed mothers talked with their children about the possible loose rabbit the same way. In fact, we (Principe et al., 2017) found that certain aspects of mothers' memory-sharing style were associated with children's false reports. Specifically, children whose mothers naturally offered high levels of elaborative structure (defined as elaborative questions and statements) and controlled the conversational agenda (defined in terms of functional control of conversational turns) rather than supporting their children's autonomy were the most likely to acquiesce to their mothers' *first* mention of the suggested activity and acquiesced to proportionally more of their mothers' questions and statements about this nonevent during the pre-interview mother–child conversation. Further, during the subsequent interview, children of mothers who provided high levels of elaborative structure and control made the greatest number of false reports of a loose rabbit and produced the most elaborate descriptions of this nonevent. Interestingly, these children also provided the highest level of overlap between things mothers uttered during the mother–child conversation and things children themselves said during the interview, demonstrating that they were particularly prone to let pieces of their mothers' contributions leak into their subsequent reports.

Why might the combination of high structure and high control be particularly damaging to children's memories when mothers have been misinformed? Examination of the mother–child dialogues indicated that the combined tendencies of a high-structure mother to offer new information consistent with a false suggestion and a high-control mother to promote a particular conversational agenda are similar to the sorts of questioning behaviors that have been found to distort children's recall in the suggestibility literature (e.g., Bruck et al., 2002). Borrowing from the vernacular of this line of research, many of these mothers' statements and questions would be characterized as conveying a bias in the veracity of the misinformation (e.g., introducing new details consistent with the misinformation, praising responses in line with the theme). These findings suggest that these mothers inadvertently had created a coercive memory-sharing environment that put their children at risk for making memory errors in line with the maternal suggestion. Further, the willingness of children of high-structure and controlling mothers to accept their mothers' suggestions during the mother–child conversations and later relay similar information during the interview suggests that these children also may behave in ways that facilitate the conversational shaping of their memory reports. Indeed, these seemingly linked maternal and child patterns are consistent with arguments made by Ornstein and colleagues (2004) that it is not merely maternal style that causes certain child behaviors but rather the interaction of tendencies of mothers and children that produces specific mnemonic outcomes.

Given that exact accuracy in recall is paramount in legal settings, we (Principe, Gardner, & Trumbull, 2016) also examined whether a focus on accuracy as a conversational goal might impact how mothers share misinformation and 3- to 5-year-old children's subsequent recollections. Considering extant work showing that mothers who focus on the goal of helping their children remember correctly are more controlling and less autonomy supportive than those who center on learning their child's perspective on an event (Cleveland, Reese, & Grolnick, 2007), we hypothesized that a focus on accuracy following exposure to false information might steer mothers' conversational agenda and consequently children's subsequent memory in the direction of misinformation. To explore this issue, we established two experimental groups that differed in mothers' goal orientation: Some mothers were asked to elicit an accurate account (accuracy-focused), while others were told to talk as they would naturally in everyday life (natural-focused).

As expected, we found that mothers focused on accuracy were more controlling and offered more suggestions consistent with the misinformation than mothers asked to proceed as they typically would. During the interview, children of accuracy-focused mothers also produced higher levels of reports of a loose rabbit and offered more fictitious elaborative detail in line with the maternal misinformation than natural-focused children. Thus, these findings suggest that a focus on the goal of "getting memory right" in conversations with their children can boost mothers' conversational control and the provision of misinformation in such a way that it increases later errors in children's independent remembering.

## Conversations about Myths

As described above, Professor Ornstein and his colleagues (Baker-Ward et al., 2020; Ornstein et al., 1998) have shown that when knowledge or beliefs are inconsistent with what happened, children are prone to report things arising from their expectations rather than their memories of experience. In one extension of this work in my lab, we explored whether children's fantasy beliefs might operate on memory in the same constructive manner as children's beliefs about the real world. To examine these issues, we centered on how children's beliefs in mythical entities, such as the Tooth Fairy, might influence how they interpret and remember certain types of experiences. Even though the supernatural powers of such beings might seem too farfetched for acceptance (e.g., the Tooth Fairy knows when and where children lose their teeth), most young children in the

United States believe in their existence (Clark, 1995; Prentice, Manosevitz, & Hubbs, 1978). Belief likely comes easy because these myths are presented ready-made by parents and widely endorsed by the community with strong demands to believe (e.g., a threat of no presents under the Christmas tree for disbelievers in Santa Claus) and accompanied by seemingly tangible evidence of their reality (e.g., teeth replaced with prizes).

In one study addressing these issues, we (Principe & Smith, 2008) asked 5- to 6-year-olds to recall their most recent tooth loss. Children also were characterized as Believers, Uncertains, or Disbelievers on the basis of a sorting task that indexed their level of belief in the Tooth Fairy. During recall, the Uncertains and Disbelievers stuck to mundane descriptions of their tooth loss and non-supernatural accounts of Tooth Fairy rituals. They talked about things like how their tooth fell out, hiding their tooth under their pillow, and waking up to find a prize. The Believers, however, told us very different stories. They relayed absolutely fantastic accounts embellished with descriptions of events that could not have occurred but nonetheless were consistent with the myth. For example, some described their memories for how the Tooth Fairy hid a prize under their pillows and others recounted how she flew in through their bedroom window.

There are two possibilities to explain these results. Either children's beliefs about the reality of the Tooth Fairy led them to construct and remember an actual experience in ways consistent with the fantasy or they simply interpreted the interview as an opportunity to indulge in pretense and fabricated a knowingly untrue story. To tease apart these two alternatives, we (Principe & Smith, 2007) altered the demands of the interview and asked some children to provide an exactly true report and others to give a fun account. Most Believers reported supernatural experiences consistent with the myth under both sets of recall instructions. By contrast, the Disbelievers recalled mainly realistic experiences regardless of condition. The Uncertains, however, evidenced a different pattern under the two sets of instructions – they described mostly realistic experiences in the truthful condition but fantastic events in the fun condition, suggesting that they were somewhat able to switch control from the make-believe to the real when motivated to do so. Given the reluctance of the Believers, but not Uncertains, to modulate their reports on the basis of recall instructions, it seems that certainty in the existence of the Tooth Fairy led to genuine memory errors.

One of the most interesting findings in these studies is that many of the Believers' fantastic statements seemed to be triggered by actual occurrences that children interpreted in ways consistent with their expectations. To illustrate, consider the following exchange with Ben:

INTERVIEWER:   Tell me what happened when you lost your baby tooth.
CHILD:         The Tooth Fairy died.
INTERVIEWER:   She died? What? What happened?
CHILD:         Fluffy ate the Tooth Fairy.
INTERVIEWER:   Fluffy? Who's Fluffy?
CHILD:         My cat!
INTERVIEWER:   Your cat? Well, now how do you know that Fluffy ate the Tooth Fairy?
CHILD:         Because I saw him. He had fairy dust all over his mouth! Everywhere!
               His tongue, his teeth, his lips. My mom said it's not true but I know Fluffy ate her.

We know that this and many other seemingly fantastic stories were based on misinterpretations of actual experiences because parents provided independent accounts of their children's tooth loss. In this case, Ben's mother scattered gold glitter (i.e., fairy dust) in his bedroom as evidence of the Tooth Fairy's visit but also forgot to exchange his tooth with a prize. Fluffy, the family cat, somehow got glitter on its muzzle, and so Ben's report of Fluffy eating the Tooth Fairy is not a fabrication based on pretense. Rather, expectations created by his parents regarding the Tooth Fairy led him to interpret a witnessed event incorrectly but nonetheless provide a reasonable explanation for a tooth left behind and a cat muzzle covered with incriminating fairy dust.

When we examined the influence of tangible evidence systematically, we found that children who were exposed to multiple forms of evidence in support of the Tooth Fairy's existence (e.g., handwritten letter, window left open) reported high levels of supernatural experiences consistent with the myth and were especially likely to claim to have actually seen the Tooth Fairy, suggesting that seemingly tangible evidence puts children at risk for formulating memories of phenomenal experiences consistent with fantastic stories perpetuated by others. To examine this possibility exper- imentally, we (Principe & Giroux, 2018) explored 5- to 6-year-olds' memory for a St. Patrick's Day event in which we manipulated children's exposure to "evidence" of a leprechaun's visit. Specially, on St. Patrick's Day, in their classrooms, children with varying levels of belief in lepre- chauns built leprechaun traps out of craft supplies and baited their traps with marshmallow four-leaf clovers. Then out of their sight, we sprung the traps and removed the bait. In some of the classrooms, four visible forms of evidence of a leprechaun's visit (i.e., gold coins, a green top hat, a trail of green four-leaf clover glitter, and a note that read "can't catch me") were placed in prominent locations.

When we planted evidence, many of the Believers later told us that not only did a leprechaun visit their classroom but that they saw him with their own eyes. So, "evidence" matters. What's more interesting is that when we paired evidence with the opportunity for natural peer interaction after finding the evidence, the Uncertains acted in many ways as those with full beliefs did. That is, when the Uncertains interacted freely with the Believers after seeing our "evidence," many of the Uncertains turned into temporary believers. Their degree of provision of fantastic detail did not differ from those of the Believers and many, like the Believers, reported memories of seeing or hearing a leprechaun.

## Implications and Conclusions

This collection of studies inspired by Ornstein's information-processing framework underscores the importance of considering how everyday conversations can affect the encoding, storage, transformation, and retrieval of information for discussions about children's memory and testimony. For example, our work shows that conversational exchanges about future events can create expectations that can lead children to interpret certain types of experiences in a fantastic manner and consequently generate event representations infused with unreal details. Likewise, our investigations show that false details invented and shared with peers can intrude into children's subsequent recollections, suggesting that such interactions can produce a period of "extended encoding" that allows pieces of peer dialogue to intrude into memory. Similarly, the incorporation of misinformation suggested to mothers into children's later accounts demonstrates that errant details shared during natural mother–child exchanges can lead to changes in information stored in memory. Finally, our data show that under certain interviewing conditions, children will relay false rumors rather than remembered experiences and indulge in pretense rather than provide a truthful account, illustrating that not everything in memory is retrieved and reported.

Importantly, our investigations go beyond demonstrations of the ways in which conversations can affect the flow of information in the memory system and reveal several conditions under which the potential of natural interactions to interfere with remembering accuracy are exacerbated. For instance, rumors picked up from peers are more mnemonically damaging than rumors spread by adults, and conversations with familiar peers pose a greater risk of contamination than exchanges with strangers. Furthermore, certain characteristics of mothers' natural conversational style, such as the provision of elaborative structure and control, are linked with increased memory error when mothers have been misinformed about their children's experiences. Likewise, tangible evidence can put children at risk for interpreting and remembering certain types of experiences in line with fantastic stories perpetuated by others. Our research also reveals developmental trends in susceptibility to others' contributions. For instance, with age children develop some resistance to conversationally conveyed misinformation when it conflicts with personal experience, but they also become more likely to generate their own causal inferences about events that can put themselves as well as their peers at increased risk of wrongly recollecting occurrences that were merely inferred.

Our work also holds some forensic relevance because it reveals an everyday source of false reports that is not readily eliminated by techniques commonly used to minimize error in forensic interviews (e.g., exclusive non-suggestive questioning, video recording interviews). Of course, some caution is needed in generalizing our findings to situations involving child witnesses because our paradigms differ in important ways from most legal experiences (e.g., we ask children about enjoyable experiences, we do not pressure children to make false claims, interviewers are not rewarded for eliciting certain information). Nonetheless, because the level of peer influence in our studies likely pales in comparison to that which occurs in cases involving multiple child witnesses, our findings underscore the importance of considering the potential contaminating influence of peers in such situations. Likewise, our findings suggest that when mothers have been exposed to unfounded claims, such as in the McMartin case referred to earlier (see Ceci & Bruck, 1995), conversations with mothers can be mnemonically risky, especially if they guide conversations with high structure and control, or focus squarely on eliciting an accurate account. Either tendency can backfire and unwittingly create a coercive remembering environment that can lead to reports of nonevents. Finally, our work reveals that the tendencies of fact finders to use certain qualities of children's testimony such as corroboration, spontaneity, elaborativeness, and consistency as markers of accuracy are unwarranted when children have been exposed to conversationally conveyed misinformation.

Our work demonstrating the potency of others on children's autobiographical recollections has significant implications for theoretical models of children's memory. Traditionally, the information-processing framework has conceptualized memory as an individual phenomenon, that is, as the product of the encoding, storage, and retrieval of information on the part of the rememberer. Indeed, this characterization makes good sense given that memories of our own lives exist within our own mental systems, and internal processes, such as personal expectations, goals, and emotions, shape our representations and reports of experience (Grant & Ceci, 2000). Yet our research showing that children's reports of experience readily are modified by what others tell them demonstrates that remembering is not solely an individual operation. Rather, our studies show that remembering is a process that commonly occurs in collaboration with others, where tellers and listeners co-construct a rendering of experience and individual memories are an amalgam of firsthand information and new content derived from others. Relevant to theory, such findings suggest that individuals do not process personal experience in the stand-alone computer-like manner described in information-processing accounts of memory. Instead such evidence of the influence of others on remembering suggests that memory works more like a collaborative enterprise, such as Wikipedia. Its content usually is close to reality but not always entirely accurate. Sometimes it includes utterly false, if not fantastic, information. And information in it can change over time. The very creator can go in there and modify its content. But so can their peers and their mothers.

# CHAPTER 10

# Commentary
## Children's Memory of Their Personal Experiences
### Maggie Bruck

It is a delight to write a commentary for the three chapters in this section on children's memory of their personal experiences. I have followed the careers and studied the research of all the contributors and conclude that these chapters represent the pinnacle of their achievements by presenting in detail the scientific evidence on children's memory of experienced events. Together the authors present a compilation and comprehensive summary of results from their respective fields of study, situate their results in terms of theoretical issues in development, and point to their importance in the forensic arena. Each chapter includes developmental designs and all focus on children in the age range of 3–9 years. These chapters are now in my right-hand drawer, and I advise all in the field to also add these chapters to their files of important articles and to assign these to your students and colleagues who are in need of a concise view of the current science on young children's memory for experienced events.

The Baker-Ward and Thomas chapter (Chapter 7) summarizes the work inspired by Peter Ornstein and his talented colleagues on children's memories of touching, mainly in the setting of a pediatric visit. Ornstein is one of the pioneers in the New Science, which began at the end of 1980s (as described below). It was a period where research was needed in the forensic arena to reveal how much children recall of meaningful experienced events and specifically about being touched. While acknowledging similar work by other colleagues who have also worked in the "vineyard" of memory development (a favorite phrase used by Peter), his is among the first to use a pediatric setting to evaluate young children's recall of touching in an ethically acceptable manner. Concurrently or since that time, the paradigm has been adapted by a number of colleagues and researchers (e.g., Bruck et al. 1995a, 1995b; Peterson and Bell, 1996; Poole & Bruck, 2012; Quas et al. 1999; Saywitz et al., 1991; Steward et al., 1996). The medical-procedure setting has been used by researchers to examine the role of a range of factors that may affect the accuracy of children's memory, including age, delay between the event and the interview, the types of questions used (open-ended vs. direct), stress, and scripts. This chapter is an excellent review of these factors.

The chapter by Principe (Chapter 9) summarizes her much-needed work on the role of parents and peers in the transmission of true and false information. Following in the footsteps of Binet (1900), Principe was among the first (and still among the few) to investigate the role of peer interactions in children's recall of experienced and non-experienced events. When I first read these articles, I was astonished by her findings that young children (3- to 5-year-olds) would spontaneously talk to each other about events they had experienced or heard about. Having spent decades in preschools and elementary schools either observing in classrooms or taking children in and out of classrooms for testing, I had never witnessed any conversations or few interactions that involved classmates talking about actual events. Principe has repeatedly shown what I was missing by examining the intricacy of the pattern and details of children's communication in the classroom that results in their reporting of actual and never-experienced events. She has also deftly extended this work to study the role of mothers' conversations with their children that result in inaccurate reports of school events. These studies are unique and demonstrate the powerful influences of peers' and adults' natural conversations in shaping children's memories of non-experienced events.

Finally, the chapter by Price and Connolly (Chapter 8) fills a gap in distilling the vast literature on children's memories of routine repeated events. They call on script theory, instance-based theories, and fuzzy-trace theory to design and then to explain children's performances on these experimental tasks. As is true of all chapters in this part, these studies are developmental and summarize how repeated events (which contain common details, but also some details unique to that repeated event) can lead to distortions or enhancements of memory. This area of inquiry reflects a common task in our daily life: It is what our daily life is about – enacting, encoding, and recalling repeated sequences of events.

The focus of my commentary is not on the theoretical value of this field of work (which is discussed in each chapter), it is on its practical value. Specifically, how do these studies inform those in the forensic arena about the accuracy and distortion of children's memory? I have been involved in this forum for more than three decades, both as a researcher and as an expert witness and consultant. My first experience as an expert witness was in 1992 where I testified for the defense in the Little Rascals case (see Ceci & Bruck, 1995), which involved preschoolers' accusations of sexual abuse at the hands of their daycare workers. At that point, research on young children's memory was sparse; there was little or no scientific research on the distortion or accuracy of young children's memory about personally experienced events, with the notable exception of Ornstein and colleagues' work, which began to appear in 1992.

Since that time, the area has exploded in part due to the number of criminal cases in the 1980s and 1990s where young children claimed that their parents or other adults, often in daycare settings, had sexually abused them. The claims were often fantastic and bizarre, involving reports of ritualistic abuse, pornography, multiple perpetrators, and multiple victims (Bottoms & Davis, 1997; Ceci & Bruck, 1995; DeYoung, 1997; Frankfurter, 2006; Nathan & Snedeker, 2001). When these cases came to trial, the defense counsel argued that the children's statements were due to community panic and to the coercive interviewing techniques used to question the children. Prosecutors relied upon the prevailing common wisdom that children do not lie about sexual abuse and that their bizarre and chilling accounts of events, which were beyond the realm of most preschoolers' knowledge and experience, had to be true. In the absence of scientific support or any framework to understand the children's state-ments, the prosecution challenged the defense's views as "hypothetical." Consequently, there was no scientific evidence that could be presented to a jury with respect to the issue of the reliability of the children's testimony and no evidentiary explanation for how and why children could make such allegations.

Prompted by the issues provoked by these daycare trials, developmental scientists began to focus on the social psychological and cognitive elements of such cases. In 1993, Stephen Ceci and I wrote the first major review of the research that had been published to date on children's suggestibility. We found a large discrepancy in the views of researchers and those involved in social policy. On the one hand, there was a group who put forth the view that while it might be possible to suggest to a child that a man they saw yesterday wore a hat (when in fact he did not wear a hat), this was not relevant to cases where children had made significant and alarming reports of body harm, thus dismissing the importance of the older literature. At the other extreme, there was the view that children were so suggestible that one should not believe a word they said.

By 1993, researchers soon reached into newer areas that were relevant to issues raised by cases of child abuse. This newer view focused on memory distortion and on memory accuracy. It focused on extraneous factors that could possibly be the source of memory distortion (e.g., biased interviews, suggestive interviewing techniques, repeated interviews, peer interaction, and contamination) as well as internal factors related to basic principles of memory (e.g., repeated exposures, knowledge base, scripts, and causal reasoning). Much of the research was developmental involving various age groups, including preschool children – an age group that had rarely been included in previous research studies. With the accumulation of this new evidence, there was a new appreciation for the strengths and weaknesses of young children's memories and reports. This new evidence on the reliability of children's recall resulted in successful legal appeals for many of those previously imprisoned (DeYoung, 1997; Nathan & Snedeker, 2001; Wood et al., 2009).

Peter Ornstein's research career was highly influenced by the history just described. Up to the middle of the 1980s, Ornstein was best known for his work on the development memory strategies (e.g., rehearsal, categorization) that underpinned children's memory skills. This changed in 1985 when he received a phone call from an attorney who led the Guardian ad Litem program in North Carolina. She described a recent case of a young child who was found wandering around her neighborhood showing signs of abuse. When asked what happened, the young children reported "Frank did it, Frank did it, with his dick." The attorney asked Ornstein for his professional opinion about what one needed to know in order to claim that the child was indeed abused. According to Ornstein, this phone call changed his life (personal communication, 2020). Calling together a group of cross-disciplinary colleagues, they began to flesh out an agenda for how to systematically explore these issues in a developmental framework. They garnered the support of local pediatricians who agreed to be part of this research program. They conducted several years of pilot studies and were finally awarded a grant for the pediatrician studies described in the Baker-Ward and Thomas chapter in this volume. In 1991, they published a paper (based on a talk from a 1989 conference at Cornell University) where they tried to make sense of the scant literature. In 1992, their first journal paper was published (Ornstein, Gordon, & Larus, 1992). The rest of the history is contained in Chapter 7 in this volume.

With the initiation of this line of study, Ornstein was urged to take his science into the courtroom. He was reticent: He didn't know enough to be an expert witness, he was too busy with his academic life, he did not think that a courtroom would allow him to communicate the subtleties of the science. Finally, one of his colleagues argued that if people like himself were reluctant to enter the forensic arena, who would convey the science and properly educate the jurors? Peter Ornstein jumped in. He assisted in many cases. He started seminars for graduate and undergraduate students to familiarize them with the scientific literature and its forensic applications. He brought in guest speakers, including attorneys and other academics, and even had one class assist with the analysis of a child's statements in a particular case.

Returning to the main theme of this commentary, I will discuss the degree to which the research described in the chapters of this section has or could make contributions to the forensic arena by informing jurors, judges, and attorneys about the basic research on children's autobiographical memory. I provide material from actual cases as examples to show the potential value of this exercise.[1]

## Forensic Applications

In discussing the forensic value of the research described in the three chapters, it is necessary to pair them with the basic structure of the case to which it might be applied. For example, research on the factors that distort children's memory is most applicable when there is evidence that external factors precede the child's statements. These cases often require an expert to present the scientific foundations for how misinformation can distort children's reports while referring to the specific instances of taint to the facts at hand. At the same time, an expert might be called to testify about how internal or basic memorial processes (e.g., the construction of scripts) may enhance or degrade a child's memory. Finally, experts should provide developmental trends showing the ages and conditions where children are best able to recall or remember certain types of information. Thus, the expert's testimony must be fine-tuned to the facts of the case. For example, the expert must speak about the literature that is pertinent to characteristics of disclosure and allegations: Did the child make spontaneous statements or did the child make accusations after several episodes of questioning? How was the child questioned? Did the adult use open-ended questions with no pressure to provide information or, at the other extreme, did the adult use repetitive leading questions? What was the delay between

---

[1] Most of the examples that I provide come from cases where there are doubts about the accuracy of the child witnesses who provide the primary evidence in the case. These cases are not necessarily representative of the many different situations where children are witnesses or participants in criminal events, but I selected these to show how psychological research such as that described in the three chapters in this section can be used in the forensic arena. They also reflect my own role in the forensic arena, which is one to testify in cases where there is evidence for the role of internal and external factors in influencing the child's testimony.

the alleged act and the disclosure by the child? Were the child's disclosures detailed and did they contain sequences of events? Were there claims of repeated events? With repeated interviews, did the child change their statements, either by contradicting previous claims, or by omitting, or adding new details? Did a parent have a specific fear or belief about abuse? Was the child interacting with siblings or peers who might influence the allegations?

### Research on Conversations as a Source of False Memories in Children

In a number of actual cases, children's allegations of wrongdoing by another adult are associated with prior conversations with a parent. Some of these examples involve very coercive questioning methods, whereas others involve less-coercive but still suggestive strategies. To date, most of the research has focused on practices that are associated with forensic interviewers or mental health practitioners when they talk to children. Although the results of these studies have often been applied to other adults who interact with children (mainly family members), until Principe's studies, there has been little research to identify the elements of parent–child conversations that may result in children's false reports or spark parental concern that something has happened to their child. The following gives a flavor of some cases, where such research would be informative to the court.

Mr. and Mrs. G. separated because Mrs. G. was worried that her husband had been abusing their kindergarten child. After 18 months of play therapy with Dr. M. and questioning by the mother, the child had not made any allegations. At that time, Mrs. G. started questioning her 5-year-old daughter, Ellie, about the sleeping arrangements when she visited her father on weekends. She implored her daughter to tell her about "the heavy thing on her chest that keeps her from flying" (this phrase was taken from a metaphorical book that the mother was reading to Ellie). The child still did not make any accusations. The mother reported the ensuing conversation.

> Ellie, I take you to Dr. M. because she is somebody who will listen to you and who will believe you. Every time I take you to Dr. M., I sit in the waiting room and I feel like it is Christmas because I'm waiting for the present that doesn't come. But it never comes. You're in so much pain and so am I. I can't do it anymore. I just don't have the energy to take you to Dr. M. and I'm tapped out. I don't have physical energy. I don't have mental energy. I don't have money . . . Please you've just got to tell her. (*At this point according to the mother, both she and her daughter are crying.*) Can you tell me what the heavy thing is in your chest?

The mother reported that Ellie replied that her father would touch her around her eyes, and he would touch her around the mouth, and that he would touch her chest. The mother then asked if Ellie would tell this to Dr. M.

Principe's studies involve providing children's mothers with misinformation about a school event. Mothers were not provided with a script or a list of questions, but rather were told to talk to their children naturally and to query them about the false event (which the mothers thought actually happened). Analysis of these interviews revealed that mothers of children who incorporated the false event conducted highly structured and controlled interviews (keeping the focus on the misinformed event). Although Principe terms this style as "coercive memory sharing with a focus on accuracy," it is interesting that this short interaction produced such large effects. In doing so, Principe has circumvented the ethically impermissible situation where children are often questioned by mothers and other family members for days or months before an allegation is made, and has shown that it is not difficult, nor does it require much pressure, for children to adopt their mothers' views of the past.

The main cornerstone of Principe's work concerns the degree to which peers indirectly or directly influence their compatriot's reports. Although Binet (1900) was among the first to note this phenomenon, subsequent studies focused on the effect of groups on adults' perceptions or memories or reports. Principe's work thus has profound implications for cases involving children (including siblings) who over time contemporaneously come to make allegations of wrongdoing. When these cases reach the legal arena, they are often interpreted as showing that all the siblings or classmates were victims of abuse, not just the first child to make the allegation. However, careful review of the case files often reveal that although one child might name a number of others who viewed or experienced the target event, the claims are not always corroborated by the named participants who subsequently made other claims involving other child victims. It seems from the case material that it takes very little suggestion to provoke a named participant to agree to their victimization. For example, the allegations made by a 7-year-old boy emerged as a result of the interviewer mentioning his older brother.

INTERVIEWER:   Did any of these men ever stick his penis up your butt?
BOB:           Na.
INTERVIEWER:   You sure about that?
BOB:           Yes.
INTERVIEWER:   I think Bruce told us that that happened. Was he...

| BOB: | Yeah. |
|---|---|
| INTERVIEWER: | Did that happen? |
| BOB: | *(No response)* |
| INTERVIEWER: | It did? |
| BOB: | Yah. |
| INTERVIEWER: | Did somebody stick a penis up your butt? |
| BOB: | Yes. |

In a group therapy session, a therapist encouraged four siblings to think of the auditory, visual, and olfactory cues that would remind them of the alleged abuse. As can be seen from the following, it appears that the children were copying the others' reports of body sensation.

CHILD 1:   The sight of Brian's house, smell of dirt and musty stuff; sound of pigeons and chickens made him think of Brian.

CHILD 2:   Brian's house, his yard, car, the sound and smell of pigeons.

CHILD 3:   Side of Brian's house, sound of a rooster in the morning, the smell of pigeons or a dusty smell.

CHILD 4:   Brian's car, rooster, smell of corn.

In another case, after many months of concern that the babysitter had molested 5-year-old Carol, she finally made an allegation. The following dialogue appeared in the ensuing forensic interview.

| CAROL: | I heard another little girl – that it happened to her before me. |
|---|---|
| INTERVIEWER: | When did you find out about that? |
| CAROL: | Because it was my friend, her name is Janie. |
| INTERVIEWER: | Did Janie say anything to you about . . . her . . . |
| CAROL: | Yeah – We went over to her house and she talked about this. |

One teacher recorded the following overheard conversation between two of her kindergarten pupils who were alleged victims of their daycare workers.

AUDREY:   They had real snakes, they went SSS, there were toys in the cage outside.

EMMY:   I saw the snakes and cage, but I ran up the steps, the snakes are called Emmy the same as me.

A few months later in the same case, the following conversation occurred between the same two children and another friend. Chris and Dawn were the accused teachers.

AUDREY:   And do you know what? Chris and Dawn kicked me.

PATTY:   Why did they kick you?

EMMY:   Cos they thought I was a pirate lady.

AUDREY:   And they slapped me cos they thought I was a doggy.   *(Both Emmy and Audrey laugh and begin to jump on a piece of equipment)*

These segments were used at trial by the prosecution as evidence that the children had been abused. Clearly, the research program headed by Principe could provide jurors with valuable information on the transmission of misinformation among children.

### Research on Children's Memory of Touching and on Memory of Repeated Events

Chapters 7 and 8 are discussed under the same heading because this research focuses on the development of memory for personally experienced events. In most of these studies, children are simply asked to recall what they remembered. With a few exceptions, there is an absence of external factors that might taint memory. Price and Connolly review the literature on children's recall of instances from repeated events where each one varies from another in terms of a detail in a complex series of activities. After a delay, children are asked to recall the details of a specific session. In the studies reviewed by Baker-Ward and Thomas, the child experiences a complex event (a medical examination) one time and then over a series of different delays is reinterviewed about its details. In all these studies, the children come into the interview situation with knowledge about what usually happens in these settings, and there are few opportunities in most of the studies for misinformation to taint these children's reports. When there are interventions between delay periods, these do not meet the standards of suggestion used in other studies[2]. These paradigms allow researchers to examine the fidelity of memory after various delays (in the case of Baker-Ward & Thomas, Chapter 7) or after acquiring a script for similar events, thus allowing for the examination of distortions due to internal mechanisms (in the case of Price & Connolly, Chapter 8). In my view, these studies allow an examination of children's memories in the "best" and most "pristine" of circumstances. In other words, they provide a metric for what one can expect in normal, natural circumstances.

The research reviewed in Chapter 7 clearly shows that even the youngest children can accurately report how the doctor or nurse touched them

---

[2] In one study reported by Baker-Ward and Thomas, children were interviewed about a recent medical examination. Sometime later they were shown a video of another child's exam that included many of the same features of their examination, but it also included new features that had not been experienced. The children were then interviewed about the examination for a second time. The video increased memory for true events, but also added errors to the second interview report due to intrusions of the doctored video (Principe et al., 2000). This is an excellent examination of how misinformation and scripts interact.

during a recent pediatric visit. The consistent findings are that (i) the youngest children are the most error-prone; (ii) accuracy decreases as a function of delay; (iii) with delay there is an increase in both errors of omission (not reporting previously mentioned items) as well as commission (newly reported information that never occurred); and (iv) the most accurate reports were spontaneous and were produced after a short delay in the absence of exposures that would lead to misinformation or lead to changes in the child's knowledge. In general, at all ages, children's memory for the exam was quite accurate with few errors about events that never happened.

Price and Connolly's review of children's memory for instances of complex repeated events shows that, as expected, this ability develops with age, but that the task remains difficult at all ages studied where accurate performance is below 50%. The children who participated in repeated presentations of the event had difficulty distinguishing between the various experienced instances (i.e., increased internal intrusion errors), but they were not more likely to confuse what did happen with what did not happen (external intrusion errors).

Both chapters report studies that present data in conditions that provide an optimal appraisal of children's memories or statements. These are most useful in forensic cases when similar parameters apply to the child and the allegation. Specifically, the interview for the event occurred within a week or a few weeks from the target experience. Also, in the case of repeated-event studies, there was only one interview, whereas in the Ornstein studies there were repeated interviews but all are quite similar (with the exception of providing the child some knowledge or misinformation in one investigation). Finally, the interviewers asked neutral open-ended and then specific questions, but did not repeat questions or provide the child with information. In other words, these researchers followed protocols that are similar to those used by forensic interviewers.

In contrast, such studies do not directly address issues and facts that describe many cases with the following features:

(i)   The child does not initially make a spontaneous comment or denies being present at such an event.
(ii)  With additional questioning, and repeated interviews, the child begins to make accusations that become more elaborated or sometimes more inconsistent with time. (Inconsistency includes adding details not previously mentioned or contradicting previous statements.) Thus, there is the opportunity for taint, practice, and

developmental cognitive changes that can influence subsequent reporting.

(iii) In some cases, children's allegations refer to events that happened more than one year ago. Sometimes children report events from three or more years ago. The scientific work on suggestibility and external memory distortion is best suited to these types of cases.

But there are other cases that do not involve the above constellation of factors, and it is here that other experts, myself included, have relied on the memory of touch and memory of repeated-events literatures to understand what is the "best" performance one might expect from children who have been questioned about repeated events or body touches, when there has been no explicit evidence or opportunity for external forces to distort the child's testimony. The following vignette is one such example:

A 3-year-old child was rushed to hospital due to injuries to her legs, which were badly broken. The child clung to her father throughout this journey and named her brother Max as the culprit. Max was jumping on the couch to touch the ceiling fan and fell on his sister. The older brother confirmed this account. Within weeks, the blame shifted to the father, in part because the medical experts at the hospital said it was impossible for Max to have had such an impact as to break the child's legs and so it had to be the father. Counseling began and all three children were put into foster homes. At trial, two experts in the field of biomechanics testified that it was highly possible for Max to have broken the child's bones. In my report to the court, I relied on the literature on children's memories of touching (where there were few opportunities for taint for her initial reports) and concluded her statements were reliable. The father was found innocent in criminal court.

Cases that involve the testimony of children who have experienced multiple events are difficult to evaluate for a number of reasons. First, children may provide imprecise and inconsistent information about the number of times that the target events occurred (ranging from 1 to 50 in one case, and these estimated frequencies may change with repeated interviews). Another difficulty in the evaluation of these cases is that children may not differentiate individual events. In other words, a child may sometimes be asked "Tell me the first time it happened," and then when asked about a second time, they will reply "The same thing." Also, there are many questions during these forensic interviews, so it is difficult to determine how much is from the child's memory, or from her guessing, or from following the interviewer's lead. Sometimes, the forensic examples put before experts are so mired in confounding variables that it is often difficult to tell the smoke from the fire.

The next section provides a glimpse of these difficulties when evaluating a 6-year-old's testimony about an alleged repeated event. The date of the alleged abuses was never established.

INTERVIEWER: Tell me about the time that he touched your private part. What happened?

CHILD: I don't remember when it happened, but it was a long time ago.

INTERVIEWER: Yeah. So, I wasn't there, but I want to know everything that happened when you say that your dad touched your private parts.

CHILD: Okay.

INTERVIEWER: Can you tell me how it happened?

CHILD: I don't know how it happened.
Oh well, how about he put his penis in my butt.
And then on other days he touched my penis.

INTERVIEWER: Tell me about another time that it happened.

CHILD: The same place it happened, the same place.

INTERVIEWER: What about your dad?

CHILD: He was wearing a white shirt and his underwear. Actually, he was wearing a white T-shirt.

INTERVIEWER: Do you remember about any other times that it happened?

CHILD: Yeah. It was the same place, he was wearing the same stuff. And he was the same age.

INTERVIEWER: Same age? How old was he?

CHILD: I don't know. I don't know how old he is now, I don't know how old he was when he did it.

INTERVIEWER: Did it happen again?

CHILD: Yeah, it happened more than one time and more than two times.

INTERVIEWER: Ooooohhh, how many times did it happen?

CHILD: I don't know.

INTERVIEWER: About how many times did it happen?

CHILD: I don't remember. I think it might've been five?

## Conclusion

The research presented in these chapters makes a tremendous contribution to our understanding of young, school-aged children's recall of personally experienced events. It elucidates the factors that both enhance children's recall as well as those that and impair their recall. Translating this field of knowledge into the courtroom is not always a straightforward task. But it can be done to advance jurors' knowledge of the strengths and weaknesses of children's testimony. It is important to keep in mind that no one study can ever mirror the many factors involved in cases involving children's testimony. There is no one study that includes such background factors as family factors and relationships, the child's psychological status, and the exact investigative procedures used in any one case. But as scientists, we can chip away at these factors and try to show that there are consistent patterns of results when certain conditions prevail.

# PART IV

# *Family Socialization of Memory*

# CHAPTER 11

# Developmental Pathways to Skilled Remembering
## Characterizing the Development of Children's Event Memory within the Family Context

*Amy M. Hedrick*

The threads of Peter Ornstein's commitment to studying the development of children's memory are woven throughout this volume. Even within this single chapter, this commitment is manifested in a methodological approach that marries longitudinal and experimental designs, a theoretical foundation that merges an information-processing approach with social-constructivist perspectives, and a dedication to memory research beyond the laboratory and into applied settings (e.g., Ornstein & Haden, 2001a; Ornstein, Haden, & San Souci, 2008). To be sure, Ornstein's body of work demonstrates an impressive and uniquely informative arc. The focus of this chapter is on a description of children's developing event-memory skills across a selection of verbal tasks and over time, with particular emphasis on characterizing the social-communicative "milieu" in which children are embedded – represented here in parent–child conversations about the present and past (Boland, Haden, & Ornstein, 2003; Haden & Ornstein, 2009; Haden et al., 2001; Haden & Ornstein, 2009; Haden et al., 2009; Hedrick, Haden, & Ornstein, 2009; Hedrick, San Souci et al., 2009; Ornstein, Haden, & Elischberger, 2006; Ornstein, Haden, & Hedrick, 2004). Much of this work was developed and carried out in collaboration with Catherine Haden (see Haden, Acosta, & Pagano, Chapter 12, for more recent developments), and this selective overview represents a program of research focused on describing children's developing skills in mother–child conversations about the past and during their recall of novel "staged" events.

## Mother–Child Conversations about the Past and Present

The extant literature is rich with research conducted over the past few decades that has established the progression of children's emerging autobiographical skills across the early years of life, including investigations that have identified the importance of socialization in supporting the development of such skills (Fivush & Nelson, 2004; Nelson, 2003; Ornstein et al., 2004; Reese & Farrant, 2003). As children become increasingly facile users of language across early childhood, they engage in interactions with others that help to shape *what* and *how* they remember. To be sure, social exchanges can serve to focus children's attention on important elements of experiences or highlight event components that may be culturally appropriate to remember (Nelson, 2003). Importantly, these behavioral interactions can occur at all stages of information processing. Research on children's memories for personal experiences has demonstrated clearly that both endogenous and exogenous factors shape children's retention of event information, and that these factors may be implicated during the *encoding* of events, while event information is *stored*, and during *retrieval* and *reporting* processes (Ornstein, Baker-Ward et al., 1997; Ornstein et al., 2004). In alignment with much of Ornstein's work across his expansive career, this chapter focuses on a program of research that is rooted within a theoretical framework reflective of both information-processing and social-constructivist perspectives (Ornstein & Haden, 2001a; Ornstein et al., 2004).

Research on mother–child reminiscing about the past, during which children have the opportunity to retrieve and recollect information about prior experiences, has demonstrated robust connections between maternal elaborative style and a host of children's cognitive, academic, and socio-emotional outcomes (see Fivush, Haden, & Reese, 2006, for a review; Salmon & Reese, 2016). Mothers who use a high-elaborative reminiscing style tend to ask more open-ended questions, provide more new information, and evaluate more positively their children's active participation in conversations about the past than mothers who use a low-elaborative style when reminiscing with their children, who instead often repeat queries or persist in a focus on the same information without adding additional details or descriptions (Fivush & Fromhoff, 1988; Reese & Fivush, 1993; Reese, Haden, & Fivush, 1993). Maternal reminiscing styles appear to be stable, as mothers demonstrate consistent use of high- or low-elaborative styles over time and even across children (Haden, 1998). Critically, maternal elaborative style is related directly to the development of children's autobiographical memory, with children of high-elaborative mothers able to remember more detailed and coherent narratives than children of low-elaborative mothers (e.g., Reese et al., 1993). Although most reminiscing research has been naturalistic and correlational in nature, some investigations have established causal connections between elaborative reminiscing style and children's subsequent language and narrative skills (Peterson, Jesso, & McCabe, 1999; Reese & Newcombe, 2007; Van Bergen et al., 2009).

In conjunction with the existing literature on the reminiscing context, an additional and related body of work has explored the extent to which conversations about the present – or during the encoding of event information – may scaffold children's understanding of novel experiences and thus support their subsequent remembering of events (Boland et al., 2003; Haden, 2003; Haden et al., 2001; Hedrick, Haden, & Ornstein, 2009; Hedrick, San Souci, et al., 2009; McGuigan & Salmon, 2006; Ornstein et al., 2004; Tessler & Nelson, 1994). To be sure, children's understanding of an experience, particularly an unfamiliar one, at the time of encoding may be influenced by their interactions with others. Further, children's understanding of a novel experience at the time of encoding may help to create a more detailed and durable event representation that, in turn, yields greater access to the memory during retrieval processes (Baker-Ward, Ornstein, & Principe, 1997; Ornstein et al., 2004). Although studies that investigate communicative exchanges during events and the effect they have on remembering have comprised a much smaller corpus of work than those that focus on reminiscing about the past, this research on what happens during children's experiences is nonetheless critical to understanding children's developing event-memory skills.

In addition to an approach that examines interactions in discussions about both the present and past, Ornstein and Haden's research also reflects a commitment to employ multiple methods to study the development of children's memory (2001a; updated in Chapter 3 by Haden). Although cross-sectional research highlights age-related changes in skills, longitudinal research remains the necessary standard by which intra-individual growth can be charted. In spite of being routinely recognized as fundamental to studying the development of memory, the challenges of longitudinal research can be prohibitive and require a keen and intentional investment of time and resources (both financial and human). Importantly, however, naturalistic longitudinal designs address descriptive and correlational claims. To demonstrate causal claims, researchers must exert control via experimental manipulation. Ornstein and Haden's approach to developmental inquiry is one that includes research on intra-individual change over time, coupled with experimental designs whereby factors identified as related in longitudinal investigations may then be brought under control so that causal mechanisms can be identified.

The selective overview that follows is a summary of the ways in which adult–child conversations about the past and present have been investigated by Ornstein, Haden, and their colleagues within a series of studies using longitudinal and experimental methods. Importantly, this program of research both replicates and extends some of the findings on reminiscing and interactions during events in the existing literature. Specifically, the research highlighted in this overview includes a small-scale longitudinal study that served as a pilot project for a larger-scale, multi-site longitudinal examination of children's memory, with two experimental studies that clarified the causal connection between children's exposure to elaborative language, during and after events, and their subsequent remembering. As such, the contributions of Ornstein's work during this particular period of his career include an assessment of *what* developmental changes occur in children's verbal event-memory reports over time and *how* these changes are influenced by conversations with others about the present and past.

## The Pilot Project

Building on research by Tessler and Nelson (1994) that determined the important role of joint attention and engagement in young children's memory for a museum experience, Haden et al. (2001) investigated children's memory for unique, "specially constructed staged events" in a small-scale longitudinal study. Twenty-one mother–child dyads were recruited when children were 30 months old and seen at two additional time points (36 and 42 months) in their homes across the next year.

At all three time points, children and their mothers took part in a host of assessments across three separate visits. During the first visits of each phase, mother–child assessments involved participation in specially constructed and staged events, which included a pretend camping trip (30 months), a birdwatching adventure (36 months), and the opening of an ice-cream shop (42 months). Children also engaged in interviews with researchers about the joint activities. All tasks were audio- and video-recorded for subsequent coding, scoring, and analysis.

To illustrate the staged events, consider the pretend camping trip (used across much of the research reviewed in this chapter; see Table 11.1 for a list of all specially constructed events created by Ornstein and Haden and used across studies). The event had three sections, such that mother–child dyads first prepared for their trip by packing up backpacks with pretend food (e.g., hamburgers, buns, lettuce), then made their way along the path to the fishing pond where they used toy fishing rods to catch fish before hiking on to their campsite, replete with a picnic area and toy grill.

Table 11.1. *Specially constructed staged events used across studies and child ages*

| Study | Child ages across events | | | | |
| --- | --- | --- | --- | --- | --- |
| | Camping Trip | Birdwatching | Ice-Cream Shop | Pirate Adventure | Archeological Dig |
| The "Pilot" Project (Haden et al., 2001) | 30 months | 36 months | 42 months | – | – |
| Developmental Pathways to Skilled Remembering (Hedrick, San Souci et al., 2009) | 36 and 42 months | 36 and 42 months | – | 54 and 60 months | 54 and 60 months |
| Experimental Training Study (Boland et al., 2003) | 46 months | – | – | – | – |
| Experimental Timing Study (Hedrick, Haden, & Ornstein, 2009) | 43 months | – | – | – | – |

Researchers introduced the mother–child dyads to the activity by stating the specific event (e.g., "Now you can go on a camping trip.") and providing a basic set of instructions for the experience (e.g., "After packing up, we would like you to hike to the fishing pond."). Importantly, mothers were not instructed to engage or talk with their children in any particular way. Because all interactions were video-recorded, accurate records of the ways in which mothers and children interacted with the features and each other were preserved, which allowed for a detailed assessment of their verbal and nonverbal engagement during each of the experiences.

To examine dyadic engagement during the events, Haden et al. (2001) coded the extent to which mothers and children independently and jointly engaged with each component feature. Engagement was further character-ized according to whether it was verbal (e.g., requesting a feature label, or providing elaborative details about the feature – such as "This fish is red.") or nonverbal (e.g., pointing, manipulating, or enacting a component of the event – such as placing a hamburger patty on a bun). A sample application of this coding system is provided in Haden et al. (2001, p. 1020):

MOTHER:   "Look. It's a fish" (*Mother Verbal* – fish)
ACTION:   Mother moves the big fish as if swimming (*Mother Nonverbal* – fish)
CHILD:    "Catch the big fish." (*Child Verbal* – fish)
ACTION:   Child "catches" the big fish. (*Child Nonverbal* – fish)

Thus, for each feature of the events with which mothers and children engaged, codes reflect the extent to which the dyadic interaction centered on that feature was individual or joint, as well as verbal or nonverbal.

At each time point, children's recall of the events was assessed in an interview with an examiner using a hierarchically structured protocol modeled after those used in prior research on children's memory for personally expe-rienced events (Baker-Ward, Gordon et al., 1993). Event-memory reports were solicited during second and third visits at each phase of the study. Hierarchically structured, or funnel, interviews used to assess children's remembering began with general open-ended questions (e.g., "Tell me about the camping trip that you had with your mom."), followed by specific open-ended prompts (e.g., "What kind of food did you pack up?"), and then yes/no questions about features of the event (e.g., "Did you have hot dogs?").

Children's recall in response to open-ended questions and prompts was scored according to the frequency of specific features they provided (i.e., Present Feature named). In addition, children's provision of additional details about the features (e.g., "The grill was hot!") and the event in general (e.g., "We had a picnic.") were coded as Extra Event Comments.

Results demonstrated that across all three time points, many of the feature interactions were coded as "joint nonverbal" engagement, in which the mothers and children jointly handled most of the present features. Moreover, when verbal engagement was recorded, most of it reflected either joint talk between mothers and children or mother-only talk, with child-only talk about features relatively rare across all three of the time points. Children's memory for the events indicated age-related changes in the percentage of features recalled during the interviews, with children recalling a greater percentage of features of the ice-cream shop event at the 42-month time point than of the birdwatching adventure when they were 36 months old. Recall of features was lowest for the camping trip at the 30-month time point. This same pattern held true for additional event details, as children provided more extra event comments during interviews about the ice-cream shop than the birdwatching adventure or the camping trip. Further, recall of both feature labels and elaborative event details decreased across the 3-week-delay intervals at all three time points. Of course, primary analyses focused on linking mother–child engagement during the events to children's subsequent recall of the experiences. At each time point, mother–child engagement during the events was associated with children's remembering, such that children were more likely to recall features of the event if the feature had been jointly discussed by the mother and child.

The findings of this study indicated that young children's recall of novel events was associated with the conversations they had with their mothers while the events occurred. This work is consistent with the view that children's understanding of an unfamiliar experience at the time of encoding may be influenced by social-communicative exchanges with others. This deeper understanding of the experience may, in turn, lead to a more elaborated and detailed remembering of the event.

The contributions of this work notwithstanding, there were a few limitations. Given that each event was included at only one time point, the effects of age on children's recall could have been due to event differences. In addition, Haden et al. (2001) emphasized the need for future research to include more microanalytic analyses of verbal communicative exchanges to investigate more fully the richness of mother–child talk about the present. A fine-grained analysis of mother–child discourse would elucidate the specific ways in which particular patterns of dialogue link to children's remembering. Their next longitudinal investigation took these considerations into account.

## Developmental Pathways to Skilled Remembering

Following the pilot project, Ornstein and Haden designed and directed a longitudinal inquiry into children's developing memory skills, described as the Developmental Pathways to Skilled Remembering project. Using a cohort-sequential design that spanned toddlerhood through early childhood, this project included a multi-task battery of language and memory assessments, with particular attention devoted to measurement of the familial linguistic context to which children were exposed.

As outlined in Grammer, Coffman, and Ornstein (2013), the challenging nature of longitudinal designs requires a commitment to best practice in using these methods. Some specific strategies include a precise selection of sampling and design techniques (e.g., preparing for and managing issues of attrition), forging positive relationships with participants to best support the time- and labor-intensive nature of the work, and building and sustaining well-trained teams of research staff. Ornstein and Haden attended to these elements in their design, implementation, and management of this project.

The initial sample included 121 families from in and around Chicago/Evanston, IL, and Chapel Hill/Durham, NC, recruited when target children were 18 and 36 months of age (Cohorts 1 and 2, respectively). Children in Cohort 1 were seen at 18, 24, 30, 36, 42, 54, and 60 months of age, whereas those in Cohort 2 participated at 36, 42, 54, 60, and 72 months. This overlapping cohort-sequential design afforded an examination of children's early expressions of nonverbal memory to their later engagement in language-based assessments of event and strategic remembering, and capitalized on a developmental period of particular importance when children demonstrate increasing linguistic competencies around the third year of age (e.g., Nelson, 2003). Further, this design reflected a strategic intent to minimize the impact of participant loss and maintain a robust sample, particularly at overlapping age points. To be sure, the overall attrition rate across both research sites was fairly low, with only 9% ($N$ = 11) of the families who originally enrolled in the study lost to attrition. The final sample yielded 53 children in Cohort 1 and 57 children in Cohort 2.

Approaches to fostering ongoing engagement in longitudinal studies include the development of strong relationships with participants, rooted in trust and cooperation, and the provision of appropriate support and incentive to participate (Cairns & Cairns, 2002; Grammer, Coffman, & Ornstein, 2013). To build those important relationships, steps were taken to provide consistency of interaction with specific research assistants for each family, such that every child was informally assigned a "lead" researcher to carry out as many of the visits as possible. This simple practice allowed for families to connect with familiar members of the research team and for research staff to demonstrate authentic interest in the children with whom they engaged, year after year. This practice was enabled further by a well-trained and collaborative team of research staff. At the culmination of each phase of data collection (i.e. at the third visit of each of the time points), children were provided with appropriate gifts, such as T-shirts and coloring picture frames with the study logo. Across the years, annual holiday cards with images of the research team and expressions of well-wishes were also provided to families. These small incentives served to demonstrate appreciation for the children and their families, and also connected them to the larger project and community in which their individual participation was embedded. Indeed, it is not unusual for a family to reach out to a member of the research team to say hello and provide an update even now – when former participants of the study are in early adulthood (personal communication)!

In this Pathways project, children and their mothers were seen in their homes every six months, with three separate visits at each phase of data collection. Visits typically lasted about an hour to 90-minutes, during which time children participated in a range of memory and language tasks. Although the project addressed multiple questions regarding the development of children's varied memory skills over time (e.g., Haden et al., 2010), only selected measures of mother–child interactions during conversations about the present and past, as well as children's verbal event-memory reports, are reviewed in detail here. As with Haden et al. (2001), all assessments were video- and audio-recorded for subsequent coding and analysis.

## Mother–Child Reminiscing

At all time points, mothers and children participated in a reminiscing task. The reminiscing task was designed to assess children's developing autobiographical memory skills and to describe how maternal style linked to children's provision of memory information both concurrently and over time. During the first visit of each phase, mothers identified several jointly experienced events (e.g., an excursion to the beach, a family visit to the zoo) that occurred in the recent past, and that they only experienced once (routine events were excluded). When children were 18 months, mothers selected two events and at all other time points, they identified and selected three events. After mothers selected the events for discussion, they were instructed to talk with their children about those events as they typically would when they engaged in conversations about the past.

The archived records of the memory conversations were subsequently transcribed verbatim from the audio-recordings. Using a coding system adapted from Haden (1998) and Reese et al. (1993), conversations were coded for maternal and child conversational code categories. Conversational codes were exhaustive and mutually exclusive, with every utterance coded by propositional unit (e.g., "We ate cookies and had cake" would be two propositions).

Maternal codes included elaborations, repetitions, and confirmations. Elaborations pertained to questions and statements about the event that requested or provided new information. Repetitions included mothers' questions or comments that repeated event information. Both elaborations and repetitions were categorized further as open-ended *Wh*-questions, yes/ no questions, or statements. Confirmations reflected mothers' affirmations of the child's prior utterance. Child codes included the use of memory elaborations (the provision of new information) and placeholders (comments that describe a conversational turn without the provision of new event information, such as a child stating, "I don't know"). Additional codes were employed to capture every utterance in the memory conversations (e.g., associative talk that connects the event under discussion to other events or the child's prior knowledge, clarification questions, etc.) but were not included in subsequent analyses highlighted in this review. Mean frequencies of each conversational code per event were calculated.

To illustrate one way in which data from this task were analyzed, Haden et al. (2009) focused on a selection of data from the younger cohort (Cohort 1; 56 dyads with no missing data) when children were 18, 24, and 30 months old. These early time points reflect some of the earliest conversations children had with their mothers about the past. Data from these phases also align with and complement some of the prior longitudinal investigations into mother–child reminiscing that span younger ages (e.g., Farrant & Reese, 2000; Reese et al., 1993). Again, this prior research demonstrated not only that mothers are consistent in their elaborative approaches to reminiscing over time but also that marked differences in reminiscing style are concurrently and longitudinally related to children's provision of memory information. For example, Harley and Reese (1999) measured maternal reminiscing style when children were 19 months old and found that maternal style predicted children's memory recall when they were 32 months of age, above and beyond children's language and nonverbal memory skills. Specifically, children of mothers who were classified as using a high-elaborative reminiscing style recalled more event information than children of mothers who used a low-elaborative style.

These robust findings notwithstanding, there are some differences in the ways in which reminiscing styles have been measured across studies in the broad literature. Some researchers have dichotomized the variable to reflect two groups of mothers who vary according to high and low elaborativeness, based on maternal ratio scores of elaborations to repetitions (e.g., Harley & Reese, 1999; Reese et al., 1993). Other researchers have focused instead on the specific forms of elaborative conversational strategies that mothers use. Open-ended *Wh*-questions (i.e., those questions that ask "who, what, where, why, or how"), in particular, may be an important element of elaborative style, as these questions request and require a specific response from the child that yes/no questions and statements do not. To be sure, Farrant and Reese (2000) found that mothers' elaborative *Wh*-questions were predictive of children's subsequent memory reports, whereas elaborative yes/no questions and statements were not.

Haden et al. (2009) expanded on the prior reminiscing research with a focus on mothers' use of elaborative open-ended questions and statements, specifically. By analyzing the frequency of these two conversational codes used by mothers when reminiscing with their children when they were 18 months old, two distinct groups were created. Mothers who had a *high-eliciting* style asked as many or more elaborative *Wh*-questions relative to their use of statement elaborations, whereas mothers in the *low-eliciting* group provided fewer elaborative *Wh*-questions and more statement elaborations. Following a meaningful characterization of maternal style, analyses focused on describing how mother–child contributions to the memory conversations changed over time and, importantly, linked children's later abilities in reminiscing to their mothers' early eliciting style.

Findings indicated a dramatic increase in children's participation in the conversations, as average frequency scores for memory elaborations increased from 18 to 24 months and doubled from 24 to 30 months of age. At 18 months, children provided very little by way of memory information. In contrast, mothers provided much of the content of these early memory conversations, and all mothers increased in their use of elaborative *Wh*-questions across time points (a finding consistent with prior research on early reminiscing). Importantly, even with this overall increase in use of questions, stylistic differences between the two groups of mothers were consistent. Specifically, mothers in the high-eliciting conversational style group (designated at 18 months) continued to use more questions relative to statements than mothers in the low-eliciting group at each of the later time points.

Linkages between mother–child talk were evident at each time point concurrently, with mothers' elaborative *Wh*- and yes/no questions, as well as their use of confirmations, associated with children's provision of memory information. Further, longitudinal linkages were also discovered and bidirectional relations between children's memory elaborations and their mothers' elaborative questions and confirmations were found at the later time points. Notably, this bidirectionality was not evident for maternal elaborative statements and children's recall. Thus, this research served to extend prior work on early reminiscing by identifying that some elements of elaborative style – particularly open-ended *Wh*-questions – may be uniquely positioned to facilitate children's early reminiscing skills.

### Conversations during Events and Children's Remembering

In addition to mother–child reminiscing, each participating dyad in the Developmental Pathways to Skilled Remembering project was also invited to take part in a novel, staged event (developed by Haden et al., 2001). These unique tasks afforded insight into the ways in which mothers and children engaged in dialogue while events were ongoing and how these interactions linked to children's remembering of the experiences. In this investigation, events included the same camping trip and birdwatching adventure used in the pilot project (counterbalanced across the 36- and 42-month time points in this study), as well as an archeological dig and pirate adventure (counterbalanced across the 54- and 60-month time points). At each time point, mother–child dyads participated in the events during the first visit, and children's recall for the experiences was solicited with the same funnel-interview protocol used in the pilot project during the second and third visits (following delay intervals of 1 day and 3 weeks).

Building on the first event coding scheme used by Haden et al. (2001), conversational codes that categorized each mother–child utterance were developed to capture a detailed account of mother–child conversations during events. Similar to the coding of reminiscing, maternal utterances included open-ended *Wh*-questions, yes/no questions, statements, evaluations, and associations. Questions and statements were further categorized as elaborative (providing or requesting new information) or repetitive. Children's participation in the conversations was coded according to the ways in which they responded to maternal queries, as well as their provision of statements and questions. This exhaustive coding system allowed for analyses of contingent response patterns. For example, consider that when mothers asked a *Wh*-question, children could respond in a number of ways. Specifically, they could provide any one of the following: a relevant response to the question (coded as either correct or incorrect based on accuracy of response), a placeholder in which they took a conversational turn without providing event information (e.g., "I don't know"), an unclassifiable response in which the coder couldn't reliably determine the child's utterance, or no response at all.

Children's memory reports were coded according to the same scheme as the pilot project. Thus, their memory for the events was scored to include their provision of feature labels in response to open-ended interview questions, as well as the additional elaborative details provided about the component features and the event in general (event elaborations).

Given that earlier research on event talk demonstrated the importance of joint verbal engagement (Haden et al., 2001), in addition to the research on reminiscing that identified the unique importance of mothers' use of elaborative *Wh*-questions (Haden et al., 2009), one approach to an analysis of mother–child discourse during events is exhibited in Hedrick, San Souci, et al. (2009). Data from the overlapping cohorts at two time points when children were 36 and 42 months old were used. Of the full sample of 110 families, 89 mother–child dyads had complete data for all relevant tasks and were included in subsequent analyses. The joint verbal interaction between the dyad was the unit of analysis in this paper, and in addition to the standard frequency counts of conversational codes used during the events, conditional probabilities that focused on children's patterns of responses to mothers' elaborative *Wh*-questions were calculated. Specifically, sequential analyses of mother–child response patterns yielded proportion scores for each dyad. These scores reflected the proportions of each child's responses to maternal elaborative *Wh*-questions across the five response options (correct response, incorrect response, placeholder, no response, and unclassifiable).

Examination of the mother–child response patterns indicated that although children frequently provided a correct response to maternal open-ended questions (roughly half the time at both the 36- and 42-month age points), it was also common for children not to respond to their mothers' queries (for example, just under one quarter of the time at 36 months). Thus, it was determined that meaningful groups of mother–child dyads could be created at the initial time point when children were 36 months of age, based on the proportion of time that children correctly responded, and did not respond, to their mothers' *Wh*-questions. One group of dyads, labeled as *high joint talk*, demonstrated a relatively high proportion of child correct responses coupled with a low proportion of no responses to mothers' open-ended questions. The other group of dyads was identified as *low joint talk,* and this group was composed of pairs who had a relatively low proportion of child correct responses and a high proportion of no responses to maternal elaborative queries. Further analysis of mother–child engagement during the events indicated that although the proportion scores shifted across the 36- and 42-month age points, such that all pairs increased in children's correct responses and decreased in their lack of responses, the two groups of mother–child pairs remained distinct in their use of these response patterns at the later time point.

Importantly, it was determined that mother–child interactions during the events were linked to children's recall of the experiences. Specifically, children who were part of the high-joint-talk group recalled more features, and event elaborations, than did children who were part of the low-joint-talk group at each time point. Additional analyses examined longitudinal linkages and used dyadic classification at 36 months to predict children's recall of the event at 42 months. Although the effect of joint talk on children's provision of feature labels weakened when controlling for feature recall at 36 months, the effect of joint talk on children's provision of additional details (event elaborations) persisted. This finding revealed a long-term effect of children's participation in high joint talk at 36 months on their provision of elaborated details of a different event at 42 months. Thus, it may be useful to consider not only mothers' use of elaborative *Wh*-questions during parent–child interactions but also the extent to which children respond to such queries.

The Pathways project served not only to corroborate earlier research on reminiscing and during-event talk but also to extend and add to those bodies of work by highlighting specific forms of conversational exchanges that support children's remembering and reporting of event information. Although these longitudinal analyses of early reminiscing and novel event memory yield important contributions to the extant literature, the results remain contextualized within a correlational framework and, as such, leave room for the establishment of clear causal linkages between parent–child interactions and children's memory reports.

### Experimental Manipulations: Determining Causal Connections

While the Developmental Pathways to Skilled Remembering project was ongoing, two ancillary experimental projects were developed to answer questions about the causal connections between conversational exchanges and children's memory reports. The first, carried out by Boland, Haden, and Ornstein (2003; recipient of the Best Article of the Year award in the *Journal of Cognition and Development*), was a simple experiment focused on training mothers to use an elaborative conversational style while engaging in the camping trip with their children. The sample included 39 preschool children (mean age = 46.82 months) and their mothers recruited from in and around Chicago, IL.

Given that prior research reported contradictory findings regarding the link between children's measures of language abilities and their contributions to conversations about the past (e.g., Farrant & Reese, 2000; Reese & Fivush, 1993), the first part of the experimental design included pretest assessments of children's receptive and expressive language (using the Preschool Language Scale-3; Zimmerman, Steiner, & Pond, 1992) and event-memory skills, which yielded groups of children with high- and low-language abilities. Children were then matched on language skills, gender, and maternal education before random assignment to maternal training or control conditions. Half of the mothers were trained to use elaborative conversational techniques during their participation in the camping trip, whereas mothers in the control condition received no training prior to the event engagement. Children were subsequently interviewed about the camping trip, after 1-day- and 3-week-delay intervals, using the same hierarchically structured protocol employed in the prior research.

The key experimental manipulation in this study involved the instructions provided to mothers prior to participation in the camping trip. Specifically, mothers in the no-training condition received no instruction, while mothers in the experimental-training condition received direct instruction in the use of four elaborative conversational strategies. Training included review of a brief pamphlet roughly 1 week prior to the event, with mothers instructed to read the pamphlet twice before the first home visit. Then, at the start of the first visit, mothers watched a video that highlighted snippets of conversations between mothers and children playing with a medical kit or toolbox. These conversations were illustrative of four elaborative techniques, including the use of *open-ended Wh-questions* that ask the child to provide information, *associations* that bridge connections between the current event and the child's prior experiences or knowledge, *follow-ins* that allow the child to direct engagement, and *positive evaluations* of the child's verbal contributions to the conversation.

All mothers and children took part in the camping event during the first home visit, with mothers in the no-training condition told to interact with their children as they typically would, while mothers in the training condition were told to incorporate the four conversational strategies into their discussions with their children during the event. The second and third home visits included children's participation in the memory interviews with the researcher. As with the prior research, all sessions were recorded for further coding and analysis.

Maternal engagement during the event was coded using a scheme adapted from Haden et al. (2001) and similar to that used by Hedrick, San Souci et al. (2009). Maternal coding categories were mutually exclusive and reflected each of the four elaborative training techniques as well as other conversational behaviors, such as yes/no questions, statements, and repetitions. In contrast to both Haden et al. (2001) and Hedrick, San Souci et al. (2009), children's participation in the event was not coded. However, their recall in the memory interviews was scored, yielding the same frequency scores for feature labels and event elaborations used in the prior studies.

Findings indicated that training mothers to use an elaborative conversational style while participating in events with their children was effective. Mothers who received training used significantly more of the four specified techniques than mothers who did not receive training. Training effects were consistent across children's language skills, such that trained mothers used the techniques similarly with children who had low- and high-language scores. Furthermore, the effect of training extended to children's memory for the event, such that children of trained mothers recalled more event elaborations than did children of untrained mothers. The effects were less robust for feature labels, which indicates that elaborative language may serve to boost remembering for elaborated and embellished details of the event as opposed to simple feature naming.

The second experimental project carried out during this time was designed to examine the role of children's exposure to elaborative language during and after an event (Hedrick, Haden, & Ornstein, 2009; recognized as the Best Article of the Year in the *Journal of Cognition and Development*). In contrast to the other studies, this is the only one that did not include mother–child engagement and instead focused on children's participation in the camping trip with a female researcher. Other research using "staged" events has identified causal connections between children's exposure to elaborative language before, during, or after an event (e.g., McGuigan & Salmon, 2004), but none had examined the potentially cumulative effect of opportunities to engage in elaborative conversations. As such, this study used a factorial experimental design to tease apart the effects of children's exposure to elaborative language during *and* after an event. Sixty children (mean age = 4 years, 1 month) were recruited from preschools in Illinois, North Carolina, and Virginia.

The procedure included three separate visits with researchers that occurred in quiet areas of the children's schools. The children were assigned randomly to one of four conditions that varied with regard to their exposure to high- or low-elaborative language during and after the camping trip. Specially constructed scripts were developed for use in the camping trip during the first visit, as well as a "memory conversation" with an unfamiliar researcher that occurred during the second visit, which occurred approximately 1 day after the first. Finally, children's memory for the events was elicited 3 weeks after the event, using the same hierarchically structured interview protocol used in each of the prior studies (Boland et al., 2003; Haden et al., 2001; Hedrick, San Souci et al., 2009).

The use of scripts afforded a high level of control over the language that children were exposed to while they engaged in the camping event with one female researcher and while they participated in the memory conversation with a different female researcher one day later. Scripts were constructed using an item-analysis of features typically recalled among a different sample of children (half of the Pathways sample of children who participated in the camping trip with their mothers when they were 36 months old; see Ornstein et al., 2004). Half of the total features of the camping trip were selected to represent features that were typically recalled (such as the backpacks and fish) and features that were less often recalled (such as the map and canteens). These features were included in scripts that varied according to the elaborative details provided by the researchers during the event and the subsequent "conversation." For example, children in the elaborative during-event talk condition were asked the following open-ended questions about the fish: 1) "What are these things in the pond?" 2) "How many fish are there?" and 3) "What color are the fish?" In contrast, children in the "informationally empty" event talk condition were exposed to these comments about the fish: 1) "What are these?" 2) "How neat, can you get one?" and 3) "I like fish." Importantly, children were exposed to the same amount of talk about each feature, but language varied with regard to how rich and elaborated it was.

Children's recall for the event was assessed in the memory conversation and the standardized memory interview. Both tasks were scored in accordance with the same systems as those used in the prior studies. However, there was a specific focus on children's comments in response to the

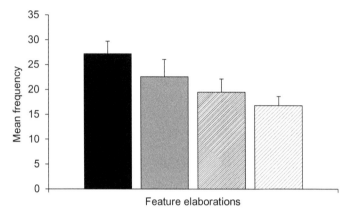

Figure 11.1 Mean feature elaborations (+*SE*) by group during the standard 3-week-delay interview.

From Hedrick, Haden, & Ornstein (2009). Copyright © 2009 by Taylor & Francis Group. Reprinted by permission.

open-ended questions and prompts categorized as the frequency of features recalled and the number of specific details about the features, or *feature* elaborations.

Results indicated a robust effect of the post-event talk during the memory conversation, such that children who were exposed to elaborative language during this conversation recalled significantly more features and feature details than children who were not exposed to elaborated talk during this assessment. Of particular interest, of course, is children's recall during the standardized memory interview after the 3-week delay. Findings indicated significant effects of during-event talk on children's recall, such that children who were exposed to elaborative language during the camping event recalled more features and feature elaborations than children who were not exposed to elaborative language during the event. Although interaction effects were not detected in the initial analysis, follow-up trend analyses were carried out to fit polynomial functions to the data. These focused contrasts suggest that the effects of exposure to elaborative language during the event were strongest when paired with exposure to elaborative language during the post-event conversation. This finding is highlighted in Figure 11.1, which displays the differences in children's feature elaborations during the memory interview as a function of experimental condition. As such, it may be that the impact of elaborative language is cumulative, with benefits detected not just at the time of encoding (or primarily during post-event talk, as was found by McGuigan & Salmon, 2004) but also with additional opportunities to retrieve information in an elaborative context.

## Conclusion

As evidenced throughout this volume, Peter Ornstein's contributions to and advancement of the broad field of memory science are noteworthy. This chapter emphasized Ornstein's commitment to studying the development of children's event memory within the family context. This selective review of his work highlights the ways in which his collaborative efforts with Catherine Haden adhered to their call to employ both naturalistic, longitudinal assessments of children's developing skills within a sociolinguistic context and experimental designs to identify whether connections between elaborative style and children's remembering are causal in nature (e.g., Ornstein & Haden, 2001a; revisited in Haden, Chapter 3).

Their work has both replicated and extended what is known about children's exposure to elaborative-style language and their subsequent event-memory skills. Critically, they have done so by not only demonstrating that maternal elaborative style is a mechanism for change in children's event memory but also refining the ways in which elaborative style is characterized. To be sure, their collective studies that investigate mother–child conversations about the present and past highlight that specific forms of elaborative language, including mothers' use of elaborative open-ended *Wh*-questions (and how children respond to them), may be particularly important for scaffolding children's understanding and subsequent remembering. This research has helped pave the way for applications to other settings, such as Haden and colleagues' investigations in museums and the ways in which adult–child conversations serve to support children's STEM learning (see Haden, Acosta, & Pagano, Chapter 12), as well as inquiries into how reminiscing can support the socialization of specific social-emotional outcomes, such as gratitude (see Langley, Coffman, & Hussong, Chapter 13). As such, Ornstein's contributions to understanding the family socialization of memory continue to set the stage for longitudinal and experimental inquiries across settings and developmental foci.

# Making Memories in Museums

Catherine A. Haden, Diana I. Acosta, and Lauren C. Pagano

The autobiographical memory stories of practicing scientists and engineers frequently refer to early experiences outside of school in museums, libraries, and at home as contributing in important ways to the developmental paths to their careers (Crowley et al., 2015; Jones, Taylor, & Forrester, 2011). A great deal of science and engineering learning takes place in such settings, collectively referred to as *informal learning environments.* Moreover, one of the strongest themes in a number of recent reports is that engaging and meaningful early experiences with science, technology, engineering, and mathematics (STEM) in early childhood can pay large dividends in terms of interest, relevant knowledge, and motivation for future STEM learning (Hurst et al., 2019; National Research Council [NRC], 2009, 2015). Research confirms the potentially formative or transformative role of early informal STEM learning in advancing skills and interests that eventually may lead to STEM educational and career pursuits. For example, children who spend time in STEM-related museum exhibits tend to show more interest in STEM, do better in STEM-related classes in school, and express more interest in STEM careers (NRC, 2009, 2015). It is also clear that family interactions in informal learning environments can boost children's future STEM achievement (Duncan et al., 2007; NRC, 2009; Haden et al., 2016).

Given that for young children, learning in informal settings is frequently social, our goal has been to elucidate and test whether and how the ways that children interact with their parents and caregivers can benefit children's informal learning. In this chapter, we describe our work conducted in a natural history museum and a children's museum in which we focus on how parent–child conversations during and after hands-on exhibit

Preparation of this chapter was supported in part by the National Science Foundation under Grant No. 1516541. Any opinions, findings, and conclusions or recommendations expressed in this material are those of the authors and do not necessarily reflect the views of the National Science Foundation.

experiences can advance children's learning and retention of information about cultural practices, and science and engineering. The work draws on research guided by sociocultural theory (Rogoff, 1990; Vygotsky, 1978) from two partially intersecting literatures. One body of work, concerned with children's memory development and including work by Peter Ornstein and his colleagues, demonstrates that parent–child conversational interactions during *and* after events can play crucial roles in children's understanding and remembering of their experiences (Fivush, Haden, & Reese, 2006; Haden, 2014; Ornstein, Haden, & Hedrick, 2004; see also Hedrick, Chapter 11). The other, focused on learning during family museum visits, points to particular forms of conversations during exhibit experiences that may be especially important for STEM learning in museums (e.g., Callanan et al., 2017; Crowley et al., 2001; Haden, 2010; Leinhardt, Crowley, & Knutson, 2002). Unique partnerships between university researchers and museum practitioners make our work possible (Haden et al., 2016). As we seek to contribute to the cognitive development literature, we also aim to identify evidence-based practices museums can use to facilitate early learning opportunities for young children and their families.

## Learning through Conversation during and after Hands-On Experiences

Experiences in museums can be key to children's developing interests and understanding of STEM, as well as other topics. One important source of learning in museums is children's direct experience interacting with objects (Leinhardt et al., 2002; Paris & Hapgood, 2002). Another is social-communicative interactions with others (Haden, 2010). Especially for young children, learning from direct experience and learning from others often are intertwined (Jant et al., 2014; NRC, 2009).

### *Learning from Hands-On Activities*

The idea that young children learn best through direct experience inter-acting with objects is one of the oldest and most consistently applied ideas in developmental psychology and education. It reflects a key tenet of Piaget's theories – that early representations of knowledge emerge from and are tied to actions (Piaget, 1970). Likewise, Bruner (1996) suggested that young children's mental representations of knowledge are first based on actions and then on mental images of those actions. More recently, work on embodied cognition has underscored the importance of physical actions for learning and representation (Glenberg, Brown, & Levin, 2007; Lakoff & Núñez, 2000). The emphasis on children's learning from direct experience with objects is also manifest in the design of school-based and informal STEM educational experiences for children. Indeed, in children's museums, many exhibits feature activities that encourage hands-on engagement with objects to enhance learning (Leinhardt et al., 2002; Paris & Hapgood, 2002). For example, while engaging with plastic materials – such as girders, beams, triangular braces, nuts, and bolts in a skyscraper-building exhibit – children can learn about ways to support their structure to keep it from toppling over. Physical engagement with objects is typical during early STEM activities, with the thought that such activity can facilitate interest and provide real-world grounding for the emergence of scientific, mathematical, and other knowledge.

Although children can learn a great deal on their own from direct experience with objects, their conversations with parents and others may determine whether children will be able to recall and use what they learn from hands-on interactions with objects in museum exhibits (Haden, 2010; Jant et al., 2014). Conversations with others about hands-on activities can support understanding of experiences and the representation of knowledge in a manner that makes it portable and applicable across contexts over time. Whereas hands-on activities in museums can capture children's attention, this alone does not ensure understanding of the underlying ideas and learning. This is because when young children engage in hands-on activities with objects, they typically focus on particular physical characteristics of the objects themselves. However, the ultimate goal is to produce knowledge that is not tied to specific actions, but rather for learning from hands-on activities to transfer to different objects in different contexts over time. What is needed is what Sigel (1993) called *distancing*, and what Goldstone and Sakamoto (2003) called *concreteness fading* – learning to focus less on concrete, action-based knowledge and more on the abstract knowledge or concepts that can facilitate understandings that are transferable across contexts and time.

### Conversations Advance Learning from Hands-On Activities

We suggest that conversations children have with others can meet the challenge of representing and recalling information in a form that will be accessible and usable beyond a hands-on activity (Haden et al., 2016; Jant et al., 2014). The idea draws on research guided by sociocultural theories that emphasize that learning is co-constructed through social and conversational exchanges (e.g., Rogoff, 1990; Vygotsky, 1978). In this section, we consider several different mechanisms through which conversations could influence whether learning through direct experiences with objects is retained, recalled, and transferred.

Research on children's memory for personally experienced events demonstrates substantial linkages between the conversations children have with their parents as events unfold and children's subsequent remembering of these experiences (e.g., Haden et al., 2001; Hedrick, San Souci et al., 2009; McGuigan & Salmon, 2006; Tessler & Nelson, 1994). Tessler and Nelson (1994) found that 3-year-old children observed as they visited a museum with their mothers later only recalled the objects the mother and child jointly talked about during the experience. Similarly, Haden et al. (2001) conducted a longitudinal investigation involving observations of parent–child conversations during three staged events (e.g., a camping event) in families' living rooms when the children were 2.5, 3, and 3.5 years old. At each age, objects (e.g., the plastic fish in the camping event) the mother and child jointly handled and jointly discussed were subsequently better recalled than those jointly handled but talked about only by the mother or only by the child, which were better recalled than those jointly handled but not discussed at all. These findings are consistent with the view advanced by Haden, Ornstein, and colleagues (Haden et al., 2001) that conversational interactions as events unfold can facilitate understanding of an experience and serve to enrich and organize the resulting representation, in turn, affecting its accessibility for retrieval over time.

Caregivers and children also engage in reminiscing about shared past experiences, and these conversations shortly after an experience transpires can especially be seen as playing a part in an extended process of family learning (Haden, 2014; Pagano et al., 2019). Whereas conversations during events can facilitate encoding, conversations after events have occurred can support consolidation and retrieval of information. Conversations shortly after hands-on experiences may be especially important for consolidation – the step in the learning process whereby labile and fleeting patterns of experience are strengthened and transformed into long-lasting memory representations (McGaugh, 2000; Wixted, 2004; see also Pagano et al., 2019 for discussion). Moreover, the content of conversations after events can reveal what was understood about an experience, which can be useful to educators, researchers, and parents in their efforts to advance learning opportunities for children (Haden et al., 2016). For example, in Pagano et al. (2019), the reminiscing conversations of families who participated in an engineering-design challenge included more talk about engineering practices, such as planning, brainstorming, testing, and teamwork. This conversation contrasted with the exchanges of families who had visited this same exhibit when the program emphasized tool use with no design challenge, who engaged in more labeling and describing of tools.

### Style and Content of Conversations That Can Support Learning

Research on children's event memory and children's learning in museums converges on a number of conversational techniques that may be especially important in supporting children's understanding of experiences as they unfold. One key technique is the use of open-ended elaborative *Wh-questions*, such as *What, How,* and *Why*. Elaborative *Wh-* questions during or after events can add new information or focus on a new aspect of an experience. These kinds of questions can encourage children to verbalize their understandings and can help parents to diagnose what children need to know more about, such as explanations of why things happen or how things work. Parents' open-ended *Wh-* questions that follow children's hands-on engagement with objects can encourage sustained engagement and learning. If parents' *Wh-* questions are followed by children's responses – such as if a parent asks, "How can we make this stronger?" and the child says, "We need to add a triangle" – this sort of joint talk can also predict learning and subsequent remembering. Overall, as Ornstein and Haden have argued, elaborative conversations involving *Wh-* questions as events unfold can have a profound impact on how young children come to make sense of and represent their experiences (Boland, Haden, & Ornstein, 2003; Haden et al., 2001). Furthermore, *Wh-* questions during reminiscing can advance understanding and the construction of meaningful and comprehensible representations of events, as well as providing practice in reporting past experiences in a detailed manner (Fivush et al., 2006).

In addition to the elaborativeness and jointness of parent–child conversations, it is also important to consider the ways that the content of parent–child conversations can support children's understanding and learning. For example, the explanations parents provide in conversations with young children can scaffold early understanding of science and may predict later skills (Callanan & Jipson, 2001; Crowley et al., 2001; Fender & Crowley, 2007; Tenenbaum et al., 2005). *Associations* that help children to link what is being experienced and what children already know or have experience with may be an especially important form of explanation for children's STEM learning (e.g., Callanan & Jipson, 2001; Palmquist & Crowley, 2007; Tenenbaum & Callanan, 2008). For example, when explaining a zoetrope in a museum, a parent might make the association, "This is how cartoons work" (e.g., Crowley et al., 2001).

Further, regarding the content of talk, research on family conversations in museums suggests that parent–child *STEM talk* during and after events can support STEM learning (Callanan & Jipson, 2001; Crowley et al., 2001; Haden, 2010; Leinhardt et al., 2002; NRC, 2009). STEM talk includes discussion of the scientific method (e.g., planning, defining problems), technology (building materials, building techniques), engineering (placement of pieces, strength, testing), and mathematics (e.g., quantity, height, distance). Prior work suggests that the frequency of specific kinds of language inputs, such as spatial and relations language (Pruden, Levine, & Huttenlocher, 2011), number words (Gunderson & Levine, 2011), and emotional and mental state talk (e.g., Rudek & Haden, 2005), predict children's skills in related domains. By extension, finding ways to increase parents' explanations and STEM talk during and after science and engineering experiences can benefit children's STEM learning from museum experiences.

## Museum Research on Supporting Family Learning Conversations

Museums provide a nearly ideal environment in which to explore children's early learning in the context of hands-on activities and conversations with others. In the following sections we discuss our work in which we focus on the ways parent–child conversations during hands-on activities may be especially important for informal learning in museums during the preschool and early school years. We generally focus on children 3 to 8 years of age, a period when there is measurable growth in both children's STEM skills (NRC, 2009) and their abilities for engaging in conversations and narratives (Ornstein et al., 2004; Reese, Haden, & Fivush, 1993). We address how parent–child conversational interactions during exhibit experiences can affect, influence, or mediate the nature of children's learning in hands-on activities. Moreover, we examine how conversations after exhibit experiences might both add layers of understanding and reveal learning from hands-on activities in museums.

### *Encouraging Parent–Child Elaborative Talk in Museums*

In a series of studies, we encouraged parents' elaborative talk with their children during experiences in museums. More specifically, we designed ways to prompt parents to incorporate particular conversational techniques associated with an elaborative conversational style into their natural ways of interacting with their children. We thought that parents' use of these elements of style would focus children's attention and increase understanding of experiences in ways that, based on prior work, should influence encoding and, in turn, subsequent remembering. The ways we introduced the conversational strategies to parents varied across projects, but our general aims were twofold. First, we examined whether and to what extent parents would demonstrate the targeted conversational techniques in their interactions with their children. Second, we addressed whether parents' use of these conversational strategies corresponded to changes in children's behavior during museum experiences and to children's learning and remembering.

*Learning and transfer:*

We conducted one of these studies at the Field Museum, Chicago's natural history museum, with funding from the Spencer Foundation (Jant et al., 2014). We involved 78 families with children between 3 and 6.5 years old (average age 5) in the research that took place in two exhibits. The first was the Southwestern Pueblo and Plaza in the children's area at the museum. Hands-on activities in the exhibit tapped the daily practices of the Pueblo people 800 years ago. The second exhibit was the Pawnee Lodge, a full-size replica of an earthen home of the Pawnee Native American people of the Great Plains in the nineteenth century. We selected these two exhibits because they depicted similarities and differences in daily living across different peoples, reflecting cultural beliefs and geographic conditions. For example, to illustrate food preparation, the Pueblo had a mano and metate for grinding corn, and the Pawnee Lodge had a mortar and a long pestle used for grinding corn and pounding meats into mush. To show how people slept, in the Pueblo, there was a straw mat on the floor, while in the Pawnee Lodge, there were beds on ledges around the perimeter of the home, draped with animal hides.

To examine the effects of object manipulation, we offered some families the opportunity to engage in hands-on exploration of several objects that figured prominently in the Pueblo. To examine the influence of conversation, other families received 4-in. × 6-in. cards with pictures of these same objects on one side and several open-ended, *Wh-* questions about these objects on the other. For example, the conversation card for the mano and metate included the following question: "What do you think this is used for?" The cards also included questions to compare the object to things the child might already be familiar with, such as for the sleeping mat, "How is this different from where you sleep?" A third group of families received both the physical objects and the conversation cards, and a fourth group (control) received fossils that were unrelated to the exhibit. We simply gave the families the objects, conversation cards, both, or neither and asked them to engage with these prior to entering the exhibit. We then gathered the objects and cards back from families who received them, and all of the families explored the two museum exhibits freely, first the Pueblo and then the Pawnee Lodge.

Although the conversation cards featured questions about objects in the Pueblo, they affected hands-on engagement and conversation in both exhibits. Compared to parents who had not received the cards, those that did asked more *Wh-* questions in the Pueblo, often in conjunction with joint parent–child hands-on engagement with the objects. For example, if the child picked up a piece of corn and the parent asked "How should we cook this?" and the child gave the corn to the parent and went to get a cooking pot, we coded this as a *Wh-* question that was accompanied by joint hands-on engagement. When they went to the Pawnee Lodge, parents and children who received the conversation cards about the Pueblo made more connections across the two exhibits, what we called *across-exhibit associations,* compared to those who had not received the cards. There were even more *joint* parent–child across-exhibit associations, such as when a parent asked, "How are these beds different from the beds we saw in the Pueblo?" and the child responded, "They have animal fur on them, not straw." Essentially, not only did the conversation cards lead parents to engage in more elaborative talk in the Pueblo, without specifically prompting them to do so, the cards were also associated with more comparisons across exhibits. The conversation cards and the forms of engagement in the Pueblo that they engendered seemed to drive understanding and representing the experience for families that received them to make information about the Pueblo more accessible and transferable to a related exhibit, the Pawnee Lodge.

We also consider how the pre-exhibit activities might have set the stage for children's subsequent remembering of their exhibit experiences. A subset of the sample (30 families) recorded parent–child reminiscing conversations 1 day and 2 weeks after the museum visit using audio recorders we had sent home with them and that they later returned to us. We thought that the combination of hands-on engagement with objects and the conversation cards would have the greatest effects on what children were able to retrieve and report across contexts (museum to home) over time. Consistent with what we observed in the museum, parents who had received the conversation cards at the museum asked significantly more *Wh-* questions when reminiscing with their children at home, compared with parents who had not received the cards. Likewise, as in the museum, those who received the cards before visiting the Pueblo engaged in the most frequent parent–child joint talk when reminiscing. Moreover, whereas children in the no-conversation-cards groups reported less about their museum visit over time, children in families who received the objects and conversation cards prior to their exhibit experience reported significantly more units of information spontaneously (not in response to parents' *Wh-* questions) 2 weeks following the museum visit than they had 1 day afterward. Rather than showing forgetting, parents and children who received the objects-plus-cards seemed to have interactions in the museum that lead to the formation of a memory for the experience that was available for reporting in even more detail weeks later. We do not know how activities and interaction patterns at home (outside of the memory conversations families recorded) may have helped to supplement these reports. Nevertheless, encouraging elaborative talk during the exhibit experiences clearly linked to children's subsequent remembering.

*Building memories:*

We conducted a similar study to encourage elaborative conversation during building activities at Chicago Children's Museum (Benjamin, Haden, & Wilkerson, 2010). A total of 121 children aged 4 to 8 (average age 6.5 years old) and their parents were randomly assigned to one of five conditions that varied according to what, if any, instructions they received prior to visiting a building construction exhibit called Skyline. Some received building information about how triangular cross-bracing makes structures strong and practiced this engineering principle by adding cross-bracing to two different wobbly structures made of materials found in the exhibit. Others in the elaborative-conversation condition were encouraged to ask open-ended *Wh-* questions and make associations connecting the exhibit experience with what their children already knew. These families practiced these conversational techniques by talking about a hard hat from the exhibit. A third group received and practiced both the building and conversation information. Two other (control) groups received no information about the building or conversation prior to visiting the exhibit.

Once in the building exhibit, all participants were encouraged to build whatever they wanted for as long as they wished. Parents and children in the conversation-only instruction group spent on average 34 minutes building, which was longer than the other groups. As we expected, parents and children who received the building information included more cross-braces in their structures compared to those who had not received building information. Parents asked more *Wh-* questions and associations if they had received the conversation information compared to those who did not. Moreover, children in the conversation information groups engaged in the most joint talk with their caregivers, responding to a greater proportion of their caregivers' *Wh-* questions. We also found that receiving information about bracing structures and elaborative talk was linked to families' engineering talk when building ("Why do you think this is wobbling?" "This isn't very sturdy.").

We asked the children to recall their building exhibit experiences, first immediately after building and then in reminiscing conversations recorded by a subsample of 45 families 1 day and 2 weeks following the museum visit. For the reports immediately after building, we asked a familiar adult who had come with the child to the museum, but who had not built with them, to ask open-ended questions to elicit the recounting. These so-called reunion narratives were intended to provide a semi-naturalistic measure of the children's initial learning from the experience. Indeed, we tried to simulate a pattern of behavior we observe in museums where family groups may split up for a while and then get back together to share what they did while apart.

Children recalled more immediately after building, and when reminiscing later, if they were in family groups who received conversation information, and in turn, engaged in elaborative talk in the exhibit. In the reunion conversations, and at both delay intervals when reminiscing, the children's reports also included the most engineering content if they were in the building-plus-conversation information group. Children in the building-plus-conversation information group recalled significantly more about the exhibit experience 2 weeks following the museum visit than they had after a 1-day delay. Therefore, the effects with regard to children's remembering were similar to what we found in the study at the natural history museum (Jant et al., 2014). Combining key exhibit information with conversation information seemed to engender interactions that boosted children's understanding and encoding and made these experiences more available for retrieval and reporting over time.

### *Facilitating Elaborative, STEM-Rich Conversations*

Our partnership with the Chicago Children's Museum has become increasingly collaborative over time (see Haden et al., 2016, for discussion). We have worked to develop programs and design ways of eliciting narratives about exhibit experiences that could become part of museum practice. One example of this is a project that involved 130 families with children an average age of 6.5 years old (Haden et al., 2014) who visited the Chicago Children's Museum's *Skyline* building exhibit. We developed a facilitated educational program to convey building and elaborative conversation information (adapted from Benjamin et al. 2010) that was modeled on the ways that museum staff daily engaged with visitors in on-the-exhibit-floor educational activities. There were two versions of the program, both involving "Inspector Sturdy" – a research assistant dressed in a white lab coat and carrying a triangle-shaped magnifying glass, playing the role of a building inspector. We randomly assigned families to the building information (only) Inspector Sturdy group, the building-plus-conversation information Inspector Sturdy group, or one of two other (control) groups.

In the building information version of the program, Inspector Sturdy began by asking families to test out the sturdiness of two model skyscrapers constructed from materials available in the exhibit, one that was wobbly and one that was sturdy. Then, Inspector Sturdy used the triangle magnifying glass to point out the differences in the ways that triangles functioned in these buildings, to brace the structure in the sturdy skyscraper but not in the wobbly one. Inspector Sturdy summed up the information by showing families a sign featuring pictures of two model structures with the words "Triangles make strong buildings"; the sign was positioned in plain sight as families built.

In the Inspector Sturdy building-plus-conversation information version of the program, families additionally received another "tip" beyond the building information. Inspector Sturdy told families that she had heard families who built strong buildings asking each other lots of questions to exchange information, such as *What?*, *Where?*, and *How?* Inspector Sturdy offered some example questions (What can we do to make this stronger?" "Where do you think we put a triangle piece?" "How can we make this stand up?"), which were also printed on a second sign that was placed in the exhibit alongside the building sign as the families built. The other two control groups did not interact with Inspector Sturdy, although for one group, the building-and-conversation information signs were placed in the exhibit but we did not draw attention to them. The other control group experienced the exhibit with no program and no special signs.

As expected, families who received the Inspector Sturdy program built the strongest buildings with the most pieces placed in ways to brace the structure. Parents in the version of the program that included conversation information asked double the number of *Wh-* questions while building with their children compared with parents in the two control groups, although across all groups children's responding to questions was equally low. Furthermore, during the building activity and without explicit instruction to do so, parents in the building-plus-conversation version of the Inspector Sturdy program demonstrated significantly more STEM talk than the other three groups. STEM talk included talk about the scientific method ("First we need to plan, then we can start to test our ideas."), technology ("How can we use the nuts to hold the bolts in place?"), engineering ("Remember, righty tighty, lefty loosey."), and mathematics ("We need 4 pieces to start.").

We also used a multimedia component in the exhibit to elicit the families' narratives after they had finished building. A camera connected to a computer kiosk took time-lapsed photos of families as they built. After, families were prompted (in English or Spanish) to sit at the computer kiosk and choose six of the photos to use to tell a narrative about their experiences. These *photonarratives* were further prompted by six questions, which we had worked with museum practitioners to design. One question was posed in connection with each photo (e.g., "How did you figure out how to start building?" "What did each of you learn from building?"). Analysis of the photonarratives families told about their building experiences revealed that children who received building information from Inspector Sturdy, with or without the conversation information, talked more about STEM than those in the control groups. Therefore, the building information provided in the program seemed to help children form a better understanding of the STEM-related aspects of the building activity that they used to tell a story about their experiences.

### Encouraging Elaborative and STEM Talk through Exhibit Design

More recently, we have been working with Chicago Children's Museum to address whether and how the design of exhibits and staff facilitation can promote families' STEM talk during and after exhibit experiences and children's STEM learning. The two projects we discuss here both took place in Chicago Children's Museum's *Tinkering Lab*. Tinkering is a creative form of open-ended problem-solving that is being widely introduced in schools and museums to provide STEM learning opportunities for children. Our work has focused on understanding the conditions of exhibit design and staff facilitation in museums that can encourage families to engage in engineering practices during tinkering, including planning, creating, testing, and iterating their designs. Moreover, we have asked how differences in programming link to differences in the STEM content of talk after children's tinkering experiences.

*Designing programs that promote STEM-related talk:*
The design of tinkering exhibits and programs includes intentionally selected tools and materials that support various creative approaches to problem-solving and diverse solutions (Pagano et al., 2019). In this work, we are interested in how the design of tinkering programs can vary as to whether and to what extent they invite engagement in engineering practices. In a recent study, we (Pagano, Haden, & Uttal, 2020) observed 61 families with 6- to 8-year-old children who participated in one of four programs that each posed an engineering design goal for families. Two of these programs specified what families' creations should do and provided places for testing progress toward the goal: wind tunnels for *Make It Fly* and ramps for *Make It Roll*. We asked whether these two programs would engender more engineering talk when compared to two programs that did not specify what the families' designs should do and did not feature places for testing: *Make a Robot* and *Make Something That Does Something*. More specifically, we investigated whether parent–child interactions during tinkering would mediate the associations between the program families engaged in and their engineering talk when reminiscing after tinkering.

This project took advantage of a unique exhibit at Chicago Children's Museum – *Story Hub: The Mini Movie Memory Maker*. In *Story Hub*, families sit at a touchscreen computer, select museum exhibits to discuss, and then video-record reminiscing conversations about their exhibit experiences. Our analyses of these conversations revealed that families who participated in the function-focused tinkering programs (*Make It Fly, Make It Roll*) talked more about engineering when reminiscing about their experiences, compared to families who participated in tinkering programs without function-focused goals (*Make a Robot, Make Something That Does Something*). The following is an example conversation recorded by a mother and her 7-year-old child after they participated in *Make It Fly*. There is substantial engineering talk in this conversation, including talk about planning, testing, redesigning, and metacognitions and evaluations (e.g., figuring things out, making mistakes, being un/successful).

MOTHER: Alright what was your mission?

CHILD: My mission was to make a plane with a propeller. The propeller kept holding it down. And I tried all kinds of different ways. Aluminum foil, um paper...

MOTHER: Cardboard.

CHILD: Cardboard and paper. Paper worked best because it was the lightest. I also used this paper bag to keep it in shape. The propeller kept holding it down because it had metal and really hard paper.

MOTHER: So how did you know if it worked or not? Talk about the testing.

CHILD: The testing was a little bit hard because I had to figure out what was keeping it down, what was keeping it from going all the way up out of the tube.

MOTHER: So what happened when you first tested it?

CHILD: When I first tested it, it did not go very far. It stayed down and its propeller was sticking down to the ground.

MOTHER: And how did you want it?

CHILD: I wanted it to go all the way up in the air flying out of the tube.

MOTHER: And you picked the materials and then when you did it..?

CHILD: It flew up in the air the last time I tested it. The second time it didn't go very far either, but it did not go face down like the first time. The third one was the best because I figured out what was keeping it down.

MOTHER: What did you learn about building something that flies? What matters?

CHILD: The light weight.

MOTHER: Mhm.

CHILD: And making sure that it's stabilized and not very heavy.

MOTHER: Great!

When reminiscing, families who participated in programs with function-focused goals talked about engineering-related information more than twice as much as families who participated in programs without function-focused goals. When we examined these families' interactions during tinkering, we found that, on the one hand, the programs all fostered collaboration, with no differences in joint engagement with materials/objects or joint talk among families participating in the different programs. However, families who participated in the function-focused programs engaged in more engineering talk during tinkering than those who participated in non-function-focused programs. What is more, our analyses revealed that with programs designed with function-focused engineering goals for tinkering, parent–child engineering talk during tinkering mediated the association between program and engineering talk during reminiscing. Therefore, this work points to ways to design exhibits to promote families' STEM-related talk. It also suggests that engaging families in reminiscing after exhibit experiences can reveal and potentially deepen engineering learning from tinkering.

*Knowledge supports STEM learning and remembering through tinkering:*
In a second project in *Tinkering Lab*, we asked how linkages between tinkering and reflection may vary as a function of the prior knowledge that is available to families to make sense of their experiences. The relevant prior knowledge that families bring with them to the museum can play a critical role in the exhibits families choose to visit, what they come to understand and find personally meaningful, and ultimately what they remember from these experiences. Further, building off prior work (Benjamin et al., 2010; Haden et al., 2014), providing families with knowledge related to the building task from the outset can help support families' engagement with the activity as well as their STEM learning and remembering. This type of knowledge can be beneficial for families who lack relevant skills or as a way to supplement families' prior knowledge.

In this project (Acosta et al., 2021), the sample included 111 families with 5- to 10-year-old children (average age 7 years old) who visited *Tinkering Lab* during the *Make It Roll* challenge. We explored rough measures of families' prior knowledge indexed by children's age, parents' level of education, and children's prior tinkering experience, based on parental reports. We also examined the role of engineering knowledge conveyed to families by museum staff with a *facilitated orientation* prior to tinkering. Families who received the orientation ($N$ = 51) gained information about wheels and axles (e.g., "For your car to roll, either the axle needs to spin or the wheels need to spin freely") as they tested model creations that either rolled or slid.

All families were video- and audio-recorded while they tinkered using the various tools and materials available in the space to make their rolling creations. Then we elicited the children's narrative reflections immediately after tinkering to gauge what children understood from their experiences. The researcher invited the child to snap a picture of their creation using a tablet computer, and then asked a series of open-ended questions to probe for what children did and learned from tinkering (e.g., "What did you do to make it?" "What did you learn?").

Analyses of the connections between STEM talk during and after tinkering revealed older children reported more STEM content in their reflections than younger children did. However, neither child age or prior tinkering experience nor parents' education levels or the facilitated orientations affected the positive associations observed between parents' STEM talk during tinkering and children's post-tinkering reflections. Further, whether children were younger or older, or whether children had parents with higher or lower levels of education, did not moderate the positive association observed between children's talk about STEM while tinkering and in their post-tinkering narrative reflections. Prior experience tinkering was a moderator, such that the association between children's STEM talk during and after tinkering was present only for children with prior tinkering experience.

Given our interest in understanding the role that museum staff might play in supporting STEM talk during and after tinkering, it was important that the facilitated orientations also moderated the relation between children's STEM talk during tinkering and their STEM talk in their reflections. This result is reflected in this excerpt of an 8-year-old child's report about their tinkering experience following participation in the *Make It Roll* program when they had received a facilitated orientation at the start.

RESEARCHER: What did you do in *Tinkering Lab* today?... Here I'll give you your creation.

CHILD: I made a car.

RESEARCHER: A car, and how did you do it? Tell me all about it.

CHILD: Um uh, I made a first hypothesis and tried to make it like one roller. And I put in two big wheels in the back but then it didn't work.

RESEARCHER: Okay.

CHILD: So then we tried another one with flaps like that but then it didn't work. So then we tried with like a thing like a tank.

RESEARCHER: Uhhuh.

CHILD: With three rollers on each side, but they didn't work. So then we put a roller and then a cap and then, um, a bottle on them.

RESEARCHER: Okay.

CHILD: And then we did it, and then we got a new high score.

RESEARCHER: Okay.

CHILD: So then we had to put some things inside there so then it could put some weight to make it go faster.

Essentially, the relation between children's STEM talk during and after tinkering was supported by receiving a facilitated orientation about engineering from a staff member – a result that is valuable in thinking about museum practices that can support STEM learning. Researchers and museum practitioners may be able to capitalize on the prior knowledge and experiences that families bring with them, as well as on opportunities to supplement this knowledge through facilitation by staff, to support children's STEM learning and remembering through tinkering.

## Conclusions: Museum Research and Practice

An important thread that ties together our different projects in museums is the idea that opportunities to reflect on experiences can advance children's learning from their experiences. It is an idea that draws heavily on the memory development literature, especially research by Ornstein and his colleagues concerning linkages between conversations during and after events. Moreover, we see parallels between our work and research by Ornstein, Coffman, and colleagues that involves partnerships with schools, and emphasizes the ways that educators can engage in conversations with children to benefit children's mnemonic and academic skills (see Coffman & Cook, Chapter 15 for details). Our research-practice partnerships with museums to continue a focus on the ways that making and eliciting memories can enhance learning outcomes for children.

# CHAPTER 13

# The Socialization of Gratitude
## How Parent–Child Conversations Impact Children's Memory for Gratitude-Related Events

*Hillary A. Langley, Jennifer L. Coffman, and Andrea M. Hussong*

A number of lines of research have highlighted the importance of the role of context for children's developing cognitive skills. This work focuses in large part on the socialization of memory and cognition (Fivush, 2018; Rogoff, 1990; Vygotsky, 1978) and began largely in research designed to examine the role of adult–child conversations in the development of children's autobiographical memory (Hedrick, Chapter 11; see also Fivush, Haden, & Reese, 2006 for a detailed review). A second line of research emerged in parallel – one that expanded the focus on parent conversations to include an exploration of teachers' language as it relates to children's deliberate memory skills (Coffman & Cook, Chapter 15).

Peter Ornstein has been involved in both lines of this research through his collaborative efforts, for example, with Haden (Ornstein & Haden, 2001a; Haden et al., 2001) and Coffman (Coffman et al., 2008; 2019), and he continues to contribute to the expansion of the field through the work of his mentees who have gone on to develop their own programs of research on relevant topics. His perspective and mentorship have been important in advancing research that has a focus on social forces that may play a role in the development of cognitive skills in children and that advance both basic knowledge and potential applications. The work described here is one extension of the parent–child conversation research, one that is rooted firmly in the literature on reminiscing and autobiographical memory, but that broadens the focus to include children's reports of gratitude-related experiences.

Through the extensive research on mother–child reminiscing, we have seen that in conversations about shared past experiences, parents help

This research was supported by the Expanding the Science and Practice of Gratitude project run by UC Berkeley's Greater Good Science Center in partnership with UC Davis with funding from the John Templeton Foundation, and by a postdoctoral fellowship provided to the first author by the National Institute of Child Health and Human Development (T32-HD07376) through the Center for Developmental Science at the University of North Carolina at Chapel Hill.

children to remember the salient aspects of prior events, identify what is important, create an explanation for why things happen in the world, and gain an understanding about what those events mean for the self and others (Fivush et al., 2006; Thompson, Laible, & Ontai, 2003; Waters et al., 2019; see Hedrick, Chapter 11). This research on children's memory skills has grown and is complemented by studies that describe linkages between the ways in which parents engage in conversations with their children and other developmental gains for children, particularly in terms of broader cognitive and socioemotional outcomes (e.g., language, theory of mind, social cognition; see Waters et al., 2019 for a meta-analytic review). In our research, we widen the lens regarding the potential benefits of parent–child reminiscing to encompass parent socialization practices related to a socio-emotional outcome of interest to many parents – gratitude.

In this chapter, we outline a new line of inquiry that is a direct extension of the rich literature on reminiscing and autobiographical memory, blended with recent research on the development of gratitude in children. This work is part of a larger set of studies focused on how parents foster gratitude in children, a widely held parenting goal (e.g., Froh et al., 2009). Following other socio-emotional socialization models (e.g., Eisenberg, Cumberland, & Spinrad, 1998), we argue that one way in which parents might socialize gratitude in children is through how they talk with their children about gratitude (Hussong et al., 2017; Hussong, Coffman, & Thomas, 2020). To the extent that children recall elements of reminiscing conversations with parents, children may internalize parental messages about gratitude. This previously untested supposition, however, assumes that findings regarding parent–child reminiscing and autobiographical memory extend to conversations about children's gratitude.

In an effort to extend the research on linkages between parents' elaborative reminiscing style and children's autobiographical memories for past, shared events, we have been carrying out research designed, in part, to investigate the ways in which parents scaffold reminiscing conversations with their children about past events that were related to gratitude. In this work, we have explored the ways in which parents talk with their children about past positive events (as a link to the general reminiscing literature) as compared to conversations about value-laden experiences, including times their children "got it right" and displayed gratitude and times when their children "missed the mark" and failed to experience or display gratitude. Additionally, we have examined the impact of elaborative style in combination with emotion-focused language and gratitude-specific content on children's memories for past events and have explored possible gender differences in these effects.

In this chapter, we explore the associations among the ways in which parents reminisce with their children about events related to gratitude and what children remember about these experiences, consistent with other emotional event reminiscing research. Specifically, we consider how parent–child reminiscing conversations may be related to how parents foster or socialize gratitude in their children. We consider effective strategies for parent–child reminiscing conversations as related to children's memory and how such strategies may be part of a larger socialization approach. We highlight the importance of parental goals and conversational contexts in linking parents' conversational strategies with levels of children's subsequent recall. In addition, we introduce conversational elements that may be critical in turning reminiscing conversations into effective socialization practices surrounding gratitude. Finally, we provide findings from the Raising Grateful Children study in which we test the associations between parent–child reminiscing conversational strategies about children's gratitude and children's recall as well as offer future directions for research.

## Parent–Child Reminiscing and Parent Socialization of Children's Gratitude

A large literature shows that parents play a critical role in the development of children's autobiographical memory capabilities (see Fivush et al., 2006; Waters et al., 2019). This research points to the importance of parents and children co-constructing narratives about past, shared events and how these reminiscing conversations influence both the organization and content of children's event memories (Haden et al., 2001; Haden, Haine, & Fivush, 1997; Sales & Fivush, 2005).

The ways in which parents structure reminiscing conversations with their children have implications for the autobiographical memories that children form about their past. Previous studies show that parents who use more elaborative styles of engaging in these conversations have children who evidence more detailed recall of past parent–child shared events, both within the same conversation and across time (Fivush et al., 2006; Langley, Coffman, & Ornstein, 2017; Schneider & Ornstein, 2015). Highly elaborative parents ask many open-ended questions that require children to embellish on the details of the shared event, provide rich descriptions about the event, confirm their children's contributions to the conversations, and make associations between aspects of the shared event and children's prior knowledge. In contrast, less-elaborative parents tend to repeat questions, rely on yes/no questions, and provide little contextual information about the shared event (Fivush et al., 2006). Children of highly elaborative parents share more detailed and coherent narratives of their personal past and display more advanced autobiographical memory skills (i.e., long-term memories that occurred in a specific time and place in one's personal past; Bauer & Fivush, 2010) than do children with less-elaborative parents (Fivush et al., 2006).

In turn, the types of details that children remember about shared events may serve a socializing function, shaping the way that children interpret the past and form expectations for the future, thereby reinforcing values and attitudes expressed by parents and internalized by children (Fivush et al., 2006; Gentzler et al., 2005). This may be particularly true when parents and children reminisce about shared *value-laden* events. However, little is known about the extent to which parents' elaborative styles when reminiscing about value-laden events (as opposed to more generic positive, neutral, and negative events) are associated with autobiographical memories in children.

Relevant studies focus on parent–child reminiscing about one-time, emotionally positive events, with only a handful of studies also examining parent–child talk about emotionally negative past experiences (e.g., Ackil et al., 2003; Sales, Fivush, & Peterson, 2003; Wang, 2001; Wang & Fivush, 2005). Most of the research on conversations about events negative in emotional valence focused on experiences that could be characterized as traumatic (e.g., a natural disaster, injury, asthma attack), with the exception of a few studies (e.g., Wang, 2001). These studies suggest that the conversational strategies used by parents change across contexts involving positive, neutral, and negative events, and presumably also when discussing value-laden events, although little research exists to date on this topic. In addition, the types of strategies that are most likely to predict recall in children may also vary as a function of the parent–child conversational context (e.g., discussions about various types of emotional or value-laden experiences). These findings have implications for optimal socialization practices that parents might use in conversations about gratitude with their children.

Conversations are undoubtedly one important mechanism through which parents work to foster gratitude in their children; however, there are other ways that parents might engage in socializing gratitude. Prior work shows that modeling grateful behavior (i.e., higher trait gratitude in parents), selecting activities or settings that promote gratitude (i.e., niche selection), daily scaffolding of gratitude moments, and how parents respond to times when children show gratitude as well as when they (in the parent's opinion) fail to do so are all aspects of socializing gratitude in children (Hussong et al., 2017, 2019, 2020; Rothenberg et al., 2017). Additionally, we argue that how parents discuss gratitude moments (i.e., particular instances when children experienced or expressed gratitude, or missed an opportunity to experience or express gratitude) with their children is another important socialization technique that parents use to teach their children about gratitude.

Our research focuses on two types of conversations (or contexts) in which parents reminisce with their children about gratitude. The first focuses on times when children demonstrate gratitude, and the second focuses on instances when children could have – but did not – demonstrate gratitude (we called these *missed opportunities for gratitude*). These two types of conversations may differ significantly, because they often differ in affective valence as well as in terms of the types of messages parents are trying to convey about their children's behavior (e.g., parental goals in reminiscing). Given that parents are likely pleased with children for showing gratitude, gratitude conversations are more likely to be positively valenced. On the other hand, parents may be disappointed with children for not showing gratitude; thus, missed-opportunity conversations are likely to be more negatively valenced in emotional tone. Based on prior literature regarding the importance of emotional valence on reminiscing, we anticipated that parent–child reminiscing about instances of child gratitude would mirror positive-event recall tasks in terms of both the strategies parents used as well as how those strategies predicted child recall. Conversely, we anticipated that parent–child resminiscing about missed opportunities would resemble negative-event tasks in the same way. To better articulate these differences, we next considered the importance of parental goals and conversational context in parent–child reminiscing conversations.

## The Importance of Parental Goals and Conversational Context for Children's Event Memory

The link between parents' high-elaborative style and children's improved autobiographical memory is well established (see Fivush et al., 2006; Waters et al., 2019 for reviews). Building on this literature, we consider additional factors that may impact parents' conversational style – factors that may, in turn, impact the strength of the association between parents' reminiscing style and children's memory for events related to gratitude. We suggest that the emotional valence of the event under discussion (e.g., positive or negative in emotional tone) as well as the extent of emotion talk and gratitude-related content used by parents in these conversations (e.g., focused on behavioral correction versus gratitude understanding) are also important variables to consider.

## Emotions and Memory

We know from the literature on memory in adults that emotion interacts critically with how we remember information, and especially events. Indeed, emotional events appear to be given a special status in memory (Carver, 2014). Memories of events associated with strong emotional responses during encoding, either positive or negative in valence (e.g., visit to a trampoline park or falling off a bike), are associated with more lasting, vivid memories than similar, neutral events (Rubin, 2005), at least in adults. Developmental theorists have also begun to discuss the impact of emotions on memory in children. Fivush (2014) notes that emotions likely play a role in how experiences are encoded, consolidated, and retrieved. She also suggests that the context in which experiences are remembered may influence children's emotional state at the point of actively remembering aspects of the experience. This may, in turn, influence encoding and recall of later events, forming a dynamic and ongoing loop (Fivush, 2014).

Parents certainly play a significant role in creating an emotional context in reminiscing conversations, which has implications for children's autobiographical recall in those discussions (e.g., Fivush, 2014). Indeed, in order to best understand the aspects of parents' conversational techniques that impact children's remembering, it is important to consider both how parents structure these conversations with their children as well as how they discuss emotions related to the experience. Previous literature suggests that parents, and mothers in particular, may structure reminiscing conversations with their children about past positive- and negative-valenced events somewhat differently. For example, research has shown that, as a whole, mothers seem to be more elaborative when discussing highly negative events, such as experiencing a natural disaster such as a tornado or visiting an emergency room after an injury, when compared to generally positive events, such as trips to the zoo or visits with relatives (Ackil et al., 2003; Sales et al., 2003). More specifically, mothers tend to ask more open-ended elaborative questions that require children to provide information and actively engage in the conversation when discussing negative compared to positive events.

In contrast, mothers ask more closed-ended (i.e., yes/no) questions when discussing positive versus negative events. In both, however, higher elaborative style by parents is associated with higher levels of recall by children, both in the same conversation and across time (Fivush et al., 2006).

In addition to elaborative reminiscing style, internal state talk – including emotion talk, or the use of words that reference and connect internal emotional experiences to the event that is the focus of the parent–child conversation – may also serve as an important determinant of event memory in children. Emotion talk may provide a window into the impact of the event on an individual and can be a way through which parents help children come to think and feel about their experiences (Bauer et al., 2005). Indeed, parents who use more emotion talk have children who also talk more about emotions in parent–child reminiscing conversations (e.g., Sales et al., 2003).

Some research suggests that parents use elaborative conversational techniques and emotion talk differently in positive- and negative-event conversations because parents have different goals in these two types of conversations. In conversations about past negative events, parents may be interested in teaching their children how to cope with previous stressful experiences or may want to correct past behavior (although little research has focused on parent–child conversations about children's previous behavioral transgressions or value-laden events). Thus, elaborative questions may attempt to engage children in reflecting on not just what happened in a shared past event but also what could have happened (i.e., if the child had not engaged in a dangerous situation that resulted in injury or if the child had picked a more appropriate behavioral response). This is consistent with findings that mothers discuss causes (e.g., antecedents of an event, why the event happened the way it did, what led to consequences for the child's injury or bad behavior) more often when reminiscing about negative than positive events (Fivush et al., 2003; Marin, Bohanek, & Fivush, 2008; Sales et al., 2003).

This finding suggests that mothers are more concerned with helping their children to recall a coherent account of negative events that may help children to understand how and what happened, whereas reminiscing about positive events may reflect a focus on creating a shared and co-constructed history of the past (Fivush et al., 2003; Sales et al., 2003). Thus, the way in which parents converse with their children about negative events may require a deeper level of cognitive processing that may lead to further encoding of event details and thus a richer autobiographical memory.

## Conversational Content and Memory

Existing studies on parent–child reminiscing suggest that elaborative style and emotion talk are two elements that predict child recall depending on the context (emotional valence) of the conversation. Extending this work, we posited that an additional element of parents' conversational style in reminiscing with their children about gratitude was the way in which parents talked about gratitude specifically. Based on conversations that we observed between parents and children, we focused on two contrasting ways in which parents presented gratitude content in these conversations: (1) behavioral correction (directed at correcting children's inappropriate behavior and/or how to behave in the future), and (2) gratitude understanding (focused on helping children better understand the construct of gratitude by explaining what gratitude means and why it is important, describing and/or pointing out the various aspects of the experience or expression of gratitude). The use of these strategies for talking about gratitude may serve as a proxy for parents' goals in reminiscing conversations. Thus the use of these strategies may differ in discussions about gratitude, which may either focus more on gratitude understanding to build co-constructed narratives or focus on behavioral correction to prepare for future challenges in the case of missed-opportunity-for-gratitude events. The use of different strategies for discussing gratitude may, in turn, differentially predict children's memory for each of these events.

In sum, nearly three decades of research suggests that parents' elaborative reminiscing style is important for children's autobiographical memory development. However, little research has focused on how parents choose to structure conversations with their children about value-laden experiences, how they discuss emotions in these conversations, and what goals they may have when scaffolding these discussions with their children. There is also little evidence regarding how variations in each of these conversational techniques affect children's recall in conversations about events related to gratitude. Based on related research, we suspected (and subsequently found in our studies of parent–child reminiscing about gratitude) that higher levels of elaborative style, higher levels of emotion talk, and more gratitude content focused on understanding the construct of gratitude would be most predictive of children's event memory.

## Gender Differences in Reminiscing

As suggested above, we anticipated that these three elements of gratitude conversations – elaborative style, emotion talk, and gratitude content – may differ in conversations focused on gratitude versus missed-opportunity events. This may be particularly true for girls, as some research suggests that mothers are more elaborative when discussing past emotional experiences with their daughters than with their sons (Fivush, 1998; Fivush et al., 2003; Reese, Haden, & Fivush, 1996; although see Waters et al., 2019 for a recent meta-analysis examining gender differences [or the lack thereof in some studies] in reminiscing). Mothers have also been shown to be more evaluative, use more emotion words, and focus more on relationships when reminiscing with girls versus boys (Fivush & Buckner, 2003). In addition, parents have been shown to be more elaborative with girls about sadness and general emotional negativity (Fivush, 1991, 1998; Fivush et al., 2000) and with boys about anger (Bird & Reese, 2006; Fivush, 1998). No research has examined gender differences in parents' elaborative style or emotional talk in parent–child conversations about children's past gratitude-related behaviors, so we examined if gender differences in parents' conversational techniques and in children's recall were present in our sample.

## Findings from the "Raising Grateful Children" Study

The Raising Grateful Children study uses a longitudinal design to examine the development of gratitude in children and the ways in which parents work to cultivate gratitude in their children. Within this study, we initially captured reminiscing conversations between parents and their 6- to 9-year-old children about previous events when children displayed gratitude as well as times when they missed an opportunity for gratitude, and then administered follow-up assessments over a series of delays, from 1 month to several years. We focus here on the initial time point.

The Raising Grateful Children study (Hussong et al., 2017, 2019, 2020; Rothenberg et al., 2017) included 101 parent–child dyads with a child aged 6–9 years ($M$ = 7.4 years, 52% female). Parents were predominantly female (85% mothers), had a mean age of 41.0 years, and were well educated. With regard to race/ethnicity, 81% of the parents self-identified as European American; 9% as Asian; 5% as African American, and 4% as Latinx. Parent–child dyads completed a series of observational tasks together and then parents completed a computerized survey in one testing room while an experimenter administered the battery of measures to the child in an adjacent room. As part of this battery, the parent–child reminiscing task (Fivush et al., 2006) was administered to assess parents' use of conversational elements of an elaborative style, emotion talk, and gratitude strategies in reminiscing conversations with their children, as well as children's recall for events discussed in these conversations (as a measure of autobiographical memory). Three novel target events (that occurred within the last month) were nominated by parents to discuss with their children: (1) a time during which his/her child experienced or expressed gratitude (i.e., gratitude event; e.g., child called Grandma and enthusiastically thanked her for gift, child used own money to buy treat for brother after he helped her when she was hurt as a way to show she was thankful); (2) a time during which the parent had hoped to or expected to see some form of gratitude in his/her child but did not (i.e., missed-opportunity-for-gratitude event; e.g., fighting with sibling over who got to open joint gift from neighbor, throwing a fit at the bowling alley for not being able to play a third game); and (3) a past event generally positive/neutral in nature (i.e., positive/neutral event; e.g., went to the trampoline park together as a family, child lost first tooth at home). These conversations were analyzed through the lens of three separate coding schemes that focused on measuring (1) parents' elaborative reminiscing style and children's autobiographical memory (adapted from a structural-functional coding system used by Reese, Haden, & Fivush, 1993); (2) parent and child emotion talk (adapted from internal states language coding scheme used by Bauer, Stennes, & Haight, 2003, and emotion coding described in Marin et al. 2008); and (3) parent and child gratitude strategies (developed by the research team of investigators).

Using these baseline data, we tested four questions that bridge the parent–child reminiscing and parent socialization of gratitude literatures. First, do parents' *reminiscing styles* differ based on the type of event? Second, does parents' use of *emotion talk* differ across types of events? Third, does parents' use of *gratitude strategies* differ across types of events? And fourth, how do parents' levels of elaborative style, emotion talk, and gratitude strategies predict children's recall in the three event conversations assessed?

## *Do Parents' Reminiscing Styles Differ Based on Type of Event?*

In our attempt to understand parents' conversational strategies across event types, we first examined whether parents displayed a more elaborative style when reminiscing about missed opportunity compared to gratitude events with their children, mirroring the literature on positive and negative emotionally valenced events. For each event (gratitude, missed-opportunity, and positive/neutral), we followed Reese et al. (1993) and coded parent talk to capture elaborative reminiscing style and child talk to assess recall of event details. For children, we coded for memory elaborations (new details about the event contributed to the conversation). For parents, we coded for use of open-ended questions, yes/no questions, and statement elaborations, as well as associative talk (linking the event under discussion to other experiences or prior knowledge), confirmations (of children's contributions to the conversation), and metamemory talk (talk about the process of remembering; see Table 13.1 for definitions). Using these codes, we created composite elaborative-style scores we used in all analyses based on our theoretical conceptualization of elaborative reminiscing style (see Langley, Coffman, & Ornstein, 2017, for a detailed description of the measure).

As can be observed in Table 13.2, aspects of parents' elaborative style were similar when comparing the positive/neutral and gratitude events for all of the components of elaborative style, and no significant differences emerged. There were, however, differences between aspects of elaborative style when comparing parents' use of associations and confirmations in the gratitude and positive/neutral event with the missed-opportunity event. Specifically, parents used significantly more associations in the missed-opportunity event conversation than in the gratitude- and positive/neutral-event conversations, whereas parents in the gratitude- and positive/neutral-event conversations provided more confirmations of their children's contributions to the conversations than in the missed-opportunity event conversations.

### Do Parents Use Emotion Talk Differently across Types of Events?

Next, we examined whether parents used more positive emotion-talk words in gratitude-event conversations, which may be more positively valenced experiences, and more negative emotion talk in missed-opportunity events, which may be more negatively valenced events. We coded for the frequency with which parents used emotion words based on coding schemes by Bauer et al. (2003) and Marin et al. (2008). Each emotion utterance was coded for valence (*positive*: happy, thankful, excited; *negative*: sad, mad, ungrateful), and we examined the frequency of positive and negative emotion talk within each event conversation.

We found differences in emotion-word use across the three events (see Table 13.2 for descriptive statistics). As expected, there were no differences in the amount of positive emotion words that parents provided in the gratitude- and positive/neutral-event conversations, but parents did provide more positive emotion words in the gratitude event and the

Table 13.1. *Definitions and examples of codes from the parent–child reminiscing task (Langley et al., 2017)*

| Code | Definitions | Examples |
|---|---|---|
| Maternal Open-Ended Question Elaborations | Open-ended questions asking the child to provide new memory information about an event. | "What did we do at the zoo?" "Who went with us to the soup kitchen?" "What did you say when you got a stuffed animal?" |
| Maternal Yes/No Question Elaborations | Questions that ask the child to confirm or deny a new piece of memory information provided by the mother. | "Were you wearing a sweatshirt?" "Was it hot or cold outside?" "Did you have fun?" "Did Alex give you a present?" |
| Maternal Statement Elaborations | Any declarative comment made by the mother that provides new information about the event. | "We ate popcorn at the zoo." "Your friend Sally came with us on the field trip." "All the girls from your class came." |
| Child Memory Elaborations | Children either move the conversations to a new aspect of the event or provide new information about the event being discussed. | "I saw a giraffe at the zoo." "I wore my favorite dress!" "I was scared of the lions." "I said 'thank you' to my teacher." |
| Maternal and Child Associative Talk | Statements or questions that are not about the particular event under discussion, but are related to the one under discussion, including talk about past or future events that are comparable to the event under discussion, as well as comments about facts about the world related to the event under discussion. | "Can we go back to the zoo again soon?" "Giraffes are my favorite animals." "A baby lion is called a cub." "You should say 'thank you' when you get a present." "What should we get Alex for her birthday next year?" |
| Maternal and Child Confirmations | Comments that in some way confirm information provided by the other conversational partner. | "Yes, you did eat popcorn at the zoo." "Yes, you're right!" "Uh huh." "Yes, you did say 'thank you.'" |
| Maternal and Child Metamemory Talk | Memory remarks about the process of remembering or about the other conversational partner's memory performance. | "I had forgotten that happened!" "I can't believe you still remember that." "Why don't you take a second to think? I bet you can remember what happened." |

Table 13.2. *Descriptive statistics from the parent–child reminiscing task: Parental reminiscing style variables, emotion talk, and gratitude strategies, and children's memory elaborations within each event*

| Variable | Gratitude Event Mean | SD | Positive/ Neutral Event Mean | SD | Missed-Opportunity Event Mean | SD |
|---|---|---|---|---|---|---|
| Parental Elaborations | | | | | | |
| Open-Ended Question Elaborations | 3.84 | 2.59 | 3.89 | 4.00 | 2.92 | 2.86 |
| Yes/No Question Elaborations | 5.10 | 3.60 | 5.74 | 4.59 | 5.02 | 3.36 |
| Statement Elaborations | 8.20 | 6.93 | 7.75 | 6.68 | 7.62 | 7.45 |
| Total Elaborations* | 17.14 | 9.30 | 17.38 | 10.41 | 15.56 | 10.01 |
| Parental Associations* | 14.77 | 11.88 | 12.94 | 12.97 | 25.66 | 19.80 |
| Parental Confirmations* | 6.67 | 5.29 | 7.54 | 6.90 | 5.28 | 4.68 |
| Parental Metamemory Talk* | 0.32 | 0.82 | 0.31 | 0.58 | 0.51 | 0.95 |
| Parent Positive Emotion Talk | 6.34 | 4.32 | 6.45 | 3.99 | 3.21 | 3.40 |
| Parent Negative Emotion Talk | 0.57 | 1.20 | 0.72 | 1.25 | 3.27 | 2.89 |
| Parent Behavioral Correction | 1.49 | 5.14 | 0.50 | 1.88 | 5.40 | 7.69 |
| Parent Gratitude Understanding | 12.03 | 9.59 | 3.87 | 6.88 | 10.25 | 9.65 |
| Children's Memory Elaborations | 7.62 | 6.30 | 9.65 | 8.18 | 6.66 | 5.90 |

*Note:* * denotes the four components of parents' reminiscing style.

positive/neutral event than in the missed-opportunity event. Parents also provided more negative emotion words in the missed-opportunity event than in the gratitude-event and positive/neutral-event conversations.

### Does Parents' Use of Gratitude Strategies Differ across Types of Events?

We sought to explore different approaches that parents employed as they talked about gratitude versus missed-opportunity events, as a function of what their possible goals for these conversations might have been. In order to do so, we identified themes regarding how parents talked to their children about gratitude in these events. Two differing conversational approaches related to gratitude were identified: (1) behavioral correction (directed at children's inappropriate behavior and/or how to behave appropriately in the future), and (2) facilitating gratitude understanding (focused on helping children better understand the construct of gratitude by defining or describing what gratitude is and why it is important, discussing aspects of the experience or expression of gratitude including verbal and nonverbal behaviors, and recognition of receiving from others). Behavioral correction included comments about children's inappropriate behavior ("I can't believe you didn't say thank you!" and "And, so, I want you to work harder on that next time... try to be grateful for what you have instead of fighting over material things and not sharing with your sister."). Messages that were coded as facilitating gratitude understanding, on the other hand, were focused on helping children understand the definition of gratitude ("I think of it as being appreciative and how you show the feelings that are inside of you"), the cognitive, emotional, and behavioral aspects of gratitude ("Why do you think Dad was so excited that we wrote him special notes and made his favorite meal for Father's Day?" and "I wonder what we can do to show Grandma that we appreciate her baking a beautiful cake for your birthday"), and why gratitude is important ("When we say 'thank you' it shows others that we are grateful for their time and effort").

We tested whether parents focused more on behavioral correction in missed-opportunity conversations, when behavioral correction may be the goal, and more facilitation of understanding the construct of gratitude in gratitude conversations, when positive reinforcement of the child's behavior may be the goal. Results revealed that gratitude strategies did differ across the three events (see Table 13.2 for descriptive statistics). As expected, parents provided more talk related to facilitating the understanding of gratitude in the gratitude and missed-opportunity conversations than in the positive/ neutral event. Parents were more likely to focus on correcting children's behavior in the missed-opportunity compared to the gratitude- and positive/ neutral-event conversations. In addition, parents were more likely to try to facilitate gratitude understanding in the gratitude event compared to the positive/neutral event and in the missed-opportunity event compared to the positive/neutral event. There were no significant differences in parents' provision of messages aimed at facilitating gratitude understanding when comparing the gratitude and missed-opportunity event conversations. Table 13.3 presents correlations among aspects of parents' reminiscing style, emotion talk, and provision of gratitude strategies across the event conversations; correlations between children's recall in each of the three event conversations is also presented in Table 13.3.

### How Do Reminiscing Style, Emotion Talk, and Gratitude Strategies Predict Children's Recall?

Finally, we focused on how aspects of parent–child conversations were related to children's recall in these event conversations and identified any

Table 13.3. *Correlations between aspects of the reminiscing conversation for parents (upper panel) and children (lower panel)*

| | 1 | 2 | 3 | 4 | 5 | 6 | 7 | 8 | 9 |
|---|---|---|---|---|---|---|---|---|---|
| **Parents' Elaborative Reminiscing Style** | | | | | | | | | |
| 1. Gratitude Event: Reminiscing Style | – | | | | | | | | |
| 2. Positive/Neutral Event: Reminiscing Style | .42** | – | | | | | | | |
| 3. Missed-Opportunity Event: Reminiscing Style | .25* | .26** | – | | | | | | |
| **Parents' Emotion Talk** | | | | | | | | | |
| 4. Gratitude Event: Total Emotion Talk | .38** | .18 | .37** | – | | | | | |
| 5. Positive/Neutral Event: Total Emotion Talk | .25* | .50** | .09 | .31** | – | | | | |
| 6. Missed-Opp. Event: Total Emotion Talk | .12 | .18 | .47** | .23* | .26** | – | | | |
| **Parents' Gratitude Content** | | | | | | | | | |
| 7. Gratitude Event: Behavioral Correction | .20* | .08 | -.07 | .06 | .04 | -.05 | – | | |
| 8. Missed-Opp. Event: Behavioral Correction | .22* | .30** | .14 | .16 | .30** | .28** | .13 | – | |
| 9. Gratitude Event: Understanding Gratitude | .46** | .07 | .12 | .16 | .15 | -.01 | .29** | .17 | – |
| 10. Missed-Opp. Event: Understanding Gratitude | .13 | .18 | .39** | .15 | .24* | .21 | .05 | .18 | .33** |

| | 1. | 2. |
|---|---|---|
| **Children's Autobiographical Memory** | | |
| 1. Gratitude Event: Memory Elaborations | – | |
| 2. Positive/Neutral Event: Memory Elaborations | .56** | – |
| 3. Missed-Opp. Event: Memory Elaborations | .25* | .36** |

*Note:* * p < .05, ** p < .01

217

possible gender differences in recall. Specifically, we tested whether aspects of elaborative style, emotion talk, and use of gratitude strategies were similarly related to recall across gratitude and missed-opportunity event conversations and made comparisons of recall to the neutral-event conversation (to provide comparisons with the larger literature).

An examination of the linkages between elements of reminiscing conversations (i.e., parents' elaborative style, positive and negative emotion-word use, and behavioral correction and facilitating understanding of gratitude strategies) and children's autobiographical memory across the three types of event conversations (see Table 13.4) revealed that regardless of conversation type, parents' elaborative style was significantly associated with children's recall. That is, consistent with the existing literature, parents with higher elaborative styles had children who reported more details in the conversation when compared to children with parents lower on the reminiscing-style continuum. Similarly, parents who talked about emotions more during each of the event conversations had children who remembered more details about that experience. Specifically, correlations between children's memory scores and parents' use of positive emotion words were statistically significant in the gratitude, positive/neutral, and the missed-opportunity event conversations, revealing that more positive emotion talk was associated with better children's recall. Similar patterns emerged when comparing children's memory scores and parents' use of negative emotion words in all three event conversations, indicating that more negative emotion talk was also associated with better memory performance in the children. Parents' greater use of facilitating gratitude understanding in the missed-opportunity conversation was also significantly associated with higher levels of children's recall during those conversations.

Regression models were run to explore the unique effects of each conversational technique used by parents on children's memory (predictors of children's memory for all models were parents' elaborative style, total positive emotion talk, total negative emotion talk, total frequency of behavioral correction messages, and total use of messages to facilitate understanding of gratitude). For the gratitude-event conversation, the model explained 32.3% of the variance in children's memory for the experience. Parents' elaborative style was the only variable that emerged as a significant predictor of children's memory, revealing that as parents' elaborative style increased, so did the children's memory performance. For the missed-opportunity-event conversation, the model explained 37.0% of the variance in children's memory for the experience. Three variables

Table 13.4. *Correlations between aspects of parents' and children's contributions to the reminiscing conversations in terms of elaborativeness, emotion word use, and gratitude strategies*

| | Gratitude Event | | | | | Missed-Opportunity Event | | | | |
|---|---|---|---|---|---|---|---|---|---|---|
| | Elaborative Style | Positive Emotion Words | Negative Emotion Words | Gratitude Behavioral Correction | Gratitude Understanding | Elaborative Style | Positive Emotion Words | Negative Emotion Words | Gratitude Behavioral Correction | Gratitude Understanding |
| **Children's Conversational Contributions** | | | | | | | | | | |
| **Gratitude Event** | | | | | | | | | | |
| Memory Elaborations | .53** | .28** | .23* | .13 | .13 | .03 | .26* | .04 | .13 | .02 |
| Pos. Emotion Words | .21* | .78** | .01 | .08 | .17 | .25* | .21* | -.03 | .11 | .04 |
| Neg. Emotion Words | .19 | .05 | .44** | .08 | -.19 | .16 | .11 | .07 | .25* | -.01 |
| **Missed-Opportunity Event** | | | | | | | | | | |
| Memory Elaborations | .19 | .15 | .20* | -.04 | .01 | .55** | .30** | .21* | -.12 | .20* |
| Pos. Emotion Words | .07 | .18 | -.03 | -.02 | .01 | .35** | .86** | .14 | .14 | .19 |
| Neg. Emotion Words | -.06 | -.09 | .08 | -.01 | -.12 | .16 | .15 | .70** | .14 | -.03 |

*Note:* * *p* < .05, ** *p* < .01

emerged as significant predictors of children's memory: higher levels of parents' elaborative style, more total positive emotion talk, and lower levels of messages related to behavioral correction when talking about gratitude.

Lastly, we examined gender differences in these associations to determine whether these predictions were stronger in girls than in boys. Overall, children articulated fewer details in the gratitude and the missed-opportunity events when compared to the positive/neutral event. In each of the three event conversations, girls remembered more unique pieces of information than did boys.

## Conclusions

A plethora of research investigating the way in which parents, and mothers in particular, reminisce with their children about previously experienced events suggests robust and long-lasting effects of parents' elaborative reminiscing style on children's autobiographical memory development. Research has also been conducted that elucidates the similarities and differences in the ways in which parents talk about past emotionally charged events with their children, with examinations of gender differences in some of this research. No prior research, to our knowledge, has examined the ways in which parents reminisce with their children – and particularly with school-aged children – about past events that are related to gratitude. The Raising Grateful Children study provides a unique opportunity to explore both the ways that parents structure these conversations with their children (by examining parents' elaborative reminiscing style) and the content of these conversations (by examining parents' provision of positive and negative emotion words as well as gratitude-specific messages) in conversations about past gratitude-related events. These results suggest that both what parents say and the way in which they say it are important in conversations with their children about previous emotional experiences, including those about gratitude and missed opportunities for gratitude.

The differences in parents' conversational techniques discussed above – including parents' elaborative reminiscing style, positive and negative emotion talk, and delivery of gratitude-specific messages (behavioral correction versus facilitating understanding of gratitude) – clearly play a role in children's recall of these experiences. These results suggest that across all event conversations, parents' elaborative reminiscing style emerged as the most significant predictor of children's memory performance. This adds to our understanding of the importance of a highly elaborative style when reminiscing with children in conversations about a range of emotionally valenced past events, including those about gratitude. Emotion talk also emerged as an important predictor of children's memory, suggesting that the more parents talk about emotions during conversations about past emotionally valenced events, the more children remember. In conversations about gratitude, it appears that more use of messages related to helping their children understand the construct of gratitude and lower levels of messages about ways to correct their children's behavior appear to be associated with better recall in the children.

Although a wealth of research has been conducted examining the impact of parents' conversational techniques on children's memory performance in reminiscing conversations (e.g., Fivush et al., 2006; Langley et al., 2017; Waters et al., 2019), this study is the first exploration of these ideas in parent–child conversations about gratitude. This extends what we know about how parents reminisce with their children about past emotional experiences, both those positive in emotional valence (gratitude event) and those more negative in nature (missed-opportunity-for-gratitude event). In addition, while much of the reminiscing literature has focused on elaborative style and emotion talk/mental-state language in separate investigations, we incorporated information about parents' elaborative reminiscing style, emotion talk, and differing strategies for talking about gratitude, and linked them to children's memory for the experiences. We also examine reminiscing conversations between parents and school-aged children, which contributes to what we know about how parents talk to children of various ages about past, shared events.

This work represents an important step in better understanding the unique constellation of parental conversational techniques that combine to most optimally predict children's memory in conversations about events that differ in terms of the emotional valence of the event. We also extend the literature about how parents talk to their children; here, about a topic never studied before in the reminiscing literature – gratitude. Importantly, given that the sample in the Raising Grateful Children study described in this chapter is relatively privileged (in terms of income and education level) and homogenous (in terms of parent gender and ethnic background), we have recently begun to explore the ways in which parents from diverse socioeconomic and ethnic backgrounds work to foster gratitude in their children (e.g., Langley et al., 2018). This is an important next step in continuing to generalize findings to populations beyond the groups that have traditionally been represented in the reminiscing literature.

Finally, this work on the role of parent–child conversations about gratitude has the potential to shed light on the role of naturalistic parent–child communicative interactions in children's developing gratitude and leads directly to the development of parental interventions aimed at facilitating children's gratitude and prosocial skills. This work – situated at the intersection of cognitive and affective functioning in children – can facilitate further understanding of the social factors that can cultivate positive outcomes for children, and can also allow for the exploration of parent–child conversations as a possible mechanism for fostering gratitude in children. This is an important next step in understanding the ways in which parents' socialization of gratitude can be supported – especially in the service of their children's prosocial or social-emotional functioning. An initial attempt at the creation and implementation of a program designed to support parents' conversations for fostering gratitude in their children (Hussong et al., 2020) has shown promise in terms of impacting parents' knowledge and use of conversational strategies and in providing preliminary linkages to children's gratitude experiences. This program is one example Connally and Powell the ways in which the basic research on the socialization of cognitive and affective development can inform intervention efforts designed to facilitate positive outcomes in children.

# CHAPTER 14

# How Memory Develops in Conversational Contexts

## Robyn Fivush

When John Flavell famously asked "What is memory development the development of?" at a 1971 symposium at the biennial meetings of the Society for Research in Child Development, memory was generally conceptualized as a cognitive system that operated according to a set of specified functions, such as encoding, storage, and retrieval, to achieve a specific mnemonic end, namely recall. Certainly, Peter Ornstein's foundational research of the development of mnemonic strategies (Ornstein, 1978/2014) both defined and clarified this conception of memory. Yet at the same time, this early research set the stage for expanding conceptualizations of memory that now permeate the field. More specifically, Ornstein's insistence that basic research be applicable to real-world settings, and that methodological approaches integrate research in the laboratory and in the field (Baker-Ward, Ornstein, & Gordon, 1993; Ornstein & Haden, 2001b) led to a remarkable blossoming of understanding the development of memory as a dynamic system that operates both "in the head" and "in the world" in ways that help the developing child achieve complex goals and objectives. Rather than memory as a unitary cognitive system, Ornstein's body of work has expanded our understanding of memory into a system that operates in concert both with other developing systems within the individual and within complicated sociocultural interactions. The three chapters in this section attest to the generativity of Ornstein's theoretical vision.

More specifically, Hedrick (Chapter 11) expands our notion of memory into the social world by detailing the role of conversational interactions before, during, and after an event occurs in shaping what children will subsequently recall about specific episodes. Haden, Acosta, and Pagano (Chapter 12) take this one step further by demonstrating how this process works in a critical real-world setting – museums – in which children's developing scientific knowledge is a complex product of conversational interactions and hands-on experience, as remembering an episode morphs into broader semantic knowledge. And Langley, Coffman, and Hussong (Chapter 13) show how remembering specific episodes can help children develop in socioemotional arenas, specifically gratitude, demonstrating that memory is not an encapsulated cognitive system, but is at the heart of all aspects of the developing mind.

## Integrating Information-Processing and Sociocultural Theories

Throughout his long and illustrious career, Peter Ornstein has maintained that memory development must be studied scientifically, in controlled laboratory experiments, and in the field, in the multiple settings in which memory is used to achieve specific goals (Baker-Ward, Ornstein, & Gordon, 1993; Ornstein & Haden, 2001b). In the early research on mnemonic strategies, Ornstein's research program engaged in a complex interplay between studying the development of strategic memory in precisely controlled laboratory experiments and studying how these results informed academic performance in school settings (Naus & Ornstein, 1983; Ornstein, Naus, & Liberty, 1975). The demonstration of both how the development of deliberate memory was shaped by formal schooling and how academic success was scaffolded by developing mnemonic abilities underscored the importance of the social and cultural contexts in which children were embedded in shaping their developmental trajectories. Whereas information-processing theories, prominent in cognitive and developmental psychology in the 1960s and 1970s (Neisser, 1967/2014; Klahr & Wallace, 1976), provided frameworks for examining and explaining the development of mnemonic abilities to encode, organize, store, and retrieve information in a more or less encapsulated memory system, Ornstein realized that this approach could not address fundamental questions about developmental process in a broader context. Two questions become paramount. First, how might deliberate memory development relate (or not) to the development of everyday memory for episodes and experiences that undergird autobiographical memory? Second, how do we best understand the process of how these various memory skills develop across childhood, and, more specifically, what is the role of the social and cultural context in facilitating memory development?

Based on emerging research, both in the lab and in the field, Ornstein and Haden (2001a) argued for integrating information-processing theories with sociocultural theories of development to provide a more comprehensive approach to the development of memory. Sociocultural theories provide insight into the ways in which social and cultural environments shape children's worlds to focus on specific activities and achievements as important (e.g., formal schooling highlights the importance of memorization as a skill; Cole, 1997; Rogoff & Mistry, 1985), whereas information-processing theories provide insight into internal mechanisms of development (Siegler, 1989). Marrying these two approaches led to a flourishing new area of research for Ornstein and his students: How might socially constructed conversations about experienced events influence the ways in which children come to recall those events? And, of course, given Ornstein's constant focus on both basic and applied research, why does this matter? This is the context in which Hedrick, Haden et al., and Langley et al. began their research programs, all of which demonstrate the crucial importance of conversational interactions in the formation of episodic memory, semantic memory, and even socio-emotional development.

## Memory of Episodes in Conversational Contexts

Early research on mnemonic strategies found that preschoolers were relatively mnemonically incompetent; deliberate interventions in order to recall presented information really did not appear until the early school years. These findings were in accord with general developmental theory that dominated at that time, stemming from Piaget (1967), claiming that the preschool mind was unordered, fragmented, and disorganized. Yet as memory research progressed, glimpses of early abilities became more apparent; although preschoolers are not very good at traditional laboratory memory tasks, such as object and list recall, they do show nascent mnemonic strategies, including looking more at items to be recalled, verbalizing items to be recalled (an early form of rehearsal), and various forms of object sorting to aid later recall (Baker-Ward, Ornstein, & Holden, 1984; DeLoache, Cassidy, & Brown, 1985). At about this same time, Katherine Nelson and her colleagues (Nelson et al., 1983; Nelson & Gruendel, 1976) found that preschoolers were able to provide well-organized, temporally sequenced, generalized reports of everyday events, such as going grocery shopping or to McDonalds. As these early abilities were documented, new conceptualizations of the preschool mind emerged, and new methodologies were called for to study the processes and products of early memory development. A critical insight gained from this research was the role of conversational interactions as a scaffold for development (Nelson, 1996).

Much of the initial research on the role of conversational context in children's memory development focused on reminiscing, examining individual differences in how parents co-constructed narratives about shared past experiences with their preschool children (see Fivush, 2019, and Fivush, Haden, & Reese, 2006, for reviews). This research established profound and enduring individual differences along a dimension of elaboration that predicted children's autobiographical memory development across childhood. Parents, and especially mothers, who reminisced with their young children in more elaborated, detailed, and coherent ways had children who recalled their own personal past in more elaborated and coherent ways both in conversation with parents and in conversation with an unfamiliar adult (see Fivush et al., 2006, for a review), and this effect held across childhood and into adolescence (Reese, Jack, & White, 2010).

Hedrick discusses three ways in which Ornstein and his colleagues and students extended this research: First, they brought an information-processing perspective to the research, thus deepening questions about exactly what aspects of a maternal elaborative style predicts children's memory development; second, whereas the initial research was naturalistic in method, asking families to discuss whatever events had occurred in their past, Ornstein and his colleagues brought experimental control to this process; and third, in bringing this control they were able to not just ask about reminiscing after the event occurred but further examine how conversational interactions both before and during the event may also shape what is subsequently remembered. All three of these innovations have added substantially to our understanding of the role of conversation interactions in different ways.

In terms of digging deeper into mechanism, Hedrick discusses the multiple specific aspects of a more elaborative reminiscing style, including asking open-ended *Wh-* questions, and not just examining the parental contributions but also performing fine-grained analyses of sequences and contingencies between parent and child within these conversations (see also Reese, Haden, & Fivush, 1993). This kind of fine-grained coding is obviously hugely labor-intensive, but provides amazing insight into the momentary dynamic interactions that produce specific outcomes. For example, we now know that mothers who ask elaborated yes/no questions with younger preschool children facilitate memory development; but later in the preschool years, open-ended *Wh*-questions are more effective (Haden et al., 2009). These kinds of results show the exquisite dance of development with parents who are sensitive to where their children are in their developmental journey and appropriately tailor their elaborative style to meet these needs, facilitating better memory development. But, of course, children are a part of this dance as well. By conducting fine-grained utterance-by-utterance coding, we learn how children begin to differentially respond to parental prompts and can analyze bidirectional developmental influences.

This bidirectionality becomes even clearer when we extend the study of conversational interactions to include conversation before and during the event as well. Ornstein and his colleagues (Haden et al., 2001; Hedrick, Haden, & Ornstein, 2009; Hedrick, San Souci et al., 2009) brought experimental control to the study of maternal reminiscing by designing a series of novel events in which the mother and child engaged. This allowed the researchers to know exactly what the event was and thus to more accurately measure recall, as well as to examine how the event was discussed while it was occurring and how this affected subsequent memory. Thus this approach emblemizes the interaction of a sociocultural approach focused on naturally occurring individual differences in mother–child conversations as a context for developmental change, with an information-processing approach that focuses on mechanisms of encoding and retrieval as operationalized in these conversations.

Intriguingly, the results underscore the need to integrate these approaches to best understand memory development. Children best remembered information that was discussed together during the event; that is, activities and objects talked about by only the mother or only the child were not as well recalled as activities and objects that mother and child had a dialogue about. This highlights both the bidirectionality of the role of conversations on recall and also the critical role of validation for the child. Objects and activities that the child was interested in enough to comment on were not recalled unless the mother validated that interest and elaborated on it. Thus, both context and mechanism are highlighted in these findings. Equally important, the role of reminiscing after the event remained critical for children's subsequent independent memory. Talk during the event may help children organize their memory, whereas talk after the event may help children rehearse or consolidate their memory, and both are important for the long-term duration of that memory.

The basic research findings set the stage for applying this knowledge in real-world settings, echoing Ornstein's commitment to pivoting between the lab and the field. Once the role of elaborative maternal reminiscing was established and the specific aspects of maternal style that were critical were identified, Ornstein and his colleagues (Boland, Haden, & Ornstein, 2003) developed a training system to help mothers become more elaborative. They devised a simple set of videos that demonstrated elaborative reminiscing and talked about the benefits of becoming more elaborative. Mothers easily adopted a more elaborative style, and their children indeed

showed benefits in that they recalled more information in more elaborative
and coherent detail weeks later. Thus, similar to the earlier work on
mnemonic strategies becoming applicable in school settings, the research
on maternal reminiscing style becomes applicable in home settings. And,
of course, applying these findings in these settings clarifies and refines the
basic knowledge obtained in the laboratory. Interventions on maternal
reminiscing have helped define the specific elements of maternal reminiscing style that are most effective for enhancing children's developing
memory skills. Together, this body of research has established the importance of socioculturally mediated conversational interactions in helping
young children form and consolidate memories of specific episodes. As
discussed in other parts of this volume, this basic work also has implications for educational (Coffman et al., 2008) and forensic (Ornstein &
Haden, 2001b) settings, again illustrating the wide reach of Ornstein's
approach to the development of memory.

### Building Semantic Knowledge in Conversational Contexts

Integration across theoretical perspectives and across the laboratory and the
field are critical elements of Ornstein's approach. We see this in the early
work on mnemonic strategies and the later work on reminiscing. Perhaps it
is no better illustrated than in Haden, Acosta, and Pagano's work on
memory in museums (Chapter 12). This research program is experimentally controlled and yet remains naturalistic, examining how conversations
between adults – both parents and museum guides – help children
comprehend and integrate knowledge about science-oriented museum
exhibits. Following Ornstein's earlier work, this research is also superbly
sensitive to both mechanism and context. It further extends the reminiscing work to examine how reminiscing about specific episodes can not just
influence memory for the episode but also help build semantic knowledge
about the topic discussed.

Based on the research examining mother–child conversations on event
memory discussed in Chapter 11 by Hedrick, Haden, Acosta, and Pagano
describe a research program that brings memory into the field to ask how
conversations between parents and children, and between museum guides
and children, both facilitate children's understanding of the exhibit and
help them to abstract semantic knowledge to build a scientific knowledge
base. Multiple aspects of Ornstein's approach to the development of
memory are incorporated into this research program. First, the research
is deeply informed by an integration of sociocultural and information-

processing theories. Children need hands-on experiences with scientific materials, and they need to bring an acute ability to attend, process, encode, and recall that information, but they also need social conversational interactions to support their understanding, to help them build more organized representations, and to help them transfer specific information into more abstract knowledge.

Second, the research combines examining real-world settings – naturally occurring museum visits – with explicit experimental control. Importantly, the work began with a more naturalistic approach, taking advantage of families who chose to visit museum exhibits and observing and collecting data on how parents and children spontaneously talked about these exhibits as they were occurring and just after, and then assessing children's subsequent memory for that visit and abstract knowledge gleaned. As in the reminiscing research, fine-grained utterance-by-utterance coding of these conversations led to discoveries about individual differences in how parents spontaneously structure these conversations, as well as information about the specific elements of conversational scaffolding that were most important for children's learning.

After demonstrating that naturally occurring individual differences in parent–child conversations about museum exhibits have similar effects as those seen in the research on everyday reminiscing, experimental control was introduced (Benjamin, Haden, & Wilkerson, 2010). Parents received instructions before coming to the museum exhibit in one of several strategies that included coordinated activities with and without conversational exchanges. As in the reminiscing research, parents who engaged in activities along with more elaborated conversations about what they were doing better facilitated children's subsequent recall and learning than parents who engaged in coordinated activities but did not engage in elaborative conversation. These findings mirror those reported by Hedrick that elaborative conversational exchanges during an event facilitate children's long-term memory of that event. The findings further extend that conclusion by demonstrating that it is not only memory of the experience that is enhanced but also aspects of learning the scientific content.

Third, the research beautifully integrates basic and applied research. Museums are a critical context for children to learn about science, engineering, and cultural diversity, and a more comprehensive approach to how and what children learn in this context is core to the educational system (Haden, 2010). Fortunately, the research findings also lend themselves to relatively easy interventions. Parents, and museum guides, can be easily instructed in more effective ways of conversing with children, both during museum visits and in reminiscing about those visits, in ways that facilitate children's learning (Haden et al., 2014; Jant et al., 2014). The melding of basic and applied research holds great promise for the future. Bringing experimental control into the everyday world of children and establishing clear principles of prediction and development confirm and extend the mission of developmental science.

## The Role of Reminiscing for Socio-emotional Skills

Although Ornstein focused on memory throughout his career, he always championed the idea that memory development unfolded within larger developing systems, both internal to the child and the external world. Perhaps this idea is best illustrated in Chapter 13 by Langley, Coffman, and Hussong, which extends the role of reminiscing into the socio-emotional arena. Langley et al. argue that children's developing understanding of the socio-emotional world must at least partly depend on how they remember and interpret previous emotional experiences (see also Fivush et al., 2006, for related arguments). In particular, they examine parent–child reminiscing conversations about specific episodes when the child either did or did not display appropriate expressions of gratitude. Gratitude has received a great deal of attention in the positive psychology literature. Individuals who express more gratitude show higher self-esteem, develop greater social support networks, access positive memories more easily, and actually show physical health benefits including greater longevity than less grateful individuals (Emmons & Mishra, 2011). Many experimental random control studies have found that encouraging people to engage in gratitude exercises, such as benefit-finding, have positive effects on both psychological and physical health (Sansone & Sansone, 2010). Being a grateful individual is clearly beneficial, yet we know little about the early development of gratitude in children or how gratitude might be cultivated during childhood (Watkins, 2004). Langley et al. take on this challenge.

More specifically, Langley et al. build on Ornstein's insistence on integrating across theories, across methods, and across basic and applied research. Gratitude, as a socio-emotional skill, is most often situated within the theoretical literature on emotional development, which is often distinct from the cognitive development literature. But in theorizing about how children might come to understand what gratitude is and how to express it, and thinking about children's everyday lives, Langley et al. posited that the ways in which parents structured conversations about past experiences of gratitude with their children might play a critical role in how children develop a sense of gratitude in their own lives. Connections to both Hedrick's work on conversational reminiscing and Haden et al.'s work on conversations about museums are clear. The underlying assumption is that parents scaffold their children's understanding of past experiences, and in so doing, help their children construct memories, understanding, and knowledge. Similar to that work, Langley et al. also examine individual differences in reminiscing styles and find that high-elaborative parents better facilitate their children's developing understanding of gratitude than less-elaborative parents (Hussong et al., 2019). Also extending the previous research programs, Langley et al. examine content of these conversations as well as structure. Just as Haden et al. found that both the structure and content of conversations about museum exhibits played a role in children's subsequent knowledge, Langley et al. find that both content and structure of conversations about gratitude, especially conversations about past experiences in which the child did not express appropriate gratitude, had positive effects on subsequent development. Further, parents who themselves were more grateful were more likely to select experiences for their children that would help build their gratitude (Rothenberg et al., 2017). Finally, and again similar to both Hedrick's and Haden et al.'s research programs, Langley et al. used initial basic research findings to develop an intervention to help parents foster gratitude in their children (Hussong, Coffman, & Thomas, 2020). This research program elegantly illustrates that, although as scientists we may divide the child up into specific systems to study, in fact, children are holistic developing organisms within sociocultural contexts that value certain kinds of experiences over others, and that the child's world is organized both by internally developing abilities to process information and the external worlds in which behavior unfolds.

## An Integrated Vision of Development

Looking across these three chapters, all focused on ways in which conversational contexts influence subsequent memory and learning, three aspects of Peter Ornstein's larger integrative vision of developmental science emerge: first, an integration of theoretical perspectives; second, an integration of basic and applied research; and third, an integration of memory with other developing systems internal and external to the child. This broad, integrative perspective provides a vision of the process of development as systematic, socially mediated, and complex. Several specific aspects of Ornstein's approach to developmental science, as illustrated in these three research programs, are noteworthy.

First, the research pays close attention to detailed fine-grained analyses of moment-by-moment interactions. This kind of painstaking work allows the researcher to examine development as it is occurring. Rather than taking a broad snapshot at different time points, this kind of work allows an investigation of development "on the ground." Moreover, through this kind of fine-grained approach, researchers gain a better understanding of the specific elements that drive development, both in terms of structure – what kinds of elaborative questions best predict outcome? What kinds of bidirectional interactions? – and content – what information is focused on and is most important in driving development?

Second, the research programs described in these three chapters consider development in the deep cultural context of what matters for the developing child. That is, what are the parental and societal goals? The early work on mnemonic strategies set the stage for placing basic research in an applied setting that described why it is important for children in the US educational system to be able to engage in deliberate memory. This was not some meaningless task, but was intrinsically related to the ways in which the culture defined educational success for its children. The same can obviously be said about the three research programs described in these chapters. Being conversant in science is highly valued by the culture, and parents and educators are anxious to discover new ways to help children build scientific knowledge skills. Similarly, being able to talk about oneself and one's experiences in coherent and elaborated ways is a critical skill in our culture, both for connecting to other people and for personal and professional flourishing (e.g., meeting romantic partners, college essays, job interviews; see Fivush, 2011, for a full discussion). And, as already mentioned, cultivating gratitude has multiple psychological and physical benefits. All three research programs are addressing questions important both for individual development and for individuals developing in ways to contribute to the social good.

In addition, in all three research programs, we see the commitment to apply basic research findings in ways to benefit children. All three programs of research have devised interventions that facilitate children's developing skills in these various arenas. Ornstein, from his early work in mnemonic strategies through his most recent work, is committed to both broadening and deepening developmental science, to examine both process and mechanism, and to drive the science to be meaningful in the everyday worlds of developing children.

Finally, a commentary on Peter Ornstein's contributions to developmental science would simply not be complete without mentioning his enormous impact as a mentor. For Ornstein, mentoring multiple generations of developmental scientists stems from the same commitments he makes in his science; just as his understanding of development involves the whole child, he is committed to mentoring the whole person. Mentoring is about integrating personal as well as professional development, integrating multiple perspectives on any given research question, and integrating researchers not formally in his lab into his research group. Each of the chapter authors discussed here was touched by Ornstein's gentle mentoring, as was I. I am eternally grateful for Peter Ornstein's vision of developmental science, and perhaps even more, his vision of what it means to grow up and become a person.

# PART V

# Classroom Socialization of Memory

# CHAPTER 15

# Overview
## The Development of Memory in the Elementary Classroom Context

### Jennifer L. Coffman and Olivia K. Cook

Peter Ornstein's central role in the field of cognitive development – especially with regard to the examination of deliberate memory skills – is evident throughout this volume. His collaborative orientation, openness to innovative ideas, and dedication to advancing the field through interdisciplinary partnerships and strong mentorship enabled multiple research teams to make considerable advances in the understanding of children's developing memory and cognitive skills. The work outlined in this chapter is one of the more recent lines of his collaborative legacy – one that builds squarely upon the copious basic research on children's strategic memory skills and that was borne out of the collaborative, interdisciplinary context in which he worked for decades. By the 1990s (as described in depth in earlier chapters in this volume), age-related changes in children's memory skills were well documented, but the bulk of the literature on children's memory was not focused on addressing questions of development – either in terms of studying intra-individual change over time or with regard to possible forces that underlie this change (see, e.g., Haden, Chapter 3; Bauer & Fivush, 2014; Ornstein & Coffman, 2020). At the same time, researchers at the Carolina Consortium on Human Development (CCHD) (e.g., Cairns, Elder, & Costello, 1996) were actively calling for developmental research – and suggesting that the study of development required both longitudinal data and multilevel analyses that would necessarily bridge across methods and paradigms.

## The Articulation of a Developmental Science Perspective on Research on Children's Memory

Influenced heavily by an emerging developmental science perspective – as articulated originally by the researchers at the CCHD – Ornstein, along

This work was supported in part by grants from the National Science Foundation (BCS-0217206 and BCS-0519153) and the Institute of Education Sciences (R305A120402). The writing of this chapter was supported in part by IES grant R305A170637.

with his colleagues and students, took on this challenge. Ornstein became convinced that a developmental evaluation of children's remembering required the exploration of factors that may influence the development of techniques for remembering. This developing perspective (as articulated, in part, in Morrison & Ornstein, 1996) contributed profoundly to the expansion of the move to interdisciplinary questions that focused on how children's memory develops in context and in the service of other cognitive, affective, and social goals. Ornstein and his students commenced research that was motivated by the question: "What forces in children's lives influence the development of strategies for remembering?" This line of work began as a sequence of small descriptive studies in elementary school classrooms (e.g., Mercer, 1996) and grew into a decades-long program of research by Ornstein, Coffman, and colleagues, currently referred to as the Classroom Memory Study.

The Classroom Memory Study serves as one example of the way in which Ornstein and his colleagues pushed toward a developmental analysis of memory, spurred in large part by the approach articulated in Ornstein and Haden's (2001a) paper that served as a challenge to the field to emphasize more on the *development* of memory through a scientific focus on factors or processes that may underlie growth in memory skills. (See Haden, Chapter 3, for an update on this perspective.) The decision to focus on the classroom context is described in detail below, but it came to be largely out of the desire to have a more developmental approach to the study of memory. As recently described in Ornstein and Coffman (2020), we were motivated by a *developmental science* approach, in which we argued for the need to provide descriptions of children's intra-individual skills over time, as well as to search for possible mediators that could underlie the observed changes in memory performance.

This chapter details the origins, findings, and future directions of this collaborative work. We highlight longitudinal findings that describe components of teachers' instruction that are associated with different facets of children's changing memory performance and outline the ways in which these correlational studies have informed the development of experimental manipulations that provide initial support for a causal relation between teachers' language and children's strategic skills. Finally, we discuss future directions for this line of research, including 1) the examination of the interplay of multiple contexts on the development of children's memory and cognitive skills, and 2) the possibility of the creation of interventions focused on teachers' instructional language – particularly language that is rich in references to metacognition and cognitive processes – that may be leveraged to facilitate the growth of students' skilled remembering.

## Origins of the Classroom Memory Study

We began this work using a socialization-of-cognition perspective (see Fivush, 2018; Rogoff, 1990; Vygotsky, 1978) to examine a set of relatively understudied developmental questions concerning the origin and refinement of deliberate memory strategies, but coupled this model with aspects of an information-processing approach, especially in terms of the memory tasks selected for use with the children in our studies. This program of research is positioned in the context of a rich literature that shows children's growing proficiency in the use of strategies such as rehearsal, organization, and elaboration and the suggestion that these age-related changes in strategy use parallel corresponding changes in remembering (Folds et al., 1990; Schneider & Ornstein, 2015). The extant data indicate that strategy use changes across the elementary school years in terms of both complexity and effectiveness (e.g., Folds et al., 1990; Schneider & Bjorklund, 1998), is associated in complex ways with children's metamnemonic understanding (Paris, Newman, & McVey, 1982; Schneider, Schlagmüller, Visé, 1998), and is causally linked to recall performance (e.g., Best & Ornstein, 1986; Bjorklund, Dukes, & Brown, 2009). At the beginning of this program of work, it was clear that skills in the use of rehearsal and organizational strategies for committing material to memory increase dramatically as children progress across elementary school grades (Ornstein, 1978); however, there was little research that spoke to questions of developmental change over time or in context. Indeed, because much of the literature on children's memory was based on cross-sectional research designs that contrasted the performance of children at different ages, little was known about intra-individual change over time, and even less was known about possible factors that may support the development of strategy use and effectiveness.

Motivated by questions about the course of memory development within individual children, as well as regarding possible factors that serve to mediate this development, our research team drew on a number of existing lines of research (that will be described in greater detail below) that together led us to a focus on the classroom setting as a possible context for the development of strategic skills. This foray into the classroom was prompted by cross-cultural studies that seemed to suggest that children who were exposed to formal Western-style schooling outperformed their non-schooled peers on measures typically studied by Western psychologists (e.g., Rogoff, 1981; Scribner & Cole, 1978; Wagner, 1978). Of particular interest was the finding that attending school seemed to be associated with children's acquisition and use of organizational techniques for remembering unrelated items. Moreover, the work of Morrison, Smith, and Dow-Ehrensberger (1995) with the "cutoff" method that enabled contrasts between "old kindergartners" and "young first graders" indicated that experience in the first grade was particularly important for the development of skilled remembering. In addition, findings from Baker-Ward, Ornstein, and Holden (1984) suggested that although kindergarteners exhibited spontaneous strategy-like behaviors, children's application of deliberate memory strategies was linked to recall only by the time children reached first grade.

Our initial work also drew on the limited information that was available about the potential linkage between classroom activities and memory development (Moely et al., 1992; Morrison et al., 1995), and the few existing longitudinal studies of children's memory (e.g., Guttentag, Ornstein, & Siemens, 1987; Haden et al., 2001; Reese, Haden, & Fivush, 1993; Schneider & Sodian, 1997; Weinert & Schneider, 1999) in the literature. Finally, we were influenced heavily by the growing literature on linkages between aspects of parent–child conversations and children's developing mnemonic skill (Reese et al., 1993). As will be described below, the basic science on children's strategic efforts (and success) paved the way for a growing perspective on the role of context in the development of strategic skill.

## Children's Memory Strategies

Since the end of the twentieth century, a rich literature has existed that provides a characterization of children's memory skills, age-related differences, and mnemonic strategies employed (Ornstein, Baker-Ward, & Naus, 1988; see Best & Folds-Bennett, Chapter 4, for a review). In the late 1960s and early 1970s, there was a rise in the focus of studying the development of children's memory strategies. Employing rather mechanistic conceptualizations of memory processes and reductionist methodologies, it had been previously assumed that children were rather nonstrategic in their deliberate memory skills. (For a review, see Ornstein et al., 1988; Baker-Ward & Ornstein, 2014.) However, it has since been shown that children's use of appropriate techniques for remembering and the effectiveness of deliberate strategies improve throughout elementary school (Ornstein, Haden, & San Souci, 2008). Children's deliberate memory development has been conceptualized as the development of children's information processing in situations in which retention-specific actions (e.g., strategies) and higher-order cognitions are activated with the intention to remember target information (Roebers, 2014). With this definition in mind, researchers were primarily interested in the mnemonic techniques and strategies employed by participants and how those techniques related to children's recall ability in tasks designed to assess deliberate memory (Ornstein et al., 2006; Schneider & Pressley, 1997).

The literature has shown convincingly that as children grow older they become proficient in the use of strategies for storing and retrieving information (Schneider & Ornstein, 2015), including rehearsal (e.g., Ornstein & Naus, 1978), organization (e.g., Lange, 1978), and elaboration (e.g., Rohwer, 1973). These data have also indicated that the complexity and effectiveness of children's strategy use change across the elementary school years (e.g., Folds et al., 1990; Schneider & Bjorklund, 1998). Additionally, strategy use has been causally linked to children's recall performance (e.g., Best & Ornstein, 1986; Bjorklund et al., 2009) and also is associated with children's metamnemonic understanding (Paris et al., 1982; Schneider et al., 1998). Nevertheless, it remained unclear from where these early strategy-like behaviors originate and how they develop both within individual children as well as over time. Some research supported the idea that the strategy-acquisition process is a swift transition from nonstrategic to strategic rather than a gradual, linear increase in strategy use (Schneider et al., 2004; Schlagmüller & Schneider, 2002). Other scholars demonstrated that children develop a complex set of strategies that they can use in varying combinations (Coyle & Bjorklund, 1997). Further, a number of studies found that when children used multiple strategies in the service of a memory goal, they exhibited higher recall scores than did single-strategy or no-strategy users (Coyle & Bjorklund, 1997; Schneider et al., 2004). However, this link between strategy use and recall is not pronounced until children begin elementary school (Ornstein et al., 2008). Building upon this early research, contemporary researchers have expanded upon lines of inquiry that focus how children's memory develops in context and in the service of other cognitive and social goals (Baker-Ward & Ornstein, 2014; Morrison & Ornstein, 1996; Wang 2018).

## The Development of Memory in the Formal School Context

One way that researchers have begun to apply a social-constructivist perspective has been through investigating children's memory as it develops in context. Since coined by White in 1965, the *5–7 shift* became a term used by teachers and researchers to describe a period in early childhood that is characterized by rapid cognitive growth. From late preschool to early elementary school, this growth has been exhibited through children's refinement of language skills (Read & Schrieber, 1982), increased metacognitive skills (Case, 1985; White, 1965), and strategic memory performance (Bjorklund, 1987; Ornstein & Naus, 1978). Over the past three decades, researchers have aimed to uncover the mechanisms that account for such change. Emerging from an era of primarily theory-driven research, contemporary cross-cultural approaches (e.g., Rogoff, 1981) have since demonstrated the relevance of school context as it relates to strides in children's memory development. The improved understanding of the ontogeny of children's strategy use notwithstanding, we are only at the beginning of our understanding of the contextual factors that are associated with the emergence and development of memory skills.

Ornstein, Coffman, and their students began their pursuit of possible contextual factors in the elementary school classroom, motivated by a number of lines of research that suggested a potential impact of formal schooling on the development of strategies for remembering. First, cross-cultural investigations contrasted the performance of children matched in chronological age but who differed in terms of their access to and participation in Western-style schooling (e.g., Scribner & Cole, 1978; Wagner, 1978). For example, in Wagner's study (1978), various cultural experiences of children in Morocco were explored as they served as antecedents to memory development. Using a design that contrasted schooled and non-schooled children in urban and rural environments, Wagner (1978) investigated variations in structural features as well as strategies for remembering. Wagner investigated three groups of subjects – Koranic students, Moroccan rug sellers, and college students – testing the hypothesis that each group may have a set of particular, culture-specific memory skills as a function of their experiences. Results from the study's first experiment, using a short-term recall task, showed that while short-term storage did not vary across age or experience (schooled vs. non-schooled, rural vs. urban), *control processes* (i.e., mnemonic techniques and strategies) were found to vary under the interaction of age and schooling experience. In the second experiment, subjects took part in a continuous recognition task that used black-and-white pictures of traditional rugs as the stimuli. Results from the second experiment suggested that although invariance of forgetting persisted across age and experience, the acquisition parameter varied as a function of specific cultural experiences. Wagner's (1978) study was one of several breakthroughs in contextually embedded research – arguing that aspects of cognition are driven by context. Further illustrated by a review of cross-cultural studies on memory performance, Rogoff (1981) concluded that non-schooled children generally do not make use of organizational techniques for remembering unrelated items and that experiences at school were related to the acquisition of these skills. Taken together, these cross-cultural findings suggested that something in the formal school context is important regarding the emergence of deliberate memorization skills.

## The Importance of First-Grade Experience

With cross-cultural research indicating that something about formal schooling encourages the development of strategic behavior, Ornstein, Coffman, and their team began to ask *when* during a child's school experience does this growth occur? To investigate what specific aspects of formal schooling play a role in children's memory development, a second area of literature has investigated the relevance of school setting on children's memory development using a different natural experiment: the School Cutoff Design. This approach allowed Morrison and his colleagues (1995) to capitalize on mandated dates for school entry, in which students need to be a specific age by a state-authorized date in order to begin school, by comparing children whose birthdays were within several weeks of that date and either just made or just missed the cutoff to begin school. Thus, the children were matched in terms of age but differed in their school experience, allowing for a comparison between a first-grade school experience (for young first graders) and a kindergarten experience (for older kindergarteners). By allowing researchers to compare the degree of change of a skill, such as memory, from pre- to posttest between children that just made or just missed the cutoff, this design has been used to assess the impact of schooling experience on the growth of various skills (for a review see Morrison et al., 2019). For example, young first graders have evidenced substantial growth in their memory skills over the first-grade year; however, in contrast, the kindergarteners' memory performance did not improve over the kindergarten year. Interestingly, these students showed improvement over the next year as a function of their experiences in the first grade. Additional studies utilizing a *between-grades regression discontinuity design* (Cahan & Davis, 1987), in which children near the cutoff are simply excluded from the sample, have yielded similar results. Although both of these approaches have provided findings that support separate age- and school-related influences on cognitive development, it remains unclear what about the classroom environment is driving memory development.

Prior to the work of Morrison and colleagues, the potential importance of the first-grade experience was suggested by the results of a study by Baker-Ward et al. (1984) in which age differences in strategic effectiveness were documented. In contrast to their performance on tasks involving rehearsal and organization (e.g., Ornstein & Naus, 1978; Lange, 1978), skills that develop during the elementary school years, Baker-Ward et al. showed that 4-, 5-, and 6-year-olds made use of a set of similar (albeit fairly simple) techniques. These children were placed in a setting in which they could interact with a set of common objects and toys for a 2-minute period. Although all children were told that they could play with the items, some of them received specific memorization instructions as well. The authors reported that even at age 4, children told to remember behaved differently from those simply instructed to play. For example, spontaneous labeling or naming occurred almost exclusively among the children instructed to remember, who also played less than the other children. The children who received instructions to remember also engaged in more visual inspection and evidenced more of what seemed to be reflection and self-testing. However, even though the memory instructions were associated with a "studious" approach to the task by the 4-, 5-, and 6-year-olds alike, only among the older children were the strategic behaviors associated with the facilitation of recall. This suggests again not only the importance of experiences in the first grade but also the role of conveying the deliberate nature of a task to child: "work to remember." As shown by the work of Baker-Ward et al. (1984), as noted above, language directed at a child may be one way in which strategies originate as well as become more reliable and effective over time.

## The Role of Teachers

Putting the cross-cultural (Rogoff, 1981; Wagner, 1978) work together with research carried out with the "cutoff" method (Morrison et al., 1995), we came to believe that participation in a Western-style school, especially in the first grade, is particularly important for the development of children's memory. But what is it about the early elementary school context that is important? Moely and her colleagues (1992) conducted classroom observations that later pointed to the relevance of teachers' instructional language on children's memory development. After examining instances of teacher instruction that included information about cognitive processing and strategy suggestions, Moely and her colleagues concluded that although explicit instruction to use strategies was rare, teachers were able to be grouped across first, second, and third grades by their level of strategy-suggestive instruction. Moreover, students in classes where teachers employed more strategy suggestions were more likely to engage in spontaneous strategic organization in recall tasks than students in other classes, but only among the first graders. In a similar endeavor, Mercer (1996) observed explicit strategy suggestions across six first-grade class-rooms. Although instances of strategy suggestions only occurred in 2.4% of the observational intervals that were coded, and an expressed goal of an ongoing activity was apparent in only 1.8% of the observational intervals, 38.8% of the intervals contained instances in which the use of remember-ing was strongly implied, if not explicitly requested.

Taken together, the work of Moely et al. (1992) and Mercer (1996) suggested that although explicit instruction in memory skills or cognitive processing language is rare, it may be quite important for students' developing memory. Teachers report that they believe that memory skills are important for their students' success in school, but indicate that they have not been trained in the teaching of these skills. These lines of research further suggest that something about the classroom – and potentially first grade in particular – is important for children's developing memory skills.

This suggestion is at the core of a question that has driven our line of work for over a decade:

> If school is important in terms of the emergence and refinement of mnemonic techniques, and if teachers value the development of memory skills, but if explicit instruction is an infrequent occurrence, then what is it about the classroom that influences the development of these skills? (Ornstein & Coffman, 2020, p. 5).

We hypothesized that elementary teachers may create a context for strategy use, or for the generalization of techniques from one area – possibly math or language arts – to remembering. With this in mind, and influenced by Rogoff's (1990, 2003) calls for the utilization of con-textually embedded approaches to examine children's memory develop-ment, we were led to a serious consideration of the possible role of the classroom context – and to teachers' instruction in particular.

Our consideration of the nature of teachers' language during instruction was reinforced by a growing literature that documented a linkage between the ways in which mothers of preschoolers structure conversations about past experiences and the memory abilities of their children. For example, Fivush and her colleagues (e.g., Fivush, 2018; Reese et al., 1993) reported that mothers classified as "high-elaborative" in their conversational style encouraged talk about past events more than "low-elaborative" mothers. Building upon this work, a sizable number of studies have since linked parents' elaborative style to children's autobiographical memory skills (for a review, see Fivush, Haden, & Reese, 2006), and more recently, their deliberate memory (Langley, Coffman, & Ornstein, 2017). Given the strong indication that "parent talk" about an event can influence children's remembering, it has been suggested that "teacher talk" may also be relevant for the development of memory strategies. Paralleling the work with pre-schoolers, both types of conversation – while a lesson is taking place and after it has occurred – may be relevant in the classroom. Thus, given the existing literature described here, The Classroom Memory Study team focused on the language that teachers used in early elementary classrooms and on trying to uncover associations between aspects of instructional language and children's memory skills.

## The Classroom Memory Study

In our initial longitudinal investigation (Coffman et al., 2008), we carried out in-depth assessments of children's memory skills and academic achievement across grades 1, 2, 4, and 5, while at the same time making comprehensive observations of their teachers during instruction in mathematics and language arts. In the course of this work, we developed the measure of cognitive processing language (CPL) that we present below in greater detail.

### Measuring Cognitive Processing Language

The measure of teacher language was developed in preparation for our initial longitudinal study (Coffman et al., 2008), in which coders observed 1 hour of instruction in language arts and a second hour in mathematics, making coding decisions every 30 seconds, and has been used in subsequent investigations. Coffman and colleagues (2008) created a Taxonomy of Teacher Behaviors (based in part of Moely et al., 1992) that aimed to characterize teachers' CPL using an index of 23 codes across four broad categories of (1) instructional activities, (2) cognitive structuring activities, (3) memory requests or demands, and (4) the provision of metacognitive information. Our Taxonomy was designed to characterize teachers' naturally occurring language and to evaluate variability across teachers in their use of this language that we believed would be important for students' skills in memory and cognition. In our original longitudinal investigation, we observed for 2 hours in each of 14 first-grade classrooms, coding 1 hour of instruction in both language arts and mathematics. Our coders made judgments every 30 seconds concerning whether or not teachers engaged in a wide range of behaviors that fell into four broad categories. Although multiple codes can occur within each interval, coders can only record each code *once* within each 30-second interval. Examples of codes and categories are below; see Coffman et al. (2008) for the complete coding scheme.

*Instruction* codes were used in instances such as a teacher's provision of specific task information (e.g., where to place materials), general information (e.g., describing a frog's habitat), or a summary of upcoming activities. *Cognitive structuring activities* captured teacher language that encourages children to engage materials in ways that have been found in laboratory studies to prompt deep levels of processing and to affect the encoding and retrieval of information (Craik & Lockhart, 1972; Hyde & Jenkins, 1969). Examples of cognitive structuring activities include attention regulation, identifying features, categorization, or connecting to previous experiences. *Memory requests* were coded when a teacher asked students to retrieve information or to prepare for future activities. Memory requests include, for example, episodic (e.g., retrieval of an event), semantic (e.g., report of a learned fact), and future prospective requests. *Metacognitive information* codes were used when teachers provided or solicited metacognitive information in the service of facilitating children's performance. Codes included, for example, when teachers offer a metacognitive rationale (e.g., "Showing your work will help you organize your thinking."), use metacognitive questioning (e.g., "How could you solve that problem?"), or make a suggestion (e.g., "Use your tens frame.").

*Describing the Classroom Context*

As would be expected, the first-grade children were exposed to a considerable amount of *instruction*, with 78.2% of the total observational intervals containing some form of instruction. The teachers also devoted much time to the provision of both *general information* (41.8% of observational intervals contained this code) and *specific task information* (40.1%). In addition, 42.6% of the intervals included *cognitive structuring activities*. Some teacher time was devoted to *attention regulation* (14.1%) and *relating new material to prior experiences* at home or school (10.1%), and some emphasis was placed on *massed repetition* (9.3%). Importantly, *memory requests* were quite frequent; 52.7% of the intervals included some demand for memory, and 47% of the intervals included occurrences of probes for *semantic* information. In contrast, the provision of *metacognitive information* was relatively rare (9.5%), although approximately half of the intervals with such information included suggestions about strategies, particularly in the context of approaching a specific question in mathematics or reading. (See Coffman et al., 2008 for detailed descriptions of descriptive data and variability.)

Although our coding system enables us to capture many features of classroom instruction that are likely important for the development of children's mnemonic skills, we have focused largely on the construction of an index of teachers' mnemonic orientation that was based on a subset of five component codes – based on two individual and three combination codes – that seemed to be particularly relevant for understanding memory in the classroom. As described in Coffman et al. (2008), the index was comprised of (a) *strategy suggestions*; (b) *metacognitive questioning*; (c) the co-occurrence of *deliberate memory demands* and *instructional activities*; (d) the co-occurrence of *deliberate memory demands* and *cognitive structuring activities*; and (e) the co-occurrence of *deliberate memory demands* and *metacognitive information*. The selection of these activities for an index of mnemonic style was based primarily on three factors. First, we observed considerable variability across teachers in each of these coded behaviors. Second, the selection of these activities was also based on their presumed role in memory and its development. Thus, for example, cognitive structuring activities influence the depth to which information is processed (Craik & Lockhart, 1972), whereas memory requests and the provision of strategy suggestions and metacognitive information impact encoding, retrieval, or both (Schneider & Pressley, 1997). And third, the teacher behaviors that provided the foundation for our characterization of mnemonic style in the classroom were observed during instruction in each of the domains in which we made observations.

There was considerable variability across teachers in their use of language captured by the five codes; the range across the 14 first-grade classrooms in *strategy suggestions* was between 0.8% and 13.8%, and in the asking of *metacognitive questions* from 0.8% to 9.6%. Interestingly, large differences were also seen in the combination codes that capture both *deliberate memory demands* and either *instructional activities* (ranging from 25.8% to 50%), *cognitive structuring activities* (10% to 35.4%), or *metacognitive information* (1.3% to 12.1%). Over subsequent studies, we have continued to see similar patterns of variability in terms of the basic rates at which aspects of language occur, and also related to teachers' differential use of these codes. In all of this work, because of the variability in the rates of occurrence of these different codes, we make use of standardized scores so that the values can be combined into a single composite indicator of teachers' CPL.

### *Linking the Classroom Context to the Children's Memory Performance*

In the initial longitudinal study, we first described the performance of the children at three points during the first grade, provided an overview of the language used by the teachers as they taught lessons in language arts and mathematics, and examined the children's performance on the Free Recall with Organizational Training Task (Moely et al., 1992) as a function of the extent to which their teachers made use of CPL. We found that initially the first graders grouped the pictures randomly, but also noted that they responded effectively to organizational training such that their category-based sorting increased across the year, along with recall. Consistent with initial observations and with Moely et al.'s (1992) report, we found that direct instruction in memory strategies was indeed rare, but we observed that the different codes that comprised the CPL measure provided an interesting look at the "mnemonic climate" of the classroom. Based on our measure of teachers' language, we then examined the patterns of various indices of children's memory performance as a function of their classroom assignment. Of the 107 first graders enrolled in our original study, 46 were taught by teachers who used low levels of CPL and 61 by teachers who used higher levels of CPL. By the end of the first-grade year, the children in classes taught by teachers with contrasting orientations differed in their use of memory strategies and their recall on several deliberate memory tasks, including an Object–Memory Task (Baker-Ward et al., 1984) and a Free Recall with Organizational Training task (Moely et al., 1992). To illustrate the findings, consider children's contrasting performance on the Free Recall with Training Task that was administered across the first and second grades. At the first assessment point in the fall of Grade 1, each child received three trials – baseline, training, and generalization – whereas at each subsequent assessment in the winter and spring only non-instructed generalization trials were administered. Similarly, when the children were in Grade 2, three assessments with non-instructed generalization trials were carried out, one each in the fall, winter, and spring.

As can be seen in Figure 15.1, the sorting performance of the children in the two types of classrooms did not differ initially on either the baseline or generalization trials at the first assessment point (Time 1) of Grade 1, but

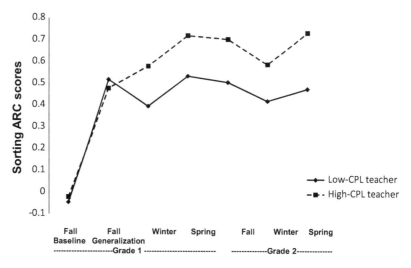

Figure 15.1    Children's mean adjusted ratio of clustering (ARC) sorting score over time as a function of first-grade teachers' use of cognitive processing language (CPL)

by the winter, the groups had diverged, with differences evident at both Time 2 and Time 3. Thus, there were significant effects of teacher CPL on the children's sorting performance (Coffman et al., 2008). Importantly, the effect of the first-grade classroom context was maintained across the second grade, when the children were taught by different teachers (Ornstein, Coffman, & Grammer, 2009).

In addition to the linkages between the instructional style of the first-grade teachers and the children's strategic abilities in the first and second grades, we have also observed some surprising long-term connections between the first-grade classroom and children's strategic performance on complex tasks in the later years of the elementary school. Interestingly, these differences in children's performance extended to their use of strategies during the second grade, even though they were taught by different teachers and were dealing with more difficult thematically organized material (Ornstein et al., 2009, 2010; Coffman et al., 2019). Moreover, these differences in children's skills were sustained and observable in later years despite being taught by different teachers. For example, the performance of 58 of the 107 children who entered the investigation in the first grade were observed in the fourth grade on tasks involving the organization of low-associated items in a Sort–Recall task (cf. Bjorklund, Ornstein, & Haig, 1977) and the deployment of techniques for acquiring information from text in a Study Skills task (cf. Brown & Smiley, 1977). In the Sort–Recall task, the children were told to sort the low-associated words into groups that would facilitate remembering, and clear differences were observed in the level of semantic organization reflected in the children's sorting patterns as a function of the CPL of their first-grade teachers. Indeed, children who had a high-CPL teacher in first grade made greater use of meaning-based sorting across the fourth-grade year (Coffman et al., 2019). Similarly, when the fourth graders were presented with a grade-appropriate science or social studies passage and given four minutes to "work to remember," differences were observed in their study behaviors as a function of their first-grade teachers. When participants' individual behaviors (e.g., highlighting, note taking, rereading) were scored on a scale from 0 (absence of the study behavior) to 3 (organized, efficient use of the strategy) and averaged, children who had been placed in a high-CPL first-grade classroom outperformed their peers who had a low-CPL first-grade teacher (Coffman et al., 2019).

Coffman et al. (2008) found that children in high-CPL classrooms were not only using spontaneous strategic behavior in an Object–Memory task at a higher rate than their peers, but they were also better at transferring the strategic knowledge that they learned to new materials. Thus, it seems as though there is something in the classroom environment that is established by teachers who use higher levels of CPL that supports children's acquisition of memory skills that are important for success in school. Children with teachers who use more CPL are exposed to greater memory demands and more strategic and metacognitive language in mathematics and language arts than are their peers with teachers who use less of this language, and perhaps this exposure is important for their emerging deliberate memory skills.

We have also continued to explore possible sources (including both child and teacher factors) of remaining variability in children's developmental trajectories, including, for example, the children's self-regulation in the classroom, as assessed by the teachers, and their performance on standardized measures of academic achievement. Indeed, children rated as low in self-regulation who were in the classes of teachers who used high levels of CPL showed markedly greater gains in organized sorting over the year than did low-regulated children in other classes (Ornstein & Coffman, 2020), as can be seen in Figure 15.2 (used with permission). As can also be seen in the figure, this interaction of first-grade teacher language and this child-level factor continued through the second grade. Similar patterns were observed in the academic achievement data such that

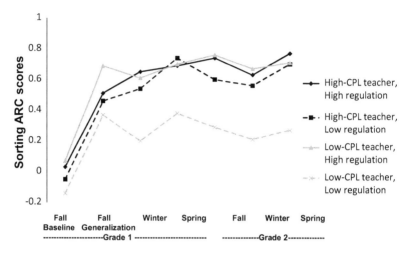

Figure 15.2    Children's mean adjusted ratio of clustering (ARC) sorting score over time as a function of first-grade teachers' use of cognitive processing language (CPL) and children's self-regulation

high-achieving children had elevated patterns of sorting, regardless of their first-grade teachers' use of CPL, whereas lower achievers' performance was strongly linked to teacher style (Ornstein et al., 2010).

### *Initial Experimental Evidence*

Building on the correlational, longitudinal work of Coffman et al. (2008, 2019) and Ornstein et al. (2009, 2010), we turned next toward an attempt to identify potential causal linkages between aspects of teacher language and children's memory performance via an experimental study in after-school programs (Grammer, Coffman, & Ornstein, 2013). In this project, we first trained teachers to use contrasting presentation styles (based on the Coffman et al., 2008 teacher groups) and then assessed students assigned to each of those conditions. Groups of first and second graders were assigned to one of two instructional conditions (high vs. low levels of memory-relevant language [CPL]) in a 2-week science and engineering unit that we called *Things That Move*, with content about building, sturdy structures, simple machines, and gears. The activities and materials were consistent across conditions – only the language of instruction was manipulated. Grammer and colleagues (2013) found that students who were exposed to higher levels of CPL not only acquired more strategic knowledge, but they were better able to apply this new knowledge in the service of a memory goal.

Although children in both conditions had essentially no knowledge concerning the facts of the *Things That Move* unit (e.g., the definition of gears) before instruction, all participants demonstrated gains in factual knowledge as a result of instruction. Children's strategic knowledge within this domain (e.g., how to choose the right gears to get a vehicle to move) was also very limited at the outset, but the children exposed to high-CPL instruction outperformed their peers in the low-CPL condition by the end of the 2-week unit of instruction. More specifically, children in both instructional conditions evidenced enhanced knowledge of facts, with children in the high-CPL condition demonstrating greater gains in strategic knowledge of how to solve problems within this domain (see Grammer, Coffman, & Ornstein, 2013).

Moreover, not only did the children who received high-CPL instruction acquire more strategic knowledge concerning *Things That Move*, they were also better able to apply this knowledge in the service of a memory goal than were the children who received low-CPL instruction. We observed these differences in the application of knowledge gained in the course of the instructional unit in their performance on a Content-Specific Sort–Recall Task. This task is essentially a modification of the baseline trial (i.e., the trial prior to any instruction in meaning-based sorting) of the Free Recall with Organizational Training task (Moely et al., 1992), in which materials drawn from the domain of instruction rather than general taxonomic categories were employed. In this task, the children were presented with sets of 15 picture cards of Lego pieces (e.g., plates, beams, gears), and their sorting patterns were scored to reflect the degree to which the cards were sorted into meaning-based groups (e.g., all of the gears placed together, regardless of color or shape). The scores ranged from 0 (sorting at random) to 4 (the majority of the groups were organized by strong semantic or functional associations). At the beginning of the instructional unit there was almost no sorting on the basis of meaning for either group, but at the end of instruction and at a 1-month posttest, there were clear differences between the two conditions, such that the children exposed to low CPL showed very little growth in the ability to make use of the material to which they were exposed in the *Things That Move* unit, whereas those in the high-CPL condition were quite skilled in doing so. Thus, it is clear that the language experienced during instruction was also linked to this ability to apply the new content knowledge in the service of a memory goal. The children in the high-CPL condition were also better able to use this knowledge to group conceptually in a Content-Specific Sort–Recall task than their peers in the low-CPL condition (Grammer, Coffman, & Ornstein, 2013).

These findings suggest that teachers' "talk" is linked causally to children's performance, but which features seem to be important in determining the outcomes? To examine this issue, we carried out two follow-up experiments in which students received instruction that emphasized contrasting components of CPL, and the findings indicated that metacognitive language is a key determinant of the outcomes that we have observed (Ornstein et al., 2016). The results of this experiment provide considerable support for view that teachers' CPL during instruction is malleable and that exposing children to a high-CPL style of teaching is associated with benefits in domain-specific strategic knowledge and utilization. What we did not find, however, is generalization of strategic skill to the taxonomic materials that have been at the foundation of much of our research. We suspect that we did not obtain this generalization because our instructional unit was short, only 2 weeks, and perhaps because we exposed children to high levels of CPL language in only one domain. In contrast, in our longitudinal research (Coffman et al., 2008), the children were exposed to the CPL of their teachers in multiple areas of instruction for the full academic year.

In order to further investigate which features of teachers' talk are important in determining the outcomes, Ornstein et al. (2016) carried out two follow-up experiments in which students received different types of instruction that carried contrasting components of CPL. The findings indicated that metacognitive language was the key determinant in the child outcomes observed (Ornstein et al., 2016). This focus on metacognition, as well as complementary emphases on other aspects of child-, home-, and teacher-level factors, will likely comprise much of the attention of the Classroom Memory Study team moving forward.

## Future Pursuits for the Classroom Memory Study Team

The research described in this chapter provides an overview of a program of study that suggests that aspects of parents' and teachers' language are important in the socialization of children's memory skills. To return to the distinction originally put forth by Ornstein and Haden (2001a), and revisited in Haden, Chapter 3 of this volume, we see this work as providing continuing information on *memory* development, that is, the memory performance of children of different ages, and as moving further along the path to understanding the *development* of memory, that is, the factors that impact developmental change in memory skills from one age to another. Seen through the lens of social-constructivist views of cognitive development, and focused primarily on the context of early elementary school classrooms, we are beginning to understand that the language of instruction that children experience in the classroom plays an important role in the development of children's skills for remembering. Moreover, we see that this is of particular importance for specific subgroups of children (related to their regulatory skills or academic achievement). Much remains to be understood, however, about the combined influence of language exposure at home and school, as well as regarding the role of teachers' CPL when it comes to both additional domain-general (e.g., executive functions or study skills) and more domain-specific (e.g., mathematics) skills that are relevant in the classroom context. The Classroom Memory Study has begun to lay the groundwork for a growing body of knowledge regarding the role of parents' and teachers' language – a body that will grow in a number of directions in the coming years. Here, we outline just a few of the questions that remain to be fully understood, including a further explication of various levels of analysis, the possible role of metacognition as a mediator of change, and plans for the development of teacher interventions that can support the development of children's cognitive skills.

First, additional evidence concerning teachers, children, and families is necessary to understand more completely the ways in which exposure to different levels of CPL may be associated with children's cognitive and academic outcomes. For example, what characteristics of teachers make it likely that they would be naturally predisposed to use high levels of CPL in their instruction or to incorporate higher levels of CPL into their teaching when they are made aware of the advantages of this style of instruction? Similarly, what characteristics of a child's basic skills and his or her family environment (especially the forms of language experienced at home) contribute to or perhaps moderate the impact of CPL on performance? The nature of the in-the-home language environment may impact children's skills at school entry and have implications for their ability to take advantage of the richness of the language environment in the classroom. Moreover, children's regulatory abilities and metacognitive skills may interact in complex ways with aspects of students' experiences at home and school.

Indeed, metacognition is one important possible mediator of change, and although the importance of metacognition has been recognized in the memory literature for some time, much remains to be explored concerning associations between students' performance and their own metacognitive understanding – as well as regarding the role of metacognitive language in the classroom. It has long been understood that metacognition has had a role in children's learning of strategic methods for remembering, but the elucidation of clear relations between metamemory and strategic performance has been difficult. For example, under some conditions, children nominate their use of a particular mnemonic strategy but then fail to use it in practice (Sodian, Schneider, & Perlmutter, 1986). Additionally, children have been found to appear as though they are using a deliberate strategy, but then fail to articulate metamnemonic understanding of this strategy (Bjorklund & Zeman, 1982). However, children's memory performance has been found to be best supported by supplementing strategy instruction with metamnemonic information (Paris et al., 1982), and numerous studies have provided significant linkages between metamemory and memory development (Schlagmuller & Schneider, 2002; Schneider et al., 1998).

The role of metacognition was also seen in the early classroom work in which Moely and colleagues (1992) investigated the connection between teacher language and children's strategic memory, focusing in part on students' metacognitive reports of their use of category organization as a study and recall strategy. Importantly, children who were enrolled in classrooms in which teachers engaged in high-strategy-use instruction were more likely to discuss their use of categorization than were children of low-strategy-use teachers. Metacognitive language is also an important component of teachers' CPL, and although it occurs at a fairly low frequency in classrooms, metacognitive language is viewed as influential in children's memory development. The importance of metacognition has also been emphasized in literature examining children's memory development in the context of mother–child reminiscing, where it has been suggested that metacognitive talk is integral in supporting children's autobiographical and deliberate memory development (Langley et al., 2017). Further support for the role of metacognition comes from preliminary experimental studies in which students received different styles of instructional language during simulated classroom instructional units (in Science or Language Arts) and that suggest that metacognitive language played a central role in children's increased strategic understanding (Ornstein et al., 2016).

These findings not only contribute to our basic understanding of the role of specific aspects of instruction that may be especially important for the development of children's skills, but they also can inform the creation of interventions that could influence teaching in the classroom as well as children's learning. Once clear linkages are established between teachers' language and children's skills – both in naturalistic observational studies and in experimental investigations – we then can move toward implementing specific professional-development programs in schools. These programs could be designed to provide teachers with instructional tools that can be leveraged to support the cognitive growth of all of their students, thus providing an application of the basic research findings on the socialization of children's cognitive skills. Although these preliminary experimental investigations can serve as directions for intervention work, in order to truly address the continued gaps in our understanding of children's memory development, researchers must continue to be creative in their scientific approach. As urged by Ornstein and Haden (2001a), two primary steps are clear for progressing the field of children's memory development: 1) the pairing of longitudinal and experimental approaches in order to gain a more enriched understanding of children's development, and 2) the continued application of both information-processing and social-constructivist perspectives, thus transcending traditional paradigms of research. By following proposed directives from Ornstein and other cognitive developmental scientists, the future of scientific inquiry in this field appears promising – both in the pursuit of basic knowledge and in the application of findings that could be used by the researchers, educators, and families involved in the process.

# CHAPTER 16

# Children's Accuracy and Strategy Use in the Context of Addition
## Extending the Impact of Metacognitive Language to Children's Academic Skills

*Kesha N. Hudson, Keadija C. Wiley, and Jennifer L. Coffman*

In preceding chapters in this volume, our colleagues considered the socialization of memory, with an emphasis on the importance of mothers' and teachers' language for the development of children's autobiographical and deliberate memory skills. Hedrick (Chapter 11) demonstrated that richly supportive and scaffolded interactions between mothers and their children support children's developing abilities to talk about previously experienced events (e.g., Haden et al., 2001; see also Fivush, Haden, & Reese, 2006 for a review of the literature) as well as children's strategic behaviors in the context of deliberate memory tasks (Langley, Coffman, & Ornstein, 2017). Coffman and Cook (Chapter 15) also showed that exposure to metacognitively rich instruction in the context of formal schooling is related to the extent to which children spontaneously use memory strategies as well as in their response to strategy training in the context of deliberate memory tasks (Coffman et al., 2008). Moreover, these differences in memory performance are sustained across elementary school, such that those students who experienced more metacognitively rich instruction in the first grade continued to engage in more strategic behaviors during a memory task in second grade and during a study-skills task in fourth grade (Coffman et al., 2019).

As the work of Ornstein, Coffman, and their colleagues on the socialization of memory moved into the classroom, it became evident that the effects of teachers' use of cognitive processing language may extend beyond domain-general skills, such as memory, to include domain-specific performance, such as mathematics. Although little is known about cross-domain associations among children's growing mastery of strategies that are important for remembering and problem-solving in mathematics, in many respects the literatures in these domains are parallel. Indeed, in much the same way that children engage in deliberate strategy use and recall efforts in the service of a memory goal, they also retrieve previously learned math facts and utilize a variety of strategies to solve mathematics problems for which they do not already know the answer. Across both domains, children have been observed using multiple strategies in the context of a single task with varying degrees of success (Coyle & Bjorklund, 1997; Lehman & Hasselhorn, 2007; Siegler & Jenkins, 1989; Siegler, Adolph, & Lemaire, 1996). Moreover, researchers have identified the important role of prior knowledge in memory and mathematical skill development. For example, a considerable amount of evidence indicates that changes with age in both the content and structure of children's underlying knowledge in permanent memory can influence strategy selection and implementation (Bjorklund, 1985; Ornstein & Naus, 1985; Ornstein, Baker-Ward, & Naus, 1988). Similarly, both conceptual and procedural knowledge impact children's abilities in mathematics. For example, at entry to school there is considerable variability in children's knowledge of numbers, which is often gained through informal experience. This basic knowledge plays an important role in the acquisition of more complex skills introduced by their elementary school teachers (Bransford, Brown, & Cocking, 1999). Educators recognize that children's mastery of early addition strategies, such as counting from a larger addend, provides a foundation on which later-developing, more sophisticated mathematical skills are based, such as those used in multidigit arithmetic and algebra (Siegler, 2003).

These cross-domain similarities led Ornstein and colleagues to consider whether aspects of mothers' and teachers' language, known to support strategy use in the context of memory tasks, may also support the emergence and refinement of children's strategic skill in mathematics. In this chapter, we begin with a brief overview of children's early mathematical competencies, focusing primarily on strategy use in the context of addition. We then present illustrative findings that highlight (1) the effects of both mothers' and teachers' language on the development of children's math skills across early elementary school, and (2) the sustained effects of teachers' instructional language on the math skills of specific subgroups of children. In doing so, we demonstrate that aspects of the home and school contexts, including mothers' and teachers' language, may be important not only for the socialization of memory but also for cognition more broadly, as evidenced by a growing number of studies focused on children's mathematics skills.

## Children's Early Mathematical Competence

When children arrive in kindergarten, they exhibit an understanding of a range of arithmetic concepts that is based on their informal experiences, and their mastery of these ideas provides the foundation for the acquisition of increasingly more complex and abstract mathematical competencies (Newcombe et al., 2009). Children as young as 2.5 years of age are able to understand number and amount, as evidenced by their nonverbal calculation abilities (Huttenlocher, Jordan, & Levine, 1994). By maintaining a mental model in which imagined transformations are mapped onto actual objects and their movements, children are able to determine how many items remained in a hidden array after items had been added into or taken away from it.

Children's numerical knowledge continues to develop as they acquire an understanding of cardinality and the cardinal principle. This process begins as children learn that number words correspond to sets of certain sizes (e.g., that "two" refers to a set of two items) and continues until they recognize the cardinal principle, namely, that the last number reached when counting a set of objects represents the numerosity of the whole set. Understanding the cardinal principle is a critical milestone in children's mathematical development because it enables them to produce a set of a given numerosity, compare sets based on their numerosities, and recognize that adding one to a set increases its numerosity by exactly one (Gelman & Gallistel, 1978; Wynn, 1992). These capacities represent the emergence of a conceptual framework that provides the foundation for learning more complex symbolic calculation procedures in later childhood. Indeed, as children transition to kindergarten, they begin to acquire rules, procedures, and problem-solving strategies that facilitate mastery of more formal arithmetical concepts through formal instruction (Baroody & Ginsburg, 1983; Carpenter, Franke, & Levi, 2003; Knuth et al., 2006).

In the context of addition, Siegler and Jenkins (1989) define a strategy as any procedure that is (1) nonobligatory, such that it does not represent the only way to solve a problem, and (2) goal-directed, insofar as it is intended to accomplish a specified purpose. Across a range of studies, researchers have observed that preschool and elementary-aged children used a variety of strategies to solve addition problems, ranging from counting fingers to retrieving facts from memory, and that the repertoire of strategies varies in a wavelike manner over time. Indeed, as new strategies emerge, older and often less-efficient ones are used less often and may be abandoned altogether (Ashcraft, 1982; Baroody & Ginsburg, 1986; Fuson, 1982; Ilg & Ames, 1951; Siegler & Jenkins, 1989; Svenson & Sjoberg, 1983)

In the strategy choice model (Siegler, 1986; Siegler & Robinson, 1982; Siegler & Shrager, 1984), Siegler and colleagues posit that children's deployment of strategies is governed by two parameters: (1) a confidence criterion, that determines whether the associative strength of an answer is sufficient to state it, and (2) a search length criterion that corresponds to the maximum number of retrieval attempts a child will make before choosing an alternative strategy. The likelihood that an answer can be directly retrieved from memory is seen as being influenced by the peakedness of the distribution of associations between a problem and all potential answers. That is, the more peaked the distribution of associations, the more strongly a single answer is associated with the problem solution, and therefore the more readily it can be retrieved. If the distribution is relatively flat, however, the associative strength is distributed among several potential answers and the use of a strategy is likely (Geary et al., 1991; Geary & Brown, 1991; Kerkman & Siegler, 1997).

To illustrate, in order to solve 9 + 5 = ___, a child would first set the confidence criterion, which determines if the associative strength of a potential answer is sufficient to state it, and then attempt to retrieve an answer. If an answer cannot be easily retrieved, or if the retrieved value does not exceed the confidence criterion, then the child will employ a strategy, such as shortcut-sum (counting from one to the first addend 1, 2, 3, 4, 5, 6, 7, 8, 9 and then continuing to count five more 10, 11, 12, 13, 14) or the decomposition procedure (breaking the problem 9 + 5 into a simpler version such as 9 + 1 = 10, so 10 + 4 = 14). These strategies differ in terms of the time required for execution, the probability of producing the correct answer, and the demands placed on working-memory resources (Siegler, 1986).

This body of work is informative in that it highlights *what* develops in terms of children's early mathematical competencies. With regard to children's early use of addition strategies, these findings indicate that young children are aware that if they do not know the answer to a problem, they can employ a variety of different strategies in an attempt to solve it. Moreover, children demonstrate facility in using multiple strategies, and over time they evidence a shift toward using more advanced techniques. In order to understand *how* children become aware of mathematical strategies as well as how to execute them, we look toward the home and school contexts in which children are embedded.

## Characterizing Mothers' and Teachers' Language

As described in previous chapters, researchers have documented consistent differences in the ways in which mothers structure and support conversations about the past with their children (Fivush et al., 2006; Hedrick, Chapter 11). In particular, mothers vary in the extent to which they use metamemory talk to reference children's memory or to acknowledge the process of remembering, as well as in their use of elaborative statements to provide additional new information to the conversation (Langley et al., 2017). Importantly, the provision of maternal metamemory talk (Coffman et al., 2011) and elaborativeness (Langley et al., 2017) have been linked to children's strategic attempts to remember and recall information in the context of deliberate memory tasks.

Similarly, teachers naturally vary in the extent to which they scaffold children's approaches to learning during instruction (Coffman et al., 2008; Coffman & Cook, Chapter 15; Grammer, Coffman, & Ornstein, 2013; Hudson, Coffman, & Ornstein, 2018). Across a series of longitudinal studies, Ornstein, Coffman, and their colleagues used an observational coding system – the Taxonomy of Teacher Behaviors – to identify the types of instructional techniques employed by teachers that may be associated with children's developing cognitive skills. Using the Taxonomy, a total of 60 minutes of mathematics and language arts instruction is coded in 30-second intervals. Variability across teachers in the use of metacognitively rich language that promotes the deep processing of information by encouraging students to actively monitor and assess their own thinking and understanding is reflected in what Coffman and Ornstein call cognitive processing language (CPL) (Coffman et al., 2008; Coffman et al., 2019; Grammer, Coffman, & Ornstein, 2013; Hudson et al., 2018). More specifically, CPL is an index of the frequency with which teachers make use of (1) strategy suggestions, (2) metacognitive questions and the co-occurrence of deliberate memory demands, (3) instructional activities, (4) cognitive structuring activities, and (5) metacognitive information. Coffman et al. (2008) documented considerable variation in teachers' provision of CPL during both mathematics and language arts instruction. As can be seen in the left-most column of Table 16.1, teachers provided strategy suggestions ($M$ = 4.9% of observational intervals) and metacognitive questions ($M$ = 4.9%) relatively infrequently. By comparison, teachers made deliberate memory demands and provided instructional information ($M$ = 37.6%) much more frequently during the course of instruction. Importantly, a comparison of the middle and right-most columns of Table 16.1 indicates that teachers were more likely to use metacognitive language during mathematics lessons than language arts lessons. For example, teachers provided strategy suggestions and posed metacognitive questions more than twice as often during mathematics instruction than they did during language arts instruction.

As a result of the naturally occurring variability in teachers' instructional language, it is possible to classify teachers as high or low in their provision

Table 16.1. *Percent occurrences of teacher behaviors*

| | First Grade | | |
| --- | --- | --- | --- |
| | Overall | Language Arts | Mathematics |
| *Taxonomy Codes* | | | |
| Strategy Suggestions | **4.9%** | **3.2%** | **6.7%** |
| | (0.8%–13.8%) | (0.0%–13.3%) | (0.0%–16.7%) |
| Metacognitive Questions | **4.9%** | **2.7%** | **7.1%** |
| | (0.8%–9.6%) | (0.0%–14.2%) | (0.0%–16.7%) |
| *Co-occurrence of Deliberate Memory Demand with* | | | |
| Instructional Activities | **37.6%** | **35.2%** | **40.2%** |
| | (25.8%–50.0%) | (21.7%–49.2%) | (25.8%–58.3%) |
| Cognitive Structuring Activities | **23.5%** | **23.7%** | **23.2%** |
| | (10.0%–35.4%) | (9.2%–39.2%) | (8.3%–36.7%) |
| Metacognitive Information | **5.9%** | **2.9%** | **8.9%** |
| | (1.3%–12.1%) | (0.0%–10.8%) | (0.0%–21.7%) |

of CPL. As can be seen in Table 16.2, teachers who are considered high in CPL place a greater emphasis on the process of problem-solving by frequently using metacognitive language (e.g., strategy suggestions, metacognitive questions) over the course of instruction. To illustrate, high-CPL teachers provided strategy suggestions in approximately 7% of intervals whereas low-CPL teachers provided strategy suggestions in approximately 2% of intervals. A similar pattern is evident for the provision of metacognitive questions and metacognitive information more broadly.

Coffman et al.'s (2008) findings provided initial support for associations between first-grade teachers' use of CPL and changes over the academic year in their students' strategy use and recall in a number of deliberate memory tasks. More precisely, students of teachers who used more CPL evidenced better performance across the first-grade year on both an Object–Memory task and a Sort–Recall task when compared to students who had teachers who used lower levels of CPL. Moreover, Coffman et al. (2019) documented the long-term linkages between children's first-grade classroom experiences and their later memory strategy performance – in both the second and the fourth grades. These findings, in conjunction with consistent linkages between aspects of mothers' language and children's memory performance, prompted further exploration of their potential association with children's domain-specific skills in mathematics.

Table 16.2. *Frequency of CPL during mathematics instruction in high- and low-CPL classrooms*

|  | Kindergarten | | First Grade | |
| --- | --- | --- | --- | --- |
|  | High CPL | Low CPL | High CPL | Low CPL |
| *Taxonomy Codes* | | | | |
| Strategy | **6.8%** | **1.9%** | **9.8%** | **3.6%** |
| Suggestions | (4.2%–13.3%) | (0.8%–3.3%) | (2.5%–16.7%) | (0.0%–11.7) |
| Metacognitive | **9.35%** | **2.7%** | **9.76%** | **4.4%** |
| Questions | (7.5%–12.5%) | (0.00%–5.0%) | (.8%–16.7%) | (0.0%–9.2%) |
| *Co-occurrence of Deliberate Memory Demand with* | | | | |
| Instructional | **53.3%** | **43.5%** | **44.4%** | **35.9%** |
| Activities | (47.5%–60.0%) | (26.7%–60.0%) | (30.8%–58.3%) | (25.8%–49.2%) |
| Cognitive | **34.3%** | **24.9%** | **24.5%** | **21.9%** |
| Structuring Activities | (27.5%–43.3%) | (9.2%–42.5%) | (13.3%–33.3%) | (8.3%–36.7%) |
| Metacognitive | **8.8%** | **1.9%** | **13.2%** | **4.5%** |
| Information | (5.8%–12.5%) | (0.0%–4.2%) | (3.3%–21.7%) | (0.0%–8.3) |

It seems necessary to consider the role of both the home and classroom environments during the transition to formal school in order to account for the substantial variation in children's mathematical knowledge that is apparent at school entry, as well as contrasting developmental trajectories that emerge during early elementary school. In the following section we present two sets of findings from the Classroom Memory Study that demonstrate (1) the influence of parents' and teachers' metacognitive language on children's accuracy and strategy use in kindergarten, as well as (2) the sustained impact of kindergarten teachers' metacognitive language on children's mathematics performance for particular subgroups of children.

### Mothers' Language and Children's Mathematics Skills

As mentioned above, maternal metamemory talk and elaborativeness are two features of mother–child conversations about the past that are consistently associated with children's ability to remember and recall information during deliberate memory tasks (Coffman et al., 2011; Langley et al., 2017). This work demonstrates that these aspects of mothers' language may play a role in children's understanding of how to get information into (e.g., encode) and out of (e.g., retrieve) memory and that they may signal the need to "do something" (e.g., engage in strategy use) when presented with a task involving remembering (Rudek & Haden, 2005). Thus, it seems possible that the ability to execute directed memory searches and employ strategic behaviors may also be necessary in domain-specific areas such as mathematics.

In an attempt to examine this relationship, Hudson et al. (2018) explored the association between maternal metamemory talk and children's math performance. A sample of kindergarten children was recruited to participate in a short-term longitudinal study that included direct assessments of math performance and a mother–child reminiscing task. In the fall and spring of the kindergarten year, children completed an Addition Strategy task (Siegler & Jenkins, 1989) in which each child was asked to solve a series of 10 single-digit addition problems (e.g., 6 + 5). An examiner read the problems aloud and the child was instructed to solve each problem using any method he or she preferred. Immediately after the child provided a response, the examiner asked for a retrospective report of how the problem had been solved (Siegler & Jenkins, 1989). Both the answer and the strategy reported by the child were recorded, such that children's performance on each trial resulted in two measures: one for accuracy, defined in terms of the number of problems answered correctly, and one for effective strategy use, defined as the percentage of times that a strategy was used to produce a correct response. Mothers' use of metamemory talk, which reflects attempts to scaffold conversations by referencing general memory processes or children's memory more specifically, was characterized during conversations with their children about previously experienced events using a coding scheme adapted from Haden (1998) and Reese, Haden, & Fivush, (1993). These mother–child conversations were gathered from a reminiscing task that was administered only in the fall of the kindergarten school year.

Hudson et al. (2018) documented associations between maternal metamemory talk and children's accuracy and strategy use on the Addition task at kindergarten entry. Children whose mothers used greater amounts of metamemory talk answered more problems correctly and also used more strategies effectively (i.e., to produce correct answers) than did their peers whose mothers used less metamemory talk. Importantly, by the end of kindergarten, the association between mothers' metamemory talk as measured in the fall and children's accuracy approached significance, but the association between metamemory talk and children's strategy use was no longer observed. The disappearance of this association suggests that aspects of the formal school environment, more specifically teachers' language, may be increasingly important for children's strategy use over time.

This exploration of the linkage between language within the home and children's math skills has recently been extended to include standardized measures of mathematics achievement. Using data from another short-term longitudinal study, Wiley et al. (2019) examined children's performance on the Calculation and Fluency subscales of the Woodcock–Johnson IV (Woodcock & Mather, 2000) at kindergarten entry in relation to maternal elaborativeness during reminiscing tasks. Consistent with previous results with a similar sample, Wiley and colleagues (2019) observed that at the beginning of kindergarten, children whose mothers were more elaborative were faster and more accurate in their responses than their peers whose mothers were less elaborative. Replicating findings from Hudson et al. (2018), results indicated that at school entry, children's math performance was associated with mothers' elaborativeness, such that children of high-elaborative mothers displayed higher math problem-solving scores, math calculation scores, and math fluency scores than children of low-elaborative parents. This pattern of results supports and extends the initial findings reported by Hudson et al. (2018) in two important ways. First, these findings confirm that the aspects of maternal language are consistently associated with children's mathematics performance across a diverse range of measures. Second, these findings indicate that additional aspects of maternal language, including mothers' efforts to scaffold conversation by elaborating on children's contributions, are related to children's mathematics achievement. Taken together, these findings provide consistent evidence to suggest that multiple aspects of mother–child conversations, which have traditionally been linked to children's recall and strategy use in the context of deliberate memory tasks, may also set the stage for children's accuracy and strategy use in academic contexts as well. Our consideration of contrasting trajectories of mathematics development that emerge during the first few years of school continues with an examination of the types of language teachers use during the course of instruction.

## Teachers' Language and Children's Mathematics Skills

As detailed above and in Tables 16.1 and 16.2, observations of teacher-led mathematics and language arts instruction indicate that teachers naturally vary in the extent to which they scaffold children's approaches to learning during instruction (Coffman et al., 2008; Grammer, Cofffman, & Ornstein, 2013; Hudson et al., 2018). This naturally occurring variation, especially in the context of mathematics instruction, provides an opportunity to examine children's mathematics performance as a function of exposure to more versus less CPL.

Efforts to examine whether exposure to greater amounts of CPL was related to academic outcomes began with an examination of children's performance on standardized assessments of mathematics achievement (Grammer et al., 2016). Data from a longitudinal study (Coffman et al., 2008) were used to investigate whether teachers' use of CPL during mathematics instruction was related to children's growth on the math fluency and calculation subscales of Woodcock–Johnson Tests of Achievement (Woodcock & Mather, 2000). Observations of teacher-led mathematics instruction were made over the course of the second-grade year using the Taxonomy, and teachers were classified as high or low in the use of CPL. Using a series of conditional hierarchical linear models (HLM), Grammer et al. (2016) demonstrated that mathematics instruction that is rich in references to cognitive processes, metacognition, and requests for remembering was related to changes in students' math achievement from the end of first grade to the end of second grade. More specifically, children whose second-grade teachers used greater amounts of CPL evidenced greater growth on both the math fluency and calculation subscales than did their peers whose teachers employed less CPL.

Hudson et al. (2018) reported a similar pattern of results for children's accuracy and strategy use on the Addition Strategy task during kindergarten. After controlling for performance at school entry, children who were exposed to higher levels of CPL during the year answered more problems correctly and used strategies more effectively than their peers who experienced lower levels of CPL. Whereas teachers' use of CPL was significantly associated with both accuracy and strategy use, the relation between CPL and strategy use was particularly strong.

As a final illustration, we consider whether teachers' instructional language may be more or less important for specific subgroups of children over time. Given the previously documented variation in children's mathematical knowledge at school entry and the established importance of teachers' CPL for mathematical growth, it seems necessary to consider whether CPL may be especially important for those students who enter school with very low mathematics knowledge. Hudson, Coffman, and Ornstein (2015) examined kindergarteners' (N = 61) performance on the

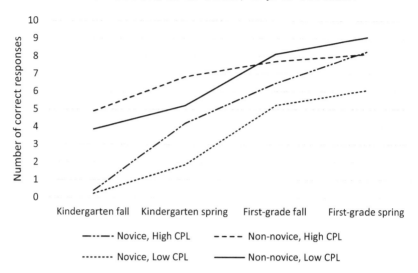

Figure 16.1   Novice and non-novice accuracy across the kindergarten and first-grade school year as a function of teachers' cognitive processing language (CPL)

Addition Strategy task (Siegler & Jenkins, 1989) and identified a subgroup of mathematical novices (N = 28). Mathematical novices were distinct from their peers in that they answered one or fewer problems correctly at the beginning of kindergarten. The left-hand sides of Figures 16.1 and 16.2 demonstrate the disparity in performance at school entry between mathematical novices and their peers both in terms of accuracy (Figure 16.1) and strategy use (Figure 16.2). Moreover, these figures also illustrate the sustained effect of teachers' CPL on students' mathematical trajectories over the first two years of school. As can be seen in Figure 16.1, although mathematical novices as a whole continued to perform more poorly than their non-novice peers at the end of kindergarten, the novices taught by kindergarten teachers high in CPL answered significantly more problems correctly at the end of kindergarten ($t = 2.48$, $p < .05$) and the first-grade year ($t = 2.41$, $p < .05$) than did novices who were taught by teachers low in CPL. A similar pattern was observed for children's strategy use. Compared to mathematical novices who experienced lower amounts of CPL during kindergarten, novices taught by teachers who used high levels of CPL used strategies more effectively at the end of the kindergarten year ($t = 2.06$, $p < .05$) and continued to do so during the first grade ($t = 1.78$, $p = .09$). Importantly, as can be seen on the right-hand side of Figures 16.1 and 16.2, at the end of first grade, mathematical

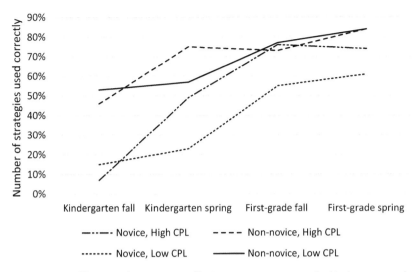

Figure 16.2    Novice and non-novice effective strategy use across the kindergarten and first-grade school year as a function of teachers' cognitive processing language (CPL)

novices who experienced high-CPL mathematics instruction in kindergarten were indistinguishable from their non-novice peers in terms of accuracy and strategy use. Taken together, these findings highlight the importance of exposure to greater amounts of CPL during kindergarten for children who enter school with limited mathematical proficiency.

## Connections and Future Directions

The studies reviewed here detail the evolution of the Classroom Memory Study to include the socialization of children's domain-specific cognitive skills more broadly. Taken together, the set of results presented above provide evidence to suggest that specific aspects of mothers' and teachers' language that have previously been linked to children's use of strategies for remembering are also associated with children's mathematical skills during the transition to formal schooling and across the early elementary school years. Specifically, these findings provide preliminary evidence to suggest that (1) the home environment, in particular aspects of mothers' language, is relevant to understanding the emergence of children's mathematical skills, and (2) aspects of teachers' instructional language are important to the development of skills over time, especially for children who enter school with limited mathematical proficiency.

These initial findings also provide a rationale for considering other aspects of the home and school contexts that may influence the development of children's strategic competences in mathematics. For example, it may be especially important to characterize the home context more broadly by measuring the home numeracy environment using parent questionnaires and observational methods that are designed to assess the frequency with which parents engage in direct (e.g., counting objects, counting simple sums, identifying written numbers) and indirect (e.g., cooking, shopping, playing card or board games) activities with their children (LeFevre et al., 2009; Thompson, Napoli, & Purpura, 2017). Observations of parent–child dyads may provide an opportunity to capture the richness of the ways in which parents provide, structure, and engage in authentic math activities with their children. Indeed, it may be useful to measure the ways in which mothers appropriately scaffold math-related conversations with their children. To illustrate, Bjorklund, Hubertz, and Reubens (2004) demonstrated that mothers' behaviors while playing board games with their children – such as prompting, instructing, and modeling – were associated with children's strategy use in the context of the game and while solving addition problems. Observations of parent–child interactions and dyadic exchanges also present a unique opportunity to consider children's contributions to math-related conversations from an early age.

Our assessment of the mathematics education literature suggests that there is considerable overlap in our conceptualization of CPL and the aspects of mathematics discourse that are thought to promote mathematical understanding through the articulation of mathematical ideas, including justifying meaning and making mathematical connections (e.g., Chapin et al., 2009; Herbel-Eisenmann, Steele, & Cirillo, 2013). However, in order to characterize the classroom context more broadly, it may be necessary to consider teacher characteristics that are not captured by the current measure of CPL. In this regard, it is important to note that teachers who use greater amounts of CPL do not tend to differ from their colleagues who use CPL less frequently in terms of education level, years of teaching, or classroom quality as assessed by the Classroom Assessment Scoring System (Pianta, La Paro, & Hamre, 2008). However, other characteristics of teachers – including their philosophy of teaching, beliefs about teaching mathematics, and mathematical content knowledge – may influence instruction and consequently contribute to variation in students' mathematical performance.

## Child-Level Measurement

Although our primary focus in mathematics has been on children's accuracy and effective strategy use in the context of addition, this perspective could be extended to include subtraction as well as alternative characterizations of strategy use. To date, we have focused on the extent to which children use strategies correctly (e.g., the percentage of time children use a strategy to produce a correct answer). Additional information about strategic competence may also be gained by supplementing measures of effective strategy use with indicators of strategy sophistication. For example, strategy use could be further classified as either overt (i.e., relying on fingers) or covert (i.e., mental math) and rank ordered from least (e.g., counting all) to most (e.g., decomposition) advanced. It may also be worthwhile to consider alternative techniques for accurately assessing strategy use. One possibility for capturing a more accurate representation of children's strategy use involves using a think-aloud or tutoring-style protocol in which students provide verbal reports while solving problems in real time or instruct other novice learners in the use of particular strategies. Using these types of protocols may allow for a richer account of children's strategic behaviors that would permit a more qualitative assessment of children's understanding of how to execute strategies. This technique has been used effectively in the memory literature (Best & Ornstein, 1986) to assess children's strategic understanding in a study of organizational strategy use. Interestingly, using an embedded think-aloud protocol in a tutoring paradigm, Best and Ornstein (1986) demonstrated that children with greater strategic skills could also provide effective instruction to younger children concerning how they should approach the task of trying to remember a list of relatively unrelated items.

At the core of this program of research is an interest in how children learn to think critically and to solve problems effectively. Our experiences observing classroom instruction and examining children's performance on a range of cognitive tasks suggests that metacognition may be key to understanding children's ability to transfer their knowledge to settings and problems that differ substantially from those involved in initial knowledge acquisition. Metacognition is believed to exert an influence on children's performance in two ways. First, metacognition affects children's initial decision to be strategic as it produces an understanding that performance will generally improve if sufficient effort is put forth in strategy selection and deployment. Second, it facilitates effective implementation of strategies and monitoring activities that enable students to evaluate performance and adapt their approach as necessary. Incorporating measures of metacognition into longitudinal designs will enable researchers to consider whether metacognition is a developmental antecedent of strategy use or whether metacognition and strategy use develop reciprocally. Preliminary findings suggest that in the context of a deliberate memory task, children's metacognition develops in advance of their use of an organizational sorting strategy and also predicts their subsequent strategy use (Grammer et al., 2011). One possibility is that a different developmental pattern emerges in the context of mathematics, where specific strategies are explicitly taught, such that children's strategy use precedes the development of their metacognitive knowledge. Embedding assessments of children's metacognition and strategy use in microgenetic and longitudinal studies designed to follow children from the transition to formal schooling throughout early elementary school will be critical to addressing these questions. A commitment to examining instructional approaches and methods of assessment that emphasize students' metacognitive understanding and flexible application of knowledge will be critical to the progression of the Classroom Memory Study and to studying the socialization of children's cognition more broadly.

The evolution of the Classroom Memory Study is a testament to the influence of Ornstein's commitment to the principles of developmental science that continue to guide his approach to studying cognition in context. As with many of his students and colleagues, under his tutelage we gained an appreciation for understanding how basic cognitive processes can inform applied developmental science research and a dedication to integrating empirical research into educational practice to enhance children's outcomes.

# CHAPTER 17

# The Socialization of Cognition in the Classroom
## Future Directions for Understanding the Role of Instruction in Brain and Behavioral Development

*Jennie K. Grammer and Remi Torres*

School-based research has elucidated a number of classroom and instructional factors that promote the development of children's abilities in content domains including literacy and mathematics. In contrast, the study of developmental changes in children's domain-general cognitive skills has historically been conducted with less emphasis on the contextual factors (e.g., the nature of teacher and student interactions) that promoted this growth (Morrison & Ornstein, 1996). As a result, the extent to which school experiences support the development of domain-general cognitive skills is less well understood. However, as results from the Classroom Memory Study clearly indicate (e.g., Coffman et al., 2008; Grammer, Coffman, & Ornstein, 2013), experiences children have in school shape children's memory skills, and interactions between teachers and students play a prominent role in fostering development.

More broadly, the Classroom Memory Study has provided a framework for examining the ways in which experiences in the classroom shape cognitive skills that children need to be successful in school (Ornstein, Grammer, & Coffman, 2010; Ornstein, Coffman et al., 2010). In this chapter, new directions in the socialization of cognition will be discussed. Specifically, in this chapter we outline the links between memory skills and those associated with self-regulated learning, including metacognition and executive functions (EF). Next, correlational and experimental studies linking schooling experience – including aspects of teacher language identified in the Classroom Memory Study – and self-regulated learning skills will be outlined. Finally, building on this, new research focusing on the impact of instruction on the neural and behavioral correlates of student attention, a key aspect of self-regulation, will be described.

## Expanding the Focus on Cognition in the Classroom: From Memory to Self-Regulation

As is outlined in previous chapters in this volume and elsewhere, as children progress through school, their use of memory strategies and memory-related metacognition increases steadily (Best & Fold-Bennett, Chapter 4; Coffman & Cook, Chapter 15; Schneider, 2010). Moreover, these memory skills have direct implications for children's academic performance – indeed, the ability to remember new information in the service of a learning goal, one's awareness of strategies for remembering, and knowledge of how and when to apply them – is useful across academic domains.

As has been revealed through a number of studies conducted by Peter Ornstein and colleagues (Ornstein, Grammer, & Coffman, 2010; Ornstein, Coffman et al., 2010), this growth in memory skills is in part due to the experiences that children have in the classroom everyday. Specifically, Ornstein and colleagues identified aspects of teachers' language during the course of instruction that are linked to elementary school children's deliberate memory performance (Coffman et al., 2008). In their original longitudinal study of the development of children's memory and academic skills, Coffman et al. (2008) developed an observational coding system for identifying instructional techniques in the context of lessons in mathematics and language arts associated with the development of cognitive processes. Although direct instruction in cognitive strategies by teachers is rare, they found that some teachers did use greater amounts of language that could promote children's skills in processing information, thinking in metacognitive terms, and remembering. These included instances where teachers would make strategy suggestions, ask metacognitive questions, and elicit information from children's memory.

Variability in the extent to which teachers made use of this type of cognitive processing language (CPL) was found to have direct implications for their students' memory development. In the initial longitudinal investigation, the findings of Coffman et al. (2008) indicated that there was a clear association between teachers' use of CPL and children's memory performance. By the end of the first grade, children who had been taught by teachers who made greater use of CPL exhibited greater use of organizational strategies than those who had been taught by teachers who did not. These associations between teacher language in first grade and children's organizational strategies also appear to have lasting implications for children's memory skills, with links between teacher language in early elementary school and students' complex memory strategy and study skills in fourth grade (Coffman et al., 2019).

Building on this observational work, linkages between teachers' language and children's cognitive skills have since further been confirmed using experimental methods, in which the use of CPL was manipulated in the context of lessons in a science unit (Grammer, Coffman, & Ornstein, 2013). In this investigation, we demonstrated that the nature of the instructional language to which children were exposed did not impact their learning of new facts. However, instructional language was very important in both the acquisition of strategic knowledge in the unit and the use of this knowledge in the service of a memory goal involving the science materials. Indeed, children who experienced the unit under conditions of high levels of CPL outperformed their peers who had less exposure. Thus, not only did exposure to instruction that contained high levels of CPL facilitate the acquisition of strategic understanding, it also enabled the children to apply what they had learned in the service of other cognitive tasks.

The school years are also characterized by rapid changes in the cognitive skills that aid in self-regulation and self-regulated learning. Self-regulation is a set of skills that are important for functional adaptation across the life span for a host of educational outcomes (Moffitt et al., 2011). While definitions of self-regulation differ (Morrison & Grammer, 2016), many accounts place emphasis on emotion and cognitive regulation (e.g., executive functions, cognitive control). Defined at a basic level, self-regulation involves the ability to take in information from the environment, evaluate choices and consequences of an action, and make an adaptive choice in the service of a goal (McClelland et al., 2015). More specifically, this includes top-down cognitive processes (i.e., executive functions that include working memory, inhibitory control, and cognitive flexibility) that modulate an individual's prepotent responses to a range of emotionally salient experiences, ranging from fear and frustration to excitement and interest. Although cognitive developmental research conducted in laboratory settings rarely focuses on this interplay, this balance between cognition and emotion is at the heart of children's everyday experiences of applying their cognitive skills in the classroom. Demands on children's self-regulation can be seen in almost everything they do in school, and even the most basic academic tasks can have emotional valence. When studying for a challenging test, for example, children must inhibit their desire to give up and instead focus their attention on the learning goal at hand. Similar levels of self-regulation are also needed to stay on task when classroom activities are exciting and enthusiasm is high.

Self-regulation is present in almost all activities that children engage in in school regardless of the emotional valence, and it is thought to play a particularly important role during the transition into elementary school as children are encountering new sets of emotional and cognitive demands (Blair & Razza, 2007). It is worth noting that memory and metacognition were implicated in early models of self-regulation for academic activities (i.e., self-regulated learning; Brown & DeLoache, 1978) and with respect to EF (Fernandez-Duque, Baird, & Posner, 2000). In more recent conceptualizations of self-regulation as it relates to children's ability to regulate their thoughts, feelings, and emotions, memory has similarly been highlighted (Cole, Ram, & English, 2019; Lewis, 2005). Although early and contemporary conceptualizations of self-regulation have included an emphasis on memory and metacognitive processes, only recently have researchers begun revisiting links between these constructs (e.g., Roebers, 2017; Roebers & Feurer, 2016).

In educational research, a widely adopted definition of self-regulation includes the skills necessary for controlling, directing, and planning of cognition, emotion, and behavior (Schunk & Zimmerman, 1997). This definition has expanded to include a range of processes that are important for adaptive success in the school setting, including the ability to set goals, persist, and remain motivated in the face of a challenge. In practical terms, these are the skills that children use to regulate their cognitive processes in the service of a learning goal (e.g., focusing attention with the goal of learning new information that will be on a test the next day), but these are also important for social interactions (e.g., regulating your frustration with having to take turns with a classmate while remembering it was your turn yesterday).

Although self-regulation is often operationalized in research as the use of a regulating strategy *or* the resulting behavioral outcome, self-regulation is perhaps most appropriately characterized as a dynamic process (Cole et al., 2019). Viewed this way, self-regulation is not just the use of a regulating strategy or the resulting behavioral outcome but instead may be best characterized as a balance between the two. Considering the dynamic interplay between regulating strategies and children's behavior, the key role of memory and metacognition in self-regulation becomes more apparent. To engage in a regulatory strategy, children must have a metacognitive understanding of when and why to apply their skills and the procedural understanding of how to apply them. This knowledge is often derived from their memory of past experiences, which contributes to children's understanding of appropriate behavioral responses. Take, for example, children who repeatedly interrupt others while working in a small group. Over time, the memory of negative feedback from their peers, combined with an understanding of how favorable interactions are when they are able to inhibit their desire to talk out of turn, can result in changes in self-regulatory behavior.

As is the case with memory strategy development (see Best & Folds-Bennett, Chapter 4), significant questions remain regarding the development of self-regulation. It is clear, however, that expectations for children's regulatory behaviors are derived from their environments at home and at school. Given correlational and experimental evidence linking aspects of memory and metacognitively rich teacher language to gains in children's memory and metacognitive understanding (Coffman et al., 2008; Grammer, Coffman, & Ornstein, 2013), it seems likely that similar factors in the classroom could play a role in self-regulation development. We next turn to evidence linking early school experiences to the development of self-regulation skills.

## The Socialization of Self-Regulation at School

With increasing evidence for the importance of self-regulation for children's school adjustment and success (Blair & Razza, 2007; McClelland et al., 2014), there has been greater focus on the part of developmental and educational researchers seeking to understand the interplay between maturational and environmental factors in shaping the development of self-regulation. The transition to school in particular has been highlighted as an important period for self-regulation development, and the experience of going to school has been shown to have an impact on this skill (Morrison, Ponitz, & McClelland, 2010; Morrison et al., 2019).

Accumulating evidence indicates that experience in school promotes the development of children's EF (Brod, Bunge, & Shing, 2017; Burrage et al., 2008; Morrison et al., 2019). These studies, including the school cutoff and regression discontinuity, have been conducted using causal inference methods that allow for inferences to be drawn regarding the impact of attending 1 year of formal schooling on children's skills discontinuity (Morrison et al., 2019). To examine the impact of school experience, both of these techniques leverage children's birthdates relative to the cutoff date that school districts determine for enrollment eligibility. Because of the cutoff date, children are either enrolled in school in a given year or wait until the following year. Thus, for example, as a function of this cutoff date, one can examine differences in growth between "older" pre-kindergarten children and "younger" kindergarten children. By comparing outcomes between the two groups of children – who are virtually the same age but differ only in the schooling experiences they receive – it is possible to draw inferences regarding the unique effect of schooling on children's outcomes.

School-cutoff research provides evidence for the link between school experience and self-regulation broadly but is unable to identify specific aspects of this environment that are driving developmental change. Thus, from this work the specific mechanisms by which experience in school impacts children's development and the extent to which individual children might benefit from different types of experiences in the classroom are not clear. Of the available studies revealing the impact of school experience on children's EF, two of these investigations (Brod et al., 2017; Grammer et al., in preparation) have identified the impact of experience on neural correlates of EF, demonstrating an impact of school experience on the brain before it can be observed in behavior. Specifically, children who had schooling experience showed greater activation in areas of the brain associated with sustained attention (Brod et al., 2017) and showed differences in neural activity associated with cognitive control (Grammer et al., in preparation) in EF tasks compared to kindergarten children of a similar age. In this work, changes in brain function associated with EF have been observed before commensurate development in behavior, further demonstrating the impact of experience in school in ways that might not even be immediately apparent to teachers and parents.

### What Factors Promote Self-Regulation Development?

Although the school-cutoff and regression discontinuity work make it clear that experience in school provides an important context for self-regulation development, far less is known about the mechanisms underlying this change. Questions about what specific factors in the school environment promote self-regulation development remain. Two lines of research have yielded hints as to experiences that might be driving this development: experimental interventions focused on training children's self-regulation (and EF more specifically) and correlational/longitudinal studies linking aspects of teacher instruction to children's self-regulation development.

As is outlined in two recent reviews published by Diamond and Ling (2016, 2019), a number of studies involving a wide range of methods for training EF skills – ranging from tightly controlled computerized programs to physical fitness – have been conducted with varying levels of success.

The evidence is clear that directly training children's self-regulation generally is possible, but the transfer of trained skills is quite narrow, and rarely leads to EF gains outside of the context of training. For instance, computerized training programs using an N-back task lead to improvement in children's working memory in computerized tasks; however, little evidence demonstrates transfer of these benefits in children's general EF skills in other settings. Thus, although children's skills might improve when tested in the context in which they are trained, these benefits do not translate into behavioral changes in the classroom. In contrast, programs that embed EF training within the classroom curriculum and routines, such as mindfulness interventions, have been shown to be more efficacious in terms of these efforts translating to children's everyday skills (Flook et al., 2010, 2015; Schonert-Reichl et al., 2015). A few other themes emerge from the training literature. First, for EF training to be effective, EF skills must be challenged and the practice must be adapted to children's level of ability. The type and duration of training is also important for the successful acquisition of these skills. In addition, although most training programs are generally brief (around 4 months on average), the longer or more intensive the training, the more EF is benefited.

Why might so many of these interventions fail to result in lasting changes in EF? One potential reason is that these efforts fail to take into account a fully developmental perspective of EF. It is telling that one characteristic of effective intervention includes the amount of time spent involved in training – the development of these skills is protracted over a relatively long developmental time course, emerging in early childhood and continuing to develop throughout the elementary school years. Self-regulation is also known to manifest differently as a function of context, as is evidenced by relatively low associations between ratings of EF offered by parents versus teachers, as well as differences observed in EF as assessed with children individually or with a group of their peers (Ahmed et al., in press). Moreover, teachers' perceptions of student EF are driven by and assessed based on behavioral cues – such as inattention, classroom wandering, and frequent interruptions (e.g., see assessments such as the BRIEF, Roth, Isquith, & Gioia, 2014) – which are far removed from discrete measures of these skills in the types of laboratory tasks often implemented in training studies. Here the utility of mindfulness in the training of EF also might be beneficial for understanding factors that promote self-regulation development. Mindfulness training with young children emphasizes a non-judgmental awareness of moment-by-moment experiences, which involves a number of direct, highly metacognitive elements that help children better understand the feelings that indicate regulation is necessary as well as the strategies that could be used to be mindful. Mindfulness training helps children notice their experience, describe it, and act with awareness. For example, upon noticing feelings of frustration, a child employing mindfulness strategies might make a mental or verbal note that they are feeling frustrated. Then, rather than allow the frustrating feelings to overwhelm them, they make a conscious choice to take a mindful breath or ask an adult for help. Several school-based mindfulness interventions have found promising improvements in children's self-regulation skills and academic achievement, especially in children who begin with low levels of self-regulation (Diamond, 2012; Flook et al., 2010, 2015; Schonert-Reichl et al., 2015).

More holistic interventions, involving teachers, parents, and children, have shown greater efficacy for changing children's self-regulation (Bierman et al., 2008; Blair & Raver, 2014; Diamond & Ling, 2019); however, there is still much to be learned about how factors within the classroom environment might be more important for the development of self-regulation. One set of evidence for this can be found in preschool-based interventions that have been conducted to train children's regulatory skills (e.g., Chicago School Readiness Project [CSRP], Raver et al., 2011; Tools of the Mind, Blair & Raver, 2014; and Promoting Alternative Thinking Strategies [PATHS], Domitrovich, Cortes, & Greenberg, 2007). These interventions included curricula with explicit instruction and activities to support children's self-regulation skills, but they also provided coaching for teachers' classroom management strategies and stress management (PATHS and CSRP). A number of insights in the classroom factors that promote self-regulation have come from the studies. For example, based on their school-based intervention, Raver and colleagues (2011) concluded that children appeared to benefit from greater levels of structure in the classroom setting, including clearer routines, and less student–teacher conflict. Children that participated in the PATHS program showed greater improvements in emotion knowledge compared to controls, although no intervention effects were found on children's inhibitory control or sustained attention (Domitrovich et al., 2007). Children who participated in the Tools of the Mind intervention showed improved executive function, attention, and academic achievement compared to controls (Blair & Raver, 2014). Results from these interventions highlight promising benefits to students; however, more research is needed to understand how specific classroom activities and teaching strategies and classroom environments impact children's self-regulation skills.

Observational studies of the school context have also yielded information regarding the specific aspects of the school experience that promote EF and self-regulation. Drawing on the Classroom Memory Study in particular, observational evidence suggests that teachers' use of specific instructional techniques that are related to aspects of children's cognitive development – including the provision of explicit goals focusing children's attention and requests for remembering – is particularly important for children who exhibit lower regulation at the beginning of the school year (Ornstein, Coffman, & Grammer, 2009). Similarly, Connor and colleagues (2010) found that although classroom instruction did not directly impact children's early self-regulation, children with lower regulatory skills benefited more from individualized instruction.

Other research has focused on sizable differences across classrooms in the ways in which teachers organize time spent in instruction and daily activities – including the amount of time devoted to describing classroom procedures and preparing the class for assignments and transitioning from one activity to the next (Cameron, Connor, & Morrison, 2005; Cameron & Morrison, 2011; Connor et al., 2010). Evidence indicates, for example, that more time spent in these organizational aspects of instruction during fall predicts fewer disruptive transitions and more time spent by children in independent, self-regulated activities in spring. In addition, in a cross-cultural investigation involving Chinese and American classrooms, the role of classroom practices – including strategies teachers use to regulate students' learning-related and behavioral actions (e.g., commands and questions during regular classroom activities) as well as the time that students in each classroom spend in transition between instructional activities for developing self-regulation – was shown to be important for student outcomes (Weixler, 2012).

Research on classroom processes (e.g., instructional techniques and classroom management) demonstrates that the context teachers create for their students can impact not only their memory or domain-specific academic skills but also their ability to regulate their cognitive skills in the service of learning and in the classroom setting. Notably, when teachers create these contexts they use metacognitively rich language and set up opportunities for children to practice regulation through managing the type and timing of instruction. Why might this matter? For many children, self-regulation is challenging. In classrooms where metacognitive discussions and questions are prevalent, children have more opportunities to hear their teachers and peers talk about how they think and learn. For children with low regulatory skills, these insights may be particularly valuable. This is also in line with many of the interventions that have proven to be effective for training EF, employing mindfulness in the school setting (e.g., Flook et al., 2010, 2015; Schonert-Reichl et al., 2015), where teachers support children's awareness of emotions, thoughts, and behaviors.

Although it is unclear how certain teaching strategies and classroom management practices support student self-regulation, it is likely that teachers who minimize time in transitions and individualize instruction to the needs of their students are providing further external scaffolding for children to practice self-regulation (Cameron & Morrison, 2011). Teachers also serve as role models for successful self-regulation behaviors to children. Teachers who are organized, control impulses, and have greater EF skills scaffold children's EF skills more often and tend to have students with greater self-regulation skills (Bardack & Obradović, 2019). Again, for those children for whom self-regulation is more effortful, extended and repeated practice has been shown to be one of the most effective ways to help them develop EF skills in direct training (Diamond & Ling, 2019). Consistently providing these opportunities in the class-room – a context in which children spend a large percentage of their time every day – would provide the extended practice preschool- and elementary-aged children need as they continue to develop these skills.

## Approaches to Examining School Factors

While school-based studies – either experimental or correlational in nature – have provided insight into aspects of the school experience that might be driving the causal link between experience in school and self-regulation gains, there is still much to be learned about how specific aspects of classroom instruction might shape self-regulation. As is exemplified in Chapter 15 (Coffman & Cook), through a series of iterative observational, longitudinal, and experimental studies, research from the Classroom Memory Project has demonstrated the impact of specific types of teacher language on children's strategic memory development. Expanding on this work, aspects of parent and teacher language known to promote the development of skilled remembering also contribute to children's abilities in academic domains, namely mathematics (see Hudson & Wiley, Chapter 16). For example, teachers who prompt children to discuss the strategies they use to solve a word problem are also drawing students' attention to strategies for focusing attention on key aspects of the problem at hand (attentional control), engaging in multiple steps of a problem while still keeping sight of the goal (working memory), and recognizing and rectifying mistakes they might make while working to derive the answer (response inhibition). These specific findings highlight the important role of the conversations children have with adults in shaping their strategic abilities.

## The Socialization of Self-Regulation: Linking School Experience with Brain Development

One of the challenges of examining factors that promote the development of self-regulation is that, although the resulting behavior is observable, the cognitive processes involved in regulation are not accessible to researchers through observation and difficult for students to report on directly. In our recent work (Grammer et al., 2014; Grammer, Gehring, & Morrison, 2018; Morrison et al., 2019), we have been focusing on the impact of school experience on a key aspect of self-regulation: cognitive control processes. Specifically, we have been examining event-related potentials (ERPs), including the error-related negativity (ERN), error positivity (Pe), N2, and P3 – ERP components that reflect a network of structures, including the anterior cingulate cortex (ACC) and lateral prefrontal cortex, involved in detecting response conflict and attention control. This recent work also represents an expansion of the study of cognitive development in context that includes a focus on brain development, but it also reflects the model laid out by Ornstein and colleagues in the Classroom Memory Study, which has provided a framework for our recent efforts to examine the impact of instructional experiences on these unobservable skills (Ornstein, Grammer, & Coffman, 2010; Ornstein, Coffman et al., 2010). Specifically, we have begun iterating between observational and experimental methods the examination of the role that experiences in the classroom play in the development of cognitive control processes. By collecting neurological data in the real-world environment of the classroom, we are looking at the role that teachers play in creating contexts that support attention regulation among the students in the classroom.

### *Why Incorporate Neuroscience into the Study of the Socialization of Cognition?*

Although there has been increasing awareness of the need to identify and examine specific environmental factors that contribute to cognitive development when examining behavioral indices of children's cognition, the same is not true for research focusing on the neural correlates of these same skills. In some ways this is an interesting case of history repeating itself – neuroscientific research involving both adults and children is heavily influenced by experimental traditions, with studies designed to emphasize rigorous experimental control and a focus on mechanistic models of basic cognitive processes. Moreover, practical limitations imposed by the methods employed in neuroscientific research have made the reality of examining neural processes in the real world challenging. However, recent advances in noninvasive methods for assessing neural activity, such as use of an electroencephalogram (EEG), have provided new opportunities for elucidating cognitive processes associated with self-regulation that have proven challenging to measure with behavior alone, particularly in young children.

### Challenges Associated with Assessing Self-Regulation

In the study of self-regulation, researchers have relied on two main modes of data collection: laboratory-based measures and indirect teacher or parent reports. However, there are limitations to each method that make examining the development of these skills more challenging. Considering first laboratory assessments, in theory, understanding cognitive processes through controlled laboratory experimentation should provide a basis on which to examine the role that broader contextual factors – including school experiences – play in their development. Many of these laboratory-based assessments of EF with children have been adapted from tasks used with adults by cognitive psychologists and neuroscientists. Reflecting the neural substrates believed to underlie the behavioral manifestations of subcomponents of EF, these computerized tasks capture differences in children's reaction time and accuracy rates in response to stimuli. Despite the rigorous control and precision afforded by these measures, it is not clear to what extent they reflect or predict behavior in the classroom (Cameron et al., 2005; Cameron & Morrison, 2011; Domitrovich et al., 2007; Bodnar et al., 2007). Contextual influences are particularly important for examining children's self-regulation and EF, in part because the expression of these skills is modulated by the emotional experiences that children have with their peers, when facing new learning challenges, and when interacting with their teachers. This limitation has very real implications for the utility of findings resulting from cognitive/neurophysiological measures for educators.

In contrast, parent and teacher reports of children's self-regulation should incorporate more information about how children engage attention in context and are often viewed as more ecologically valid than observations of children's behavior in the laboratory or classroom setting. These methods too have limitations. Evidence for consistency across teacher reports and performance-based measures is not always found in individual investigations, and these reports also fail to capture aspects of children's attention that cannot be directly observed. For example, a child could exhibit behavior akin to attending (e.g., sitting still, eyes focused on an activity) but actually be disengaged from a lesson. An additional, related, concern is the extent to which bias might impact teacher evaluations of children. Teachers' perceptions based on their students' appearance, particularly in terms of differences in children's racial/ethnic group, gender, and perceived socioeconomic status, have been related to how engaged and academically competent they perceive students to be in their classrooms (Derks, Hudziak, & Boomsma, 2009; Fitzpatrick, Côté-Lussier, & Blair, 2016; Ready & Wright, 2011).

These issues of potential rater bias go beyond issues of measurement validity. The implications for children's experiences in the classroom – and for the development of their self-concept regarding their academic and cognitive abilities – have the potential to be far more long-lasting and problematic. Although the majority of research on classroom factors that promote memory development have focused on the impact of teacher instruction on all students in the classroom, evidence from extensive observations of elementary literacy instruction – and some focused on aspects of self-regulation as well – has demonstrated that individual children in classrooms have variable instructional experiences. The alignment of these classrooms experiences – characterized as child × instruction interactions – with the educational needs of children has been shown to promote growth in reading and self-regulation skills (Connor, 2016; Connor et al., 2010). Thus, it is not just the broad instructional context that drives development, but rather the attunement of that environment to the specific developmental needs of individual students that contributes to development.

The ways that teachers attune the instructional goals that they have for children are often informed by their perceptions of children's cognitive or academic skills. These bidirectional interactions between teachers and students are not yet well studied; however, there is some indication that children who are perceived as being less engaged or cognitively competent may be afforded fewer opportunities for learning and teacher engagement in the classroom (Hughes & Kwok, 2007; Hughes, Gleason, & Zhang, 2005). This treatment in turn influences children's academic self-concept, motivation, and ultimately academic success (Ryan & Deci, 2000). Given these challenges in measurement and the implications of potential bias for children's long-term academic outcomes, it is important to develop tools to help us more directly and accurately measure the capabilities of diverse groups of students.

Perception of student self-regulation, and attention more specifically, is particularly hard to judge in the classroom based on behavior alone. Previous observational studies have quantified attention in broad terms, with trained observers coding children's on-task versus off-task behaviors (Kofler, Rapport, & Alderson, 2008). Although these types of measures have been used to reliably differentiate children with and without a diagnosis of ADHD (Rapport et al., 2009), even highly trained researchers can find it challenging to quantify the behaviors associated with attention, which is a largely unobservable cognitive process. Young children also have trouble reporting on their attentional states or identifying learning environments or strategies that can help support their attention.

### Approaching Measurement Challenges with Neuroscience: Examining the Neural Correlates of Self-Regulation

Neuroscientific methods, including EEG, present one approach to measuring attention that is less influenced by limitations posed by observational or self-report methods. EEG measures electrical activity that propagates to the scalp, reflecting neural activity. EEG methods are particularly well suited to tracking dynamic fluctuations in attention given the high temporal resolution of these data (on the order of milliseconds). In addition, as compared to other neuroscientific methods such as functional magnetic resonance imaging (fMRI), which require children to be still for long periods of time and are quite expensive, EEG assessments are relatively easy to conduct with children in a wide variety of settings including the laboratory and at school (Grammer et al., 2014).

Within the past few years there have been substantial advances in remotely amplified EEG equipment, which allows for the collection of high-quality data without needing to have a participant tethered to an amplifier. Thus, it is possible to move outside of the laboratory and collect data in the naturalistic environments where learning occurs. By pushing the boundaries of EEG technology, it is possible for the first time to examine the neural correlates of cognitive processes, including attention, while children are interacting in the real world, engaged with teachers and peers in everyday tasks. Using this approach – in combination with measures of classroom instruction – we are now able to directly link classroom experience to brain function and explore directly the ways in which classroom experience impacts students' attention (Grammer et al., under revision; Xu et al., invited submission in revision).

In our first efforts to characterize student attention using neural measures, our group employed remotely amplified EEG in a study with undergraduates who were engaged in classroom instruction (Grammer et al., under review). By simultaneously collecting EEG data from multiple participants at a time and synchronizing these data with videos of classroom instruction, for the first time we have been able to track the neural correlates of attention of multiple students and link these EEG data with specific events occurring during classroom instruction. Thus, we are able to examine the classroom instructional factors – teacher moves and activities – that create the social context in which attention is being deployed.

In our first investigation, EEG data were collected while the undergraduates were presented with experimentally controlled lessons that included lectures, video-watching, peer work, and individual work. In this research we have used "alpha" range (8-12Hz) neural oscillations, or alpha power, in EEG data to quantify attentional engagement of undergraduate students. Alpha oscillations are the most dominant of oscillatory patterns observed in the human brain and are the only frequency domain that responds to stimuli within the environment, including the need for attention. There is a wealth of empirical evidence from carefully controlled laboratory studies for the functional association of alpha oscillations with attention (Lenartowicz et al., 2016; Pfurtscheller, 1992; Sadaghiani & Kleinschmidt, 2016), and it is this rich evidence base that we leverage as we have taken EEG methods into real-world settings. This measure allowed us to assess neural correlates of student attention during a college lecture across four types of instructional context (instructor-initiated: lecture, video-watching; student-initiated: group work, and independent work). We predicted that passive academic activities – listening to a lecture and watching a video – would result in lower attentional engagement than active academic activities – engaging in a discussion with peers and working independently on a written test.

In this initial study, we found that student attention during lectures, as indexed by alpha power, varied significantly as a function of the types of activities that the teacher set in place during instruction. Students were most attentive during peer work and independent work – activities that were structured by the teacher but directed by the student. Attention decreased during teacher-led lecture, but was by far the lowest during video-watching, in spite of a stated preference for video-watching on the part of students who indicated that including these types of materials in lecture enhanced learning.

Notably, the EEG data revealed a different, more nuanced story than that which was provided by behavioral coding alone and also differed from analyses of student self-reports of activity preference. Independent, reliable coders rated student attention as being highest during lecture. Ratings of attention were lowest (and most variable) during peer interactions. This finding was in direct contrast of the EEG measures, which revealed that these activities were associated with the strongest indicators of attention in the EEG data.

These results provided promising evidence for the utility of EEG methods for assessing attention in real-world settings, which provide access to understanding cognitive processes that are difficult for teachers to observe directly. Given the particular challenges associated with using behavioral and report measures of cognitive control, these results gave us confidence that we could understand similar processes in children as well. Thus, with this preliminary work as a foundation, we have recently extended this work to focus on the ways in which teachers support and promote attention in early elementary students. In this work (Xu et al., invited submission in revision), we are examining attentional EEG and event-related potentials (ERP) while children are engaged in lessons in school. Beginning first with experimentally controlled lessons, we have been tracking children's attention with EEG and ERP measures, balancing experimental control afforded by scripted lessons and activities with increases in ecological validity afforded by interactions with peers and distractions that cannot be modeled in the laboratory.

Although this work is still underway, we anticipate that the results will allow us to make concrete recommendations to teachers around basic aspects of student attention in the classroom. Focusing on the potential mechanisms driving the development of self-regulation outlined above, including teacher metacognitive language and the type and time of instruction, we are linking observations from the classroom directly with EEG data collected while children are engaged in lessons and activities. For example, we are currently analyzing data to understand the amount of time, on average, that children can attend to lessons during whole-group instruction, as well as the activities that best support student engagement. We hope that employing EEG methods for examining these skills in the classroom context has the potential to broaden our understanding of individual differences in children's performance, reduce bias introduced by parent and teacher report measures, and gain insight into the mechanisms by which teacher instructional practices are driving children's self-regulation development.

## Conclusion

Research conducted by Ornstein and colleagues in the Classroom Memory Study, as reviewed by Coffman and Cook in Chapter 15, clearly demonstrated the important role that teachers play in socializing young children's cognitive development. Expanding on this work, new efforts are underway to better understand how the development of other core cognitive skills might be socialized – including the development of self-regulation. Previous self-regulation interventions have demonstrated that training children's EF is possible, but it requires a large dose of training and is most successful when embedded within existing classroom processes. While the results of these programs are promising, as we move to expand our understanding of the socialization of these skills such as self-regulation and attention, incorporating neuroscientific methods provides new promise for understanding cognitive phenomena that are challenging to measure in the classroom setting. In doing so, ultimately we hope that it will be possible to understand how classroom experiences impact individual students in both behavior and brain function. Our recent work is already providing evidence that the inclusion of neuroscientific methods has a potential for doing so – neural measures of attention are revealing patterns of individual differences that are not evident from behavior alone. There is still much to learn about individual differences and preferences in attentional engagement in children. As we work toward linking aspects of the classroom experience with the brain and behavioral correlates of children's self-regulation, we ultimately hope to be able to inform teachers' understanding of how to promote the development of cognition in their students.

# CHAPTER 18

# Creating a Life in Science

## Fredrick J. Morrison

The modern era of developmental psychology emerged 60–70 years ago, alongside a series of revolutionary changes across the broader field of psychology itself. Most prominent was a reemergence of a scientific focus on human thinking, which extricated itself from the theoretical strictures of the neo-behaviorist era (see Cox, Chapter 2). For scientists interested in learning and development, this new direction meant that research studies could be conducted directly with humans (including children), as opposed to the earlier behaviorist emphasis on experimenting on animals.

During the same period, a pioneering group of psychologists began by exploring the growth of thinking in children, initially to ascertain how feasible and reliable experimental studies could be with young children, to systematically charting the extent and nature of developmental changes, to asking what the sources of those changes might be (including neurobiological), and eventually to developing interventions to facilitate acquisition of thinking skills.

One of those pioneers was Peter Ornstein, whose early education cut across that transitional era, and whose body of work in the ensuing decades did much to shape and influence the dramatic shifts in developmental science that we have witnessed. From one perspective, to borrow a current methodological term, Ornstein's evolution can be seen as an example of a "crossed-lagged panel" scientific life, with Ornstein's work and that of the general field evolving along parallel lines, with mutual, bidirectional influences intermingling over time.

In my commentary, I would like to first sketch the historical and theoretical changes that have occurred in the study of development over the last half century or so. In so doing, it should be clear how central Ornstein's work has been to the dramatic progress we have seen in our field. Second, I will comment on the exciting work presented in the chapters in this section, hoping to illustrate how tightly the research simultaneously reflected and created the important trends seen in our field. Finally, I would like to comment on what Peter Ornstein's work tells us about creating a life in science and making a difference in the world.

## Trends in the Study of Development

Most observers would agree, I feel, that the modern-day discipline encompassing the study of development looks very different from the nascent efforts of the 1960s and early 1970s. In essence, three salient developments can be identified that culminated in the dynamic nature of the current field.

### The Cognitive Revolution

Emanating initially within the parent discipline of mainstream experimental psychology, research gradually began to focus on human thinking, with particular emphasis on human memory. Remembering was a natural choice, in part because of its long history in traditional psychology, including seminal studies by Ebbinghaus and Bartlett. The first major model of memory, developed by Atkinson and Shiffrin in 1968, posited three major memory structures – sensory registers, short-term memory (STM), and long-term memory (LTM). Likewise, it posited a series of control processes including rehearsal, chunking, and elaboration, that facilitated manipulation, control, and transfer of information across structures. In his initial forays on the development of memory, Ornstein chose to examine the role of rehearsal in age differences in short-term memory performance (Ornstein & Naus, 1978). Across a series of groundbreaking studies, he not only established the critical role of rehearsal in explaining age differences in STM performance, he pioneered a number of ingenious techniques for rendering observable the normally covert rehearsal process, but also devised a series of "training" studies to improve memory skills that served as precursors to recent, more large-scale intervention studies. Taken together, these early studies laid a solid empirical foundation for the importance of memory and its development in understanding children's cognitive growth (Ornstein, 1978).

### From Developmental Psychology to Developmental Science

The science of developmental psychology that emerged during this period began to emulate the style and methods of experimental psychology, emphasizing laboratory-based research, experimental isolation and manipulation of individual cognitive processes, and quantitative analytic techniques. A robust set of findings emerged from this effort, documenting major age-related changes in rehearsal and other memory strategies, especially across the range from 5 to 12 years of age (Bjorklund, 1987). That these age-related changes tracked closely with children's entry into and progression through school was not lost on scientists. Consequently, as they naturally began to ask about where these developmental changes came from, the potential role of schooling (as well as the accompanying role of parenting) came immediately to mind (Morrison & Ornstein, 1996).

Unfortunately, the developmental psychology dominant at the time was not easily equipped to study environmental sources of developmental change. Most research was conducted in laboratories in academic settings, primarily with white middle-class samples, utilizing simple experimental designs and relatively elementary analytic techniques. Fortuitously, across the broader field, a group of scholars was calling for a radically different conceptualization of the nature and sources of developmental change, one that emphasized the need to include multiple sources of environmental influence in a fuller understanding of human development. In a series of groundbreaking papers, prominent scientists such as Urie Bronfenbrenner, Robert Cairns, Gilbert Gottlieb, and Glen Elder elaborated a complex, multilevel, interactive view of human growth and development that laid out a very different methodological strategy for studying developmental change (Cairns, Elder, & Costello, 1996). The new approach emphasized studying children in their natural environment (preschools, schools, homes, after-care centers) and put as much emphasis on studying their environments as on their individual cognitive or social skills (Rogoff, 1990).

Compelled by his own findings to pose the developmental question, Ornstein was also driven by the new theoretical "contextualism," some of whose leading exponents were his colleagues at the University of North Carolina, Chapel Hill. As he began to study the classroom environment, several new insights emerged, which would serve to redirect and guide ensuing research strategies (Ornstein, Coffman et al., 2010). First, it became clear that studying the classroom was neither simple nor easy. Few rigorous observational tools were available to capture the complexity of classroom instruction and activity. Moreover, working with children, teachers, and principals posed a very different set of challenges than testing in a laboratory. Studying the "feral environment" was messy, but it was the only way to make progress in examining the sources of developmental change. As we shall see below, the success of the Classroom Memory Study (CMS) is direct testimony to Peter's creativity, ingenuity, and persistence.

Second, observations of teachers in classrooms rapidly revealed large individual differences in their instructional and other behaviors that seemed linked to subsequent memory skills. Successfully documenting the extent, nature, and consequences of that teacher variability for children's development represented a true empirical breakthrough in realizing the value of the contextualist perspective.

Finally, the CMS was responsible in part for one final advance, namely documenting that the influence of teacher behavior varied with the skill level and other characteristics of the child (Coffman et al., 2008, 2019). These "child × instruction" interactions, once elucidated, paved the way for a more complex, nuanced view of classroom interactions but also set the stage for classroom interventions that would ultimately individualize instruction for each child.

## *The Final Link: Neurobiology*

In its initial formulations, the role of biology was central to understanding developmental change. While early research tended to focus on animal studies, the rapid development of neurobiological methods such as functional magnetic resonance imaging (fMRI) and electroencephalogram (EEG) opened the door to research on humans. As we shall see below, advances in EEG technology made possible direct testing of children in schools and, with it, the possibility of linking classroom processes with brain changes (Grammer et al., 2014; Kim et al. 2017). The critical challenge for this new thrust was to discover biological mechanisms for the psychological processes underlying developmental change in cognitive skills. Ornstein's work laid the foundation for his students to take on the challenge of incorporating neurobiological perspectives into the contextualist work on development. This nascent thrust holds the promise of radically redirecting our view of how and when the environment causes change in development (Morrison et al., 2019).

## The Present Chapters

The work summarized in the chapters in this section clearly and dramatically illustrates the pioneering nature of Peter Ornstein's work and his influence on the field over the last five decades.

## *Coffman and Cook*

Ornstein's decades-long collaboration with Jennifer Coffman, highlighted in this chapter and Chapter 16, has produced some of the most dramatic discoveries and systematic advances in the field of developmental psychology. The Classroom Memory Study has served as a professional and methodological foundation for insights about the extent and nature of variability in teacher language to children in the classroom and its impact on children's knowledge and memory. The mere finding of meaningful differences across teachers in their use of cognitive processing language (CPL) constitutes a noteworthy discovery itself. But, across a series of studies, Coffman and colleagues go on to establish a connection between CPL and children's strategic knowledge and the application of that knowledge for memory goals. Enhanced memory performance in first and second grade was sustained into fourth grade. Finally, they found that the impact of CPL was not uniform across children. Students with lower self-regulation scores improved significantly from teachers who used higher CPL both in memory performance and achievement levels. Taken together the pattern of findings emerging from this work established beyond a doubt the interactive connections between teacher behavior, child characteristics, and children's memory development.

## *Hudson, Wiley, and Coffman*

Following the success of the memory research in classrooms, recent efforts, summarized in this illuminating chapter, have extended the work into homes and on academic skills. In one study, maternal metacognitive language predicted children's math skills in fall and spring of kindergarten. Likewise, teacher CPL showed similar relations to children's math performance. Consistent with the memory work, Hudson et al. (2018) demonstrated that at the beginning of kindergarten, children identified as math novices who were exposed to high-CPL teachers improved in math performance and strategy use at the end of kindergarten and into first grade. In contrast, higher-performing children did not show improvement with high-CPL teachers.

Combined with the memory research, the work summarized here raises a central question in education, namely, what is effective instruction? The prevailing answer emanating from Ornstein's work is an emphatic "It depends." The most effective instructional regimen will vary depending on the child's initial skills levels and other characteristics, such as self-regulation.

The most recent extension into neurobiological mechanisms in growth of self-regulation is best considered a work in progress, but may hold truly surprising discoveries about the nature of brain development and its relation to behavioral growth.

Recapitulating the original behavioral work, Grammer and colleagues first demonstrated the feasibility of conducting EEG studies with very young children, some as young as 4 (Grammer et al., 2014)! They also verified the validity and reliability of collecting EEG data directly in schools, paving the way for future studies to include much larger samples and atypical groups of participants. More substantively, Grammer et al. (2014) discovered two important neural processes underlying executive function, the error-related negativity (ERN) and error positivity (Pe), that were previously thought to emerge only in later childhood. Following demonstration of age changes between preschool and early elementary school in these responses, the stage was set to examine the potential role of schooling in changes at the brain level. Indeed, in initial research, Grammer has shown that early schooling modifies the ERN and Pe, in the absence of a schooling effect on overt behavior (Grammer et al., 2021). Although preliminary, this dramatic finding implies that brain changes as a function of schooling experience may precede changes seen at the behavioral level. If confirmed, this phenomenon could redefine what we mean by learning (Morrison et al., 2019). Specifically, learning in the brain may not be identical to learning that manifests itself in behavior. More generally, the trajectory of brain learning may be asynchronous with that seen in behavior, at least at some times or with some skills. Following this logic, individual differences among children in the rate of brain changes may not reveal themselves in behavior immediately. Conversely, lack of individual differences in behavior may not reveal important underlying differences among children in their level of brain learning. The solution would be to assess both brain and behavior directly in the classroom during normal classroom instruction, exactly what Grammer and colleagues are currently doing, using wireless EEG. Stay tuned!

## Creating a Life in Science

There are many deeper lessons to be learned from immersing oneself in Peter Ornstein's work over a lifetime in science. I will highlight a special few.

First, be a mensch! A person of honor and integrity. Throughout his life (both in science and out), Peter has consistently demonstrated the highest ideals of conduct – as a researcher, mentor, and professional colleague.

Second, always be asking "What is the next, most important question?" Following his original studies of age differences in memory and rehearsal, Ornstein was faced with the question of what to do next. Clearly, one answer was to look for the sources of developmental change in schooling experiences. At the time, there was almost no quantitative research on classroom observations to rely on. But it was clear that further progress in understanding memory development dictated that Peter take the next step and attempt to study the classroom directly.

Finally, believe in the work and plunge ahead. There are peaks and troughs in science, and at best, we receive steady doses of partial reinforcement. Once when I had a grant turned down, I was disheartened and discouraged from continuing. Peter, sensing my mood, uttered the above advice. As I pondered it later, I realized that I did indeed believe in the work and should keep going. It set the course for the rest of my career.

Other qualities include his dedication to his students, his healthy work–life balance, and, of course, his keeping Yiddish alive.

All in all, well done, my friend, well done.

# PART VI

# Perspective

# CHAPTER 19

# Fifty Years of Research in Memory Development and Its Impact on Conceptions of Cognitive Development

## David F. Bjorklund

Memory sits at center stage of cognition and its development. It is not too much of an exaggeration, if it is at all, to say that memory is involved in all lower-level, automatic, and unconscious processes, and also in all higher-level, mostly conscious, deliberate cognitive processes, such as reasoning, planning, and problem-solving. It is little wonder that memory has been one of the most studied topics in cognition and cognitive development.

The field of memory development has grown up over the last 50 years, and Peter Ornstein was there at its birth and contributed significantly to its maturation. The birth (or perhaps conception) of the modern field of memory development can be traced to a 1966 paper by Flavell, Beach, and Chinsky that showed age differences in how frequently children repeated words they were asked to remember. The study was couched in terms of *mediation theory*, not memory development per se. From this perspective, learning could be explained, not based on the then-dominant paradigm of stimulus–response relationships, but in terms of intervening mediators – covert stimuli and responses that operated between observable stimuli and behaviors. But new ways of thinking about cognition and its development were in the air (see Cox, Chapter 2; Morrison, Chapter 18), and the formal field of memory development took shape at a 1971 symposium organized by John Flavell at the meeting of the Society for Research in Child Development (SRCD) titled, "What Is Memory Development the Development of?" Initial research focused on children's memory strategies, and Peter Ornstein was less an early traveler on the memory development bandwagon than a pioneering driver. He had work in progress when the SRCD symposium was held on age differences in children's use of an organizational strategy (Liberty & Ornstein, 1973). Over the next decade Ornstein published groundbreaking papers documenting age-related changes in children's use of organizational and rehearsal strategies and factors influencing children's use and effectiveness of those strategies (e.g., Bjorklund, Ornstein, & Haig, 1977; Corsale & Ornstein, 1980; Ornstein, Naus, & Liberty, 1975).

As the field of memory development matured and new issues became the focus of research, Ornstein and his collaborators were again at the forefront, investigating topics such as "what are supposedly nonstrategic preschoolers doing when they try to remember information?" (Baker-Ward, Ornstein, & Holden, 1984); children's testimony for complex events (e.g., Baker-Ward, Gordon et al., 1993); mother–child conversational style and children's memory performance (e.g., Haden et al., 2001); and children's use of memory strategies in school (e.g., Coffman et al., 2008). Ornstein's research on these diverse topics in memory development reflects his broader vision of developmental science, stressing the importance of integrating across theoretical perspectives, methods, and basic and applied research (see Fivush, Chapter 14). He, his students, and colleagues continued to investigate these and other topics into the twenty-first century, and as the chapters in this volume attest, Ornstein and his former students remain leaders in the field of memory development research.

## Five "Truths" of Memory Development

There are a number of "truths" or (to use a less-grandiose term) themes about cognitive development, and one way to evaluate the state of the art in memory development is in terms of these "truths." Five that I think are particularly relevant to memory development are listed here (cf. Bjorklund, 2013)[1]:

1. Developmental and individual differences in cognition proceed via the dynamic and reciprocal transaction of children's biological constitutions and their physical and social environments.
2. Cognitive development involves changes in the way information is represented.
3. Children develop increasing intentional control over their thoughts and actions.

---

[1] This of course is a partial list. Other "truths" worthy of making this list include the following: (a) children play an active role in the construction of their own minds; (b) cognitive development involves both stability and plasticity over time; (c) cognition is multifaceted, and different cognitive skills show different patterns of developmental function and stability of individual differences; (d) cognitive development involves changes in both domain-general and domain-specific skills. I'm confident readers could come up with additional "truths" if they were so inclined.

4.  Background knowledge has a significant influence on children's cognition.
5.  Cognitive development occurs within a social context.

In addition to these "truths," most developmental scientists tend to emphasize *meliorism*, the fostering of development (Charlesworth, 1992). For memory development researchers, this has usually involved enhancing children's academic performance or investigating children's eyewitness abilities, especially when children are victims of a possible crime.

In the next two major sections of this chapter I examine what we've learned over the last 50 years for the topics of strategic memory and autobiographical memory development, areas in which Ornstein and his colleagues have been centrally involved, keeping in mind the five truths listed here plus the concept of meliorism. In the final section, I take an assessment of the state of the art of memory development, its impact on conceptions of cognitive development, and a look to the future. I also briefly reflect on Peter Ornstein's five-decade scientific journey in the field of memory development.

## The Development of Memory Strategies

At its beginning, memory development *was* strategy development. The two most researched strategies were rehearsal and organization, and dozens of studies documented that children used more and more effective strategies with age, with corresponding improvements in amount recalled (for reviews see Bjorklund, Dukes, & Brown, 2009; Roebers, 2014; Best & Folds-Bennett, Chapter 4, Esposito & Bauer, Chapter 5, and Schneider, Chapter 6).

### *Developing Mnemonics*

With respect to rehearsal, Ornstein and colleagues developed the *overt rehearsal procedure* in which children were given time between the presentation of successive words and told they must repeat out loud the most recently presented word at least once, and, if they wished, they could practice any other words they liked. Using this procedure, Ornstein showed that young children would use what they called a *passive* strategy, rehearsing a single word at a time, whereas older children would use an *active*, or *cumulative*, strategy, including several different words per rehearsal set (e.g., Naus, Ornstein, & Aivano, 1977; Ornstein et al.,

1975). Levels of recall were predicted not so much by how many words a child rehearsed but by the *style* (passive versus cumulative) of rehearsal. The results of these and other studies (e.g., Lehmann & Hasselhorn, 2012; Ornstein & Naus, 1978) suggested that rehearsal facilitates recall primarily by strengthening associations between items in a list. Moreover, young children who did not spontaneously use a cumulative rehearsal strategy could be trained to use one, with corresponding improvements in memory performance (e.g., Cox et al., 1989; Ornstein, Naus, & Stone, 1977). This finding suggests that children display what Flavell (1970) called a *production deficiency*, in which they fail to produce an appropriate mediator (or in more modern terms, a strategy), but can benefit from the strategy when one is provided for them.

Similar age-related patterns were found for organization. Young children tended not to sort related words or pictures together in preparation for a memory test, nor did they remember related words together when recalling the list items (clustering). Older children were more apt to do both, and levels of recall tended to be correlated with levels of organization, both for sorting (at input) and clustering (at output) (e.g., Bjorklund et al., 1977; Schwenck, Bjorklund, & Schneider, 2009). And as with rehearsal, children who did not spontaneously use an organizational strategy could be trained to use one with corresponding increases in memory performance (e.g., Corsale & Ornstein, 1980). However, for both rehearsal and organization, training rarely resulted in young children attaining the levels of recall shown by equally strategic older children, and young children frequently failed to transfer trained strategies to new materials (see Bjorklund et al., 1997).

The picture painted by scores of rehearsal and organizational memory studies of increasingly strategic performance with age is only partially accurate, however. Although most studies found that preschool-age children were essentially astrategic, displaying chance levels of organization, for example (e.g., Schwenck et al., 2009), other studies demonstrated that young children did do things in preparation for a memory test. For example, 3- and 4-year-old children will selectively attend to items they are trying to remember (e.g., Baker-Ward et al., 1984). However, despite showing some selectivity, children in this and other studies rarely remembered more of the items than less-selective children did. Miller (1990; Miller & Seier, 1994) argued that such children are displaying a *utilization deficiency*, using a strategy that does not improve performance. Such deficiencies are not limited to preschoolers but have been found in older children as well. In fact, Miller and Seier (1994) reported strong or partial evidence for utilization deficiencies in greater than 90% of all experiments examining children's spontaneous use of memory strategies. Utilization deficiencies were similarly found in more than 50% of memory training studies conducted during a 30-year period (Bjorklund et al., 1997).

Other research showed that children actually use a variety of memory strategies on any particular task, with both the number and sophistication of those strategies increasing with age (e.g., Coyle & Bjorklund, 1997; Schwenck et al., 2009). For example, in one study the average number of strategies (sorting by category, category naming, rehearsal, clustering at recall) second-, third-, and fourth-grade children used on a series of Sort–Recall trials increased with age, although even the youngest children used more than one (*Ms* = 1.61, 1.91, and 2.40 for second, third, and fourth graders, respectively). Moreover, the number of strategies children used was positively correlated with how much they remembered (Coyle & Bjorklund, 1997; DeMarie et al., 2004).

Most strategy development studies used cross-sectional designs, and results from these studies suggested gradual change in strategic functioning. This interpretation, however, was not supported by longitudinal research that showed that changes in memory strategy development were not always gradual, but that children often "jumped" from being non-strategic to highly strategic, not over several years, but over much shorter periods of time (e.g., Schneider & Bullock, 2009; see Haden, Chapter 3). For instance, in one study the organizational strategies of 8- to 12-year-old children were assessed on a series of Sort–Recall tasks over 11 consecutive weeks (Schlagmuller & Schneider, 2002). The researchers reported that children transitioned quickly, not gradually, from using no organizational strategies to being strategic, and that once children started to be strategic, they continued to be so and also showed corresponding improvements in their memory performance.

Memory strategies can be useful in a broad range of everyday situations, but they are particularly useful in school. It is somewhat surprising, however, that teachers rarely explicitly teach memory strategies, with several researchers reporting that the absolute frequency of strategy instruction in elementary school classrooms is noted on fewer than 3% of the teacher observations (Coffman et al., 2008; Moely et al., 1992). However, the type of language teachers use in talking to young children does have a significant impact on children's current and future use of memory strategies and classroom performance. For example, first-grade children with teachers who have a "mnemonic orientation," or what Coffman and her colleagues (2008, 2019) call cognitive processing language (e.g., asking children, "How did you study those words?"; "If you make a picture in your mind, it will help you to remember"), showed elevated memory strategy use relative to children with less–"mnemonically oriented" teachers. This benefit extended to the second and later to the fourth grade when children were taught by other teachers, with these effects being especially large for children with low self-regulation abilities (Ornstein, Grammer, & Coffman, 2010; Coffman et al., 2019; see Ornstein, Coffman et al., 2010; Coffman & Cook, Chapter 15; Hudson, Wiley, & Coffman, Chapter 16; and Grammer & Torres, Chapter 17). Educators have used these and other research findings to generate academic curricula to enhance student learning (e.g., Bernstein & Greenhoot, 2014).

### Factors That Influence Strategy Development

Researchers have focused on three factors that contribute significantly to children's tendencies to use and benefit from memory strategies: *mental capacity*, *knowledge*, and *metamemory*, and I examine each of these factors briefly here (see Schneider, Chapter 6).

The idea of limited mental capacity is central to information-processing models of cognition. People can only process so much information at any single time. Using a variety of measures, including speed of processing, working memory, span of apprehension, and dual-task interference, researchers have shown that mental capacity increases with age and predicts performance on a host of tasks (e.g., Case, 1985; Ornstein, Baker-Ward, & Naus, 1988). For example, using a dual-task paradigm, Bjorklund and Harnishfeger (1987) showed that third-grade children who were required to tap on the space bar of a keyboard as fast as they could while being trained to use an organizational memory strategy subsequently used the trained strategy but showed no corresponding improvement in memory performance, illustrative of a utilization deficiency. The authors interpreted these results as indicating that the children expended too much of their limited mental capacity in executing the strategy to have enough left over for other aspects of the memory task, such as retrieving specific words. Strategies are effortful, and their use may not always be associated with improvements in performance. To some extent, levels of neural maturity limit how effectively children can process information, and this will affect all subsequent aspects of cognitive performance (e.g., Vergauwe et al., 2015).

Capacity can account for only a portion of the developmental and individual differences seen in children's strategy use and memory performance, however. Memory span and working memory, for example, vary with a child's knowledge of the to-be-remembered materials (e.g., Chi, 1978); levels of recall and strategy use are greater when children have detailed knowledge of the items they are asked to remember (e.g., Best, 1993; Schwenck et al., 2009); and integration and later retention of information is greater when semantic content is similar between contexts (e.g., Bauer et al., 2012; see Esposito & Bauer, Chapter 5). Bjorklund (1987) proposed that knowledge may enhance children's memory performance by (1) increasing the accessibility of specific items (item-specific effects); (2) the relatively effortless activation of relations among sets of items (nonstrategic organization); and (3) facilitating the use of deliberate strategies. Consistent with Bjorklund's proposal, Ornstein and his colleagues (Folds et al., 1990; Ornstein et al., 1988) argued that the use of memory strategies is facilitated by the automatic execution of certain parts of a task, even in very young children. Later in development, when children have a more elaborated knowledge base and more experience, entire problem-solving routines can become automated.

Concerning metamemory – knowledge of the workings of one's memory – researchers dating back to Flavell's early work (e.g., Kreutzer, Leonard, & Flavell, 1975) have shown a relationship between children's understanding of how their memory works and memory performance. For instance, children who are aware of the connection between memory strategies and memory performance often have better recall than children with less metamemory knowledge (Justice et al., 1997), and children with greater metamemory awareness are more likely to transfer a trained strategy to a new context than less-aware children (e.g., Ringel & Springer, 1980). This pattern was demonstrated in a longitudinal study of first- and second-grade children, which showed that high levels of metamemory preceded sophisticated use of strategies over time (Grammer et al., 2011; see Coffman & Cook, Chapter 15).

There are many factors that influence children's strategy use and effectiveness, and they function in transaction. For example, children who are experts in a domain (e.g., soccer) perform better in that domain than less-expert children (e.g., Schneider, Körkel, & Weinert, 1989), although children's performance is greatest when they also have substantial metacognitive knowledge (e.g., Schneider, Schlagmüller, & Visé, 1998).

The memory development literature, perhaps more than any other body of research, shows clearly the processes whereby children take increasing intentional control of their cognition and actions, with older children needing fewer supports to implement techniques to facilitate their performance than younger children. Strategy use and effectiveness are affected by biologically paced events as reflected by various measures of capacity; by children's abilities to represent and apply their cognitive skills as reflected by metamemory; and by experience, especially as reflected by knowledge. With respect to knowledge, the memory development literature has led the field of cognitive development in demonstrating its important role in intellectual performance.

## The Development of Autobiographical Memory

Research into strategic memory development involves asking children to intentionally remember information and then explicitly retrieve that information at a later time. Much of what children learn and later remember in everyday life is not done intentionally, however. Rather, children go through their day experiencing the world, usually in a social context, acquiring information without conscious awareness or specific intention to store that information for later retrieval. The storage and recall of information about events, even if people had no explicit intention to remember those events, is referred to as *autobiographical memory*. Autobiographical memory emerges over the preschool years and is a major milestone in cognitive development (Nelson, 1996).

Autobiographical memory is a form of episodic, or *explicit* (conscious and declarative), *memory* and is contrasted with infants' memory using visual preference/habituation or operant-conditioning paradigms, which most researchers (but not all, see e.g., Rovee-Collier & Giles, 2010) believe reflect *implicit memory* (memory without awareness; Schneider & Ornstein, 2019). One exception seems to be memory for novel actions using *deferred-imitation* techniques, observed in infants as young as 6 months old (see Bauer, 2007). People with hippocampal damage, who cannot form new declarative memories, also cannot learn new actions via deferred imitation (McDonough et al., 1995), suggesting that deferred imitation involves the same, or highly similar, representational system used for more conventional declarative-memory tasks. The existence of autobiographical memories requires a representational system different than the implicit system characteristics of infants, as well as a somewhat sophisticated sense of self (the "auto" in autobiographical; See Ross, Hutchison, & Cunningham, 2019).

One indication of the onset of autobiographical memory is the offset of *infantile amnesia*, the inability to remember experiences from early childhood. Few people can recall with any accuracy events in their life much before the age of 3.5 or 4 years; and when people have memories extending much beyond these ages (such as my memory of having the croup as a baby), they turn out to be false (in my case, a recollection of my sick younger brother). Two- and 3-year-old children can remember events for days and even weeks, yet their memories seem qualitatively different from those of only slightly older children. According to Gopnik (2009),

> [Two and 3-year-old children] do not experience their lives as a single time line stretching back into the past and forward into the future. They don't send themselves backward and forward along this time line as adults do ... Instead, the memories, images, and thoughts pop in and out of consciousness as they are cued by present events, or by other memories, images, and thoughts (pp. 153–154).

The beginnings of autobiographical memory may be related to children's developing language proficiency. This was illustrated in a study by Simcock and Hayne (2002) in which 2- and 3-year-old children experienced a novel event and were then questioned about the experience half a year later. The authors reported that children's recall 6 months after experiencing the event was related to their language proficiency *at the time of the event*, not at the time of retrieval. Children with more advanced language abilities during the initial experience were apparently able to represent that experience in a language code similar to one they would use 6 months in the future to recall the event. According to Simcock and Hayne (2002, p. 229), "children's verbal reports were frozen in time, reflecting their verbal skill at time of encoding, rather than at time of test." (But see Morris & Baker-Ward [2007] for evidence that some early, preverbal memories can be translated into words at a subsequent time.)

Infants' and young children's limited declarative memories should not necessarily be viewed as a deficit, however, but may reflect an evolutionary adaptation. Rovee-Collier and Giles (2010) argued that infants' lack of long-term declarative memory represents *"rapid forgetting ... an evolutionarily selected survival-related strategy* that facilitates young infants' adaptation to their rapidly changing niche and enables them to shed the excessive number of recent, rapidly formed associations that are potentially useless, irrelevant, or inappropriate" (p. 203) (see also Bjorklund & Green, 1992; Sellers & Bjorklund, 2014). Rovee-Collier and Giles suggested that the first 9 or 10 months of life is a time of "exuberant learning" accompanied by rapid synaptogenesis and pruning, which reflects a transition to a period of perceptual tuning.

Young children's earliest autobiographical memories tend to be in the form of *scripts*, real-world events organized in terms of their causal and temporal characteristics (Nelson, 1996). Children learn what typically happens in a situation (e.g., visiting a fast-food restaurant), and remember novel information in the context of these familiar events (see Bauer, 2007; Fivush, Kuebli, & Clubb, 1992). Two-year-old children's reliance on scripts often results in their recalling only script-consistent information when asked about an event, failing to recall much that was novel about the experience (e.g., Fivush & Hamond, 1990). Nelson (1996, 2005) proposed that young children's reliance on scripts is adaptive for their particular time in development, in that it helps children predict the probability of events in the future. According to Nelson (1996),

> Memory for a single, one-time occurrence of some event, if the event were not traumatic or life-threatening, would not be especially useful, given its low probability. Thus, a memory system might be optimally designed to retain information about frequent and recurrent events – and to discard information about unrepeated events – and to integrate new information about variations in recurrent events into a general knowledge system (p. 174).

With age, children are increasingly better at recalling novel aspects of an experience occurring within a scripted event (see Fivush, 2014).

Age-related changes in brain structures, particularly the frontal cortex and hippocampus, are related to children's increasing abilities to retrieve autobiographical (declarative) memories (e.g., Akers et al., 2014; Monk, Webb, & Nelson, 2001). The hippocampus goes through rapid neurogenesis and pruning in the first year of life (e.g., Akers et al., 2014), but other brain areas (prefrontal lobe, temporal lobe) must mature before infants can retain more complicated information for longer periods. The relatively gradual development of these brain structures is associated with the improvement in long-term retention of infants assessed by deferred-imitation tasks during this same period (e.g., Bauer et al., 2000).

Autobiographical memory involves representing the self in the past, retrieving experiences from some minutes, days, or years earlier. This is referred to as *retrospective memory*. In recent decades, psychologists have examined the development of *prospective memory*, or remembering to do something in the future. Prospective memory, sometimes referred to as *mental time travel* or *episodic future thought* (Atance, 2015; Suddendorf & Corballis, 2007), requires representing the self in the future. This seemingly requires a more sophisticated representational system than that used for autobiographical memory, but one surely related to it and requiring greater metacognitive awareness. Although even 2-year-olds are able to engage in limited "time traveling" when delays are short and motivation is high, the ability to remember to do something in the future develops with age, as children's representational abilities, memories, and executive functions improve (e.g., Voigt et al., 2015; see Mahy, Moses, & Kliegel, 2014, for a review).

### *The Role of Parents in Fostering Autobiographical Memory*

Although young children typically store autobiographical information without intention to later remember that information, what they encode and what they later remember are influenced by their social environment, particularly their parents. Parents and their young children often engage in *shared remembering*, with parents frequently prompting their children to recall recent events. Gauvain (2001) provided a number of functions of shared remembering, some of them cognitive (e.g., learning about memory processes, learning about narrative structures) and others social (e.g., learning values important to the family and the community, that is, what is worth remembering). Through shared remembering, parents show children how to construct narratives about important things they see and do, which they in turn use to share their experiences with others (see Langley, Coffman, & Hussong, Chapter 13; Fivush, Chapter 14). Not surprisingly, there are cultural and individual differences in how parents scaffold children's remembering (e.g., Haden et al., 2009; Schröder et al., 2013). For example, American mothers talk more to their 3-year-old children than Korean mothers do (Mullen & Yi, 1995), which may explain the fact that American children talk more about the past than Korean children and that American adults have earlier first memories than Korean adults (Han, Leitchman, & Wang, 1998; Mullen, 1994).

When children are first learning to talk about the past, parents provide substantial scaffolding to facilitate their children's reminiscing by asking them *Wh-* questions – the who, what, where, and when of the event (e.g., Who did we see? What did we do next?). As children's language and memory abilities improve, parents provide less support, consistent with Vygotsky's (1978) idea of working within the zone of proximal development (Fivush, 2014; Haden & Ornstein, 2009). Some parents provide more support than others, with corresponding differences in their children's recollections. For example, the children of mothers who use more elaborative language when talking about memory with their young children and who provide comments that confirm or negate children's statements (*elaborative* mothers) tend to remember past events better than children with less-elaborative mothers (e.g., Boland, Haden, & Ornstein, 2003; Fivush, Haden, & Reese, 2006; Ornstein, Haden, & Hedrick,

2004; Waters et al., 2019). In a 1-year longitudinal study in which children, beginning at 30 months of age, and their mothers carried out joint activities, mothers who were more involved in jointly carrying out the activities with their children and who used more elaborative language had children who better remembered aspects of the events than children with less-involved and verbal mothers (Haden et al., 2001; Hedrick, Haden, & Ornstein, 2009; see Hedrick, Chapter 11, Haden, Acosta, & Pagano, Chapter 12, and Langley, Coffman, & Hussong, Chapter 13).

Although most parent–child talk involves discussion of everyday activities, occasionally the context supports pedagogy, specifically learning new facts or principles about socially or educationally important topics. Museums are places parents have opportunities to discuss the various displays with their children, often hoping their children will learn something in the process (e.g., Haden et al., 2016; see Haden, Acosta, & Pagano, Chapter 12). Most research on parent–child conversation during museum visits has focused on STEM (science, technology, engineering, and mathematics) talk, some with hands-on exhibits in which both parents and children interact with materials (e.g., Haden et al., 2016; Pagano et al., 2019; Pagano, Haden, & Uttal, 2020). For example, in one study, parents who were encouraged to ask questions of their children for specific hands-on museum exhibits later engaged in more frequent parent–child joint talk and asked more *Wh-* questions when reminiscing about the museum visit with their children at home than non-encouraged parents. The children of prompted parents in turn remembered more about the exhibit 2 weeks after visiting the museum than they had only 1 day after their visit (Jant et al., 2014; Pagano et al., 2020; see Haden, Acosta, & Pagano, Chapter 12).

Children's memory develops in a social context. How parents share experiences with children influences not only what children remember but also how they remember. Although most of the time parents may not have the explicit goal of "teaching" their children specific content, sometimes they do, and museum visits provide ideal contexts for studying such interactions and providing parents with tools to facilitate their children's acquisition of specific content and developing a love of science.

## Children as Eyewitnesses

In the 1990s, there was a spate of legal cases with young children being interviewed about alleged abuse by adults, usually preschool staff (see Cox, Chapter 2; Baker-Ward & Taylor, Chapter 7; Bruck, Chapter 10). At the time, there was little scientifically valid information about the reliability of children as witnesses, either as victims or observers of crimes, and little understanding of the factors that influenced children's eyewitness testimony. How well do children recall details of events they experience or witness pertinent to a possible crime? What role do children's background knowledge, interviewing techniques used, and repeated questioning have on the quantity and accuracy of children's recollections? How susceptible are children to interviewers' suggestions and to forming false memories? These and other issues were of vital social and legal importance, and memory development scientists began extensive research programs to address these and related questions about this particular type of autobiographical memory.

Early research established that preschool children who witnessed forensic-relevant events recall relatively few details in response to open-ended questions, but what they do recall is typically accurate (e.g., Ornstein, Gordon, & Larus, 1992). Young children recall more information when asked cued questions, although they are more likely to assent to the suggestion of an interviewer for both positively leading questions (questions that probed for events that really did happen) and negatively leading questions (questions that suggested events that did not happen) than older children, resulting in a decline in overall accuracy. With increasing age, children remember more information to open-ended questions and are generally less susceptible to the suggestions of interviewers (for a review, see Ceci, Hritz, & Royer 2016). When interviewed over delays of a month or less, children of all ages and adults remember about the same proportion of accurate and inaccurate information as they do originally (e.g., Baker-Ward, Gordon et al., 1993); however, the accuracy of young children's recall declines relative to that of adults for longer delays, especially for less-salient items (e.g., Ornstein, Baker-Ward et al., 2006), although it often remains high for more salient items (e.g., Burgwyn-Bailes et al. 2001). Children who experience repeated episodes of a similar event (as might be the case in child abuse) tend to recall fewer correct details and sometimes have difficulty distinguishing between the various experienced instances of the event, but they report relatively few details never experienced (see Woiwod et al., 2019; Price & Connolly, Chapter 8). Preschool children are also susceptible to forming false memories when they are repeatedly asked whether they had experienced a specific novel event (e.g., taking a ride in a hot air balloon, Ceci et al., 1994) or when other children in their classroom relate events that the target children themselves had not experienced (e.g., a magician's rabbit got loose in a classroom, Principe et al., 2012; see Principe, Chapter 9).

How much and how accurately children remember autobiographical information is affected by a host of factors. For example, as with strategic memory, age and individual differences in knowledge base are strong predictors of children's autobiographical memory performance. In a series of studies examining children's memories for stressful and invasive medical procedures, Ornstein and his colleagues reported that the more children knew about the procedures they underwent, the more accurate was their recall of the procedures (e.g., Clubb et al., 1993; Ornstein, Baker-Ward et al., 1997; Ornstein, Baker-Ward et al., 2006; see Baker-Ward & Taylor, Chapter 7). For example, in one study 4- and 6-year-old children were given a standard well-child medical exam, although in addition to typical features of an exam (e.g., the doctor listened to children's heart with a stethoscope), the exam also included unexpected features (e.g., the doctor measured children's head circumference), as well as omitted some expected features (e.g., measuring blood pressure). Children were interviewed about the exam both immediately and after a 12-week delay, first with open-ended questions followed by increasingly specific questions, some suggesting events that actually happened and others suggesting events that did not happen (Ornstein, Merritt et al., 1998). At the 12-week interview, children correctly recalled more expected than unexpected features and correctly rejected most unexpected features. However, both the 4- and 6-year-olds remembered expected features of an exam that were not actually experienced. Knowing what usually happens caused children to falsely remember what did happen, at least when their memory was tested 12 weeks after the event. Other research has confirmed that although having detailed knowledge of the to-be-remembered events often facilitates memory, at other times it can cause children (and adults) to falsely remember typical events that actually did not occur (e.g., Otgaar et al., 2018).

Of particular importance for children's eyewitness memory are characteristics of the interviewer and the structure of the interview process. For example, children recall more correct and less incorrect information when they are interviewed by a warm and supportive interviewer (e.g., Quas, Bauer, & Boyce, 2004). The use of props, such as anatomically correct dolls, can also influence the accuracy of children's recall. For instance, in one study only about half of 3-year-olds who had received a genital exam by the doctor as part of a well-child check-up correctly reported the exam when dolls were used (e.g., "Did the doctor touch you there?"). More problematic, about half of the children who did *not* receive a genital exam reported incorrectly that they had "been touched there" when shown the doll (Bruck, Ceci, Francoeur, & Renick, 1995; see also Greenhoot et al., 1999; Poole, Bruck, & Pipe, 2011).

Research into children's eyewitness testimony has not only expanded our knowledge of the processes involved in the development of autobiographical memory but also influenced how legal professionals interview children (e.g., Bruck, Ceci, & Principe, 2006; see Cox, Chapter 2; Baker-Ward & Taylor, Chapter 7; Bruck, Chapter 10). The endeavors by scores of developmental memory researchers provide a clear example of how basic science can contribute to social policy and the better treatment of children. As Professor Ornstein has been heard to say, this reflects developmental scientists "giving psychology away" for the public good.

* * *

Whereas research into the development of strategic memory mostly assesses processes involved in remembering context-independent information, important for children in schooled cultures but otherwise lacking ecological validity (what Ebbinghaus called "memory proper," see Cox, Chapter 2), research into the development of autobiographical memory examines the acquisition, storage, and retrieval of "meaningful" information related to the self (what Ebbinghaus called "reminiscence, self-conscious recollection," see Cox, Chapter 2). That autobiographical memory develops in a social context is obvious, with differences in characteristics of cultures and mothers influencing both how and what children remember. The onset of autobiographical memory reflects a clear distinction between the implicit memory representations of infants and the explicit representations of toddlers and preschoolers. The distinction seems not to be all-or-none, however, with children's developing language abilities and sense of self affecting how and what they remember (and what they will remember to do in the future). Importantly, knowledge plays a critical role in children's autobiographical memory, much as it did in children's strategic memory. And because autobiographical memory is for "real-life" experiences, opportunities to study it in ecologically relevant contexts (e.g., museums, doctors' offices, courthouses, classrooms) have led to improved ways of interacting with and facilitating the development of children.

## Memory Development: Past, Present, and Future

I was fortunate enough to begin working with Peter Ornstein not long after the "official" beginning of the modern field of memory development research in the early 1970s. It was exciting to be on the cutting edge of new discoveries, working with a pioneer in the field. Since that time, much has been learned about memory development and its application to educational and legal settings, and Ornstein, his students, and colleagues have contributed substantially to our growing knowledge.

As the Ur-topic, strategy development has become a mature field, with contemporary research building on the findings from rehearsal and organizational studies and expanding to assess other memory strategies. Much contemporary research is especially relevant to pedagogical settings, including self-derived knowledge through integration (Bauer, Esposito, & Daly, 2020; Esposito & Bauer, Chapter 5), use of massed versus spaced learning (e.g., Vlach, Bredemann, & Kraft, 2019), and showing that motor-imagery rehearsal can sometimes produce memory performance superior to verbal researsal (Yang et al., 2020). Some memory strategy research examines topics that provide greater insight into the lower-level processes underlying memory development (e.g., part-list cuing impairment, John & Aslan, 2020; age differences in encoding of indivdual items versus categorical clusters, Horn, Bayen, & Michalkiewicz, 2020), whereas others, such as examinations of children's off-loading memory – using artifacts to aid their subsequent memory (e.g., Bulley et al., 2020) – may be related to children's developing use of tools to solve problems; a feature that is, if not unique to humans, one that develops early and is of great evolutionary significance to our species. Continued research into these and related topics should advance our understanding of cognitive development, as well as contribute to improved pedagogy (see Coffman & Cook, Chapter 15; Hudson, Wiley, & Coffman, Chapter 16; Grammer & Torres, Chapter 17; Morrison, Chapter 18).

Our understanding of the development of autobiographical memory has also expanded substantially since its early beginnings, and we've learned much about the many factors that affect the development of and individual differences in autobiographical memory (see Baker-Ward & Taylor, Chapter 7; Price & Connolly, Chapter 8; and Principe, Chapter 9; Bruck, Chapter 10). Basic developmental science in children's autobiographical memory has made substantial contributions to the legal system, helping to know when children's memories for witnessed or experienced events are apt to be accurate, conditions under which children are susceptible to suggestion, and forensic techniques for interviewing children as witnesses. Basic research continues on ways to get the most complete and accurate information from children as witnesses (e.g., Rezmer et al., 2020); and the cognitive underpinnings of autobiographical memory – of remembering the past and testifying to our experiences – may be clues to humans' intellectual uniqueness and of great theoretical significance (Mahr & Csibra, 2020). Recent research has even identified particular genetic polymorphisms associated with individual differences in autobiographical memory in interaction with characteristics of children's mothers (Tõugu et al., 2016), pointing to a new line of research examining the transaction of children's biological constitutions and their social environment.

### Five "Truths" Revisted

The study of memory and memory development are worthwhile pursuits unto themselves. But memory is always used to *do* something – to perform everyday tasks or solve problems, simple and complex, and for this reason the study of memory and its development have greater implications to human intellectual functioning than other cognitive mechanisms. This realization harkens back to the earliest days of memory development research, with John Flavell's (1970, p. 275) statement that "memory development is largely the development of the mind itself, but the mind as viewed from a certain angle, or with respect to one of its numerous adaptational acts."

I began this chapter listing five "truths" about cognitive development. When the question is asked, "how has research in memory development over the past half century contributed to advancing our understanding of the broader field of cognitive development with respect to these truths?" the answer, I believe, is substantially.

(1) Both strategic and autobiographical memory develop as a result of the interaction of experience and brain-based changes, such as the underlying cognitive abilities associated with self-regulation (see Grammer & Torres, Chapter 17) and the ability to hold and operate on information in working memory. As a measure of capacity, *working memory*, the ability to store and transform information being held in the short-term store, has been widely applied to understanding children's cognition as part of the tripartite division of executive function – inhibition, cognitive flexibility, and working memory (or updating) (Miyake & Friedman, 2012). The working-memory portion of executive function has been identified as a major contributor to many more advanced forms of cognition, including reading, mathematics, intelligence as measured by IQ, and academic performance. For example, in one longitudinal study, working memory measured at age 5 predicted academic performance at age 11 better

than IQ measured either at age 5 or at age 11 (Alloway & Alloway, 2010). Research continues on both the components of children's working memory (e.g., Mathy & Friedman, 2020) and the effects of working memory on higher-level cognition (e.g., Gordon et al., 2020) and promises to provide new insights into cognitive development in the future. Other cutting-edge research is examining brain functioning associated with students' real-time classroom behavior and promises to bring neuroscience into the schoolhouse (Grammer & Torres, Chapter 17).

(2)    The canonical example of age-related changes in mental representation can be found in the transition from the implicit memory of infants to the onset of explicit memory systems, first seen in deferred imitation and later with the beginnings of autobiographical memory, followed by the ability to "mental time travel" via prospective memory.

(3)    Children's increasing ability to "remember on their own" – whether it be for lists of categorically related words or for what happened on the playground earlier in the day – reflects a larger ability to intentionally control their thoughts and actions, and this is clearly reflected in both the strategic memory and autobiographical memory development literatures.

(4)    A major contribution of memory development research to the broader field of cognitive development is perhaps no better illustrated than by the effects of children's developing knowledge base on cognitive performance. The effects of knowledge are robust in both memory strategy and autobiographical memory development literatures and serve as the basis for research and theorizing in other subdisciplines of cognitive development.

(5)    Finally, Vygotsky's (1978) emphasis on the social construction of cognition is exemplified in the development of autobiographical memory, whether it be for socially conventional routines, such as what happens during a well-child doctor's visit; for how parents scaffold children's memory functioning, showing them what is worth remembering in their culture and how to go about remembering it; or for how interactions with other people can create false memories that are highly resistant to forgetting. In this vein, Principe's proposal for a Wikipedia model of memory (Principe, Chapter 9), with content changing over time – sometimes due to other people's contributions – may be a promising guide for future research and theorizing. The socialization of memory is also seen in how teachers' language and emphasis on metacognition influences children's strategic memory and their study skills.

*A Career in Retrospect*

To say that Peter Ornstein's 50-year scientific career closely mirrors the course of memory development research more broadly would be accurate, but an understatement. In many ways, Professor Ornstein anticipated changes in how memory development would be studied, leading the way in performing rigorously designed experiments for important research questions (see Morrison, Chapter 18). During my tenure in the Ornstein Lab in the mid-1970s – while he was conducting field-leading research in the development of strategic memory – Peter was already talking about and planning longitudinal studies (the "true" developmental approach) of memory and of conducting research in schools where memory strategies could be examined in real-world contexts. I still have on my bookshelf a copy of F. C. Bartlett's *Remembering: A Study in Experimental and Social Psychology*, purchased and discussed during my time in the Chapel Hill lab. Ornstein's interest in Bartlett early in his career is a recognition that, even while doing groundbreaking work on research stemming from the Ebbinghaus tradition, he was aware of the essentially social nature of remembering, anticipating his research decades later on children's recollections of experiences during a doctor's office visit and memory stemming from parent–child and teacher–child talk.

In the best tradition of the emerging information-processing paradigm, Peter Ornstein's early work in strategy development began looking at internal processes (encoding, storage, retrieval) and how they affected children's memory and development. But even then, he was mindful of how developmental and individual differences in what children know affect what strategies they use and what they remember. His lab was among the first to investigate the role of knowledge base on children's use of rehearsal and organizational strategies (e.g., Bjorklund et al., 1977; Liberty & Ornstein, 1973), cognizant that meaning (here reflected by word knowledge and words' associations with other words) played an important role in what and how children remembered. His understanding of the importance of meaning and the social context of remembering is apparent in his research on children's memory for a visit to the doctor, some of the first research to apply rigorous methodology to children's long-term retention of complex and forensically relevant events (Baker-Ward, Gordon et al., 1993; Ornstein, Gordon, & Larus, 1992). His research continued to increasingly focus on memory development as the product of the child-within-social-context, recognizing that internal cognitive processes are executed and developed within social (e.g., parents) and cultural (e.g., schools) milieus, all the while emphasizing the importance of doing "true" (i.e., longitudinal) research. As Robyn Fivush (Chapter 14) wrote in her commentary, Ornstein's "integrative perspective provides a vision of the process of development as systematic, socially mediated, and complex" (p. 213).

As I hope the chapters by Ornstein's former students and collaborators in this volume indicate, Peter Ornstein's contribution to our understanding of memory development has been substantial and constant over a five-decade career. Moreover, his students and colleagues are continuing the Ornstein tradition of conducting methodologically sound and innovative research, extending the work of their mentor into new realms of investigations. As a result, contemporary research on children's memory is making, and will continue to make in the future, important contributions not only to our understanding of memory development and its application but also to cognitive development more generally.

# References

Ackil, J. K., Van Abbema, D. L., & Bauer, P. J. (2003). After the storm: Enduring differences in mother–child recollections of traumatic and nontraumatic events. *Journal of Experimental Child Psychology, 84*, 286–309. https://doi.org/10.1016/S0022-0965(03)00027-4 (Chapter 13)

Acosta, D. I., Polinsky, N. J., Haden, C. A., & Uttal, D. H. (2021). Whether and how knowledge moderates linkages between parent–child conversations and children's reflections about tinkering in a children's museum. *Journal of Cognition and Development.* https://doi.org/10.1080/15248372.2020.1871350 (Chapter 12)

Adams, L. T., & Worden, P. E. (1986). Script development and memory organization in preschool and elementary school children. *Discourse Processes, 9*, 149–166. https://doi.org/10.1080/01638538609544637 (Chapter 8)

Ahmed, S., Grammer, J., & Morrison, F. (in press). Cognition in context: Validating group-based executive function assessments in young children. *Journal of Experimental Child Psychology.* (Chapter 17)

Akers, K. G., Martinez-Canabal, A., Restivo, L., Yiu, A. P., De Cristofaro, A., Hsiang, H. L. L., ... Ohira, K. (2014). Hippocampal neurogenesis regulates forgetting during adulthood and infancy. *Science, 344*(6184), 598–602. https://doi.org/10.1126/science.1248903 (Chapter 19)

Alba, J. W., & Hasher, L. (1983). Is memory schematic? *Psychological Bulletin, 93*, 203–231. https://doi.org/10.1037//0033-2909.93.2.203 (Chapter 8)

Alloway, T. P., & Alloway, R. G. (2010). Investigating the predictive roles of working memory and IQ in academic attainment. *Journal of Experimental Child Psychology, 106*, 20–29. https://doi.org/10.1016/j.jecp.2009.11.003 (Chapter 19)

American Psychological Association, Working Group on Investigation of Memories of Childhood Abuse. (1998). Final conclusions of the American Psychological Association Working Group on Investigation of Memories of Child Abuse. *Psychology, Public Policy, and Law, 4*, 933–940. https://psycnet.apa.org/doi/10.1037/1076-8971.4.4.933 (Chapter 1)

Chapter numbers are given in parentheses after each reference to indicate where in the book they are cited.

Ashcraft, M. H. (1982). The development of mental arithmetic: A chronometric approach. *Developmental Review, 2*, 213–236. https://doi.org/10.1016/0273-2297(82)90012-0 (Chapter 16)

Atance, C. M. (2015). Young children's thinking about the future. *Child Development Perspectives, 9*, 178–182. https://doi.org/10.1111/cdep.12128 (Chapter 19)

Atkinson, R. C., & Shiffrin, R. M. (1968). Human memory: A proposed system and its control processes. In K. W. Spence & J. T. Spence (Eds.), *The psychology of learning and motivation: II.* New York, NY: Academic Press. https://doi.org/10.1016/S0079-7421(08)60422-3 (Chapters 2, 4, 18)

Baker-Ward, L. E., Gordon, B. N., Ornstein, P. A., Larus, D. M., & Clubb, P. A. (1993). Young children's long-term retention of a pediatric examination. *Child Development, 64*, 1519–1533. https://doi.org/10.1111/j.1467-8624.1993.tb02968.x (Chapters 2, 5, 7, 8, 11, 19)

Baker-Ward, L. E., & Ornstein, P. A. (2014). The coaction of theory and methods in the study of the development of memory. In P. J. Bauer & R. Fivush (Eds.), *The Wiley-Blackwell handbook on the development of children's memory* (pp. 41–64). New York, NY: Wiley-Blackwell. https://doi.org/10.1002/9781118597705.ch3 (Chapters 2, 3, 5, 15)

Baker-Ward, L. E., Ornstein, P. A., & Gordon, B. N. (1993). A tale of two settings: Young children's memory performance in the laboratory and the field. In G. Davis & R. H. Logie (Eds.), *Memory in everyday life* (pp. 13–41). Amsterdam: North-Holland. https://doi.org/10.1016/S0166-4115(08)61089-4 (Chapter 14)

Baker-Ward, L. E., Ornstein, P. A., Gordon, B. N., Follmer, A., & Clubb, P. A. (1995). How shall a thing be coded? Implications of the use of alternative procedures for scoring children's verbal reports. In M. S. Zaragoza, J. R. Graham, G. C. N. Hall, R. Hirschman, & Y. S. Ben-Porath (Eds.), *Memory and testimony in the child witness* (pp. 61–85). Thousand Oaks, CA: Sage. (Chapter 2)

Baker-Ward, L. E., Ornstein, P. A., & Holden, D. J. (1984). The expression of memorization in early childhood. *Journal of Experimental Child Psychology, 37* (3), 555–575. https://doi.org/10.1016/0022-0965(84)90076-6 (Chapters 4, 5, 6, 14, 15, 19)

Baker-Ward, L. E., Ornstein, P. A., & Principe, G. F. A. (1997). Revealing the representation: Evidence from children's reports of events. In P. van den Broek, P. Bauer, & T. Bourg (Eds.), *Developmental spans in event comprehension and representation: Bridging fictional and actual events* (pp. 79–101). Hillsdale, NJ: Erlbaum. (Chapters 5, 11)

Baker-Ward, L E., Ornstein, P. A., & Starnes, L. P. (2009). Children's understanding and remembering of stressful experiences. In J. A. Quas & R. Fivush (Eds.), *Emotion in memory and development* (pp. 28–59). New York, NY: Oxford University Press. https://doi.org/10.1093/acprof:oso/9780195326932.003.0002 (Chapters 5, 7, 9)

Baker-Ward, L E., Ornstein, P. A., & Thomas, T. E. (in press). Children's memory for forensically relevant experiences. In G. Calloway & S. Margaret Lee (Eds.), *A handbook of children in the legal system: A guide for forensic and mental health practitioners*. New York, NY: Taylor & Francis/ Routledge. (Chapter 7)

Baker-Ward, L. E., Quinonez, R., Milano, M., Lee, S., Langley, H., Brumley, B., & Ornstein, P. A. (2015). Predicting children's recall of a dental procedure: Contributions of stress, preparation, and dental history. *Applied Cognitive Psychology*, *29*(5), 775–781. https://doi.org/10.1002/acp.3152 (Chapter 2)

Baker-Ward, L. E., Tyler, C. S., Coffman, J. L., Merritt, K. A., & Ornstein, P. A. (2020). Children's expectations and episodic reports over 12 weeks: Influences on memory for a specially designed pediatric examination. *Applied Cognitive Psychology*, *34*, 1–13. https://doi.org/10.1002/acp.3619 (Chapters 7, 8, 9)

Baltes, P. B., Reese, H. W., & Lipsitt, L. P. (1980). Life-span developmental psychology. *Annual Review of Psychology*, *31*(1), 65–110. https://doi.org/10.1146/annurev.ps.31.020180.000433 (Chapter 7)

Bardack, S., & Obradović, J. (2019). Observing teachers' displays and scaffolding of executive functioning in the classroom context. *Journal of Applied Developmental Psychology*, *62*, 205–219. https://doi.org/10.1016/j.appdev.2018.12.004 (Chapter 17)

Baroody, A. J., & Ginsburg, H. (1983). The effects of instruction on children's understanding of the "equals" sign. *The Elementary School Journal*, *84*(2), 199–212. https://doi.org/10.1086/461356 (Chapter 16)

(1986). The relationship between initial meaningful and mechanical knowledge of arithmetic. In J. Hiebert (Ed.), *Conceptual and procedural knowledge: The case of mathematics*. Hillsdale, NJ: Erlbaum. (Chapter 16)

Bartlett, F. C. (1923). *Psychology and primitive culture*. London: Cambridge University Press. (Chapters 2, 9)

(1932). *Remembering: A study in experimental and social psychology*. London: Cambridge University Press. (Chapters 2, 9)

Bauer, P. J. (2007). *Remembering the times of our lives: Memory in infancy and beyond*. Mahwah, NJ: Erlbaum. (Chapter 19)

(2012). Facilitating learning and memory in infants and young children: Mechanisms and methods. In S. L. Odom, E. P. Pungello, & N. Gardner-Neblett (Eds.), *Infants, toddlers, and families in poverty: Research implications for early child care*. New York, NY: Guilford. (Chapter 5)

(2014). Insights from longitudinal studies. In P. J. Bauer & R. Fivush (Eds.), *The Wiley-Blackwell handbook on the development of children's memory* (pp. 943–946). New York, NY: Wiley-Blackwell. (Chapter 3)

Bauer, P. J., Blue, S. N., Xu, A., & Esposito, A. G. (2016). Productive extension of semantic memory in school-aged children: Relations with reading comprehension and deployment of cognitive resources. *Developmental Psychology*, *52*(7), 1024–1037. https://doi.org/10.1037/dev0000130. (Chapter 5)

Bauer, P. J., Esposito, A. G., & Daly, J. J. (2020). Self-derivation through memory integration: A model for accumulation of semantic knowledge. *Learning and Instruction, 66,* 101271. https://doi.org/10.1016/j.learninstruc.2019.101271. (Chapters 5, 19)

Bauer, P. J., & Fivush, R. (2010). Context and consequences of autobiographical memory development. *Cognitive Development, 25,* 303–308. https://doi.org/10.1016/j.cogdev.2010.08.001 (Chapter 13)

Bauer, P. J., & Fivush, R. (Eds.) (2014). *The Wiley-Blackwell handbook on the development of children's memory.* New York, NY: Wiley-Blackwell. https://doi.org/10.1002/9781118597705 (Chapters 3, 4, 15)

Bauer, P. J., King, J. E., Larkina, M., Varga, N. L., & White, E. A. (2012). Characters and clues: Factors affecting children's extension of knowledge through integration of separate episodes. *Journal of Experimental Child Psychology, 111*(4), 681–694. https://doi.org/10.1016/j.jecp.2011.10.005. (Chapters 5, 19)

Bauer, P. J., & Larkina, M. (2017). Realizing relevance: The influence of domain-specific information on generation of new knowledge through integration in 4- to 8-year-old children. *Child Development, 88*(1), 247–262. https://doi.org/10.1111/cdev.12584. (Chapter 5)

Bauer, P. J., & San Souci, P. (2010). Going beyond the facts: Young children extend knowledge by integrating episodes. *Journal of Experimental Child Psychology, 107*(4), 452–465. https://doi.org/10.1016/j.jecp.2010.05.012 (Chapter 5)

Bauer, P. J., Stark, E. N., Lukowski, A. F., Rademacher, J., Van Abbema, D. L., & Ackil, J. K. (2005). Working together to make sense of the past: Mothers' and children's use of internal states language in conversations about traumatic and nontraumatic events. *Journal of Cognition and Development, 6,* 463–488. https://doi-org.ezproxy.shsu.edu/10.1207/s15327647jcd0604_2 (Chapter 13)

Bauer, P. J., Stennes, L., & Haight, J. C. (2003). Representation of the inner self in autobiography: Women's and men's use of internal states language in personal narratives. *Memory, 11,* 27–42. https://doi.org/10.1080/741938176 (Chapter 13)

Bauer, P. J., Wenner, J. A., Dropik, P. L., & Wewerka, S. S. (2000). Parameters of remembering and forgetting in the transition from infancy to early childhood. *Monographs of the Society for Research in Child Development, 65* (4, Serial No. 263). https://doi.org/10.1111/1540-5834.00103 (Chapters 3, 19)

Bauer, P. J., Wenner, J. A., & Kroupina, M. G. (2002). Making the past present: Later verbal accessibility of early memories. *Journal of Cognition and Development, 3*(1), 21–47. https://doi.org/10.1207/S15327647JCD0301_3 (Chapter 3)

Belmont, J. M., & Butterfield, E. C. (1971). What the development of short-term memory is. *Human Development, 14,* 236–248. https://doi.org/10.1159/000271218 (Chapter 4)

Bender, R. H., Wallsten, T. S., & Ornstein, P. A. (1996). Age differences in encoding and retrieving details of a pediatric examination. *Psychonomic Bulletin and Review, 3,* 188–198. https://doi.org/10.3758/BF03212417 (Chapter 8)

Benjamin, N., Haden, C. A., & Wilkerson, E. (2010). Enhancing building, conversation, and learning through caregiver–child interactions in a children's museum. *Developmental Psychology, 46*(2), 502–515. https://doi.org/10.1037/a0017822 (Chapters 12, 14)

Bernstein, D., & Greenhoot, A. F. (2014). Team-designed improvement of writing and critical thinking in large undergraduate courses. *Teaching & Learning Inquiry: The ISSOTL Journal, 2,* 39–61. https://doi.org/10.20343/teachlearninqu.2.1.39 (Chapter 19)

Best, D. L. (1993). Inducing children to generate mnemonic organizational strategies. *Developmental Psychology, 29,* 324–336. https://doi.org/10.1037/0012-1649.29.2.324 (Chapters 4, 19)

Best, D. L., & Ornstein, P. A. (1986). Children's generation and communication of mnemonic organizational strategies. *Developmental Psychology, 22*(6), 845–853. https://doi.org/10.1037/0012–1649.22.6.845 (Chapters 4, 5, 6, 7, 15, 16, 19)

Bierman, K. L., Nix, R. L., Greenberg, M. T., Blair, C., & Domitrovich, C. E. (2008). Executive functions and school readiness intervention: Impact, moderation, and mediation in the Head Start REDI program. *Development and Psychopathology, 20*(3), 821–843. https://doi.org/10.1017/S0954579408000394 (Chapter 17)

Bikel, O. (Director & Producer) (1993, July 20 & 21). Innocence Lost. *Frontline.* New York, NY: Public Broadcasting Service. (Chapter 7)

Binet, A. (1900). *La suggestibilité* (Vol. 3). Paris: C. Reinwald. (Chapter 10)

Binet, H., & Henri, V. (1884a). La memoire des mots. *L'Année Psychologique, 1,* 1–23. https://doi.org/10.3406/psy.1894.1044 (Chapter 4)

(1884b). La memoire des phrases. *L'Année Psychologique, 1,* 24–59. https://doi.org/10.3406/psy.1894.1045 (Chapters 3, 4)

Bird, A., & Reese, E. (2006). Emotional reminiscing and the development of an autobiographical self. *Developmental Psychology, 42,* 613–626. https://doi-org.ezproxy.shsu.edu/10.1037/0012-1649.42.4.613 (Chapter 13)

Bjorklund, D. F. (1985). The role of conceptual knowledge in the development of organization in children's memory. In C. J. Brainerd & M. Pressley (Eds.), *Basic processes in memory development: Progress in cognitive development research* (pp. 103–142). New York, NY: Springer-Verlag. https://doi.org/10.1007/978-1-4613-9541-63 (Chapters 4, 6, 16)

(1987). How age changes in knowledge base contribute to the development of children's memory: An interpretive review. *Developmental Review, 7*(2), 93–130. https://doi.org/10.1016/0273-2297(87)90007-4 (Chapters 2, 4, 5, 6, 15, 18, 19)

(1988). Acquiring a mnemonic: Age and category knowledge effects. *Journal of Experimental Child Psychology, 45,* 71–87. https://doi.org/10.1016/0022-0965(88)90051-3 (Chapter 4)

Bjorklund, D. F. (Ed.) (1990). *Children's strategies: Contemporary views of cognitive development*. Hillsdale, NJ: Erlbaum. https://doi.org/10.4324/9780203771648 (Chapter 4)

  (2013). Cognitive development: An overview. In P. D. Zelazo (Ed.), *Oxford handbook of developmental psychology* (pp. 447–476). Oxford, UK: Oxford University Press. https://doi.org/10.1093/oxfordhb/9780199958450.013 .0016 (Chapter 19)

Bjorklund, D. F., & Buchanan, J. J. (1989). Developmental and knowledge base differences in the acquisition and extension of a memory strategy. *Journal of Experimental Child Psychology*, *48*, 451–471. https://doi.org/10.1016/0022-0965(89)90052-0 (Chapter 4)

Bjorklund, D. F., & Coyle, T. R. (1995). Utilization deficiencies in the development of memory strategies. In F. E. Weinert & W. Schneider (Eds.), *Memory performance and competencies: Issues in growth and development* (pp. 161–180). Mahwah, NJ: Erlbaum. (Chapters 4, 6)

Bjorklund, D. F., Dukes, C., & Brown, R. D. (2009). The development of memory strategies. In M. Courage & N. Cowan (Eds.), *The development of memory in infancy and childhood* (pp. 145–175). New York, NY: Psychology Press. (Chapters 4, 6, 15, 19)

Bjorklund, D. F., & Green, B. L. (1992). The adaptive nature of cognitive immaturity. *American Psychologist*, *47*, 46–54. https://doi.org/10.1037/0003-066X.47.1.46 (Chapter 19)

Bjorklund, D. F., & Harnishfeger, K. K. (1987). Developmental differences in the mental effort requirements for the use of an organizational strategy in free recall. *Journal of Experimental Child Psychology*, *44*, 109–125. https://doi.org/10.1016/0022-0965(87)90025-7 (Chapter 19)

Bjorklund, D. F., Hubertz, M., & Reubens, A. (2004). Young children's arithmetic strategies in social context: How parents contribute to children's strategy development while playing games. *International Journal of Behavioral Development*, *28*(4), 347–357. https://doi.org/10.1080/01650250444000027 (Chapters 3, 16)

Bjorklund, D. F., Miller, P. H., Coyle, T. R., & Slawinski, J. L. (1997). Instructing children to use memory strategies: Evidence of utilization deficiencies in memory training studies. *Developmental Review*, *17*(4), 411–441. https://doi.org/10.1006/drev.1997.0440 (Chapters 2, 19)

Bjorklund, D. F., Ornstein, P. A., & Haig, J. R. (1977). Developmental differences in organization and recall: Training in the use of organizational techniques. *Developmental Psychology*, *13*(3), 175–183. https://doi.org/10.1037/0012-1649.13.3.175. (Chapters 4, 5, 6, 15, 19)

Bjorklund, D. F., Schneider, W., Cassel, W. S., & Ashley, E. (1994). Training and extension of a memory strategy: Evidence for utilization deficiencies in the acquisition of an organizational strategy in high- and low-IQ children. *Child Development*, *65*(3), 951–965. https://doi.org/10.1111/j.1467-8624 .1994.tb00795.x. (Chapter 5)

Bjorklund, D. F., & Zeman, B. R. (1982). Children's organization and meta-memory awareness in the recall of familiar information. *Child Development*, *53*, 799–810. https://doi.org/10.2307/1129394 (Chapter 15)

Blair, C., & Raver, C. C. (2014). Closing the achievement gap through modification of neurocognitive and neuroendocrine function: Results from a cluster randomized controlled trial of an innovative approach to the education of children in kindergarten. *PLOS ONE*, *9*(11), e112393. https://doi.org/10.1371/journal.pone.0112393 (Chapter 17)

Blair, C., & Razza, R. P. (2007). Relating effortful control, executive function, and false belief understanding to emerging math and literacy ability in kindergarten. *Child Development*, *78*(2), 647–663. https://doi.org/10.1111/j.1467-8624.2007.01019.x (Chapter 17)

Bodnar, L. E., Prahme, M. C., Cutting, L. E., Denckla, M. B., & Mahone, E. M. (2007). Construct validity of parent ratings of inhibitory control. *Child Neuropsychology*, *13*(4), 345–362. https://doi.org/10.1080/09297040600899867 (Chapter 17)

Boland, A. M., Haden, C. A., & Ornstein, P. A. (2003). Boosting children's memory by training mothers in the use of an elaborative conversational style as an event unfolds. *Journal of Cognition and Development*, *4*(1), 39–65. https://doi.org/10.1207/S15327647JCD4,1-02 (Chapters 3, 11, 12, 14, 19)

Bottoms, B. L., & Davis, S. L. (1997). The creation of satanic ritual abuse. *Journal of Social and Clinical Psychology*, *16*(2), 112–132. https://doi.org/10.1521/jscp.1997.16.2.112 (Chapter 10)

Bousfield, A. K., & Bousfield, W. A. (1966). Measurement of clustering and of sequential constancies in repeated free recall. *Psychological Reports*, *19*, 935–942. https://doi.org/10.2466/pro.1966.19.3.935 (Chapter 4)

Bousfield, W. A. (1953). The occurrence of clustering in the recall of randomly arranged associates. *Journal of General Psychology*, *49*, 229–240. https://doi.org/10.1080/00221309.1953.9710088 (Chapter 2)

Bousfield, W. A., Esterson, J., & Whitmarsh, G. A. (1958). A study of developmental changes in conceptual and perceptual associative clustering. *The Journal of Genetic Psychology: Research and Theory on Human Development*, *92*, 95–102. https://doi.org/10.1080/00221325.1958.10532378 (Chapters 2, 4)

Brainerd, C. J., & Reyna, V. F. (2012). Reliability of children's testimony in the era of developmental reversals. *Developmental Review*, *32*, 224–267. https://doi.org/10.1016/j.dr.2012.06.008 (Chapters 7, 8, 9)

Brainerd, C. J. & Reyna, V. F. (2019). Fuzzy-trace theory, false memory, and the law. *Policy Insights from Brain and Behavioral Sciences*, *6*, 79–86. https://doi.org/10.1177/2372732218797143 (Chapter 9)

Brainerd, C. J., Reyna, V. F., & Ceci, S. J. (2008). Developmental reversals in false memory: A review of data and theory. *Psychological Bulletin*, *134*, 343–382. https://doi.org/10.1037/0033-2909.134.3.343 (Chapter 8)

Bransford, J. D., Brown, A. L., & Cocking, R. R. (1999). *How people learn: Brain, mind, experience, and school*. Washington, DC: National Academic Press. (Chapter 16)

Braun, K., & Rubin, D. C. (1998). The spacing effect depends on an encoding deficit, retrieval, and time in working memory: Evidence from once-presented words. *Memory*, *6*, 37–65. https://doi.org/10.1080/741941599 (Chapter 8)

Broadbent, D. E. (1958). *Perception and communication*. New York, NY: Oxford University Press. https://doi.org/10.1037/10037-000 (Chapter 4)

Brod, G., Bunge, S. A., & Shing, Y. L. (2017). Does one year of schooling improve children's cognitive control and alter associated brain activation? *Psychological Science*, *28*(7), 967–978. https://doi.org/10.1177/095679 7617699838 (Chapter 17)

Brown, A. L., Bransford, J. D., Ferrara, R. A., & Campione, J. C. (1983). Learning, remembering, and understanding. In P. H. Mussen (Series Ed.), J. H. Flavell, & E. M. Markman (Eds.), *Handbook of child psychology (4th ed.): Cognitive development* (4th ed., Vol. 3, pp. 77–166). New York, NY: Wiley. (Chapter 5)

Brown, A. L., & DeLoache, J. S. (1978). *Skills, plans, and self-regulation*. In R. S. Siegler (Ed.), *Children's thinking: What develops?* (pp. 3–35). Hillsdale, NJ: Erlbaum. (Chapter 17)

Brown, A. L., & Smiley, S. S. (1977). Rating the importance of structural units of prose passages: A problem of metacognitive development. *Child Development*, *48*(1), 1–8. https://doi.org/10.2307/1128873 (Chapter 15)

Brown, D. A., Salmon, K., Pipe, M. E., Rutter, M., Craw, S., & Taylor, B. (1999). Children's recall of medical experiences: The impact of stress. *Child Abuse & Neglect*, *23*(3), 209–216. https://doi.org/10.1016/S0145-2134(98) 00127-6 (Chapters 2, 3)

Brubacher, S. P., Earhart, B., Roberts, K. P., & Powell, M. B. (2018). Effects of label training and recall order on children's reports of a repeated event. *Applied Cognitive Psychology*, *32*, 600–609. https://doi.org/10.1002/acp .3440 (Chapter 8)

Brubacher, S. P., Glisic, U., Roberts, K. P., & Powell, M. B. (2011). Children's ability to recall unique aspects of one occurrence of a repeated event. *Applied Cognitive Psychology*, *25*, 351–358. https://doi.org/10.1002/acp.1696 (Chapter 8)

Brubacher, S. P., Powell, M. B., & Roberts, K. P. (2014). Recommendations for interviewing children about repeated experiences. *Psychology, Public Policy, and Law*, *20*, 325–335. https://doi.org/10.1037/law0000011 (Chapter 8)

Brubacher, S. P., Roberts, K. P., & Powell, M. B. (2011). Effects of practicing episodic versus scripted recall on children's subsequent narratives of a repeated event. *Psychology, Public Policy, and Law*, *17*, 286–314. https://doi .org/10.1037/a0022793 (Chapter 8)

(2012). Retrieval of episodic versus generic information: Does the order of recall affect the amount and accuracy of details reported by children about repeated events? *Developmental Psychology*, *48*, 111–122. https://doi.org/10 .1037/a0025866 (Chapter 8)

Bruck, M., & Ceci, S. J. (1999). The suggestibility of children's memory. *Annual Review of Psychology*, *50*, 419–439. https://doi.org/10.1146/annurev.psych .50.1.419 (Chapter 7)

Bruck, M., Ceci, S. J., Francoeur, E., & Barr, R. (1995). "I hardly cried when I got my shot": Influencing children's reports about a visit to their pediatrician. *Child Development, 66*(1), 193–208. https://doi.org/10.2307/1131200 (Chapters 2, 10)

Bruck, M., Ceci, S. J., Francoeur, E., & Renick, A. (1995). Anatomically detailed dolls do not facilitate preschoolers' reports of a pediatric examination involving genital touching. *Journal of Experimental Psychology: Applied, 1*, 95–109. https://doi.org/10.1037/1076-898X.1.2.95 (Chapters 10, 19)

Bruck, M., Ceci, S. J., & Hembrooke, H. (2002). The nature of children's true and false narratives. *Developmental Review, 22*, 520–554. https://doi.org/10.1016/S0273-2297(02)00006-0 (Chapter 9)

Bruck, M., Ceci, S. J., & Principe, G. F. (2006). The child and the law. In W. Damon & R. M. Lerner (Series Ed.), K. A. Renniger & I. E. Sigel (Vol. Eds.), *Handbook of child psychology: Child psychology in practice* (6th ed., Vol. 4, pp. 776–816). New York, NY: Wiley. https://doi.org/10.1002/9780470147658.chpsy0419 (Chapters 9, 19)

Bruner, J. S. (1996). *The culture of education.* Cambridge, MA: Harvard University Press. (Chapter 12)

Bulley, A., McCarthy, T., Gilbert, S. J., Suddendorf, T., & Redshaw, J. (2020). Children devise and selectively use tools to offload cognition. *Current Biology, 30.* https://doi.org/10.1016/j.cub.2020.06.035 (Chapter 19)

Burgwyn-Bailes, E., Baker-Ward, L. E., Gordon, B. N., & Ornstein, P. A. (2001). Children's memory for emergency medical treatment after one year: The impact of individual difference variables on recall and suggestibility. *Applied Cognitive Psychology, 15*(7), S25–S48. https://doi.org/10.1002/acp.833 (Chapters 2, 3, 5, 7, 19)

Burrage, M. S., Ponitz, C. C., McCready, E. A., Shah, P., Sims, B. C., Jewkes, A. M., & Morrison, F. J. (2008). Age- and schooling-related effects on executive functions in young children: A natural experiment. *Child Neuropsychology, 14*(6), 510–524. https://doi.org/10.1080/09297040701756917 (Chapter 17)

Cahan, D. (2019). *Helmholtz: A life in science.* Chicago, IL: Chicago University Press. https://doi.org/10.7208/chicago/9780226549163.001.0001 (Chapter 2)

Cahan, S., & Davis, D. (1987). A between-grade-levels approach to the investigation of the absolute effects of schooling on achievement. *American Educational Research Journal, 24*(1), 1–12. https://doi.org/10.3102/00028312024001001 (Chapter 15)

Cairns, R., & Cairns, B. (2002). Plotting developmental pathways: Methods, measures, models, and madness. In E. Phelps, F. Furstenberg, & A. Colby (Eds.), *Looking at lives: American longitudinal studies of the twentieth century* (pp. 267–296). New York, NY: Russell Sage Foundation. (Chapter 11)

Cairns, R. B., Elder, G. H., Jr., & Costello, E. J. (Eds.) (1996). *Development science.* Cambridge studies in social and emotional development. New York, NY: Cambridge University Press. https://doi.org/10.1017/CBO9780511571114 (Chapters 1, 15, 18)

Calkins, M. W. (1896). Association: An essay analytic and experimental. *Psychological Review Monograph Supplement, 1*(2), 1–56. https://doi.org/10.1037/h0092984 (Chapter 2)

Callanan, M. A., Castañeda, C. L., Luce, M. R., & Martin, J. L. (2017). Family science talk in museums: Predicting children's engagement from variations in talk and activity. *Child Development, 88*(5), 1492–1504. https://doi.org/10.1111/cdev.12886 (Chapter 12)

Callanan, M. A., & Jipson, J. (2001). Explanatory conversations and young children's developing scientific literacy. In K. Crowley, C. D. Schunn, & T. Okada (Eds.), *Designing for science: Implications from everyday, classroom, and professional science* (pp. 21–49). Mahwah, NJ: Erlbaum. (Chapter 12)

Cameron, C. E., Connor, C. M., & Morrison, F. J. (2005). Effects of variation in teacher organization on classroom functioning. *Journal of School Psychology, 43*(1), 61–85. https://doi.org/10.1016/j.jsp.2004.12.002 (Chapter 17)

Cameron, C. E., & Morrison, F. J. (2011). Teacher activity orienting predicts preschoolers' academic and self-regulatory skills. *Early Education & Development, 22*(4), 620–648. https://doi.org/10.1080/10409280903544405 (Chapter 17)

Caramazza, A., Hersh, H., & Torgerson, W. S. (1976). Subjective structures and operations in semantic memory. *Journal of Verbal Learning & Verbal Behavior, 15*, 103–117. https://doi.org/10.1016/S0022–5371(76)90011-6 (Chapter 4)

Carpenter, T. P., Franke, M. L., & Levi, L. (2003). *Thinking mathematically: Integrating arithmetic and algebra in elementary school.* Portsmouth, NH: Heinemann. (Chapter 17)

Carr, M., & Schneider, W. (1991). Long-term maintenance of organizational strategies in kindergarten children. *Contemporary Educational Psychology, 16*, 61–72. https://doi.org/10.1016/0361-476X(91)90006-7 (Chapter 6)

Carver, L. J. (2014). Cognitive neuroscience of emotion and memory development. In P. J. Bauer & R. Fivush (Eds.), *The Wiley-Blackwell handbook on the development of children's memory* (Vols. I–III, pp. 709–723). New York, NY: Wiley-Blackwell. https://doi.org/10.1002/9781118597705.ch31 (Chapter 13)

Case, R. (1985). *Intellectual development: Birth to adulthood.* Orlando, FL: Academic Press. (Chapters 15, 19)

Ceci, S. J., & Bruck, M. (1993). Suggestibility of the child witness: A historical review and synthesis. *Psychological Bulletin, 113*(3), 403–439. https://doi.org/10.1037/0033-2909.113.3.403 (Chapters 7, 10)

   (1995). *Jeopardy in the courtroom: A scientific analysis of children's testimony.* Washington, DC: American Psychological Association. https://doi.org/10.1016/S0885–2014(93)80006-F (Chapters 2, 7, 9, 10)

Ceci, S., Hritz, A., & Royer, C. (2016). Understanding suggestibility. In W. T. O'Donohue & M. Fanetti (Eds.), *Forensic interviews regarding child sexual abuse: A guide to best practices* (pp. 141–153). New York, NY: Springer. https://doi.org/10.1007/978-3-319-21097-1_8 (Chapter 19)

Ceci, S. J., Loftus, E. F., Leichtman, M., & Bruck, M. (1994). The role of source misattributions in the creation of false beliefs among preschoolers. *International Journal of Clinical and Experimental Hypnosis, 62*, 304–320. https://doi.org/10.1080/00207149408409361 (Chapter 19)

Chapin, S. H., O'Connor, C., O'Connor, M. C., & Anderson, N. C. (2009). *Classroom discussions: Using math talk to help students learn, Grades K-6.* Sausalito, CA: Math Solutions. (Chapter 16)

Charlesworth, W. R. (1992). Darwin and developmental psychology: Past and present. *Developmental Psychology, 28,* 5–16. https://doi.org/10.1037/0012-1649.28.1.5 (Chapter 19)

Cheatham, C., & Bauer, P. (2005). Construction of a more coherent story: Prior verbal recall predicts later verbal accessibility of early memories. *Memory, 13* (5), 516–532. https://doi.org/10.1080/09658210444000205 (Chapter 3)

Chi, M. T. H (1978). Knowledge structure and memory development. In R. Siegler (Ed.), *Children's thinking: What develops?* (pp. 73–96). Hillsdale, NJ: Erlbaum. (Chapters 4, 19)

Chi, M. T. H., & Koeske, R. D. (1983). Network representation of a child's dinosaur knowledge. *Developmental Psychology, 19*(1), 29–39. https://doi.org/10.1037/0012-1649.19.1.29 (Chapter 4)

Clark, C. D. (1995). *Flights of fancy, leaps of faith: Children's myths in contemporary America.* Chicago, IL: University of Chicago Press. (Chapter 9)

Cleveland, E. E., Reese, E., & Grolnick, W. S. (2007). Children's engagement and competence in personal recollection: Effects of parents' reminiscing goals. *Journal of Experimental Child Psychology, 96,* 131–149. https://doi.org/10.1016/j.jecp.2006.09.003 (Chapter 9)

Clubb, P. A., Nida, R. E., Merritt, K., & Ornstein, P. A. (1993). Visiting the doctor: Children's knowledge and memory. *Cognitive Development, 8,* 361–372. https://doi-org/10.1016/S0885-2014(93)80006-F (Chapters 2, 7, 8, 19)

Coffman, J. L., Grammer, J. K., Hudson, K. N., Thomas, T. E., Villwock, D., & Ornstein, P. A. (2019). Relating children's early elementary classroom experiences to later skilled remembering and study skills. *Journal of Cognition and Development, 20*(2), 203–221. https://doi.org/10.1080/15248372.2018.1470976 (Chapters 2, 3, 5, 6, 13, 15, 16, 17, 18, 19)

Coffman, J. L., Mugno, A., Zimmerman, D. A., Langley, H. A., Howlett, K., Grammer, J. K., & Ornstein, P. A. (2011, April). *A longitudinal examination of kindergarteners' memory performance.* Poster session presented at the biennial meeting of the Society for Research in Child Development, Montreal, Quebec, Canada. (Chapter 16)

Coffman, J. L., Ornstein, P. A., McCall, L. E., & Curran, P. J. (2008). Linking teachers' memory-relevant language and the development of children's memory skills. *Developmental Psychology, 44*(6), 1640–1654. https://doi.org/10.1037/a0013859 (Chapters 2, 3, 5, 13, 14, 15, 16, 17, 18, 19)

Cole, M. (1997). Cultural mechanisms of cognitive development. In E. Amsel & K. A. Renninger (Eds.), *Change and development: Issues of theory, method, and application* (pp. 245–263). New York, NY: Psychology Press. (Chapter 14)

Cole, P. M., Ram, N., & English, M. S. (2019). Toward a unifying model of self-regulation: A developmental approach. *Child Development Perspectives, 13*(2), 91–96. https://doi.org/10.1111/cdep.12316 (Chapter 17)

Connolly, D. A., Chong, K., Coburn, P. I., & Lutgens, D. (2015). Factors associated with delays of days to decades to criminal prosecutions of child sexual abuse. *Behavioral Sciences and the Law, 33*, 546–560. https://doi.org/10.1002/bsl.2185 (Chapter 8)

Connolly, D. A., & Gordon, H. M. (2014). Can order of general and specific memory prompts help children to recall an instance of a repeated event that was different from the others? *Psychology, Crime & Law, 20*, 852–864. https://doi.org/10.1080/1068316X.2014.885969 (Chapter 8)

Connolly, D. A., Gordon, H. M., Woiwod, D. M., & Price, H. L. (2016). What children recall about a repeated event when one instance is different from the others. *Developmental Psychology, 52*, 1038–1051. https://doi.org/10.1037/dev0000137 (Chapter 8)

Connolly, D. A., & Lindsay, D. S. (2001). The influence of suggestions on children's reports of a unique experience versus an instance of a repeated experience. *Applied Cognitive Psychology, 15*, 205–223. https://doi.org/10.1002/1099-0720(200103/04)15:2<205::AID-ACP698>3.0.CO;2-F (Chapter 8)

Connolly, D. A., & Price, H. L. (2006). Children's suggestibility for an instance of a repeated event versus a unique event: The effect of degree of association between variable options. *Journal of Experimental Child Psychology, 93*, 207–223. https://doi.org/10.1016/j.jecp.2005.06.004 (Chapter 8)

Connolly, D. A., Price, H. L., Lavoie, J. A. A., & Gordon, H. M. (2008). Perceptions and predictors of children's credibility of a unique event and an instance of a repeated event. *Law and Human Behavior, 32*, 92–112. https://doi.org/10.1007/s10979-006-9083-3 (Chapter 8)

Connor, C. M. (2016). A lattice model of the development of reading comprehension. *Child Development Perspectives, 10*(4), 269–274. https://doi.org/10.1111/cdep.12200 (Chapter 17)

Connor, C. M., Ponitz, C. C., Phillips, B. M., Travis, Q. M., Glasney, S., & Morrison, F. J. (2010). First graders' literacy and self-regulation gains: The effect of individualizing student instruction. *Journal of School Psychology, 48* (5), 433–455. https://doi.org/10.1016/j.jsp.2010.06.003 (Chapter 17)

Corsale, K., & Ornstein, P. A. (1980). Developmental changes in children's use of semantic information in recall. *Journal of Experimental Child Psychology, 30*(2), 231–245. https://doi.org/10.1016/0022-0965(80)90060-0 (Chapters 2, 4, 6, 19)

Cox, B. D. (1989). *The effects of feedback on the transfer of mnemonic strategies in young children: The importance of individual differences in response to training.* Unpublished doctoral dissertation, University of North Carolina, Chapel Hill. (Chapter 2)

(1997) The rediscovery of the active learner in adaptive contexts: A developmental-historical analysis of transfer of training. *Educational Psychologist, 32*, 41–55. https://doi.org/10.1207/s15326985ep3201_4 (Chapter 2)

(2019). *The history and evolution of psychology: A philosophical and biological perspective*. New York, NY: Routledge/Taylor and Francis. https://doi.org/10.4324/9781315462295 (Chapter 2)

Cox, B. D., Ornstein, P. A., Naus, M. J., Maxfield, D., & Zimler, J. (1989). Children's concurrent use of rehearsal and organizational strategies. *Developmental Psychology*, *25*(4), 619–627. https://doi.org/10.1037/0012-1649.25.4.619 (Chapters 2, 6, 19)

Cox, B. D., Ornstein, P. A., & Valsiner, J. (1991). The role of internalization in the transfer of mnemonic abilities. In L. Oppenheimer and J. Valsiner (Eds.), *The origins of action: International perspectives*. New York, NY: Springer-Verlag. https://doi.org/10.1007/978-1-4612-3132-5_4 (Chapter 2)

Cox, D., & Waters, H. S. (1986). Sex differences in the use of organization strategies: A developmental analysis. *Journal of Experimental Child Psychology*, *41*(1), 18–37. https://doi.org/10.1016/0022-0965(86)90048-2 (Chapter 6)

Coyle, T. R., & Bjorklund, D. F. (1997). Age differences in, and consequences of, multiple- and variable-strategy use on a multitrial sort-recall task. *Developmental Psychology*, *33*(2), 372–380. https://doi.org/10.1037/0012-1649.33.2.372 (Chapters 15, 16, 19)

Craik, F. I. M., & Lockhart, R. S. (1972). Levels of processing: A framework for memory research. *Journal of Verbal Learning and Verbal Behavior*, *11*, 671–684. https://doi.org/10.1016/S0022–5371(72)80001-X (Chapter 15)

Crossman, A. M., Powell, M. B., Principe, G. F., & Ceci, S. J. (2002). Child testimony in custody cases: A review. *Journal of Forensic Psychology Practice*, *2*, 1–31. https://doi.org/10.1300/J158v02n01_01 (Chapter 9)

Crowley, K., Barron, B., Knutson, K., & Martin, C. K. (2015). Interest and the development of pathways to science. In K. A. Renninger, M. Nieswandt, & S. Hidi (Eds.), *Interest in mathematics and science learning* (pp. 297–313). Washington, DC: AERA. https://doi.org/10.3102/978-0-935302-42-4_17 (Chapter 12)

Crowley, K., Callanan, M. A., Jipson, J. L., Galco, J., Topping, K., & Shrager, J. (2001). Shared scientific thinking in everyday parent–child activity. *Science Education*, *85*(6), 712–732. https://doi.org/10.1002/sce.1035 (Chapter 12)

Danby, M., Sharman, S. J., Brubacher, S. P., & Powell, M. B. (2018). The effects of episode similarity on children's reports of a repeated event. *Memory*, *27*(4), 1–7. https://doi.org/10.1080/09658211.2018.1529798 (Chapter 8)

Danby, M., Sharman, S. J., Brubacher, S. P., Powell, M. B., & Roberts, K. P. (2017). Differential effects of general versus cued invitations on children's reports of a repeated event episode. *Psychology Crime and Law*, *23*, 794–811. https://doi.org/10.1080/1068316X.2017.1324028 (Chapter 8)

Danziger, K. (2008). *Marking the mind: A history of memory*. New York, NY: Cambridge University Press. (Chapter 2)

Deese, J., & Kaufman, R. A. (1957). Serial effects in recall of unorganized and sequentially organized verbal material. *Journal of Experimental Psychology*, *54*(3), 180–187. https://doi.org/10.1037/h0040536 (Chapter 2)

DeLoache, J. S. (1990). Young children's understanding of models. In R. Fivush and J. A. Hudson (Eds.), *Knowing and remembering in young children*, Emory symposia in cognition (Vol. 3, pp. 94–126). New York, NY: Cambridge University Press. (Chapter 7)

DeLoache, J. S., Cassidy, D. J., & Brown, A. L. (1985). Precursors of mnemonic strategies in very young children's memory. *Child Development*, 125–137. https://doi.org/10.2307/1130180 (Chapter 14)

DeMarie, D., Miller, P. H., Ferron, J., & Cunningham, W. R. (2004). Path analysis tests for theoretical models of children's memory performance. *Journal of Cognition and Development*, *5*, 461–492. https://doi.org/10.1207/s15327647jcd0504_4 (Chapter 19)

Derks, E. M., Hudziak, J. J., & Boomsma, D. I. (2009). Genetics of ADHD, hyperactivity, and attention problems. In *Handbook of behavior genetics* (pp. 361–378). New York, NY: Springer. https://doi.org/10.1007/978-0-387-76727-7_25 (Chapter 17)

DeYoung, M. (1997). The devil goes to day care: McMartin and the making of a moral panic. *Journal of American Culture*, *20*, 19–26. https://doi.org/10.1111/j.1542-734X.1997.00019.x (Chapter 10)

Diamond, A. (2012). Activities and programs that improve children's executive functions. *Current Directions in Psychological Science*, *21*(5), 335–341. https://doi.org/10.1177/0963721412453722 (Chapter 17)

Diamond, A., & Ling, D. S. (2016). Conclusions about interventions, programs, and approaches for improving executive functions that appear justified and those that, despite much hype, do not. *Developmental Cognitive Neuroscience*, *18*, 34–48. https://doi.org/10.1016/j.dcn.2015.11.005 (Chapter 17)

(2019). Review of the evidence on, and fundamental questions about, efforts to improve executive functions, including working memory. In J. M. Novick, M. F. Bunting, R. W. Engle, & M. R. Dougherty (Eds.), *Cognitive and working memory training: Perspectives from psychology, neuroscience, and human development* (pp. 145–389). New York, NY: Oxford University Press. https://doi.org/10.1093/oso/9780199974467.003.0008 (Chapter 17)

Domitrovich, C. E., Cortes, R. C., & Greenberg, M. T. (2007). Improving young children's social and emotional competence: A randomized trial of the preschool "PATHS" curriculum. *The Journal of Primary Prevention*, *28*(2), 67–91. https://doi.org/10.1007/s10935-007-0081-0 (Chapter 17)

Dugan, J. A., Menkes, M. W., Esposito, A. G., & Bauer, P. J. (2017). Knowing is some of the battle: Metacognitive awareness improves self-derivation performance. Poster presented at the Cognitive Development Society Biennial Conferences, Portland, OR. (Chapter 5)

Duncan, G. J., Claessens, A., Huston, A. C., Pagani, L. S., Engel, M., Sexton, H., et al. (2007). School readiness and later achievement. *Developmental Psychology*, *43*(6), 1428–1446. https://doi.org/0.1037/0012-1649.43.6.1428 (Chapter 12)

Ebbinghaus, H. (1913) *Memory: A contribution to experimental psychology*. New York, NY: Teachers College. (H. A Ruger and C. E. Busenius, Tr. Original work published in 1885 as *Uber das Gedächtnis: Untersuchungen zur experimentellen Psychologie.*) https://doi.org/10.1037/10011-000 (Chapter 2)

Ebert, E., & Meumann, E. (1905). Über einige grundfragen der psychologie der übungsphdnomene im bereiche des geddchtnisses. *Archiv fur Gesamte Psychologie, 4,* 1–232. (Chapter 2)

Eisenberg, N., Cumberland, A., & Spinrad, T. L. (1998). Parental socialization of emotion. *Psychological Inquiry, 9,* 241–273. https://doi.org/10.1207/s15327965pli0904_1 (Chapter 13)

Emmons, R. A., & Mishra, A. (2011). Why gratitude enhances well-being: What we know, what we need to know. In K. M. Sheldon, T. B. Kashdan, & M. F. Steger (Eds.), *Designing positive psychology: Taking stock and moving forward.* Series in positive psychology (pp. 248–262). New York, NY: Oxford University Press. https://doi.org/10.1093/acprof:oso/9780195373585.003.0016 (Chapter 14)

Erskine, A., Markham, R., & Howie, P. (2001). Children's script-based inferences: Implications for eyewitness testimony. *Cognitive Development, 16,* 871–887. https://doi.org/10.1016/S0885-2014(01)00068-5 (Chapter 8)

Esposito, A. G., & Bauer, P. J. (2017). Going beyond the lesson: Self-generating new factual knowledge in the classroom. *Journal of Experimental Child Psychology, 153,* 110–125. https://doi.org/10.1016/j.jecp.2016.09.003 (Chapter 5)

(2018). Building a knowledge base: Predicting self-derivation through integration in 6- to 10-year-olds. *Journal of Experimental Child Psychology, 176,* 55–72. https://doi.org/10.1016/j.jecp.2018.07.011 (Chapter 5)

(2019a). From bench to classroom: Collaborating within a dual-language education model. *Journal of Cognition and Development, 20*(2), 165–181. https://doi.org/10.1080/15248372.2018.1483374 (Chapter 5)

(2019b). Self-derivation through memory integration under low surface similarity conditions: The case of multiple languages. *Journal of Experimental Child Psychology, 187,* 104661. https://doi.org/10.1016/j.jecp.2019.07.001 (Chapter 5)

Esposito, A. G., Lee, K. A., Dugan, J. A., Lauer, J. E., & Bauer, P. J., (2021). *The gap between a picture and a 1000 words: Self-derivation through integration within and across presentation formats.* Manuscript submitted for publication. (Chapter 5)

Farrant, K., & Reese, E. (2000). Maternal style and children's participation in reminiscing: Stepping stones in children's autobiographical memory development. *Journal of Cognition and Development, 1*(2), 193–225. https://doi.org/10.1207/S15327647JCD010203 (Chapters 3, 11)

Farrar, M. J., & Boyer-Pennington, M. E. (1999). Remembering specific episodes of a scripted event. *Journal of Experimental Child Psychology, 73,* 266–288. https://doi.org/10.1006/jecp.1999.2507 (Chapter 8)

Farrar, M. J., & Goodman, G. S. (1990). Developmental differences in the relation between scripts and episodic memory: Do they exist? In R. Fivush & J. A. Hudson (Eds.), *Knowing and remembering in young children* (pp. 30–64). New York, NY: Cambridge University Press. (Chapter 8)

(1992). Developmental changes in event memory. *Child Development, 63,* 173–187. https://doi.org/10.2307/1130911 (Chapter 8)

Fender, J. G., & Crowley, K. (2007). How parent explanation changes what children learn from everyday scientific thinking. *Journal of Applied Developmental Psychology, 28*(3), 189–210. https://doi.org/10.1016/j.appdev.2007.02.007 (Chapter 12)

Fernandez-Duque, D., Baird, J. A., & Posner, M. I. (2000). Executive attention and metacognitive regulation. *Consciousness and Cognition, 9*(2), 288–307. https://doi.org/10.1006/ccog.2000.0447 (Chapter 17)

Fitzpatrick, C., Côté-Lussier, C., & Blair, C. (2016). Dressed and groomed for success in elementary school: Student appearance and academic adjustment. *The Elementary School Journal, 117*(1), 30–45. https://doi.org/10.1086/687753 (Chapter 17)

Fivush, R. (1984). Learning about school: The development of kindergartners' school scripts. *Child Development, 55,* 1697–1709. https://doi.org/10.2307/1129917 (Chapters 2, 8)

(1991). Gender and emotion in mother–child conversations about the past. *Journal of Narrative & Life History, 1,* 325–341. https://doiorg.ezproxy.shsu.edu/10.1075/jnlh.1.4.04gen (Chapter 13)

(1993). Emotional content of parent–child conversations about the past. *Memory and affect in development* (Vol. 26, pp. 39–77). Hillsdale, NJ: Erlbaum. (Chapter 2)

(1997). Event memory in early childhood. In N. Cowan (Ed.), *The development of memory in childhood* (pp. 139–161). London: Psychology Press. (Chapter 8)

(1998). Gendered narratives: Elaboration, structure, and emotion in parent-child reminiscing across the preschool years. In C. P. Thompson, D. J. Herrmann, D. Bruce, J. D. Read, D. G. Payne, & M. P. Toglia (Eds.), *Autobiographical memory: Theoretical and applied perspectives* (pp. 79–103). Mahwah, NJ: Erlbaum. https://doi.org/10.4324/9781315784250-6 (Chapter 13)

(2002). Scripts, schemas, and memory of trauma. In N. L. Stein, P. J. Bauer, & M. Rabinowitz (Eds.), *Representation, memory, and development: Essays in honor of Jean Mandler* (pp. 53–74). Mahwah, NJ: Erlbaum. (Chapter 8)

(2011). The development of autobiographical memory. *Annual Review of Psychology, 62,* 559–582. https://doi.org/10.1146/annurev.psych.121208.131702 (Chapters 7, 14)

(2014). Maternal reminiscing style: The sociocultural construction of autobiographical memory across childhood and adolescence. In P. J. Bauer & R. Fivush (Eds.), *The Wiley-Blackwell handbook on the development of children's memory* (pp. 568–585). New York, NY: Wiley-Blackwell. https://doi.org/10.1002/9781118597705.ch24 (Chapters 3, 13, 19)

(2018). The sociocultural functions of episodic memory. *Behavioral and Brain Sciences, 41,* e14. https://doi.org/10.1017/S0140525X17001352 (Chapters 13, 15)

(2019). Sociocultural approaches to autobiographical memory. *Applied Cognitive Psychology*, *33*, 489–497. https://doi.org/10.1002/acp.3512 (Chapter 14)

Fivush, R., Berlin, L. J., Sales, J. M., Mennuti-Washburn, J., & Cassidy, J. (2003). Functions of parent–child reminiscing about emotionally negative events. *Memory*, *11*, 179–192. https://doi.org/10.1080/741938209 (Chapter 13)

Fivush, R., Brotman, M. A., Buckner, J. P., & Goodman, S. H. (2000). Gender differences in parent–child emotion narratives. *Sex Roles: A Journal of Research*, *42*(3–4), 233–253. https://doi.org/10.1023/A:1007091207068 (Chapters 2, 13)

Fivush, R., & Buckner, J. P. (2003). Creating gender and identity through autobiographical narratives. In R. Fivush & C. A. Haden (Eds.), *Autobiographical memory and the construction of a narrative self: Developmental and cultural perspectives* (pp. 149–167). Mahwah, NJ: Erlbaum. https://doi.org/10.4324/9781410607478 (Chapter 13)

Fivush, R., & Fromhoff, F. (1988). Style and structure in mother–child conversations about the past. *Discourse Processes*, *11, 337–355.* https://doi.org/10.1080/01638538809544707 (Chapter 11)

Fivush, R., & Haden, C. A. (Eds.) (2003). *Autobiographical memory and the construction of a narrative self: Developmental and cultural perspectives.* Mahwah, NJ: Erlbaum. https://doi.org/10.4324/9781410607478 (Chapter 3)

Fivush, R., Haden, C. A., & Adam, S. (1995). Structure and coherence of preschoolers' personal narratives over time: Implications for childhood amnesia. *Journal of Experimental Child Psychology*, *60*(1), 32–56. https://doi.org/10.1006/jecp.1995.1030 (Chapter 3)

Fivush, R., Haden, C. A., & Reese, E. (2006). Elaborating on elaborations: Role of maternal reminiscing style in cognitive and socioemotional development. *Child Development*, *77*(6), 1568–1588. https://doi.org/10.1111/j.1467-8624.2006.00960.x (Chapters 2, 3, 11, 12, 13, 14, 15, 16, 19)

Fivush, R., & Hamond, N. R. (1990). Autobiographical memory across the preschool years: Toward reconceptualizing childhood amnesia. In R. Fivush & J. A. Hudson (Eds.), *Knowing and remembering in young children* (pp. 223–248). Cambridge, UK: Cambridge University Press. (Chapter 19)

Fivush, R., & Hudson, J. A. (Eds.) (1990). *Knowing and remembering in young children.* New York, NY: Cambridge University Press. (Chapters 7, 8, 16)

Fivush, R., Kuebli, J., & Clubb, P. A. (1992). The structure of events and event representations: A developmental analysis. *Child Development*, *63*, 188–201. https://doi.org/10.2307/1130912 (Chapter 19)

Fivush, R., & Nelson, K. (2004). Culture and language in the emergence of autobiographical memory. *Psychological Science*, *15*(9), 573–577. https://doi.org/10.1111/j.09567976.2004.00722.x (Chapter 11)

Fivush, R., Sales, J., Goldberg, A., Bahrick, L., & Parker, J. (2004). Weathering the storm: Children's long-term recall of Hurricane Andrew. *Memory*, *12*(1), 104–118. https://doi.org/10.1080/09658210244000397 (Chapter 3)

Flavell, J. H. (1970). Developmental studies of mediated memory. In H. W. Reese & L. P. Lipsitt (Eds.), *Advances in child development and behavior* (pp. 181–211). New York, NY: Academic Press. https://doi.org/10.1016/S0065-2407(08)60467-X (Chapters 2, 4, 19)

(1971). First discussant's comments: What is memory development the development of? *Human Development, 14*(4), 272–278. https://doi.org/10.1159/000271221 (Chapters 2, 4, 6, 14)

(1979). Metacognition and cognitive monitoring: A new area of cognitive-developmental inquiry. *American Psychologist, 34*(10), 906–911. https://doi.org/10.1037/0003-066X.34.10.906 (Chapter 5)

Flavell, J. H., Beach, D. R., & Chinsky, J. M. (1966). Spontaneous verbal rehearsal in a memory task as a function of age. *Child Development, 37*(2), 283–299. https://doi.org/10.2307/1126804 (Chapters 2, 3, 4, 6, 19)

Flavell, J. H., Friedrichs, A. G., & Hoyt, J. D. (1970). Developmental changes in memorization processes. *Cognitive Psychology, 1*(4), 324–340. https://doi.org/10.1016/0010-0285(70)90019-8 (Chapter 2)

Flavell, J. H., Miller, P. H., & Miller, S. A. (1993). *Cognitive development* (3rd ed.). Englewood Cliffs, NJ: Prentice-Hall. (Chapter 4)

Flavell, J. H., & Wellman, H. M. (1977). *Metamemory*. In R. Kail & W. Hagen (Eds.), *Perspectives on the development of memory and cognition* (pp. 3–31). Hillsdale, NJ: Erlbaum. (Chapters 3, 6)

Flook, L., Goldberg, S. B., Pinger, L., & Davidson, R. J. (2015). Promoting prosocial behavior and self-regulatory skills in preschool children through a mindfulness-based kindness curriculum. *Developmental Psychology, 51*(1), 44–51. https://doi.org/10.1037/a0038256 (Chapter 17)

Flook, L., Smalley, S. L., Kitil, M. J., Galla, B. M., Kaiser-Greenland, S., Locke, J., Ishijima, E., & Kasari, C. (2010). Effects of mindful awareness practices on executive functions in elementary school children. *Journal of Applied School Psychology, 26*(1), 70–95. https://doi.org/10.1080/15377900903379125 (Chapter 17)

Folds, T., Footo, M., Guttentag, R., & Ornstein (1990). When children mean to remember: Issues of context specificity, strategy effectiveness, and intentionality in the development of memory. In D. F. Bjorklund (Ed.), *Children's strategies: Contemporary views of cognitive development* (pp. 67–91). Hillsdale, NJ: Erlbaum. (Chapters 4, 6, 15, 19)

Frankfurter, D. (2006). *Evil incarnate: Rumors of demonic conspiracy and ritual abuse in history*. Princeton, NJ: Princeton University Press. https://doi.org/10.1515/9780691186979 (Chapter 10)

Friendly, M. L. (1977). In search of the M-gram: The structure of organization in free recall. *Cognitive Psychology, 9*, 188–249. https://doi.org/10.1016/0010-0285(77)90008-1 (Chapter 4)

Froh, J. J., Kashdan, T. B., Ozimkowski, K. M., & Miller, N. (2009). Who benefits the most from a gratitude intervention in children and adolescents? Examining positive affect as a moderator. *The Journal of Positive Psychology, 4*, 408–422. https://doi.org/10.1080/17439760902992464 (Chapter 13)

Fuson, K. C. (1982). An analysis of the counting-on solution procedure in addition. In T. P. Carpenter, J. M. Moser, & T. A. Romberg (Eds.), *Addition and subtraction: A cognitive perspective* (pp. 67–81). Hillsdale, NJ: Erlbaum. https://doi.org/10.1201/9781003046585-6 (Chapter 16)

Gaultney, J. F., Bjorklund, D. F., & Schneider, W. (1992). The role of children's expertise in a strategic memory task. *Contemporary Educational Psychology, 17* (3), 244–257. https://doi.org/10.1016/0361-476X(92)90063-5 (Chapter 5)

Gauvain, M. (2001). *The social context of cognitive development.* New York, NY: Guilford. (Chapter 19)

Geary, D. C., & Brown, S. C. (1991). Cognitive addition: Strategy choice and speed-of-processing differences in gifted, normal, and mathematically disabled children. *Developmental Psychology, 27*(3), 398–406. https://doi.org/10 .1037/0012-1649.27.3.398 (Chapter 16)

Geary, D. C., Brown, S. C., & Samaranayake, V. A. (1991). Cognitive addition: A short longitudinal study of strategy choice and speed-of-processing differences in normal and mathematically disabled children. *Developmental Psychology, 27*(5), 787–797. https://doi.org/10.1037/0012-1649.27.5.787 (Chapter 16)

Geisel, T. S. (1990). *Oh, the places you'll go!* New York, NY: Random House Books for Young Readers. (Chapter 5)

Gelman, R., & Gallistel, C. R. (1978). *The child's understanding of number.* Cambridge, MA: Harvard University Press. (Chapter 16)

Gentzler, A. L., Contreras-Grau, J. M., Kerns, K. A., & Weimer, B. L. (2005). Parent–child emotional communication and children's coping in middle childhood. *Social Development, 14,* 591–612. https://doi-org.ezproxy.shsu .edu/10.1111/j.1467-9507.2005.00319.x (Chapter 13)

Ghetti, S., & Bauer, P. J. (Eds.) (2012). *Origins and development of recollection: Perspectives from psychology and neuroscience.* New York, NY: Oxford University Press. (Chapter 3)

Gibson, E. J. (1940). A systematic application of the concepts of generalization and differentiation to verbal learning. *Psychological Review, 47*(3), 196–229. https://doi.org/10.1037/h0060582 (Chapter 2)

Gilbert, D. T., & Malone, P. S. (1995). The correspondence bias. *Psychological Bulletin, 117,* 21–38. https://doi.org/10.1037/0033-2909.117.1.21 (Chapter 9)

Glenberg, A., Brown, M., & Levin, J. R. (2007). Enhancing comprehension in small reading groups using a manipulation strategy. *Contemporary Educational Psychology, 32*(3), 389–399. https://doi.org/10.1016/j.cedpsych .2006.03.001 (Chapter 12)

Goldstone, R. L., & Sakamoto, Y. (2003). The transfer of abstract principles governing complex adaptive systems. *Cognitive Psychology, 46*(4), 414–466. https://doi.org/10.1016/S0010-0285(02)00519-4 (Chapter 12)

Goodman, G. S., & Quas, J. A. (1997). Trauma and memory: Individual differences in children's recounting of a stressful experience. In N. L. Stein, P. A. Ornstein, B., Tversky, & C. Brainerd (Eds.), *Memory for everyday and emotional events* (pp. 267–294). Hillsdale, NJ: Erlbaum. https://doi.org/10.4324/9781315789231-11 (Chapters 8, 19)

Goodman, G. S., Quas, J. A., Batterman-Faunce, J. M., Riddlesberger, M. M., & Kuhn, J. (1994). Predictors of accurate and inaccurate memories of traumatic events experienced in childhood. *Consciousness and Cognition*, *3*, 269–294. https://doi.org/10.1006/ccog.1994.1016 (Chapter 8)

Gopnik, A. (2009). *The philosophical baby: What children's minds tell us about truth, love, and the meaning of life*. New York, NY: Farber, Straus, and Giroux. (Chapter 19)

Gordon, B. N., Baker-Ward, L. E., & Ornstein, P. A. (2001). Children's testimony: A review of research on memory for past experiences. *Clinical Child and Family Psychology Review*, *4*, 157–181. https://doi.org/10.1023/A:1011333231621 (Chapters 7, 9)

Gordon, B. N., & Follmer, A. (1994). Developmental issues in judging the credibility of children's testimony. *Journal of Clinical Child Psychology*, *23*(3), 283–294. https://doi.org/10.1207/s15374424jccp2303_6 (Chapter 7)

Gordon, B. N., Ornstein, P. A., Nida, R., Follmer, A., Crenshaw, M., & Albert, G. (1993). Does the use of dolls facilitate children's memory of visits to the doctor? *Applied Cognitive Psychology*, *7*, 459–474. https://doi.org/10.1002/acp.2350070602 (Chapter 7)

Gordon, R., Smith-Spark, J. H., Newton, E. J., & Henry, L. A. (2020). Working memory and high-level cognition in children: An analysis of timing and accuracy in complex span tasks. *Journal of Experimental Child Psychology*, *191*, 104736. https://doi.org/10.1016/j.jecp.2019.104736 (Chapter 19)

Goswami, U. (2002). Phonology, reading development, and dyslexia: A cross-linguistic perspective. *Annals of Dyslexia*, *52*(1), 139–163. https://doi.org/10.1007/s11881-002-0010-0 (Chapter 5)

Grammer, J. K., Carrasco, M., Gehring, W. J., & Morrison, F. J. (2014). Age-related changes in error processing in young children: A school-based investigation. *Developmental Cognitive Neuroscience*, *9*, 93–105. https://doi.org/10.1016/j.dcn.2014.02.001 (Chapters 17, 18)

Grammer, J., Coffman, J. L., & Ornstein, P. (2013). The effect of teachers' memory-relevant language on children's strategy use and knowledge. *Child Development*, *84*(6), 1989–2002. https://doi.org/10.1111/cdev.12100 (Chapters 2, 3, 5, 15, 16, 17)

Grammer, J. K., Coffman, J. L., Ornstein, P. A., & Morrison, F. J. (2013). Change over time: Conducting longitudinal studies of children's cognitive development. *Journal of Cognition and Development*, *14*(4), 515–528. https://doi.org/10.1080/15248372.2013.833925 (Chapter 11)

Grammer, J. K., Coffman, J. L., Sidney, P., & Ornstein, P. A. (2016). Linking teacher instruction and student achievement in mathematics: The role of teacher language. *Journal of Cognition and Development*, *17*(3), 468–485. https://doi.org/10.1080/15248372.2015.1068777 (Chapters 2, 16)

Grammer, J. K., Gehring, W. J., & Morrison, F. J. (2018). Associations between developmental changes in error-related brain activity and executive functions in early childhood. *Psychophysiology*, *55*(3). https://doi.org/10.1111/psyp.13040 (Chapter 17)

Grammer, J. K., Isbell, E., Kim, M. H., Hazlett, C., Gehring, W., & Morrison, F. J. (2021, April). The impact of school experience on cognitive control processes. In Shing, Y. L. (Chair), Causal impacts of schooling on children's cognitive and brain development. Paper presented at the Society for Research in Child Development (SRCD) Biennial Meeting. (Chapter 17, 18)

Grammer, J. K., Kim, M., Moser, J. S., Durbin, C. E., Hajcak, G., Klein, D. N., Gehring, W. J., & Morrison, F. J. (in preparation). *Schooling effects of error-related brain activity.* (Chapter 17)

Grammer, J. K., Purtell, K. M., Coffman, J. L., & Ornstein, P. A. (2011). Relations between children's metamemory and strategic performance: Time-varying covariates in early elementary school. *Journal of Experimental Child Psychology*, *108*(1), 139–155. https://doi.org/10.1016/j.jecp.2010.08.001 (Chapters 3, 16, 19)

Grammer, J. K., Xu, K., & Lenartowicz, A. (under review). *Effects of context on the neural correlates of attention in a college classroom.* (Chapter 17)

Grant, E. R., & Ceci, S. J. (2000). Memory: Constructive processes. In A. E. Kasdin (Ed.), *Encyclopedia of Psychology* (pp. 166–169). New York, NY: Oxford University Press. https://doi.org/10.1037/10520-080 (Chapter 9)

Greene, R. L. (1989). Spacing effects in memory: Evidence for a two-process account. *Journal of Experimental Psychology: Learning, Memory, and Cognition*, *15*, 371–377. https://doi.org/10.1037/0278-7393.15.3.371 (Chapter 8)

Greenhoot, A. F. (2000). Remembering and understanding: The effects of changes in underlying knowledge on children's recollections. *Child Development*, *71*, 1309–1328. https://doi.org/10.1111/1467-8624.00230 (Chapters 7, 9, 19)

Greenhoot, A. F., Ornstein, P. A., Gordon, B. N., & Baker-Ward, L. E. (1999). Acting out the details of a pediatric check-up: The impact of interview condition and behavioral style on children's memory reports. *Child Development*, *70*(2), 363–380. https://doi.org/10.1111/1467–8624.00027 (Chapter 7, 19)

Guadagno, B. L., Powell, M., & Wright, R. (2006). Police officers' and legal professionals' perceptions regarding how children are, and should be, questioned about repeated abuse. *Psychiatry, Psychology, and Law*, *13*, 251–260. https://doi.org/10.1375/pplt.13.2.251 (Chapter 8)

Güler, O. E., Larkina, M., Kleinknecht, E., & Bauer, P. J. (2010). Memory strategies and retrieval success in preschool children: Relations to maternal behavior over time. *Journal of Cognition and Development*, *11*(2), 159–184. https://doi.org/10.1080/15248371003699910 (Chapter 3)

Gunderson, E. A., & Levine, S. C. (2011). Some types of parent number talk count more than others: Relations between parents' input and children's cardinal-number knowledge. *Developmental Science*, *14*(5), 1021–1032. https://doi.org/10.1111/j.1467-7687.2011.01050.x (Chapter 12)

Guttentag, R. E. (1984). The mental effort requirement of cumulative rehearsal: A developmental study. *Journal of Experimental Child Psychology*, *37*, 92–106. https://doi.org/10.1016/0022-0965(84)90060-2 (Chapter 4)

Guttentag, R. E., Ornstein, P. A., & Siemens, L. (1987). Children's spontaneous rehearsal: Transitions in strategy acquisition. *Cognitive Development*, *2*(4),

307–326. https://doi.org/10.1016/S0885-2014(87)80010-2 (Chapters 3, 4, 5, 6, 15)

Haden, C. A. (1998). Reminiscing with different children: Relating maternal stylistic consistency and sibling similarity in talk about the past. *Developmental Psychology, 34*, 99–114. https://doi.org/10.1037/0012-1649 .34.1.99 (Chapters 11, 16)

(2003). Joint encoding and joint reminiscing: Implications for young children's understanding and remembering of personal experiences. In R. Fivush & C. A. Haden (Eds.), *Autobiographical memory and the construction of a narrative self: Developmental and cultural perspectives* (pp. 49–69). Mahwah, NJ: Erlbaum. (Chapter 11)

(2010). Talking about science in museums. *Child Development Perspectives, 4*(1), 62–67. https://doi.org/10.1111/j.1750-8606.2009.00119.x (Chapters 12, 14)

(2014). Interactions of knowledge and memory in the development of skilled remembering. In P. Bauer & R. Fivush (Eds.), *The Wiley-Blackwell handbook on children's memory* (pp. 809–835). New York, NY: Wiley-Blackwell. https://doi.org/10.1002/9781118597705.ch35 (Chapter 12)

Haden, C. A., Cohen, T., Uttal, D., Marcus, M. (2016). Building learning: Narrating and transferring experiences in a children's museum. In D. M. Sobel & J. J. Jipson (Eds.), *Cognitive development in museum settings: Relating research and practice* (pp. 84–103). London: Routledge. (Chapters 12, 19)

Haden, C. A., Haine, R. A., & Fivush, R. (1997). Developing narrative structure in parent–child reminiscing across the preschool years. *Developmental Psychology, 33*(2), 295–307. https://doi.org/10.1037/0012-1649.33.2.295 (Chapters 3, 13)

Haden, C. A., Jant, E. A., Hoffman, P. C., Marcus, M., Geddes, J. R., & Gaskins, S. (2014). Supporting family conversations and children's STEM learning in a children's museum. *Early Childhood Research Quarterly, 29*(3), 333–344. https://doi.org/10.1016/j.ecresq.2014.04.0041 (Chapters 12, 14)

Haden, C. A. & Ornstein, P. A. (2009). Research on talking about the past: The past, present, and future. *Journal of Cognition and Development, 10*, 135–142. https://doi.org/10.1080/15248370903155718 (Chapter 19)

Haden, C. A., Ornstein, P. A., Eckerman, C. O., & Didow, S. M. (2001). Mother–child conversational interactions as events unfold: Linkages to subsequent remembering. *Child Development, 72*(4), 1016–1031. https:// doi.org/10.1111/1467-8624.00332 (Chapters 3, 11, 12, 13, 14, 15, 16, 19)

Haden, C. A., Ornstein, P. A., O'Brien, B. S., Elischberger, H. B., Tyler, C. S., & Burchinal, M. J. (2010). The development of children's early memory skills. *Journal of Experimental Child Psychology, 108*(1), 44–60. https://doi.org/10 .1016/j.jecp.2010.06.007 (Chapter 11)

Haden, C. A., Ornstein, P. A., Rudek, D. J., & Cameron, D. (2009). Reminiscing in the early years: Patterns of maternal elaborativeness and children's remembering. *International Journal of Behavioral Development, 33*(2), 118–130. https://doi.org/10.1177/0165025408098038 (Chapters 3, 11, 14, 19)

Han, J. J., Leitchman, M. D., & Wang, Q. (1998). Autobiographical memory in Korean, Chinese, and American children. *Developmental Psychology, 34,* 701–713. https://doi.org/10.1037/0012-1649.34.4.701 (Chapter 19)

Harley, K., & Reese, E. (1999). Origins of autobiographical memory. *Developmental Psychology, 35*(5), 1338–1348. https://doi.org/10.1037/0012-1649.35.5.1338 (Chapters 3, 11)

Hasselhorn, M. (1992). Task dependency and the role of category typicality and metamemory in the development of an organizational strategy. *Child Development, 63,* 202–214. https://psycnet.apa.org/doi/10.2307/1130913 (Chapter 6)

Hedrick, A. M., Haden, C. A., & Ornstein, P. A. (2009). Elaborative talk during and after an event: Conversational style influences children's memory reports. *Journal of Cognition and Development, 10*(3), 188–209. https://doi.org/10.1080/15248370903155841 (Chapters 2, 3, 11, 14, 19)

Hedrick, A. M., San Souci, P., Haden, C. A., & Ornstein, P. A. (2009). Mother–child joint conversational exchanges during events: Linkages to children's memory reports over time. *Journal of Cognition and Development, 10,* 143–161. https://doi.org./10.1080=15248370903155791 (Chapters 2, 11, 12, 16)

Herbel-Eisenmann, B. A., Steele, M. D., & Cirillo, M. (2013). (Developing) teacher discourse moves: A framework for professional development. *Mathematics Teacher Educator, 1*(2), 181–196. https://doi.org/10.5951/mathteaceduc.1.2.0181 (Chapter 16)

Hintzman, D. L. (1986). "Schema abstraction" in a multiple-trace memory model. *Psychological Review, 93,* 411–428. https://doi.org/10.1037/0033-295X.93.4.411 (Chapter 8)

Horn, S. S., Bayen, U. J., & Michalkiewicz, M. (2020) The development of clustering on episodic memory: A cognitive modeling approach. *Child Development.* https://doi.org/10.1111/cdev.13407 (Chapter 19)

Hudson, K. N., Coffman, J. L., & Ornstein, P. A. (2015, March). *Sustained effects of kindergarten instruction on mathematics performance across the first two years of elementary school.* Poster presented at the Society for Research in Child Development (SRCD), Philadelphia, PA. (Chapter 16)

(2018). Addition in kindergarten: The role of mothers' and teachers' language. *Journal of Cognition and Development, 19*(1), 65–86. https://doi.org/10.1080/15248372.2017.1415900 (Chapter 16)

Hudson, J. A., Fivush, R., & Kuebli, J. (1992). Scripts and episodes: The development of event memory. *Applied Cognitive Psychology, 6,* 483–505. https://doi.org/10.1002/acp.2350060604 (Chapter 8)

Hudson, J. A., & Grysman, A. (2014). Extending the life of a memory: Effects of reminders on children's long-term event memory. In P. J. Bauer & R. Fivush (Eds.), *The Wiley-Blackwell handbook on the development of children's memory* (pp. 255–284). New York, NY: Wiley-Blackwell. https://doi.org/10.1002/9781118597705.ch12 (Chapter 3)

Hudson, J. A., & Mayhew, E. M. (2009). The development of memory for recurring events. In M. Courage & N. Cowan (Eds.), *The development of memory in infancy and childhood* (pp. 69–92). New York, NY: Psychology Press. (Chapter 8)

(2018). Addition in kindergarten: The role of mothers' and teachers' language. *Journal of Cognition and Development, 19*(1), 65–86. https://doi.org/10.1080/15248372.2017.1415900 (Chapters 2, 3, 16)

Hughes, J., & Kwok, O. (2007). Influence of student–teacher and parent–teacher relationships on lower achieving readers' engagement and achievement in the primary grades. *Journal of Educational Psychology, 99*(1), 39–51. https://doi.org/10.1037/0022-0663.99.1.39 (Chapter 17)

Hughes, J. N., Gleason, K. A., & Zhang, D. (2005). Relationship influences on teachers' perceptions of academic competence in academically at-risk minority and majority first grade students. *Journal of School Psychology, 43*(4), 303–320. https://doi.org/10.1016/j.jsp.2005.07.001 (Chapter 17)

Hurst, M., Polinsky, N., Haden, C., Levine, S., & Uttal, D. (2019). Advancing STEM learning by starting early: Leveraging research to inform policy. *Social Policy Report, 32*(3), 1–33. https://srcd.onlinelibrary.wiley.com/doi/pdf/10.1002/sop2.5 (Chapter 12)

Hussong, A. M., Coffman, J. L., & Thomas, T. E. (2020). Gratitude conversations: An experimental trial of an online parenting tool. *The Journal of Positive Psychology, 15*(2), 267–277. https://doi-org.libproxy.uncg.edu/10.1080/17439760.2019.1610484 (Chapters 13, 14)

Hussong, A. M., Langley, H. A., Coffman, J. L., Halberstadt, A. G., & Costanzo, P. R. (2017). Parent socialization of children's gratitude. In J. Tudge & L. Freitas (Eds.), *Developing gratitude* (pp. 199–219). New York, NY: Cambridge University Press. https://doi.org/10.1017/9781316863121.010 (Chapter 13)

Hussong, A. M., Langley, H. A., Rothenberg, W. A., Coffman, J. L., Halberstadt, A. G., Costanzo, P. R., & Mokrova, I. (2019). Raising grateful children one day at a time. *Applied Developmental Science, 23*(4), 371–384. https://doi-org.ezproxy.shsu.edu/10.1080/10888691.2018.1441713 (Chapters 13, 14)

Huttenlocher, J., Jordan, N., & Levine, S. (1994). A mental model for early arithmetic. *Journal of Experimental Psychology, 123*(3), 284–284. https://doi.org/10.1037/0096-3445.123.3.284 (Chapter 16)

Hyde, T. S., & Jenkins, J. J. (1969). The differential effects of incidental tasks on the organization of recall of a list of highly associated words. *Journal of Experimental Psychology, 82*, 472–481. https://doi.org/10.1037/h0028372 (Chapter 15)

Ilg, F., & Ames, L. B. (1951). Developmental trends in arithmetic. *Journal of Genetic Psychology, 79*(1), 3–28. https://doi.org/10.1080/08856559.1951.10533584 (Chapter 16)

Jack, F., MacDonald, S., Reese, E., & Hayne, H. (2009). Maternal reminiscing style during early childhood predicts the age of adolescents' earliest memories. *Child Development, 80*(2), 496–505. https://doi.org/10.1111/j.1467-8624.2009.01274.x (Chapter 3)

Jack, F., Simcock, G., & Hayne, H. (2012). Magic memories: Young children's verbal recall after a 6-year delay. _Child Development, 83_(1), 159–172. https://doi.org/10.1111/j.1467-8624.2011.01699.x (Chapter 3)

Jacobs, J. (1887). Experiments on "prehension." _Mind, 12_, 75–79. https://doi.org/10.1093/mind/os-12.45.75 (Chapters 3, 4)

James, W. (1985). _Principles of psychology._ Cambridge, MA: Harvard University Press. (Original work published in 1890.) (Chapter 2)

Jant, E. A., Haden, C. A., Uttal, D. H., & Babcock, E. (2014). Conversation and object manipulation influence children's learning in a museum. _Child Development, 85_(5), 1771–2105. https://doi.org/10.1111/cdev.12252 (Chapters 12, 14, 19)

John, T., & Aslan, A. (2020). Age differences in the persistence of the part-list cuing impairment: The role of retrieval inhibition and strategy disruption. _Journal of Experimental Child Psychology, 191_, 104746. https://doi/org/10.1016/j.jecp.2019/104746 (Chapter 19)

Johnson, M. K., Hashtroudi, S., & Lindsay, D. S. (1993). Source monitoring. _Psychological Bulletin, 114_, 3–28. https://doi.org/10.1037/0033-2909.114.1.3 (Chapter 9)

Jones, G., Taylor, A., & Forrester, J. H. (2011). Developing a scientist: A retrospective look. _International Journal of Science Education, 33_(12), 1653–1673. https://doi.org/10.1080/09500693.2010.523484 (Chapter 12)

Justice, E. M., Baker-Ward, L. E., Gupta, S., & Jannings, L. R. (1997). Means to the goal of remembering: Developmental changes in awareness of strategy use-performance relations. _Journal of Experimental Child Psychology, 65_, 293–314. https://doi.org/10.1006/jecp.1997.2368 (Chapter 19)

Kail, R. V., & Hagen, J. W. (1977). _Perspectives on the development of memory and cognition._ Hillsdale, NJ: Erlbaum. (Chapter 3)

Kee, D. W., Bell, T. S., & Davis, B. R. (1981). Developmental changes in the effects of presentation mode on the storage and retrieval of noun pairs in children's recognition memory. _Child Development, 52_(1), 268–279. https://doi.org/10.2307/1129240 (Chapter 6)

Keeny, T. J., Cannizzo, S. R., & Flavell, J. H. (1967). Spontaneous and induced verbal rehearsal in a recall task. _Child Development, 38_(4), 953–966. https://doi.org/10.2307/1127095 (Chapter 2)

Kendler, T. S., & Kendler, H. H. (1959). Reversal and nonreversal shifts in kindergarten children. _Journal of Experimental Psychology, 58_(1), 56–60. https://doi.org/10.1037/h0041855 (Chapter 2)

(1962). Inferential behavior in children as a function of age and subgoal constancy. _Journal of Experimental Psychology, 64_(5), 460–466. https://doi.org/10.1037/h0042038 (Chapter 2)

Keppel, G. (1964). Verbal learning in children. _Psychological Bulletin, 61_(1), 63–80. https://doi.org/10.1037/h0043153 (Chapter 2)

Kerkman, D. D., & Siegler, R. S. (1997). Measuring individual differences in children's addition strategy choices. _Learning and Individual Differences, 9_(1), 1–18. https://doi.org/10.1016/01421599979185 (Chapter 16)

Kim, M. H., Marulis, L. M., Grammer, J. K., Morrison, F. J., & Gehring, W. J. (2017). Motivational processes from expectancy-value theory are associated with variability in the error positivity in young children. *Journal of Experimental Child Psychology*, *155*, 32–47. https://doi.org/10.1016/j.jecp .2016.10.010 (Chapter 18)

Kirkpatrick, E. A. (1894). An experimental study of memory. *Psychological Review*, *1*, 602–609. https://doi.org/10.1037/h0068244 (Chapter 4)

Klahr, D., & Wallace, J. G. (1976). *Cognitive development: An information-processing view*. Mahwah, NJ: Erlbaum. (Chapter 14)

Knuth, E. J., Stephens, A. C., McNeil, N. M., & Alibali, M. W. (2006). Does understanding the equal sign matter? Evidence from solving equations. *Journal for Research in Mathematics Education*, *37*(4), 297–312. https://doi .org/10.1207/s15326909xci2403_3 (Chapter 16)

Kofler, M. J., Rapport, M. D., & Alderson, R. M. (2008). Quantifying ADHD classroom inattentiveness, its moderators, and variability: A meta-analytic review. *Journal of Child Psychology and Psychiatry*, *49*(1), 59–69. https://doi .org/10.1111/j.1469-7610.2007.01809.x (Chapter 17)

Kreutzer, M. A., Leonard, C., & Flavell, J. H. (1975). An interview study of children's knowledge about memory. *Monographs of the Society for Research in Child Development*, *40*(1), 1–60. https://doi.org/10.2307/1165955 (Chapters 2, 4, 19)

Kron-Sperl, V., Schneider, W., & Hasselhorn, M. (2008). The development and effectiveness of memory strategies in kindergarten and elementary school: Findings from the Würzburg and Göttingen longitudinal memory studies. *Cognitive Development*, *23*(1), 79–104. https://doi.org/10.1016/j.cogdev .2007.08.011 (Chapters 4, 5, 6)

Kuenne, M. R. (1946). Experimental investigation of the relation of language to transposition behavior in young children. *Journal of Experimental Psychology*, *36*(6), 471–490. https://doi-10.1037/h0054770 (Chapter 2)

Lakoff, G., & Núñez, R. (2000). *Where mathematics comes from: How the embodied mind brings mathematics into being*. New York, NY: Basic Books. (Chapter 1)

Lamb, M. E., Brown, D. A., Hershkowitz, I., Orbach, Y. & Esplin, P, W. (2018). *Tell me what happened: Questioning children about abuse* (2nd ed.). New York, NY: Wiley (Chapters 2, 9)

Lamb, M. E., La Rooy, D. J., Malloy, L. C., & Katz, C. (Eds.) (2011). *Children's testimony: A handbook of psychological research and forensic practice*. Chichester, UK: Wiley. https://doi.org/10.1002/9781119998495 (Chapter 8)

Lamb, M. E., Orbach, Y., Hershkowitz, I., & Epstein, P. W. & Horowitz, D. (2007). Structured forensic interview protocols improve the quality and informativeness of investigative interviews with children: A review of research using the NICHD Investigative Interview Protocol. *Child Abuse and Neglect*, *3*, 1201–1231. https://doi.org/10.1016/j.chiabu.2007.03.021 (Chapter 7)

Lange, G. (1978). Organization-related processes in children's recall. In P. A. Ornstein (Ed.), *Memory development in children*. Hillsdale, NJ: Erlbaum. (Chapters 4, 15)

Lange, G., & Pierce, S. H. (1992). Memory-strategy learning and maintenance in preschool children. *Developmental Psychology*, *28*, 453–462. https://psycnet.apa.org/doi/10.1037/0012-1649.28.3.453 (Chapter 6)

Langley, H. A., Chumchal, M., Billeiter, K., & Smith, M. (October, 2018). How do race/ethnicity and privilege differences predict parents' ideas about children's gratitude? Poster presented at the SRCD Special Topic Meeting: Promoting Character Development Among Diverse Children and Adolescents: The Roles of Families, Schools, and Out-Of-School-Time Youth Development Programs, Philadelphia, PA. (Chapter 13)

Langley, H. A., Coffman, J. L., & Ornstein, P. A. (2017). The socialization of children's memory: Linking maternal conversational style to the development of children's autobiographical and deliberate memory skills. *Journal of Cognition and Development*, *18*(1), 63–86. https://doi.org/10.1080/15248372.2015.1135800 (Chapters 3, 13, 15, 16)

LeFevre, J., Skwarchuk, S. L., Smith-Chant, B. L., Fast, L., Kamawar, D., & Bisanz, J. (2009). Home numeracy experiences and children's math performance in the early school years. *Canadian Journal of Behavioural Science*, *41*, 55–66. https://doi.org/10.1037/a0014532 (Chapter 16)

Lehman, M., & Hasselhorn, M. (2007). Variable memory strategy use in children's adaptive intratask learning behavior: Developmental change and working memory influences on free recall. *Child Development*, *78*(4), 1068–1082. https://doi.org/10.1111/j.1467-8624.2007.01053.x (Chapter 16)

Lehmann, M., & Hasselhorn, M. (2012). Rehearsal dynamics in elementary school children. *Journal of Experimental Child Psychology*, *111*, 552–560. https://doi.org/10.1016/j.jecp.2011.10.013 (Chapters 4, 6, 19)

Leichtman, M. D., & Ceci, S. J. (1995). The effects of stereotypes and suggestions on preschoolers' reports. *Developmental Psychology*, *31*(4), 568–578. https://doi.org/10.1037/0012-1649.31.4.568 (Chapter 2)

Leinhardt, G., Crowley, K., & Knutson, K. (2002). *Learning conversations in museums*. Mahwah, NJ: Erlbaum. https://doi.org/10.4324/9781410606624 (Chapter 12)

Lenartowicz, A., Lu, S., Rodriguez, C., Lau, E. P., Walshaw, P. D., McCracken, J. T., … & Loo, S. K. (2016). Alpha desynchronization and frontoparietal connectivity during spatial working memory encoding deficits in ADHD: A simultaneous EEG-fMRI study. *NeuroImage: Clinical*, *11*, 210–223. https://doi.org/10.1016/j.nicl.2016.01.023 (Chapter 17)

Lenartowicz, A., Xu, K., Torres, R., Torgrimson, S. J., & Grammer, J. K. (invited submission in prep). Tracking the neural correlates of attention in the classroom: Evidence from elementary and college classrooms. *Mind, Brain, and Education*. (Chapter 17)

Lepore, S. J., & Sesco, B. (1994). Distorting children's reports and interpretations of events through suggestion. *Journal of Applied Psychology*, *79*(1), 108–120. https://doi.org./10.1037/0021-9010.79.1.108 (Chapter 2)

Lewis, M. D. (2005). Bridging emotion theory and neurobiology through dynamic systems modeling. *Behavioral and Brain Sciences, 28*(2), 169–194. https://doi.org/10.1017/S0140525X0500004X (Chapter 17)

Liberty, C., & Ornstein, P. A. (1973). Age differences in organization and recall: The effects of training in categorization. *Journal of Experimental Child Psychology, 15*(1), 169–186. https://doi.org/10.1016/0022-0965(73)90140-9 (Chapters 2, 4, 6, 19)

Lipsitt, L. P., & Ornstein, P. A. (2002). Harriet Lange Rheingold (1908-2000): Obituary. *American Psychologist, 57*(5), 366. https://doi.org/10.1037/0003-066X.57.5.366 (Chapter 1)

Lomas, T., Froh, J. J., Emmons, R. A., Mishra, A., & Bono, G. (2014). Gratitude interventions. In A. C. Parks & S. Schueller (Eds.), *The Wiley-Blackwell handbook of positive psychological interventions* (pp. 3–20). New York, NY: Wiley. https://doi.org/10.1002/9781118315927.ch1 (Chapter 14).

London, K., Bruck, M., Ceci, S. J., & Shuman, D. W. (2005). Disclosure of child sexual abuse: What does the research tell us about the ways that children tell? *Psychology, Public Policy, and Law, 11*, 194–226. https://doi.org/10.1037/0033-2909.114.1.3 (Chapter 9)

London, K., Bruck, M., Wright, D. B., & Ceci, S. J. (2008). Review of the contemporary literature on how children report sexual abuse to others: Findings, methodological issues, and implications for forensic interviewers. *Memory, 16*, 29–47. https://doi.org/10.1080/09658210701725732 (Chapter 9)

Luria, A. R. (1961). The genesis of voluntary movements. In N. O'Connor (Ed.), *Recent Soviet psychology* (pp. 165–185). New York, NY: Macmillan (Pergamon). https://doi.org/10.1016/B978–0-08-009575-2.50012-3 (Chapter 2)

Maccoby, E. E. (1964). Developmental psychology. *Annual Review of Psychology, 15*, 203–230. https://doi.org/10.1146/annurev.ps.15.020164.001223 (Chapter 2)

Mahr, J. B., & Csibra, G. (2020). Witnessing, remembering, and testifying: Why the past is special for human beings. *Perspectives on Psychological Science, 15*, 428–443. https://doi.org/10.1177/1745691619879167 (Chapter 19)

Mahy, C. E., Moses, L. J., & Kliegel, M. (2014). The development of prospective memory in children: An executive framework. *Developmental Review, 34*, 305–326. https://doi.org/10.1016/j.dr.2014.08.001 (Chapter 19)

Mandler, G. (1967). Organization and memory. In K. W. Spence & J. T. Spence (Eds.), *The psychology of learning and motivation* (Vol. 1, pp. 328–372). New York, NY: Academic Press. https://doi.org/10.1016/S0079–7421(08)60516-2 (Chapter 4)

Marin, K. A., Bohanek, J. G., & Fivush, R. (2008). Positive effects of talking about the negative: Family narratives of negative experiences and preadolescents' perceived competence. *Journal of Research on Adolescence, 18*, 573–593. https://doi.org/10.1111/j.1532-7795.2008.00572.x (Chapter 13)

Mathy. F., & Friedman, O. (2020). Working memory develops at a similar rate across diverse stimuli. *Journal of Experimental Child Psychology, 191*, 104735. https://doi.org/10.1016/j.jecp.2019.104735 (Chapter 19)

McClelland, M. M., Cameron, C. E., Duncan, R., Bowles, R. P., Acock, A. C., Miao, A., & Pratt, M. E. (2014). Predictors of early growth in academic achievement: The head-toes-knees-shoulders task. *Frontiers in Psychology*, *5*. https://doi.org/10.3389/fpsyg.2014.00599 (Chapter 17)

McClelland, M. M., Geldhof, G. J., Cameron, C. E., & Wanless, S. B. (2015). Development and self-regulation. In W. Overton & P. C. M. Molenaar (Eds.), *Handbook of child psychology and developmental science* (pp. 1–43). New York, NY: Wiley. http://onlinelibrary.wiley.com/doi/10.1002/9781118963418.childpsy114/abstract (Chapter 17)

McDonough, L., Mandler, J. M., McKee, R. D., & Squire, L. R. (1995). The deferred imitation task as a nonverbal measure of declarative memory. *PNAS*, *92*, 7580–7584. https://doi.org/10.1073/pnas.92.16.7580 (Chapter 19)

McGaugh, J. L. (2000). Memory: A century of consolidation. *Science*, *287*(5451), 248–251. https://doi.org/10.1126/science.287.5451.248 (Chapter 12)

McGuigan, F., & Salmon, K. (2004). The time to talk: The influence of the timing of adult–child talk on children's event memory. *Child Development*, *75*(3), 669–686. https://doi.org/10.1111/j.1467-8624.2004.00700.x (Chapters 3, 11)

(2006). The influence of talking on showing and telling: Adult–child talk and children's verbal and nonverbal event recall. *Applied Cognitive Psychology*, *20*(3), 365–381. https://doi.org/10.1002/acp.1183 (Chapters 11, 12)

Mercer, J. G. (1996). *Developing a taxonomy of memory relevant classroom experiences*. Unpublished honors thesis, University of North Carolina, Chapel Hill. (Chapter 15)

Merritt, K. A., Ornstein, P. A., & Spicker, B. (1994). Children's memory for a salient medical procedure: Implications for testimony. *Pediatrics*, *94*(1), 17–23. (Chapters 3, 7)

Miller, P. H. (1990). The development of strategies of selective attention. In D. F. Bjorklund (Ed.), *Children's strategies: Contemporary views of cognitive development* (pp. 157–184), Hillsdale: NJ: Erlbaum. (Chapters 4, 5, 19)

(2014). The history of memory development research: Remembering our roots. In P. J. Bauer & R. Fivush (Eds.), *The Wiley-Blackwell handbook on the development of children's memory* (Vol I, pp. 19–40). Chichester, UK: Wiley. https://doi.org/10.1002/9781118597705.ch2 (Chapter 4)

Miller, P. H., & Seier, W. L. (1994). Strategy utilization deficiencies in children: When, where, and why. In H. W. Reese (Ed.), *Advances in child development and behavior* (Vol. 25, pp. 107–156). New York, NY: Academic. https://doi.org/10.1016/S0065-2407(08)60051-8 (Chapters 6, 19)

Miyake, A., & Friedman, N. P. (2012). The nature and organization of individual differences in executive: Four general conclusions. *Current Directions in Psychological Sciences*, *21*, 8–14. https://doi.org/10.1177/0963721411429458 (Chapter 19)

Moely, B. E., Hart, S. S., Leal, L., Santulli, K. A., Rao, N., Johnson, T., & Hamilton, L. B. (1992). The teacher's role in facilitating memory and study strategy development in the elementary school classroom. *Child Development*, *63*(3), 653–672. https://doi.org/10.2307/1131353 (Chapters 2, 15, 19)

Moely, B. E., Olson, F. A., Halwes, T. G., & Flavell, J. H. (1969). Production deficiency in young children's clustered recall. *Developmental Psychology*, *1*, 26–34. https://doi.org/10.1037/h0026804 (Chapter 4)

Moely, B. E., Santulli, K. A., & Obach, M. S. (1995). Strategy instruction, metacognition, and motivation in the elementary school classroom. In F. Weinert & W. Schneider (Eds.), *Memory performance and competencies: Issues in growth and development* (pp. 301–321). Hillsdale, NJ: Erlbaum. (Chapter 6)

Moffitt, T. E., Arseneault, L., Belsky, D., Dickson, N., Hancox, R. J., Harrington, H., Houts, R., Poulton, R., Roberts, B. W., Ross, S., Sears, M. R., Thomson, W. M., & Caspi, A. (2011). A gradient of childhood self-control predicts health, wealth, and public safety. *Proceedings of the National Academy of Sciences of the United States of America*, *108*(7), 2693–2698. https://doi.org/10.1073/pnas.1010076108 (Chapter 17)

Monk, C. S., Webb, S. J., & Nelson, C. A. (2001). Prenatal neurobiological development: Molecular mechanisms and anatomical change. *Developmental Neuropsychology*, *19*, 211–236. https://doi.org/10.1207/S15326942DN1902_5 (Chapter 19)

Morris, G., & Baker-Ward, L. (2007). Fragile but real: Children's capacity to use newly acquired words to convey preverbal memories. *Child Development*, *78*(2), 448–458. https://doi.org/10.1111/j.1467-8624.2007.01008.x (Chapters 3, 19)

Morrison, F. J. & Grammer, J. K. (2016). Conceptual clutter and measurement mayhem: A proposal for a cross disciplinary approach to conceptualizing and measuring executive function. In J. A. Griffin, L. S. Freund, & P. McArdle (Eds.), *Executive function in preschool-age children: Integrating measurement, neurodevelopment, and translational research* (pp. 327–348). Washington, D.C.: APA. (Chapter 17)

Morrison, F. J., Kim, M. H., Connor, C. M., & Grammer, J. K. (2019). The causal impact of schooling on children's development: Lessons for developmental science. *Current Directions in Psychological Science*, *28*(5), 441–449. https://doi.org/10.1177/0963721419855661 (Chapters 15, 17, 18)

Morrison, F. J., & Ornstein, P. A. (1996). Cognitive development. *Developmental Science*, 121–134. https://doi.org/10.1017/cbo9780511571114.008 (Chapters 15, 17, 18)

Morrison, F. J., Ponitz, C. C., & McClelland, M. M. (2010). Self-regulation and academic achievement in the transition to school. In S. D. Calkins & M. A. Bell (Eds.), *Child development at the intersection of emotion and cognition* (pp. 203–224). Washington, DC: American Psychological Association. https://doi.org/10.1037/12059-011 (Chapter 17)

Morrison, F. J., Smith, L., & Dow-Ehrensberger, M. (1995). Education and cognitive development: A natural experiment. *Developmental Psychology*, *31*(5), 789–799. https://doi.org/10.1037/0012-1649.31.5.789 (Chapters 3, 15)

Mullen, M. K. (1994). Earliest recollections of childhood: A demographic analysis. *Cognition*, *52*, 55–79. https://doi.org/10.1016/0010-0277(94)90004-3 (Chapter 19)

Mullen, M. K., & Yi, S. (1995). The cultural context of talk about the past: Implications for the development of autobiographical memory. *Cognitive Development*, *10*, 407–419. https://doi.org/10.1016/0885-2014(95)90004-7 (Chapter 19)

Myers, J. E. B., Diedrich, S., Lee, D., Fincher, K., & Stern, R. (1999). Professional writing on child sexual abuse from 1900 to 1975: Dominant themes and impact on prosecution. *Child Maltreatment*, *4*, 201–216. https://doi.org/10.1177/1077559599004003002 (Chapter 8)

Myles-Worsley, M., Cromer, C., & Dodd, D. (1986). Children's preschool script reconstruction: Reliance on general knowledge as memory fades. *Developmental Psychology*, *22*, 22–30. https://doi.org/10.1037/0012-1649.22.1.22 (Chapter 8)

Nathan, D., & Snedeker, M. R. (2001). *Satan's silence: Ritual abuse and the making of a modern American witch hunt*. Lincoln, NE: iUniverse. (Chapter 10)

National Research Council [NRC]. (2009). *Learning science in informal environments: People, places, and pursuits*. Washington, DC: The National Academies Press. https://doi.org/10.17226/12190 (Chapter 12)

(2012). *A framework for K-12 science education: Practices, crosscutting concepts, and core ideas*. Washington, DC: The National Academies Press. https://doi.org/10.17226/13165 (Chapter 12)

(2015). *Identifying and supporting productive STEM programs in out-of-school settings*. Washington, DC: The National Academies Press. https://doi.org/10.17226/21740 (Chapter 12)

Naus, M. J., & Ornstein, P. A. (1978). Rehearsal processes in children's memory. In P. A. Ornstein (Ed.), *Memory development in children*. Hillsdale, NJ: Erlbaum. (Chapter 4)

(1983). Development of memory strategies: Analysis, questions, and issues. In M.T.H. Chi (Ed.), *Trends in memory development research*. New York, NY: Karger. (Chapters 4, 14)

Naus, M. J., Ornstein, P. A., & Aivano, S. (1977). Developmental changes in memory: The effects of processing time and rehearsal instructions. *Journal of Experimental Child Psychology*, *23*(2), 237–251. https://doi.org/10.1016/0022-0965(77)90102-3 (Chapters 4, 5, 6, 19)

Naus, M. J., Ornstein, P. A., & Kreshtool, K. (1977). Developmental difference in recall and recognition: The relationship between rehearsal and memory as test expectations change. *Journal of Experimental Child Psychology*, *23*, 252–265. https://doi.org/10.1016/0022-0965(77)90103-5 (Chapter 4)

Neisser, U. (1967/ 2014). *Cognitive psychology: Classic edition*. New York, NY: Psychology Press. https://doi.org/10.4324/9781315736174 (Chapter 14)

Nelson, K. (Ed.) (1986). *Event knowledge: Structure and function in development*. Hillsdale, NJ: Erlbaum. (Chapters 7, 8)

Nelson, K. (1989). *Narratives from the crib*. Cambridge, MA: Harvard University Press. (Chapters 2, 3)

(1996). *Language in cognitive development: The emergence of the mediated mind*. New York, NY: Cambridge University Press. https://doi.org/10.1017/CBO9781139174619 (Chapters 14, 19)

(2003). Narrative and self, myth and memory: Emergence of the cultural self. In R. Fivush & C. A. Haden (Eds.), *Autobiographical memory and the construction of a narrative self: Developmental and cultural perspectives* (pp. 3–28). Mahwah, NJ: Erlbaum. (Chapter 11)

(2005). Evolution and development of human memory systems. In B. J. Ellis & D. F. Bjorklund (Eds.), *Origins of the social mind: Evolutionary psychology and child development* (pp. 354–382). New York, NY: Guilford. (Chapter 19)

Nelson, K., Fivush, R., Hudson, J., & Lucariello, J. (1983). Scripts and the development of memory. In Chi, M. T. (Ed.), *Trends in memory development research* (Vol. 9, pp. 52–70). New York, NY: Karger. https://doi.org/10.1159/000407966 (Chapter 14)

Nelson, K., & Gruendel, J. M. (1976). At morning, it's lunchtime: A scriptal view of children's dialogues. *Discourse Processes*, 2, 73–94. https://doi.org/10.1080/01638537909544456 (Chapters 2, 14)

Nelson, T. O., & Narens, L. (1990). Metamemory: A theoretical framework and new findings. In G. H. Bower (Ed.), *The psychology of learning and motivation* (Vol. 26, pp. 125–141). San Diego, CA: Academic. https://doi.org/10.1016/S0079-7421(08)60053-5 (Chapter 5)

Newcombe, N., Ambady, N., Eccles, J., Gomez, L., Klahr, D., Linn, M., Miller, K., & Mix, K. (2009). Psychology's role in mathematics and science education. *American Psychologist*, 64(6), 538–538. https://doi.org/10.1037/a0014813 (Chapter 16)

Ornstein, P. A. (1970). Role of prior-list organization in a free recall transfer task. *Journal of Experimental Psychology*, 86, 32–37. https://doi.org/10.1037/h0029801 (Chapter 4)

Ornstein, P. A. (Ed.) (1978/2014). *Memory development in children*. Hillsdale, NJ: Erlbaum. (Chapters 3, 4, 14, 15, 18)

(1995). Children's long-term retention of salient personal experiences. *Journal of Traumatic Stress*, 8, 581–605. https://doi.org/10.1002/jts.2490080405 (Chapter 9)

Ornstein, P. A., Baker-Ward, L. E., Gordon, B. N., & Merritt, K. A. (1997). Children's memory for medical experiences: Implications for testimony. *Applied Cognitive Psychology*, 11, S87–S104. https://doi.org/10.1002/%28SICI%291099-0720%28199712%2911:7%3CS87::AID-ACP556%3E3.0.CO;2-Z (Chapters 7, 8, 9, 11, 19)

Ornstein, P. A., Baker-Ward, L. E., Gordon, B. N., Pelphrey, K. A., Tyler, C. S., & Gramzow, E. (2006). The influence of prior knowledge and repeated questioning on children's long-term retention of a pediatric examination. *Developmental Psychology*, 42, 332–344. https://doi.org/10.1037/0012-1649.42.2.332 (Chapters 2, 7, 8, 19)

Ornstein, P. A., Baker-Ward, L. E., & Naus, M. (1988). The development of mnemonic skill. In F. E. Weinert & M. Perlmutter (Eds.), *Memory development: Universal changes and individual differences* (pp. 31–50). Hillsdale, NJ: Erlbaum. (Chapters 4, 15, 16, 19)

Ornstein, P. A. & Coffman, J. L. (2020). Toward an understanding of the development of skilled remembering: The role of teachers' instructional language. *Current Directions in Psychological Science, 29*, 445–452. (Chapter 15)

Ornstein, P. A., Coffman, J. L., & Grammer, J. K. (2009). Learning to remember. In O. Barbarin & B. Wasik (Eds.), *Handbook of developmental science and early schooling: Translating basic research into practice* (pp. 103–122). New York, NY: Guilford Press. (Chapters 15, 17)

Ornstein, P. A., Coffman, J. L., Grammer, J. K., McCall, L. E., & San Souci, P. P. (2010). Linking the classroom context and the development of children's memory skills. In J. Meece & J. Eccles (Eds.), *Handbook of research on schools, schooling, and human development* (pp. 42–59). New York, NY: Routledge. https://doi.org/10.1037/a0013859 (Chapters 15, 17, 18, 19)

Ornstein, P. A., & Corsale, K. (1979). Organizational factors in children's memory. In C. R. Puff (Ed.), *Memory organization and structure*. New York, NY: Academic Press. (Chapter 4)

Ornstein, P. A., Gordon, B. N., & Baker-Ward, L. E. (1992). Children's memory for salient events: Implications for testimony. In M. L. Howe, C. J. Brainerd, & V. F. Reyna (Eds.), *Development of long-term retention* (pp. 135–157). New York, NY: Springer. https://doi.org/10.1007/978-1-4612-2868-4_4 (Chapter 7)

Ornstein, P. A., Gordon, B. N., & Larus, D. M. (1992). Children's memory for a personally experienced event: Implications for testimony. *Applied Cognitive Psychology, 6*(1), 49–60. https://doi.org/10.1002/acp.2350060103 (Chapters 2, 7, 10, 19)

Ornstein, P. A., Grammer, J. K., & Coffman, J. L. (2010). Teachers' "mnemonic" style and the development of skilled memory. In H. S. Waters & W. Schneider (Eds.), *Metacognition, strategy use, and instruction* (pp. 23–53). New York, NY: Guilford Press. (Chapters 3, 6, 15, 17, 19)

Ornstein, P. A., & Greenhoot, A. F. (2000). Remembering the distant past: Implications of research on children's memory for the recovered memory debate. In D. F. Bjorklund (Ed.), *False memory creation in children and adults* (pp. 203–237). Mahwah, NJ: Erlbaum. (Chapter 9)

Ornstein, P. A., & Haden, C. A. (2001a). Memory development or the development of memory? *Current Directions in Psychological Science, 10*, 202–205. https://doi.org/10.1111/1467-8721.00149 (Chapters 1, 3, 11, 13, 14, 15, 19)

(2001b). The development of memory: Toward an understanding of children's testimony. In M. L. Eisen, J. A. Quas, & G. S. Goodman (Eds.), *Memory and suggestibility in the forensic interview* (pp. 43–76). New York, NY: Routledge. (Chapter 14)

Ornstein, P. A., Haden, C. A., & Coffman, J. L. (2011). Learning to remember: Mothers and teachers talking with children. In N. L. Stein & S. Raudenbush

(Eds.), *Developmental science goes to school* (pp. 69–83). New York, NY: Taylor & Francis. (Chapter 3)

Ornstein, P. A., Haden, C. A., & Elischberger, H. B. (2006). Children's memory development: Remembering the past and preparing for the future. In E. Bialystok & F. I. M. Craik (Eds.), *Lifespan cognition: Mechanisms of change* (pp. 143–161). Oxford, UK: Oxford University Press. https://doi.org/10 .1093/acprof:oso/9780195169539.003.0010 (Chapters 3, 5, 9, 11, 15)

Ornstein, P. A., Haden, C. A., & Hedrick, A. M. (2004). Learning to remember: Social-communicative exchanges and the development of children's memory skills. *Developmental Review, 24*(4), 374–395. https://doi.org/10.1016/j.dr .2004.08.004 (Chapters 3, 9, 11, 12, 19)

Ornstein, P. A., Haden, C. A., & San Souci, P. P. (2008). The development of skilled remembering in children. In H. Roediger (Ed.), *Cognitive psychology of memory* (pp. 715–745). New York, NY: Elsevier. https://doi.org/10.1016/ B978–012370509-9.00136-4 (Chapters 3, 5, 15)

Ornstein, P. A., Hale, G. A., Morgan, J. S. (1977). Developmental differences in recall and output organization. *Bulletin of the Psychonomic Society, 9,* 29–32. https://doi.org/10.3758/BF03336919 (Chapter 4)

Ornstein, P. A., Larus, D. M., & Clubb, P. A. (1991). Understanding children's testimony: Implications of research on the development of memory. In R. Vasta (Ed.), *Annals of child development* (Vol. 8, pp. 145–176). London: Jessica Kingsley Publishers. (Chapters 7, 8, 9)

Ornstein, P. A., Medlin, R. G., Stone, B. P., & Naus, M. J. (1985). Retrieving for rehearsal: An analysis of active rehearsal in children's memory. *Developmental Psychology, 21*(4), 633–641. https://doi.org/10.1037/0012-1649.21.4.633 (Chapters 4, 5, 7)

Ornstein, P. A., Merritt, K. A., Baker-Ward, L. E., Furtado, E., Gordon, B. N., & Principe, G. (1998). Children's knowledge, expectation, and long-term retention. *Applied Cognitive Psychology, 12,* 387–405 https://doi.org/10 .1002/(sici)1099-0720(199808)12:4%3C387::aid-acp574%3E3.0.co;2-5 (Chapters 7, 8, 19)

Ornstein, P. A., & Naus, M. J. (1978). Rehearsal processes in children's memory. In P. A. Ornstein (Ed.), *Memory development in children* (pp. 69–99). Hillsdale, NJ: Erlbaum. (Chapters 4, 15, 18, 19)

(1985). Effects of the knowledge base on children's memory strategies. In H. W. Reese (Ed.), *Advances in child development and behavior* (Vol. 19, pp. 113–148). Orlando, FL: Academic Press. https://doi.org/10.1016/ S0065–2407(08)60390-0 (Chapters 4, 5, 6, 7, 15, 16)

Ornstein, P. A., Naus, M. J., & Liberty, C. (1975). Rehearsal and organizational processes in children's memory. *Child Development, 46* 818–830. https://doi .org/10.1037/0012-1649.21.4.633 (Chapters 2, 4, 5, 6, 14, 19)

Ornstein, P. A., Naus, M. J., & Miller, T. D. (1977). The effects of list organization and rehearsal activity on children's free recall. *Child Development, 48,* 292–295. https://doi.org/10.2307/1128385 (Chapter 5)

Ornstein, P. A., Naus, M. J., & Stone, B. P. (1977). Rehearsal training and developmental differences in memory. *Developmental Psychology*, *13*(1), 15–24. https://doi.org/10.1037/0012-1649.13.1.15 (Chapters 2, 5, 19)

Ornstein, P. A., Shapiro, L. B., Clubb, P. A., Follmer, A., & Baker-Ward, L. E. (1997). The influence of prior knowledge on children's memory for salient medical experiences. In N. L. Stein, P. A. Ornstein, B. Tversky, & C. Brainerd (Eds.), *Memory for everyday and emotional events* (pp. 83–112). Mahwah, NJ: Erlbaum. https://doi.org/10.4324/9781315789231-4 (Chapter 8)

Ornstein, P. A., Thomas, T. E., Hudson, K. N., & Coffman, J. L. (2016, April). The impact of teachers' instructional style on children's strategic understanding. In R. McGill Wilkinson, & E. Higgins (Chairs), *Identifying and utilizing effective encoding and retrieval processes for improving student learning*. Symposium presented at the meeting of the American Educational Research Association, Washington, DC. (Chapter 15)

Otgaar, H., Howe, M. L., Merckelbach, H., & Muris, P. (2018). Who is the better eyewitness? Sometimes adults but at other times children. *Psychological Science*, *27*, 378–385. https://doi.org/10.117/0963721418770998 (Chapter 19)

Oura, Y. & Hatano, G. (1988). Memory for melodies among subjects differing in age and experience in music. *Psychology of Music*, *16*, 91–109. https://doi.org/10.1177/0305735688162001 (Chapter 4)

Pagano, L. C., Haden, C. A., & Uttal, D. H. (2020). Setting goals to support parent–child interactions during tinkering and reminiscing in museums. *Journal of Experimental Child Psychology*. https://doi.org/10.1016/j.jecp.2020.104944 (Chapters 12, 19)

Pagano, L. C., Haden, C. A., Uttal, D. H., & Cohen, T. (2019). Conversational reflections about tinkering experiences in a children's museum. *Science Education*, *103*(6), 1493–1512. https://doi.org/10.1002/sce.21536 (Chapters 12, 19)

Palmer, S. E., & Ornstein, P. A. (1971). Role of rehearsal strategy in serial probed recall. *Journal of Experimental Psychology*, *88*(1), 60–66. https://doi.org/10.1037/h0030658 (Chapter 4)

Palmquist, S. D., & Crowley, K. (2007). From teachers to testers: How parents talk to novice and expert children in a natural history museum. *Science Education*, *91*(5), 783–804. https://doi.org/10.1002/sce.20215 (Chapter 12)

Paris, S. G., & Hapgood, S. E. (2002). Children learning with objects in informal learning environments. In S. G. Paris (Ed.), *Perspectives on object-centered learning in museums* (pp. 37–54). Mahwah, NJ: Erlbaum. https://doi.org/10.4324/9781410604132 (Chapter 12)

Paris, S. G., Newman, R. S., and McVey, K. A. (1982). Learning the functional significance of mnemonic actions: A microgenetic study of strategy acquisition. *Journal of Experimental Child Psychology*, *34*, 490–509. https://doi.org/10.1016/0022-0965(82)90073-X (Chapter 15)

Paterson, H. M., & Kemp, R. I. (2006a). Co-witnesses talk: A survey of eyewitness discussion. *Psychology, Crime & Law, 12*, 181–191. https://doi.org/10.1080/10683160512331316334 (Chapter 9)

(2006b). Comparing methods of encountering post-event information: The power of co-witness suggestion. *Applied Cognitive Psychology, 20*, 1083–1099. https://doi.org/10.1002/acp.1261 (Chapter 9)

Perner, J. (1991). *Understanding the representational mind.* Cambridge, MA: MIT Press. https://doi.org/10.7551/mitpress/6988.001.0001 (Chapter 9)

Perry, L. C., Ornstein, P. A., Watters, W. C., & Grant, D. A. (1971). Effects of number and type of verbal conditioned stimuli upon differential eyelid conditioning. *Journal of Verbal Learning & Verbal Behavior, 10*(4), 459–469. https://doi.org/10.1016/S0022–5371(71)80047-6 (Chapter 2)

Peterson, C. (1999). Children's memory for medical emergencies: 2 years later. *Developmental Psychology, 35*(6), 1493–1506. https://doi.org/10.1037/0012-1649.35.6.1493 (Chapter 7)

(2002). Children's long-term memory for autobiographical events. *Developmental Review, 22*, 370–402. https://doi.org/10.1016/S0273-2297 (02)00007-2 (Chapter 3)

Peterson, C., & Bell, M. (1996). Children's memory for traumatic injury. *Child Development, 67*(6), 3045–3070. https://doi.org/10.2307/1131766 (Chapters 2, 10)

Peterson, C., Jesso, B., & McCabe, A. (1999). Encouraging narratives in preschoolers: An intervention study. *Journal of Child Language, 26*, 49–67. https://doi.org/10.1017/S0305000998003651 (Chapters 3, 11)

Peterson, C., & Rideout, R. (1998). Memory for medical emergencies experienced by 1- and 2-year-olds. *Developmental Psychology, 34*(5), 1059–1072. https://doi.org/10.1037/0012-1649.34.5.1059 (Chapter 3)

Peterson, L., & Peterson, M. J. (1959). Short-term retention of individual verbal items. *Journal of Experimental Psychology, 58*(3), 193–198. https://doi.org./10.1037/h0049234 (Chapter 2)

Pfurtscheller, G. (1992). Event-related synchronization (ERS): An electrophysiological correlate of cortical areas at rest. *Electroencephalography and Clinical Neurophysiology, 83*, 62–69. https://doi.org/10.1016/0013-4694(92)90133-3 (Chapter 17)

Piaget, J. (1967). *On the development of memory and identity.* Worcester, MA: Clark University Press. (Chapter 14)

(1970). *Science of education and the psychology of the child.* (D. Coltman, Trans.). London: Longman. (Chapter 12)

Pianta, R. C., La Paro, K. M., & Hamre, B. K. (2008). *Classroom Assessment Scoring System™: Manual K-3.* Baltimore, MD: Paul H Brookes Publishing. (Chapter 16)

Poole, D. A., & Bruck, M. (2012). Divining testimony? The impact of interviewing props on children's reports of touching. *Developmental Review, 32* (3), 165–180. https://doi-org./10.1016/j.dr.2012.06.007 (Chapters 2, 10)

Poole, D. A., Bruck, M., & Pipe, M.-E. (2011). Forensic interview aids: Do props help children answer questions about touching? *Current Directions in Psychological Science*, *20*, 11–15. https://doi.org/10.1177/0963721411038880 04 (Chapters 7, 19)

Poole, D. A., & Lamb, M. E. (1998). *Investigative interviews of children: A guide for helping professionals*. Washington, DC: American Psychological Association. https://doi.org/10.1037/10301-000 (Chapters 2, 7)

Poole, D. A., & Lindsay, D. S. (2001). Children's eyewitness reports after exposure to misinformation from parents. *Journal of Experimental Psychology: Applied*, *7*, 27–50. https://doi.org/10.1037/1076-898X.7.1.27 (Chapter 9)

Poole, D. A., & White, L. T. (1991). Effects of question repetition on the eyewitness testimony of children and adults. *Developmental Psychology*, *27* (6), 975–986. https://doi.org/10.1037/0012-1649.27.6.975 (Chapter 2)

(1993). Two years later: Effect of question repetition and retention interval on the eyewitness testimony of children and adults. *Developmental Psychology*, *29* (5), 844–853. https://doi.org/10.1037/0012–1649.29.5.844 (Chapter 2)

Powell, M. B., Roberts, K. P., Ceci, S. J., & Hembrooke, H. (1999). The effects of repeated experience on children's suggestibility. *Developmental Psychology*, *35*, 1462–1477. https://doi.org/10.1037/0012-1649.35.6.14622 3 (Chapter 8)

Powell, M. B., & Thomson, D. M. (1996). Children's memory of an occurrence of a repeated event: Effects of age, repetition, and retention interval across three question types. *Child Development*, *67*(5), 1988–2004. https://doi.org/ 10.1111/j.1467-8624.1996.tb01839.x (Chapter 8)

(1997). The effect of an intervening interview on children's ability to remember one occurrence of a repeated event. *Legal and Criminological Psychology*, *2*, 247–262. https://doi.org/10.1111/j.2044-8333.1997.tb00346.x (Chapter 8)

Prentice, N. M., Manosevitz, M., & Hubbs, L. (1978). Imaginary figures of early childhood: Santa Claus, Easter Bunny, and the tooth fairy. *American Journal of Orthopsychiatry*, *48*, 618–628. https://doi.org/10.1111/j.1939-0025.1978 .tb02566.x (Chapter 9)

Pressley, M. (1982). Elaboration and memory development. *Child Development*, *53*, 296–309. http://doi.org/10.2307/1128972. (Chapter 5)

Pressley, M., Borkowski, J. G., & Schenider, W. (1989). Good information processing: What it is and how education can promote it. *Journal of Educational Research*, *14*, 857–867. https://doi.org/10.1016/0883-0355(89) 90069-4 (Chapters 4, 6)

Pressley, M., & Levin, J. R. (1977). Developmental differences in subjects' associative learning strategies and performance: Assessing a hypothesis. *Journal of Experimental Child Psychology*, *24*, 431–439. https://doi.org/10 .1016/0022-0965(77)90089-3 (Chapter 4)

Pressley, M., Ross, K. A., Levin, J. R., & Ghatala, E. S. (1984). The role of strategy utility knowledge in children's strategy decision making. *Journal of*

*Experimental Child Psychology, 38*(3), 491–504. https://doi.org/10.1016/0022-0965(84)90091-2 (Chapters 2, 6)

Price, D. W., & Goodman, G. S. (1990). Visiting the wizard: Children's memory for a recurring event. *Child Development, 61*, 664–680. https://doi.org/10.2307/1130952 (Chapter 8)

Price, H. L., & Connolly, D. A. (2007). Anxious and non-anxious children's reports of a repeated or unique event. *Journal of Experimental Child Psychology, 98*, 94–112. https://doi.org/10.1016/j.jecp.2007.05.002 (Chapter 8)

(2008). Children's recall of emotionally arousing, repeated events: A review and call for further investigation. *International Journal of Law and Psychiatry, 31*, 337–346. https://doi.org/10.1016/j.ijlp.2008.06.002 (Chapter 8)

(2013). Suggestibility effects persist after one year in children who experienced a single or repeated event. *Journal of Applied Research in Memory and Cognition, 2*, 89–94. https://doi.org/10.1016/j.jarmac.2013.03.001 (Chapter 8)

Price, H. L., Connolly, D. A., & Gordon, H. M. (2006). Children's memory for complex autobiographical events: Does spacing of repeated instances matter? *Memory, 14*, 977–989. https://doi.org/10.1080/09658210601009005 (Chapter 8)

(2016). Children who experienced a repeated event only appear less accurate in a second interview than those who experienced a unique event. *Law and Human Behavior, 40*, 362–373. https://doi.org/10.1037/lhb0000194 (Chapter 8)

Principe, G. F., & Ceci, S. J. (2002). "I saw it with my own ears": The influence of peer conversations and suggestive questions on preschoolers' event memories. *Journal of Experimental Child Psychology, 83*, 1–25. https://doi.org/10.1016/s0022-0965(02)00120-0 (Chapter 9)

Principe, G. F., Cherson, M., DiPuppo, J., & Schindewolf, E. (2012). Children's natural conversations following exposure to a rumor: Linkages to later false reports. *Journal of Experimental Child Psychology, 113*, 383–400. https://doi.org/10.1016/j.jecp.2012.06.006 (Chapters 9, 19)

Principe, G. F., Daley, L., & Kauth, K. (2010). Social processes affecting the mnemonic consequences of rumors on children's memory. *Journal of Experimental Child Psychology, 107*, 479–493. https://doi.org/10.1016/j.jecp.2010.05.011 (Chapter 9)

Principe, G. F., DiPuppo, J., & Gammel, J. (2013). Effects of mothers' receipt of misinformation and conversation style on children's event reports. *Cognitive Development, 28*, 260–271. https://doi.org/10.1016/j.cogdev.2013.01.012 (Chapter 9)

Principe, G. F., Gardner, G., & Trumbull, J. (2016, April). Children's memory and suggestibility for a past event is influenced by mother's memory sharing style and goal orientation. Poster presented at the meetings of the Association for Psychological Science, Chicago, IL. (Chapter 9)

Principe, G. F., & Giroux, M. (2018). Fantasy beliefs and false reports: The role of visual evidence and peer interaction. *Cognitive Development, 48*, 244–255. https://doi.org/10.1016/j.cogdev.2018.09.002 (Chapter 9)

Principe, G. F., Guiliano, S., & Root, C. (2008). Rumormongering and remembering: How rumors originating in children's inferences can affect memory. *Journal of Experimental Child Psychology, 99*, 135–155. https://doi.org/10.1016/j.jecp.2007.10.009 (Chapter 9)

Principe, G. F., Haines, B., Adkins, A., & Guiliano, S. (2010). False rumors and true belief: Memory processes underlying children's errant reports of rumored events. *Journal of Experimental Child Psychology, 107*, 407–422. https://doi.org/10.1016/j.jecp.2010.05.007 (Chapter 9)

Principe, G. F., Kanaya, T., Ceci, S. J., & Singh, M. (2006). Believing is seeing: How rumors can engender false memories in preschoolers. *Psychological Science, 17*, 243–248. https://doi.org/10.1111/j.1467-9280.2006.01692.x (Chapter 9)

Principe, G. F., Myers, J. T., Furtado, E. A., Merritt, K. A., & Ornstein, P. A. (1996, March). The relationship between procedural information and young children's recall of an invasive medical procedure. In L. E. Baker-Ward (Chair), The role of individual differences in young children's reports of salient personal experiences. Symposium paper presented at the meetings of the Conference on Human Development, Birmingham, AL. (Chapter 9)

Principe, G. F., Ornstein, P. A., Baker-Ward, L. E., & Gordon, B. N. (2000). The effects of intervening experiences on children's memory for a physical examination. *Applied Cognitive Psychology, 14*(1), 59–80. https://doi.org/10.1002/(SICI)1099-0720(200001)14:1%3C59::AID-ACP637%3E3.0.CO;2-4. (Chapters 5, 7, 9, 10)

Principe, G. F., & Smith, E. (2007). The tooth, the whole tooth, and nothing but the tooth: How belief in the Tooth Fairy can engender false memories. *Applied Cognitive Psychology, 21*, 1–18. https://doi.org/10.1002/acp.1402 (Chapter 9)

(2008). Seeing things unseen: Fantasy beliefs and false reports. *Journal of Cognition and Development, 9*, 1–23. https://doi.org/10.1080/15248370701836618 (Chapter 9)

Principe, G. F., Tinguely, A., & Dobkowski, N. (2007). Mixing memories: The effects of rumors that conflict with children's experiences. *Journal of Experimental Child Psychology, 98*, 1–19. https://doi.org/10.1016/j.jecp.2007.04.002 (Chapter 9)

Principe, G. F., Trumbull, J., Gardner, G., Van Horn, E., & Dean, A. (2017). The role of maternal structure and control on children's memory and suggestibility for a past event. *Journal of Experimental Child Psychology, 163*, 15–31. https://doi.org/10.1016/j.jecp.2017.06.001 (Chapter 9)

Pruden, S. M., Levine, S. C., & Huttenlocher, J. (2011). Children's spatial thinking: Does talk about the spatial world matter? *Developmental Science, 14*(6), 1417–1430. https://doi.org/10.1111/j.1467-7687.2011.01088.x (Chapter 12)

Quas, J. A., Bauer, A., & Boyce, W. T. (2004). Physiological reactivity, social support, and memory in early childhood. *Child Development, 75*, 797–814. https://doi.org/10.1111/j.1467-8624.2004.00707.x (Chapter 19)

Quas, J. A., Goodman, G. S., Bidrose, S., Pipe, M. E., Craw, S., & Ablin, D. S. (1999). Emotion and memory: Children's long-term remembering, forgetting, and suggestibility. *Journal of Experimental Child Psychology*, *72*(4), 235–270. https://doi.org/10.1006/jecp.1999.2491 (Chapter 10)

R v. B (G), [1990] 2 SCR 30. (1990). (Chapter 8)

Rabinowitz, M., Ornstein, P. A., Folds-Bennett, T. H., & Schneider, W. (1994). Age-related differences in the speed of processing: Unconfounding age and experience. *Journal of Experimental Child Psychology*, *57*, 449–459. https://doi.org/10.1006/jecp.1994.1021 (Chapter 4)

Rapport, M. D., Kofler, M. J., Alderson, R. M., Timko, T. M., & DuPaul, G. J. (2009). Variability of attention processes in ADHD: Observations from the classroom. *Journal of Attention Disorders*, *12*(6), 563–573. https://doi.org/10.1177/1087054708322990 (Chapter 17)

Raver, C. C., Jones, S. M., Li-Grining, C., Zhai, F., Bub, K., & Pressler, E. (2011). CSRP's impact on low-income preschoolers' preacademic skills: Self-regulation as a mediating mechanism. *Child Development*, *82*(1), 362–378. https://doi.org/10.1111/j.1467-8624.2010.01561.x (Chapter 17)

Read, C., & Schreiber, P. (1982). In E. Wanner & L. Gleitman (Eds.), *Language acquisition: The state of the art*. Cambridge, UK: Cambridge University Press. (Chapter 1)

Ready, D. D., & Wright, D. L. (2011). Accuracy and inaccuracy in teachers' perceptions of young children's cognitive abilities: The role of child background and classroom context. *American Educational Research Journal*, *48*(2), 335–360. https://doi.org/10.3102/0002831210374874 (Chapter 17)

Reese, E. (1999). What children say when they talk about the past. *Narrative Inquiry*, *9*(2), 215–241. https://doi.org/10.1075/ni.9.2.02ree (Chapter 3)

(2014). Taking the long way: Longitudinal approaches to autobiographical memory development. In P. J. Bauer & R. Fivush (Eds.), *The Wiley-Blackwell handbook on the development of children's memory* (pp. 972–995). New York, NY: Wiley-Blackwell. (Chapter 3)

(2018). Encouraging collaborative remembering between young children and their caregivers. In M. L. Meade, C. B. Harris, P. Van Bergen, J. Sutton, & A. J. Barnier (Eds.), *Collaborative remembering: Theories, research, and applications* (pp. 317–333). Oxford, UK: Oxford University Press (Chapter 3)

Reese, E., & Farrant, K. (2003). Social origins of reminiscing. In R. Fivush & C. A. Haden (Eds.), *Autobiographical memory and the construction of a narrative self: Developmental and cultural perspectives* (pp. 29–48). Mahwah, NJ: Erlbaum. (Chapter 11)

Reese, E., & Fivush, R. (1993). Parental styles of talking about the past. *Developmental Psychology*, *29*(3), 596–606. https://doi.org/10.1037/0012-1649.29.3.596 (Chapters 2, 11)

Reese, E., Haden, C. A., & Fivush, R. (1993). Mother–child conversations about the past: Relationships of style and memory over time. *Cognitive Development*, *8*, 403–430. https://doi.org/10.1016/S0885-2014(05)80002 (Chapters 3, 11, 12, 13, 14, 15, 16)

Reese, E., Haden, C. A., & Fivush, R. (1996). Mothers, fathers, daughters, sons: Gender differences in autobiographical reminiscing. *Research on Language and Social Interaction*, *29*, 27–56. https://doi.org/10.1207/s15327973rlsi2901_3 (Chapter 13)

Reese, E., Jack, F., & White, N. (2010). Origins of adolescents' autobiographical memories. *Cognitive Development, 25*(4), 352–367. https://doi.org/10.1016/j.cogdev.2010.08.006 (Chapters 3, 14)

Reese, E., Macfarlane, L., McAnally, H., Robertson, S. J., & Taumoepeau, M. (2020). Coaching in maternal reminiscing with preschoolers leads to elaborative and coherent personal narratives in early adolescence. *Journal of Experimental Child Psychology, 189*, 104707 https://doi.org/10.1016/j.jecp.2019.104707 (Chapter 3)

Reese, E., & Newcombe, R. (2007). Training mothers in elaborative reminiscing enhances children's autobiographical memory and narrative. *Child Development, 78*(4), 1153–1170. https://doi.org/10.1111/j.1467-8624.2007.01058.x (Chapters 3, 11)

Reese, E., & Robertson, S. J. (2019). Origins of adolescents' earliest memories. *Memory, 27*(1), 79–91. https://doi.org/10.1080/09658211.2018.1512631 (Chapter 3)

Reese, H. W. (1962). Verbal mediation as a function of age level. *Psychological Bulletin, 59*(6), 502–509. https://doi.org/10.1037/h0040739 (Chapter 2)

Rezmer, B. E., Trager, L. A., Catlin, M., & Poole, D. A. (2020). Pause for effect: A 10-s interviewer wait time gives children time to respond to open-ended prompts. *Journal of Experimental Child Psychology, 194*, 104824. https://doi.org/10.1016/j.jecp.2020 (Chapter 19)

Riggins, T., Geng, F., Blankenship, S. L., & Redcay, E. (2016). Hippocampal functional connectivity and episodic memory in early childhood. *Developmental Cognitive Neuroscience, 19*, 58–69. https://doi.org/10.1016/j.dcn.2016.02.002 (Chapter 3)

Ringel, B. A., & Springer, C. J. (1980). On knowing how well one is remembering: The persistence of strategy use during transfer. *Journal of Experimental Child Psychology, 29*, 322–333. https://doi.org/10.1016/0022-0965(80)90023-5 (Chapter 19)

Roberts, K. P., & Powell, M. B. (2005). Evidence of metacognitive awareness in young children who have experienced a repeated event. *Applied Cognitive Psychology, 19*, 1019–1031. https://doi.org/10.1002/acp.1145 (Chapter 8)

Roberts, K. P., Brubacher, S. P., Powell, M. B., & Price, H. L. (2011). Practice narratives. In M. E. Lamb, D. La Rooy, L. C. Malloy, & C. Katz (Eds.), *Children's testimony: A handbook of psychological research and forensic practice* (pp. 129–145). Chichester, UK: Wiley. https://doi.org/10.1002/9781119998495.ch7 (Chapter 8)

Robinson, E. S., & Brown, M. A. (1926). Effect of serial position on memorization. *The American Journal of Psychology, 37*, 538–552. https://doi.org/10.2307/1414914 (Chapter 2)

Roebers, C. M. (2014). Children's deliberate memory development: The contribution of strategies and metacognitive processes. In P. J. Bauer & R. Fivush (Eds.), *The Wiley-Blackwell handbook on the development of children's memory* (pp. 865–894). https://doi.org/10.1002/9781118597705.c New York, NY: Wiley-Blackwell. (Chapters 4, 5, 6, 15, 19)

(2017). Executive function and metacognition: Towards a unifying framework of cognitive self-regulation. *Developmental Review, 45*, 31–51. https://doi.org/10.1016/j.dr.2017.04.001 (Chapter 17)

Roebers, C. M., & Feurer, E. (2016). Linking executive functions and procedural metacognition. *Child Development Perspectives, 10*(1), 39–44. https://doi.org/10.1111/cdep.12159 (Chapter 17)

Roenker, D. L., Thompson, C. P., & Brown, S. C. (1971). Comparison of measures for the estimation of clustering in free recall. *Psychological Bulletin, 76*, 45–48. https://doi.org/10.1037/h0031355 (Chapter 4)

Rogoff, B. (1981). Schooling and the development of cognitive skills. In H. C. Triandis & A. Heron (Eds.), *Handbook of cross-cultural psychology* (Vol. 4, pp. 233–294). Boston, MA: Allyn & Bacon. (Chapter 15)

(1990). *Apprenticeship in thinking: Cognitive development in social context.* Oxford, UK: Oxford University Press. (Chapters 12, 13, 15, 18)

(2003). *The cultural nature of human development.* New York, NY: Oxford University Press. (Chapter 15)

Rogoff, B., Dahl, A., & Callanan, M. (2018). The importance of understanding children's lived experience. *Developmental Review, 50*(Part A), 5–15. https://doi.org/10.1016/j.dr.2018.05.006 (Chapter 15)

Rogoff, B., & Mistry, J. (1985). Memory development in cultural context. In M. Pressley & C. J. Brainerd (Eds.), *Cognitive learning and memory in children* (pp. 117–142). New York, NY: Springer. (Chapter 15)

Rohwer, W. D. (1973). Elaboration and learning in childhood and adolescence. In H. W. Reese (Ed.), *Advances in child development and behavior* (Vol. 8, pp. 1–57). New York, NY: Academic Press. (Chapter 15)

Rosnow, R. L. (1991). Inside rumor: A personal journey. *American Psychologist, 46*, 484–496. https://doi.org/10.1037/0003-066X.46.5.484 (Chapter 9)

Ross, J., Hutchison, J., & Cunningham, S. J. (2019). The me in memory: The role of the self in autobiographical memory development. *Child Development, 91*, e299–e314. https://doi.org/10.1111/cdev.13211 (Chapter 19)

Ross, M. (1989). Relation of implicit theories to the construction of personal histories. *Psychological Review, 96*, 341–357. https://doi.org/10.1037/0033-295X.96.2.341 (Chapter 7)

Roth, R. M., Isquith, P. K., & Gioia, G. A. (2014). Assessment of executive functioning using the Behavior Rating Inventory of Executive Function (BRIEF). In L. Meltzer (Ed.), *Handbook of executive functioning* (pp. 301–331). New York, NY: Springer Science + Business Media. https://doi.org/10.1007/978-1-4614-8106-5_18 (Chapter 17)

Rothenberg, W. A., Hussong, A. M., Langley, H. A., Egerton, G. A., Halberstadt, A. G., Coffman, J. L., ... & Costanzo, P. R. (2017).

Grateful parents raising grateful children: Niche selection and the socialization of child gratitude. *Applied Developmental Science, 21*(2), 106–120. https://doi10.1080/10888691.2016.1175945 (Chapters 13, 14)

Rovee-Collier, C., & Giles, A. (2010). Why a neuromaturational model of memory fails: Exuberant learning in early infancy. *Behavioural Processes, 83*, 197–206. (Chapter 19)

Rubin, D. C. (2005). A basic-systems approach to autobiographical memory. *Current Directions in Psychological Science, 14*, 79–83. https://doi-org.ezproxy .shsu.edu/10.1111/j.0963-7214.2005.00339.x (Chapter 13)

Rudek, D. J., & Haden, C. A. (2005). Mothers' and preschoolers' mental state language during reminiscing over time. *Merrill-Palmer Quarterly, 51*(4), 523–549. https://doi.org/10.1353/mpq.2005.0026 (Chapters 3, 12, 16)

Ryan, R. M., & Deci, E. L. (2000). Intrinsic and extrinsic motivations: Classic definitions and new directions. *Contemporary Educational Psychology, 25*(1), 54–67. https://doi.org/10.1006/ceps.1999.1020 (Chapter 17)

S *v.* R. 168 CLR 266 (1989). (Chapter 8)

Sadaghiani, S., & Kleinschmidt, A. (2016). Brain networks and proportional to-oscillations: structural and functional foundations of cognitive control. *Trends in Cognitive Sciences, 20*, 805–817. https://doi.org/10.1016/j.tics .2016.09.004 (Chapter 17)

Sales, J. M., & Fivush, R. (2005). Social and emotional functions of mother–child reminiscing about stressful events. *Social Cognition, 23*(1), 70–90. https://doi .org/10.1521/soco.23.1.70.59196 (Chapter 13)

Sales, J. M., Fivush, R., Parker, J., & Bahrick, L. (2005). Stressing memory: Long-term relations among children's stress, recall and psychological outcome following Hurricane Andrew. *Journal of Cognition and Development, 6*(4), 529–545. https://doi.org/10.1207/s15327647jcd0604_5 (Chapters 3, 13)

Sales, J. M., Fivush, R., & Peterson, C. (2003). Parental reminiscing about positive and negative events. *Journal of Cognition and Development, 4*, 185–209. https://doi.org/10.1207/S15327647JCD0402_03 (Chapter 13)

Salmon, K., & Reese, E. (2016). The benefits of reminiscing with young children. *Current Directions in Psychological Science, 25*(4), 233–238. https://doi.org/ 10.1177/0963721416655100 (Chapter 11)

Sameroff, A. (2009). The transactional model. In A. Sameroff (Ed.), *The transactional model of development: How children and contexts shape each other* (pp. 3–21). Washington, DC: American Psychological Association. https://doi .org/10.1037/11877-001 (Chapter 1)

Sansone, R. A., & Sansone, L. A. (2010). Gratitude and well being: The benefits of appreciation. *Psychiatry (Edgmont), 7*(11), 18–22. (Chapter 14)

Saywitz, K. J., Goodman, G. S., Nicholas, E., & Moan, S. F. (1991). Children's memories of a physical examination involving genital touch: Implications for reports of child sexual abuse. *Journal of Consulting and Clinical Psychology, 59* (5), 682–691. https://doi.org/10.1037/0022-006X.59.5.682 (Chapters 7, 10)

Schlagmüller, M., & Schneider, W. (2002). The development of organizational strategies in children: Evidence from a microgenetic longitudinal study.

*Journal of Experimental Child Psychology, 81,* 298–319. https://doi.org/10.1006/jecp.2002.2655 (Chapters 4, 15, 19)

Schmidt, C. R., & Paris, S. G. (1978). Operativity and reversibility in children's understanding of pictorial sequences. *Child Development, 49,* 1219–1222. https:/doi.org/10.1111/j.1467-8624.1978.tb04093.x (Chapter 9)

Schneider, L., Price, H. L., Roberts, K. P., & Hedrick, A. H. (2011). Children's episodic and generic reports of alleged abuse. *Applied Cognitive Psychology, 25,* 862–870. https://doi.org/10.1002/acp.1759 (Chapter 8)

Schneider, W. (1985). Developmental trends in the metamemory-memory behaviour relationship: An integrative review. In D. L. Forrest-Pressley, G. E. MacKinnon, & T. G. Waller (Eds.), *Cognitive, metacognitive, and human performance* (Vol. VIII, pp. 2–57). New York, NY: Academic Press. (Chapter 4)

(1999). The development of metamemory in children. In D. Gopher & A. Koriat (Eds.), *Attention and performance XVII: Cognitive regulation of performance: Interaction of theory and application* (pp. 487–513). Cambridge, MA: MIT Press. (Chapter 5)

(2010). Metacognition and memory development in childhood and *strategy use, and instruction* (pp. 54–81). New York, NY: Guilford Press. (Chapter 17)

(2014). Individual differences in memory development and educational implications: Cross-sectional and longitudinal evidence. In P. J. Bauer & R. Fivush (Eds.), *The Wiley-Blackwell handbook on the development of children's memory* (pp. 947–971). New York, NY: Wiley-Blackwell. https://doi.org/10.1002/9781118597705.ch4 (Chapters 3, 4, 6)

(2015). *Memory development from early childhood through emerging adulthood.* Cham, Switzerland: Springer. https://doi.org/10.1007/978-3-319-09611-7 (Chapters 4, 6)

Schneider, W., & Bjorklund, D. F. (1998). Memory. In W. Damon (Series Ed.), D. Kuhn & R. Siegler (Vol. Eds.), *Handbook of child psychology: Cognition, perception, and language* (5th ed., Vol. 2, pp. 467–521). New York, NY: Wiley. (Chapters 6, 15)

Schneider, W., & Bullock, M. (Eds.) (2009). *Human development from early childhood to early adulthood: Findings from a 20-year longitudinal study.* New York, NY: Psychology Press. (Chapter 19)

Schneider, W., Korkel, J., & Weinert, F. E. (1989). Domain-specific knowledge and memory performance: A comparison of high- and low-aptitude children. *Journal of Educational Psychology, 81,* 306–312. https://doi.org/10.1037/0022-0663.81.3.306 (Chapters 4, 19)

Schneider, W., Kron, V., Hünnerkopf, M., & Krajewski, K. (2004). The development of young children's memory strategies: First findings from the Würzburg Longitudinal Memory Study. *Journal of Experimental Child Psychology, 88*(2), 193–209. https://doi.org/10.1016/j.jecp.2004.02.004. (Chapters 5, 15)

Schneider, W., & Ornstein, P. A. (2015). The development of children's memory. *Child Development Perspectives, 9*(3), 190–195. https://doi.org/10.1111/cdep.12129 (Chapters 3, 4, 6, 13, 15)

Schneider, W. & Ornstein, P. A. (2019). Determinants of memory development in childhood and adolescence. *International Journal of Psychology, 45,* 307–315. https://doi.org/10.1002/ijop.12503 (Chapters 4, 6, 19)

Schneider, W., & Pressley, M. (1989). *Memory development between 2 and 20* (1st ed.). New York, NY: Springer-Verlag. https://doi.org/10.1007/978-1-4613-9717-5 (Chapter 4)

(1997). *Memory development between two and twenty* (2nd ed.). Mahwah, NJ: Erlbaum. (Chapters 5, 6, 15)

Schneider, W., Schlagmüller, M., & Visé, M. (1998). The impact of metamemory and domain-specific knowledge on memory performance. *European Journal of Psychology of Education, 13*(1), 91–103. http://doi.org/10.1007/BF03172815 (Chapters 5, 6, 15, 19)

Schneider, W., & Sodian, B. (1997). Memory strategy development: Lessons from longitudinal research. *Developmental Review, 17*(4), 442–461. https://doi.org/10.1006/drev.1997.0441 (Chapters 6, 15)

(1999). Memory strategy development-gradual increase, sudden insight, or roller coaster? In F. E. Weinert, & W. Schneider (Eds.), *Individual development from 3 to 12: Findings from the Munich Longitudinal Study* (pp. 61–77). Cambridge, UK: Cambridge University Press. (Chapters 5, 15)

Schonert-Reichl, K. A., Oberle, E., Lawlor, M. S., Abbott, D., Thomson, K., Oberlander, T. F., & Diamond, A. (2015). Enhancing cognitive and social–emotional development through a simple-to-administer mindfulness-based school program for elementary school children: A randomized controlled trial. *Developmental Psychology, 51*(1), 52–66. https://doi.org/10.1037/a0038454 (Chapter 17)

Schrank, F. A. (2011). Woodcock-Johnson III Tests of cognitive abilities. In A. S. Davis (Ed.), *Handbook of pediatric neuropsychology* (pp.415–434). New York, NY: Springer. (Chapter 5)

Schröder, L., Keller, H., Kärtner, J., Kleis, A., Abeld, M., Yvosi, R. D., Chaudhary, N., Jensen, H., & Papaligoura, Z. (2013). Early reminiscing in cultural contexts: Cultural models, maternal reminiscing styles, and children's memories. *Journal of Cognition and Development, 14,* 10–34. (Chapter 19)

Schunk, D. H., & Zimmerman, B. J. (1997). Social origins of self-regulatory competence. *Educational Psychologist, 32*(4), 195–208. https://doi.org/10.1207/s15326985ep3204_1 (Chapter 17)

Schwenck, C., Bjorklund, D. F., & Schneider, W. (2009). Developmental and individual differences in young children's use and maintenance of a selective memory strategy. *Developmental Psychology, 45*(4), 1034–1050. https://doi.org/10.1037/a0015597. (Chapters 5, 6, 19)

Scribner, S., & Cole, M. (1978). Literacy without schooling: Testing for intellectual effects. *Harvard Educational Review, 48,* 448–461. https://doi.org/10.17763/haer.48.4.f44403u05l72x375 (Chapter 15)

Sellers, P. D. II, & Bjorklund, D. F. (2014). The development of adaptive memory. In B. L. Schwartz, M. L. Howe, M. P. Toglia, & H. Otgaar

(Eds.), *What's adaptive about adaptive memory?* (pp. 286–307). New York, NY: Oxford University Press. (Chapter 19)

Siegler, R. S. (1986). Unities across domains in children's strategy choices. In M. Perlmutter (Ed.), *Perspectives for intellectual development: Minnesota symposia on child psychology* (Vol. 19, pp. 1–48). Hillsdale, NJ: Erlbaum. (Chapter 16)

(1987). The perils of average data over strategies: An example from children's addition. *Journal of Experimental Psychology: General, 116*(3), 250–264. https://doi.org/10.1037/0096-3445.116.3.250 (Chapter 16)

(1989). Mechanisms of cognitive development. *Annual Review of Psychology, 40*(1), 353–379. https://doi.org/10.1146/annurev.ps.40.020189.002033 (Chapters 5, 14)

(1991). *Children's thinking.* Englewood Cliffs, NJ: Prentice-Hall. (Chapter 4)

(1996). *Emerging minds: The process of change in children's thinking.* New York, NY: Oxford University Press. (Chapter 4)

(2003). Implications of cognitive science research for mathematics education. In Kilpatrick, J., Martin, W. G., & Schifter, D. E. (Eds.), *A research companion to principles and standards for school mathematics* (pp. 219–233). Reston, VA: National Council of Teachers of Mathematics. (Chapter 16)

Siegler, R. S., Adolph, K. E., & Lemaire, P. (1996). Strategy choices across the lifespan. In L. Reder (Ed.), *Implicit memory and metacognition.* Mahwah, NJ: Erlbaum. (Chapter 16)

Siegler, R. S., & Jenkins, E. A. (1989). *How children discover new strategies.* Hillsdale, NJ: Erlbaum. (Chapter 16)

Siegler, R. S., & Robinson, M. (1982). The development of numerical understandings. In H. W. Reese & L. P. Lipsett (Eds.), *Advances in child development and behavior* (Vol. 16, pp. 242–312). New York, NY: Academic Press. (Chapter 16)

Siegler, R. S., & Shrager, J. (1984). A model of strategy choice. In C. Sophian (Ed.), *Origins of cognitive skills* (pp. 229–293). Hillsdale, NJ: Erlbaum. (Chapter 16)

Sigel, I. E. (1993). The centrality of a distancing model for the development of representational competence. In R. Cocking & A. Renninger (Eds.), *The development and meaning of psychological distance* (pp. 141–158). Mahwah, NJ: Erlbaum. (Chapter 12)

Simcock, G., & Hayne, H. (2002). Breaking the barrier? Children fail to translate their preverbal memories into language. *Psychological Science, 13*(3), 225–231. https://doi.org/10.1111/1467-9280.00442 (Chapters 3, 19)

Slackman, E., & Nelson, K. (1984). Acquisition of an unfamiliar script in story form by young children. *Child Development, 55,* 329–340. https://doi.org/10.2307/1129946 (Chapter 8)

Sloutsky, V. M. (2010). From perceptual categories to concepts: What develops? *Cognitive Science, 34*(7), 1244–1286. https://doi.org/10.1111/j.1551%966709.2010.01129.x. (Chapter 5)

Sodian, B., & Schneider, W. (1999). Memory strategy development – Gradual increase, sudden insight or roller coaster? In F. E. Weinert & W. Schneider

(Eds.), *Individual development from 3 to 12: Findings from the Munich Longitudinal Study* (pp. 61–77). Cambridge, UK: Cambridge University Press. (Chapter 4)

Sodian, B., Schneider, W., & Perlmutter, M. (1986). Recall, clustering, and metamemory in young children. *Journal of Experimental Child Psychology*, *41*, 395–410. https://doi.org/10.1016/0022-0965(86)90001-9 (Chapter 15)

Sophian, C., & Huber, A. (1984). Early developments in children's causal judgments. *Child Development*, *55*(2), 512–526. https://doi.org/10.2307/1129962. (Chapter 9)

Steward, M. S., Steward, D. S., Farquhar, Myers, J. E. B. Reinhart, M., Welker, J. Joye, N., Driskill, J., Morgan, J., McGough, L. S., Bruck, M., Ceci S. J., & Ornstein, P. A. (1996). Interviewing young children about body touch and handling. *Monographs of the Society for Research in Child Development*, *61* (Serial No. 248). https://doi.org/10.2307/1166205 (Chapter 10)

Studdert-Kennedy, M. (1998). The particulate origins of language generativity: From syllable to gesture. In J. R. Hurford, M. Studdert-Kennedy, & C. Knight (Eds.), *Approaches to the evolution of language: Social and cognitive bases* (pp. 202–221). Cambridge, UK: Cambridge University Press. (Chapter 5)

Suddendorf, T., & Corballis, M. C. (2007). The evolution of foresight: What is mental time travel, and is it unique to humans? *Behavioral and Brain Sciences*, *30*, 299–313. (Chapter 19)

Svenson, O., & Sjoberg, K. (1983). Evolution of cognitive processes for solving simple additions during the first three school years. *Scandinavian Journal of Psychology*, *24*(1), 117–124. https://doi.org/10.1111/j.1467-9450.1983.tb00483.x (Chapter 16)

Tenenbaum, H. R., & Callanan, M. A. (2008). Parents' science talk to their children in Mexican-descent families residing in the USA. *International Journal of Behavioral Development*, *32*(1), 1–12. https://doi.org/10.1177/0165025407084046 (Chapter 12)

Tenenbaum, H. R., Snow, C. E., Roach, K. A., & Kurland, B. (2005). Talking and reading science: Longitudinal data on sex differences in mother–child conversations in low-income families. *Journal of Applied Developmental Psychology*, *26* (1), 1–19. https://doi.org/10.1016/j.appdev.2004.10.004 (Chapter 12)

Tessler, M., & Nelson, K. (1994). Making memories: The influence of joint encoding on later recall by young children. *Consciousness and Cognition*, *3* (3–4), 307–326. https://doi.org/10.1006/ccog.1994.1018 (Chapters 11, 12)

Thompson, R., Laible, D., & Ontai, L. (2003). Early understandings of emotion, morality, and self: Developing a working model. In R. V. Kail (Ed.), *Advances in child development and behavior* (Vol. 31, pp. 139–172). San Diego, CA: Academic. (Chapter 13)

Thompson, R. J., Napoli, A. R., & Purpura, D. J. (2017). Age-related differences in the relation between the home numeracy environment and numeracy skills. *Infant and Child Development*, *26*(5). https://doi.org/10.1002/icd.2019 (Chapter 16)

Thorndike, E. L. (1913). *Educational Psychology: The psychology of learning* (Vol. 2). New York, NY: Teacher's College, Columbia University Press. (Chapter 2)

Thorndike, E. L., & Woodworth, R. S. (1901). The influence of improvement in one mental function upon the efficiency of other functions: III Functions involving attention, observation and discrimination. *Psychological Review, 8* (6), 553–564. https://doi.org/10.1037/h0071363 (Chapter 2)

Tõugu, P., Vaht, M., Tulviste, T., Veidebaum, T., & Harro, J., (2016). The association between the COMT gene Val[158]Met polymorphism and pre-schooler's autobiographical memory details and narrative cohesiveness. *Cognitive Development, 39,* 181–188. https://doi/org/10.1016/j.cogdev.so16.06.002 (Chapter 19)

Trocmé, N., Fallon, B., MacLaurin, B., Sinha, V., Black, T. & Fast, E. et al. (2010). *Canadian Incidence Study of Reported Child Abuse and Neglect –2008: Major Findings*, chapters 1–5. Public Health Agency of Canada (Eds.), Ottawa. (Chapter 8)

Tulving, E. (1962). Subjective organization in free recall of "unrelated" words. *Psychological Review, 69,* 344–354. https://doi.org/10.1037/h0043150 (Chapter 4)

(1968). When is recall higher than recognition? *Psychonomic Science, 10,* 53–54. https://doi.org/10.3758/BF03331403 (Chapter 4)

Tulving, E., & Madigan, S. A. (1970). Memory and verbal learning. *Annual Review of Psychology, 21,* 437–484. https://doi.org/10.1146/annurev.ps.21.020170.002253 (Chapter 2)

United States v. Cruikshank, 92 U.S. 542, 558 (1875). (Chapter 8)

Van Bergen, P., Salmon, K., Dadds, M., & Allen, J. (2009). Training mothers in emotion-rich elaborative reminiscing: Facilitating children's autobiographical memory and emotion knowledge. *Journal of Cognition and Development, 10*(3), 162–187. https://doi.org/10.1080/15248370903155825 (Chapters 3, 11)

Varga, N. L., & Bauer, P. J. (2013). Effects of delays on 6-year-old children's self-generation and retention of knowledge through integration. *Journal of Experimental Child Psychology, 115*(2), 326–341. https://doi.org/10.1016/j.jecp.2013.01.008. (Chapter 5)

(2014). Conceptual knowledge extension: An examination of its development and the underlying cognitive processes involve. In R. Chen (Ed.), *Cognitive development: Theories, stages, and processes and challenges* (pp. 1–16). Huntington, NY: Nova Science. (Chapter 5)

(2017). Young adults self-derive and retain new factual knowledge through memory integration. *Memory & Cognition, 45*(6), 1014–1027. https://doi.org/10.3758/s13421-017-0711-6. (Chapter 5)

Varga, N. L., Esposito, A. G., & Bauer, P. J. (2019). Cognitive correlates of memory integration across development: Explaining variability in an educationally relevant phenomenon. *Journal of Experimental Psychology: General, 148*(4), 739–762. https://doi.org/10.1037/xge0000581. (Chapter 5)

Vergauwe, E., Hartstra, E., Barrouillet, P., & Brass, M. (2015). Domain-general involvement of the posterior frontolateral cortex in time-based resource-sharing in working memory: An fMRI study. *NeuroImage, l15*, 104–116. https://doi.org/10.1016/j.neuroimage.2015.04.059 (Chapters 4, 19)

Virj, A., Pannell, H., & Ost, J. (2005). The influence of social pressure and black clothing on crime judgments. *Psychology, Crime, & Law, 11*, 265–274. https://doi.org/10.1080/10683160410001680780 (Chapter 9)

Vlach, H. A., Bredemann, C. A., & Kraft, C. (2019). To mass or space? Young children do not process adults' incorrect bias about spaced learning. *Journal of Experimental Child Psychology, 183*, 115–133. https://doi.org/10.1016/j./jhecp.2019.02.033 (Chapter 19)

Voigt, B., Aberle, I., Schönfeld, J., & Kliegel, M. (2015). Time-based prospective memory in schoolchildren. *Zeitschrift für Psychologie, 38*, 162–174. (Chapter 19)

Vygotsky, L. S. (1978). *Mind in society: The development of higher psychological processes*. Cambridge, MA: Harvard University Press. (Chapters 12, 13, 15, 19)

Wagner, D. A. (1978). Memories of Morocco: The influence of age, schooling, and environment on memory. *Cognitive Development, 45*, 389–396. (Chapter 15)

Wang, Q. (2001). "Did you have fun?" American and Chinese mother–child conversations about shared emotional experiences. *Cognitive Development, 16*, 693–715. https://doi-org.ezproxy.shsu.edu/10.1016/S0885–2014(01)00055-7 (Chapter 13)

(2013). *The autobiographical self in time and culture*. New York, NY: Oxford. (Chapter 3)

(2018). Studying cognitive development in cultural context: A multi-level analysis approach. *Developmental Review, 50*(Part A), 54–64. https://doi.org/10.1016/j.dr.2018.03.002 (Chapter 15)

Wang, Q., & Fivush, R. (2005). Emotion talk in mother–child conversations of the shared past: The effects of culture, gender, and event valence. *Journal of Cognition and Development, 6*(4), 489–506. https://doi.org/10.1207/s15327647jcd0604_3 (Chapter 13)

Waters, T. E. A., Camia, C., Facompré, C. R., & Fivush, R. (2019). A meta-analytic examination of maternal reminiscing style: Elaboration, gender, and children's cognitive development. *Psychological Bulletin, 145*(11), 1082–1102. https://doi-org.ezproxy.shsu.edu/10.1037/bul0000211 (Chapters 13, 19)

Watkins, P. C. (2004). *Gratitude and subjective well-being*. In R. A. Emmons & M. E. McCullough (Eds.), *Series in affective science: The psychology of gratitude* (pp. 167–192). New York, NY: Oxford University Press. (Chapter 14)

Weinert, F. E., & Schneider, W. (Eds.) (1999). *Individual development from 3 to 12: Findings from the Munich Longitudinal Study*. Cambridge, UK: Cambridge University Press. (Chapter 15)

Weinsheimer, C. C., Coburn, P. I., Chong, K., MacLean, C. L., & Connolly, D. A. (2017). Perceptions of credibility for a memory report of a single versus repeated event. *Applied Cognitive Psychology, 31(4)*, 414–423. https://doi-rg .libproxy.lib.unc.edu/10.1002/acp.3340 (Chapter 8)

Weixler, L. H. B. (2012). *The contributions of preschool attendance and kindergarten experience to executive functioning in Chinese and American children.* University of Michigan, Ann Arbor, MI. https://deepblue.lib.umich.edu/ bitstream/handle/2027.42/96108/lhbell_1.pdf?sequence=1&isAllowed=y (Chapter 17)

Wellman, H. (1983). Metamemory revisited. In M. T. H. Chi (Ed.), *Trends in memory development research* (pp. 31–51). Basel: Karger. https://doi.org/10 .1159/000407965 (Chapter 4)

White, S. (1965). Evidence for a hierarchical arrangement of learning processes. In L. Lipsitt & C. Spiker (Eds.), *Advances in child development and behavior* (pp. 187–220). New York, NY: Academic Press. https://doi.org/10.1016/ S0065-2407(08)60483-8 (Chapters 1, 15)

Wiley, K. C., Cook, O. K., Thomas, T. E., Ornstein, P. A., & Coffman, J. L., (2019, October). *The role of parents' conversational style in children's mathematics achievement.* Cognitive Development Society, Louisville, KY. (Chapter 16)

Willoughby, T., Porter, L., Belsito, L., & Yearsley, T. (1999). Use of elaboration strategies by students in grades two, four, and six. *The Elementary School Journal, 99*(3), 221–231. https://doi.org/10.1086/461924 (Chapter 5)

Wixted, J. T. (2004). On common ground: Jost's (1897) law of forgetting and Ribot's (1881) law of retrograde amnesia. *Psychological Review, 111*(4), 864–879. https://doi.org/10.1037/0033-295X.111.4.864 (Chapter 12)

Woiwod, D. M., & Connolly, D. A. (2017). Continuous child sexual abuse: Balancing defendants' rights and victims' capabilities to particularize individual acts of repeated abuse. *Criminal Justice Review, 42*, 206–225. https:// doi.org/o.1177/0734016817704700 (Chapter 8)

Woiwod, D. M., Fitzgerald, R. J., Sheahan, C. L., Price, H. L., & Connolly, D. A. (2019). A meta-analysis of differences in children's memory for single and repeated events. *Law and Human Behavior, 43*, 99–116. https://doi.org/10 .1037/lhb0000312 (Chapters 8, 19)

Wood, J. M., Nathan, D., Nezworski, M. T., & Uhl, E. (2009). Child sexual abuse investigations: Lessons learned from the McMartin and other daycare cases. In B. L. Bottoms, C. J. Najdowski, & G. S. Goodman (Eds.), *Children as victims, witnesses, and offenders: Psychological science and the law* (pp. 81–101). New York, NY: Guilford. (Chapter 10)

Woodcock, R. W., & Mather, N. (2000). *Woodcock Johnson Psycho-Educational Battery-III.* Itasca, IL: Riverside. (Chapter 16)

Woodworth, R. S., & Thorndike, E. (1900). Judgments of magnitude by comparison with a mental standard. *Psychological Review, 7*(4), 344–355. https:// doi.org/10.1037/h0064288 (Chapter 2)

Wynn, K. (1992). Children's acquisition of the number words and the counting system. *Cognitive Psychology, 24*(2), 220–220. https://doi.org/10.1016/0010- 0285(92)90008-P (Chapter 16)

Xu, K., Torres, R., Torgrimson, S. J., Lenartowicz, A., & Grammer, J. K. (in revision). Tracking the neural correlates of attention in the classroom: Evidence from elementary and college classrooms. Mind, Brain, and Education. (Chapter 17)

Yang, T-x., Allen, R., Waterman, A., Zhang, S-y., & Chan, R. C. K. (2020). Comparing motor imagery and verbal rehearsal strategies in children's ability to follow spoken instructions. *Journal of Experimental Child Psychology*. (Chapter 19)

Zimmerman, I. L., Steiner, V. G., & Pond, R. E. (1992). *Preschool language scale–3*. San Antonio, TX: Psychological Corporation. (Chapter 11)

# Index

Abuse and Prevention Act, U.S. (1988), 94
accuracy, of memory
  for repeated events, 122–123
  socialization of memory and, 271–272
Acosta, Diana, 7
adaptive memory
  child court systems and, 26
  development of, 20–28
    Bartlett and, 20–22
adult-generated rumors, as source of suggestion, 149–150
American Psychological Association, Ornstein, P., as Co-chair of, 9
analogy, 67
"At Morning It's Lunchtime" (Nelson, K.), 22
autobiographical memory skills
  children as eyewitnesses, 310–313
  definition of, 306–310
  development of, 306–313
  explicit memory, 306
  implicit memory, 306
  infantile amnesia and, 306–307
  language proficiency and, 307
  longitudinal research studies on
    deliberate memory skills and, linkages with, 37–38
    parent–child interactions in, 37–38
  parent–child interactions as influence on, 203
  parents' roles in, 309–310
    shared remembering, 309
  prospective memory and, 308–309
  reminiscing and, 204–205
  retrospective memory and, 308–309
  scripts and, 307–308
  socialization of gratitude and, 205–207

Baker-Ward, Lynne, 97
Bartlett, Frederic, 11, 21, 317
  on adaptive use of memory, 20–22
  developmental memory studies, 21–28
    in child court contexts, 25–27

cultural stories, 21–22
real-life applications of, 27–28
on event memory, 22–25
  meaning and, 22–23
  memory proper and, 25
  in natural cultural contexts, 23–25
  scripts in, 23
  schema notion, 21
basic capacities, in memory strategies, 79
Bauer, Patricia, 6
Best, Deborah L., 6
between-grades regression discontinuity design, 243
Bjorklund, David F., 5
brain development, self-regulation and, 283–284
  measurement challenges for, 286–289
  neural correlates for, 286–289
  neuroscientific applications for, purpose of, 283–284
Bruck, Maggie, 5

Cairns, Robert B., 4–5, 292
Calkins, Mary Whiton, 13
Carolina Consortium on Human Development (CCHD), 4–5, 237
categorization, 18–19
CCHD. See Carolina Consortium on Human Development
Ceci, Stephen, 154
Center for Developmental Science, 4–5
child sexual abuse
  under Abuse and Prevention Act, 94
  in media, 94
  testimony by children for, 94
    conversations and, non-experienced events from, 135
    global context for, 94
    institutional support for, 93–94
    societal controversy over, 94
child-generated rumors, 139–140
  group classifications for, 138–141

Milton Keynes UK
Ingram Content Group UK Ltd.
UKHW051543310723
426057UK00014B/182